The Ruins of Rome

The beguiling ruins of Rome have a long history of allure. They first engaged the attention of later mediaeval tourists, just as they do today. The interest of travellers was captured in the Renaissance by artists, architects, topographers, antiquarians, archaeologists and writers. Once the ruins were seen to appeal to visitors, and to matter for their aesthetic quality, their protection and attractive presentation became imperative. Rome's ruins were the first to be the object of preservation orders, and novel measures were devised for their conservation in innovative archaeological parks. The city's remains provided models for souvenirs; paintings of them decorated the walls of eighteenth-century English country houses; and picturesque sham Roman ruins sprang up in landscape gardens across Europe. Writers responded in various ways to their emotional appeal. Roland Mayer's attractive new history will delight all those interested in the remarkable survival and preservation of a unique urban environment.

ROLAND MAYER is Emeritus Professor of Classics at King's College London.

John Goldicutt (1793–1842), view in Rome, 1820, watercolour over pencil, 14⅜ × 11¼ in. (36.5 × 28.6 cm), The Huntington Library, Art Museum, and Botanical Gardens. Gilbert Davis Collection.

The Ruins of Rome

A Cultural History

———

ROLAND MAYER
King's College London

Shaftesbury Road, Cambridge CB2 8EA, United Kingdom

One Liberty Plaza, 20th Floor, New York, NY 10006, USA

477 Williamstown Road, Port Melbourne, VIC 3207, Australia

314–321, 3rd Floor, Plot 3, Splendor Forum, Jasola District Centre, New Delhi – 110025, India

103 Penang Road, #05–06/07, Visioncrest Commercial, Singapore 238467

Cambridge University Press is part of Cambridge University Press & Assessment, a department of the University of Cambridge.

We share the University's mission to contribute to society through the pursuit of education, learning and research at the highest international levels of excellence.

www.cambridge.org
Information on this title: www.cambridge.org/9781009430104

DOI: 10.1017/9781009430074

© Roland Mayer 2025

This publication is in copyright. Subject to statutory exception and to the provisions of relevant collective licensing agreements, no reproduction of any part may take place without the written permission of Cambridge University Press & Assessment.

When citing this work, please include a reference to the DOI 10.1017/9781009430074

First published 2025

A catalogue record for this publication is available from the British Library.

Library of Congress Cataloging-in-Publication Data
Names: Mayer, Roland, 1947– author.
Title: The ruins of Rome : a cultural history / Roland Mayer, King's
   College London.
Description: Cambridge, United Kingdom ; New York, NY : Cambridge
   University Press, 2025. | Includes bibliographical references and index.
   | Contents: Ruins in Antiquity – How Rome Became Ruinous – Mediaeval
   Responses to the Ruins of Rome – The Watershed: Petrarch and His
   Successors – The Battle for the Ruins – From Topographical Treatise to
   Guidebook – The Ruins Visualized: Paintings and Vedute, Drawings and
   Engravings, Photographs – 'Virtual' Rome: Rome Reconstructed-Visionary
   Archaeology – Remembering the Grand Tour: Paintings, Models and Other
   Souvenirs – Ruins in the Landscape Garden – Conservation, Restoration
   and Presentation of Ruins – Literary Responses to the Ruins,
Identifiers: LCCN 2024020559 | ISBN 9781009430104 (hardback) | ISBN
   9781009430111 (paperback) | ISBN 9781009430074 (ebook)
Subjects: LCSH: Rome (Italy) – Antiquities. | Classical antiquities in art.
   | Architecture, Roman, in art. | Ruins in art. | Ruins in literature. |
   Rome – In literature.
Classification: LCC DG807 .M39 2025 | DDC 937–dc23/eng/20240502
LC record available at https://lccn.loc.gov/2024020559

ISBN 978-1-009-43010-4 Hardback

Cambridge University Press & Assessment has no responsibility for the persistence or accuracy of URLs for external or third-party internet websites referred to in this publication and does not guarantee that any content on such websites is, or will remain, accurate or appropriate.

Contents

List of Figures   *page* [*vi*]
Preface   *xv*
Acknowledgements   [*xix*]
List of Abbreviations   [*xxi*]

1 Ruins in Antiquity   [1]

2 How Rome Became Ruinous   [14]

3 Mediaeval Responses to the Ruins of Rome   [34]

4 The Watershed: Petrarch and His Successors   [53]

5 The Battle for the Ruins   [67]

6 From Topographical Treatise to Guidebook   [95]

7 The Ruins Visualised: Paintings and *Vedute*, Drawings and
   Engravings, Photographs   [119]

8 'Virtual' Rome: Rome Reconstructed – Visionary
   Archaeology   [158]

9 Remembering the Grand Tour: Paintings, Models and Other
   Souvenirs   [179]

10 Ruins in the Landscape Garden   [212]

11 Conservation, Restoration and Presentation of Ruins   [241]

12 Literary Responses to the Ruins   [277]

Epilogue   [308]
Notes   [311]
Bibliography   [340]
Index   [365]

Figures

Frontispiece: John Goldicutt (1793–1842), view in Rome, 1820,
watercolour over pencil, 14⅜ × 11¼ in. (36.5 × 28.6 cm),
The Huntington Library, Art Museum, and Botanical
Gardens. Gilbert Davis Collection   *page* [ii]

1.1   *Rustic Sanctuary*, State Collections of Antiquities and Glyptothek
Munich, Inv. 455 WAF. Photo: Christa Koppermann   [8]

1.2   *Chateaubriand Meditating upon the Ruins of Rome* by Anne-Louis
Girodet de Roussy-Trioson   [11]

2.1   Remains of the Circus Maximus. Photo: Luciano Tronati – own
work, CC BY-SA 4.0   [15]

2.2   Panorama of the Baths of Caracalla. Photo: Massimo Baldi – own
work, CC BY-SA 3.0   [15]

2.3   Basilica of Maxentius. Photo: Wikimedia Commons – public
domain   [17]

2.4   Loading animals for *Venatio*, Villa Romana del Casale, Sicily.
Photo: Getty Images   [21]

2.5   The nave of San Pietro in Vincoli. Photo: C. Suceveanu,
CC BY-SA 4.0   [26]

2.6   Ancient doors of the Temple of Romulus. Photo: Joris,
CC BY-SA 3.0   [27]

3.1   Allegorical relief of a Roman province. Photo: Wikimedia
Commons – Carole Raddato, CC BY-SA 2.0   [39]

3.2   J.-G. Moitte, terracotta sculpture after a relief on the Arch of Titus.
Photo: Los Angeles County Museum of Art/public domain   [48]

3.3   Tabularium. Photo: Rita1234 – own work, CC BY-SA 3.0   [50]

4.1   Lafréry, *The Septizodium of Severus*. Photo: Metropolitan Museum
of Art/public domain   [59]

4.2   Roma in Fazio's *Dittamondo*. Photo: Sonia Halliday/Alamy   [62]

4.3   Mérigot, *Temple of Venus and Cupid*. Photo: Wikimedia
Commons – Internet Archive Book Images   [66]

5.1   The Casa dei Crescenzi. Photo: Wikimedia Commons –
Daderot/Creative Commons CCO 1.0, universal public domain
dedication   [68]

5.2 Brunelleschi, S. Spirito interior. Photo: Wikimedia Commons – Sailko, CC BY-SA 3.0 [72]

5.3 Alberti, Palazzo Rucellai, Florence. Photo: Wikimedia Commons – Benjamin Núñez González – own work/CC BY-SA 4.0 [74]

5.4 Arch of Trajan, Ancona. Photo: Wikimedia Commons – Claudio. stanco, CC BY-SA 4.0 [77]

5.5 Strozzi, *Map of Ancient Rome*, 1474. Photo: Wikimedia Commons – public domain [81]

5.6 Temple of Antoninus and Faustina. Photo: Wikimedia Commons – ThePhotografer – own work, CC BY-SA 4.0 international; the staircase is modern [89]

5.7 Herman Posthumus (1512–66), *Landscape with Roman Ruins*, 1536, LIECHTENSTEIN, The Princely Collections – Vaduz-Vienna. Photo: 2024 © LIECHTENSTEIN, The Princely Collections – Vaduz-Vienna/Scala, Florence [90]

5.8 Cancelleria nuova, Rome. Photo: Wikimedia Commons – Lalupa/public domain [93]

5.9 Cancelleria nuova, courtyard. Photo: I, Sailko, CC BY-SA 3.0 [94]

6.1 Romulan Rome in Calvo's *Simulachrum*, 1532. Photo: Metropolitan Museum of Art/public domain [99]

6.2 The Tenth Region of ancient Rome in Calvo's *Simulachrum*. Photo: Wikimedia Commons/public domain [99]

6.3 Pirro Ligorio, map of Ancient Rome, 1552. Photo: Metropolitan Museum of Art/public domain [103]

6.4 Coin depicting Nero's *Macellum Magnum*. Photo: Dirk Sonnenwald, Berlin, Münzkabinett der Staatlichen Museen, 18204470, public domain mark 1.0 [104]

6.5 Ligorio, *Rometta Fountain*, Villa d'Este, Tivoli. Photo: Palickap – own work, CC BY-SA 4.0 [105]

6.6 Venturini, *Ligorio's Rometta*. Photo: Metropolitan Museum of Art/public domain [106]

7.1 Maso di Banco, *Pope Sylvester and the Dragon*. Photo: Wikimedia Commons – Sailko, CCA 3.0 [121]

7.2 Masaccio, *Holy Trinity*. Photo: Wikimedia Commons – Web Gallery of Art 14208/public domain [122]

7.3 Mantegna, *S. Sebastian*. Photo: Wikimedia Commons – public domain [123]

7.4 Botticelli, *Nativity*. Photo: Wikimedia Commons – public domain [124]

7.5   Parmigianino, *Madonna and Child*. Photo: Wikimedia
        Commons – public domain   [127]

7.6   Caron, *Massacres*. Photo: author   [128]

7.7   Palazzo Spada, picture gallery. Photo: Wikimedia Commons –
        Kent Wang, CC BY-SA 2.0   [130]

7.8   Matthijs Bril the Younger, *Forum of Nerva 1570–80*. Photo:
        Metropolitan Museum of Art/public domain   [131]

7.9   Van Poelenburgh, *Figures Dancing Near a Ruin*. Photo: Detroit
        Institute of Arts – public domain   [132]

7.10   Claude Lorrain, *Landscape with the Arch of Titus*. Photo: National
        Gallery of Victoria, Melbourne – public domain   [133]

7.11   Lorrain, *Ascanius Shooting a Stag*. Photo: Getty Images   [134]

7.12   Lorrain, *Drawing of Ascanius*. Photo: Getty Images   [135]

7.13   Panini, *Capriccio* of ruins and sculpture. Photo: Yale University
        Art Gallery/public domain   [137]

7.14   Panini, *Ancient Rome*. Photo: Metropolitan Museum of Art/public
        domain   [138]

7.15   Robert, *A Hermit Praying in the Ruins of a Roman Temple*. Photo:
        Getty Open Content Program   [139]

7.16   Robert, *Ruins of the Grande Galerie*. Photo: Web Gallery of Art/
        public domain   [141]

7.17   Gandy, *A Bird's-Eye View of the Bank of England*. Photo: © Sir John
        Soane's Museum, London   [142]

7.18   Heemskerck, *Panorama with the Abduction of Helen amidst the
        Wonders of the World*. Photo: Walters Art Museum/Creative
        Commons Licence   [144]

7.19   Lafréry, title page for the *Speculum*. Photo: Metropolitan Museum
        of Art/public domain   [146]

7.20   Cock, *Baths of Diocletian*. Photo: Los Angeles County Museum of
        Art/public domain   [148]

7.21   Hendrick van Cleve III, *Interior of the Colosseum*, Colisei
        prospectus. Harvard Art Museums/Fogg Museum, Light-
        Outerbridge Collection, Richard Norton Memorial Fund.
        Photo © President and Fellows of Harvard College,
        M24480.16   [149]

7.22   Dupérac, *View of the Campidoglio from the Forum*, 1584. Photo:
        Metropolitan Museum of Art/public domain   [149]

7.23   Piranesi, *The 'Temple of Peace'*. Photo: Yale University Art
        Gallery – The Arthur Ross Collection/public domain   [153]

7.24   Macpherson, *Theatre of Marcellus*, 1858. Photo: Metropolitan
        Museum of Art/public domain   [156]

7.25   Lamy, stereogram of the Column of Phocas, 1861–78. Photo: Rijksmuseum – CC0/public domain   [157]

8.1   Golden Bull of Ludwig IV the Bavarian. Photo: Lutz-Jürgen Lübke, Münzkabinett, Staatliche Museen zu Berlin – public domain mark   [159]

8.2   Bordone, *Colosseum in the Triumph of Caesar*, 1504. Photo: Berlin State Museums, Kupferstichkabinett/Volker-H. Schneider – public domain mark 1.0   [161]

8.3   Frieze from Castillo de Vélez Blanco. Photo: author   [162]

8.4   Serlio, Temple of Vesta, Tivoli. Photo: Wikimedia Commons – public domain   [162]

8.5   Lauro, *The Circus Flaminius*, Harvard Art Museums/Fogg Museum, Gift of Max Falk. Photo © President and Fellows of Harvard College, M24967.78   [164]

8.6   Fischer von Erlach, *The Forum of Trajan*. Photo: Wikimedia Commons – public domain   [165]

8.7   Unger, Belvedere, Potsdam. Photo: Wikimedia Commons – Krückstock, CC BY-SA 3.0   [166]

8.8   Canina, *Forum of Julius Caesar*. Photo: © Royal Academy of Arts, London. Photographer: Prudence Cuming Associates Limited   [167]

8.9   Warren and Wetmore, Grand Central Terminal, New York City. Photo: Metropolitan Transportation Authority of the State of New York, CCBY-SA 2.0   [169]

8.10   (a) Staccioli, reconstruction of the Forum of Julius Caesar. Photo: author; (b) Staccioli, ruins of the Forum of Julius Caesar. Photo: author   [171]

8.11   Bigot, *maquette* of Rome. Photo: Q. Keysers, CCBY-SA 3.0   [174]

8.12   Gismondi, *Plastico*. Photo: J.-P. Dalbéra, CCA 2.0   [175]

9.1   Batoni, *Portrait of Sir Gregory Turner*. Photo: David Munro   [180]

9.2   Piranesi, *Pantheon*. Photo: Metropolitan Museum of Art/public domain   [181]

9.3   Ricci, *Monument to Sir Clowdisley Shovell*. Photo: The National Gallery of Art, Washington, DC, Samuel H. Cress Collection/public domain   [182]

9.4   Ricci, *Classical Ruins with Equestrian Statue and Round Temple*. Photo: Los Angeles County Museum of Art/public domain   [183]

9.5   Shugborough Hall, former drawing room. Photo: Tony Hisgett, CCBY-SA 2.0   [184]

9.6   Ducros, *Temple of Peace*. Photo: Yale Center for British Art/public domain   [186]

9.7   Harewood House, Music Room. Photo: Daderot/public domain   [187]

9.8   Kedleston Hall, the Saloon. Photo: The Roaming Picture Taker, CC BY-SA 2.0   [189]

9.9   South Wall, Print Room, Woodhall Park, Hertfordshire. Photo: Matthew Hollow, courtesy of Paul Mellon Centre for Studies in British Art   [190]

9.10   Wallpaper, Boston Manor, Hounslow. Photo: Rick Morgan   [190]

9.11   Dodd, *Arch of Titus*. Photo: author   [191]

9.12   Cole, *A View Near Tivoli (Morning)*. Photo: Metropolitan Museum of Art/public domain   [192]

9.13   Moglia, micromosaic view of the Pantheon. Photo: Wikimedia Commons/public domain   [194]

9.14   Raffaelli, micromosaic view of the Arch of Janus Quadrifrons. Photo: © Victoria and Albert Museum, London   [195]

9.15   Princess Augusta's fan. Photo: Royal Collection Trust/© His Majesty King Charles III 2023   [196]

9.16   Rosa, cork model of the Arch of Constantine. Photo: Wolfgang Fuhrmannek, © Hessisches Landesmuseum Darmstadt, CC BY-SA 4.0   [197]

9.17   Carl May, cork model of the Arch of the Argentarii. Photo: Los Angeles County Museum of Art/public domain   [199]

9.18   Georg May, cork model of the restored Arch of Titus. Photo: Lutz Hartmann, CC BY-SA 3.0   [199]

9.19   Soane's cork model of the Temple of Fortuna Virilis. Photo: © Sir John Soane's Museum, London   [200]

9.20   Dubourg, cork model of the Colosseum. Photo: Jon Augier, © Museums Victoria, CC BY licensed as Attribution 4.0 International   [202]

9.21   Lucangeli, model of the Colosseum. Photo: Wikimedia Commons – Jean-Pierre Dalbéra from Paris, France, CC BY-SA 2.0   [203]

9.22   The Bellis, Arch of Constantine. Photo: Royal Collection Trust/© His Majesty King Charles III 2023   [204]

9.23   The Sarcophagus of Scipio. Photo: Getty Images   [205]

9.24   Model of the Sarcophagus in *rosso antico* marble, ca. 1810. Photo: author   [205]

9.25   Tomb of Thomas Skarratt Hall. Photo: No Swan So Fine – own work, CC BY-SA 4.0   [206]

9.26   Eli Whitney's sarcophagus in New Haven. Photo: Wikimedia
        Commons – Noroton/public domain   [207]

9.27   Robert Hancock, transfer print on Worcester Porcelain Punch-
        bowl. Photo: © Victoria and Albert Museum, London   [208]

9.28   Prattware dish with ruins *capriccio*. Photo: author   [209]

9.29   Theo Fennell, Colosseum ring. Photo: author   [210]

10.1   Langley, plate XX of *New Principles of Gardening*, 1728. Photo:
        author   [214]

10.2   The Mausoleum, Painshill Park, Surrey. Photo: author   [216]

10.3   Chambers, arch at Kew. Photo: Patche99z, CC BY-SA 3.0   [218]

10.4   Wilson, sketch of Kew Arch. Photo: Getty Images   [218]

10.5   Goathurst, Temple of Harmony. Photo: Stronach at English
        Wikipedia – Transferred from en.wikipedia to Commons,
        CC0 1.0 universal public domain dedication, https://commons
        .wikimedia.org/w/index.php?curid=32927719   [219]

10.6   Adam, design for a *capriccio* of a Roman ruin. Photo: © Victoria
        and Albert Museum   [220]

10.7   Basevi, *Garden Ruins at Pitzhanger Manor*. Photo: © Sir John
        Soane's Museum, London   [221]

10.8   Wyatville, Roman ruins at Virginia Water: The Avenue. Photo: US
        Library of Congress/public domain   [222]

10.9   Gibberd, ruins of a Roman temple. Photo: author   [223]

10.10   La Naumachie, Parc Monceau. Photo: Patrick Janicek, CC BY-SA
        2.0 generic   [224]

10.11   Arkadia Park, aqueduct. Photo: Jolanta Dyr – own work, CC
        BY-SA 3.0   [225]

10.12   Theatre ruin, Lazienki Park, Warsaw. Photo: Ken Eckert – own
        work, CC BY-SA 4.0   [226]

10.13   Knobelsdorff, Ruinenberg, Potsdam. Photo: DerFotogfraf – own
        work, CC BY-SA 4.0   [227]

10.14   Schlossküche, Marmorpalais. Photo: Oursana/public
        domain   [227]

10.15   Piranesi, Temple of Jupiter Tonans, Jupiter the Thunderer,
        actually the Temple of Vespasian and Titus. Photo: Harvard Art
        Museums/Fogg Museum, permanent transfer from the Fine Arts
        Library, Harvard University, Gift of Thomas Palmer, Esq., of
        Boston, 1772. Photo © President and Fellows of Harvard College,
        2008.312.44   [228]

10.16   Ruin cluster at Schloss Klein-Glienicke. Photo: Andreas F. E.
        Bernhard, CC BY-SA 3.0   [229]

10.17   Three columns of Jupiter Tonans, Hohenheim. Photo:
        Weltenspringerin – own work, CC BY-SA 4.0   [229]

10.18   Sham ruin at Schloss Hohenheim. Photo: Creazilla/public
        domain   [230]

10.19   'Roman Ruin' in the Georgium, Dessau. Photo MH.DE – own
        work, CC BY-SA 3.0   [231]

10.20   Ruined aqueduct, Wilhemshöhe. Photo: A. Savin,
        WikiCommons   [232]

10.21   Shrine to Mercury, Schloss Schwetzingen. Photo: Dguendel – own
        work, CC BY 4.0   [232]

10.22   Karthago, Vienna. Photo: Jorge Valenzuela A, CC BY-SA 3.0   [233]

10.23   Petitot, Tempietto d'Arcadia, Parma. Photo: Lex2/public
        domain   [234]

10.24   Petitot's drawing of the *tempietto*. Photo: Metropolitan Museum of
        Art/public domain   [234]

10.25   Island temple at Caserta. Photo: Marcok, CC BY-SA 3.0   [235]

10.26   Villa Borghese, ruined temple. Photo: Daderot/public domain
        CC0 1.0   [237]

10.27   Temple of Flora, Washington, DC. Photo: AgnosticPreachersKid,
        CC BY-SA 3.0   [239]

11.1   Heemskerck, view of the Sacra via, ca. 1536. Photo: Staatliche
        Museen zu Berlin, Kupferstichkabinett/Jörg P. Anders – public
        domain mark 1.0   [243]

11.2   Caneva, columns of the Temple of Castor and Pollux. Photo: This
        file was donated to Wikimedia Commons as part of a project
        by the Metropolitan Museum of Art. See the Image and Data
        Resources Open Access Policy, CC0, https://commons.wikimedia
        .org/w/index.php?curid=60498286   [243]

11.3   Cruyl, view of the Forum, 1665. Photo: The Cleveland Museum of
        Art, Dudley P. Alan Fund/public domain   [244]

11.4   Rossini, Arch of Septimius Severus in 1820. Photo: The Art
        Institute of Chicago/CCO public domain designation   [246]

11.5   Stern, Colosseum buttress. Photo: Alessandroferri,
        CC BY-SA 4.0   [247]

11.6   Forum of Trajan. Photo: Mattis – own work, CC BY-SA 4.0   [251]

11.7   The Roman Forum ca. 1850. Photo: ImageZeno.org, ID number
        20001877704, public domain, https://commons.wikimedia.org/w/
        index.php?curid=64901839   [254]

11.8   The Shrine of Juturna. Photo: author   [255]

11.9   The reconstructed Arch of Titus, 1853–6. Photo: Wikimedia
        Commons courtesy of the Metropolitan Museum of Art, Jane
        Martha St John, CC0 1.0   [256]

11.10   Valadier's buttress. Photo: Wknight94, CC BY-SA 3.0   [257]

11.11   Taylor and Cresy, plate XC, *Capital of the Temple of Jupiter Stator*.
        Photo: author   [258]

11.12   Reconstructed pier in Basilica Julia. Photo: Wikimedia
        Commons – MM/public domain   [259]

11.13   Reconstructed Portico of the Harmonious Gods. Photo: Lalupa –
        own work, CC BY-SA 4.0   [260]

11.14   Catel, 'Inside the Colosseum, 1822'. Photo: The Art Institute of
        Chicago/CCO public domain designation   [263]

11.15   Toadflax in a wall in Frensham, Surrey, UK. Photo: author   [264]

11.16   Richter, *View of the Temple of Minerva Medica*. Photo: Ablakok –
        own work/public domain – CCA-SA 4.0 International   [266]

11.17   Contemporary view of the Temple of Minerva Medica. Photo:
        Lalupa, CC BY-SA 3.0   [266]

11.18   Temples in the Largo Argentina. Photo: Wikimedia Commons –
        Jastrow/public domain   [269]

11.19   The Theatre of Marcellus. Photo: Palickap – own work,
        CC BY-SA 4.0   [270]

11.20   Via del Teatro romano, Trieste. Photo: author   [271]

11.21   Meier, pavilion of the Ara Pacis. Photo: Manfred Heyde – own
        work, CC BY-SA 3.0   [273]

11.22   Pavement of the Senate House. Photo: Rodrigo Caballero R. – own
        work, public domain   [273]

11.23   The Forum of Julius Caesar. Photo: Carole Raddato from
        FRANKFURT, Germany, CC BY-SA 2.0   [274]

11.24   The Temple of Vesta, Roman Forum. Photo: Jebulon – own work,
        CC01.0 universal public domain dedication   [275]

12.1   Chernetsov, *The Colosseum by Moonlight*, 1842. Photo: Wikimedia
        Commons/public domain   [291]

12.2   Jane Martha St John, *The Pyramid of Cestius*. Photo: Jane Martha
        St John – Getty Open Content   [295]

12.3   The Pont du Gard, Gard, France. Photo: author   [303]

12.4   The Temple of Deified Hadrian. Photo: Following Hadrian – own
        work, CC BY-SA 4.0   [304]

Preface

In the introduction to her recent book, Susan Stewart pertinently asked how Roman ruins came to be prototypical: was it something to do with their scale, or did the continuous presence of visitors ensure that they were seen? The answer to both questions, as she demonstrates, is in the positive, and so 'the representation of Roman ruins has proved to be a paradigm for the apprehension of ruins' more generally (2020: 18–19). Stewart's gaze is fixed chiefly upon the pictorial representation of ruins, and especially the prototypical images of the ruins of Rome. But more can be said about how those ruins, rather than any others, came to be so greatly esteemed that they were depicted in paintings and engravings, and imitated in gardens. What is even more exceptional and unusual for any decayed structures, the ruins of Rome were the first to be conserved and protected for future ages to study and enjoy. The present book aims to survey more comprehensively the origins of the attraction of Rome's ruins and the outcomes of that attraction in the study, depiction and conservation of the ancient city's material remains. In effect this is an extended essay in reception, centred exclusively on the ruins of Rome itself.

Many of the chapters of this book originated over twenty years ago as lectures to second-year undergraduates at King's College London. The students were following the non-linguistic Classical Studies programme, and the course for which the lectures were prepared was compulsory for all of them. The title of the course was 'Views of Rome', and my Head of Department, Professor Henrik Mouritsen, gave me one piece of advice: 'Make it entertaining, Roland.' Of course, he didn't mean that the content should be meagre or the coverage superficial, but that I should always keep in mind the diverse interests of a large group of students who had no choice in the matter, and came to the programme with different levels of knowledge of Roman antiquity. Thus little could be taken for granted. Still, many of the students had visited Rome, or were determined to do so, and so they were at least to some degree 'on my side' already. The issue then was to ensure that their interest in the ancient city of Rome and its remains, as actually seen or imagined down the ages, did not flag – that was why the entertainment factor was important. I have tried to follow Henrik's advice in working up my material for a wider audience.

'Views of Rome' was a helpfully baggy concept. In some cases it could be taken literally – what could be seen materially in Rome at various times in the city's long history. It was this literal viewing that pushed the ruins into prominence in the lecture programme as it took shape over the years. We have accounts in ancient literature of what the city looked like, and how it struck those who saw it, but we can only imagine what the reality was. That sparked an investigation of modern imaginative reconstructions of Rome, either in drawings and engravings or in three-dimensional models, or nowadays in films and computer-generated imagery. Now all these reconstructions are based on the physical evidence of the ruins. But the ruins cannot tell their own story, which has to be mined from texts, and so the topographical researches on the ancient city which began in earnest in the fifteenth century had to be sifted (keeping in mind that my target audience then and now will not read the original works in Latin or perhaps even in Italian).

At the time that topographical treatises were being produced in Italy, artists working in Rome began to depict ruins in their paintings, and that pictorial 'view' of the ruins, upon which Susan Stewart has so fruitfully focussed, raised an obvious question: why depict a ruin; what was the attraction? The question became even more comprehensive when Italian architecture of the period was taken into account: why was Gothic style repudiated by some architects in favour of a restored 'Roman' style, based on careful drawing and study of the ruins? The answer to the question seemed simple enough, namely that the Roman style began to make an appeal to the eye of the painter and of the architect, an appeal generated and sustained by autopsy of the ruins. The ruins of Rome thus began to have an importance unlike any other ruins in the world; they became, as Stewart put it, prototypical. It was my attempt to unpack the implications of this conviction that led me, long after the lecture course from which so many of this book's topics are derived, to settle down to sorting out the issues into some sort of coherent order. The order had to be roughly chronological, since my aim is to chart the enlargement of the sentiment which Rose Macaulay felicitously dubbed 'ruin-mindedness'.

Ruin-mindedness is not an ancient or a universal sentiment, as I will show in the first chapter. This raises the fundamental question: why did the ruins of Rome come to matter so much and in so many ways? The second chapter accounts for the ruination of the city despite attempts at maintenance of the built environment. A number of the city's generally nameless ruins surviving from the pagan past acquired legendary accounts in the Middle Ages, the *Mirabilia*. These accounts, the subject of the third chapter, kept alive the sense that antique Rome had been an extraordinary place, filled with wonders: *Mirabilia*. Shattered and slighted though the city became, it had a mystique and a glamour attested to by these works of popular story-telling. But none of this really counts as 'ruin-mindedness', since the ruins were pretty much taken for granted and left to shift for themselves, integrated as they were into the contemporary urban fabric.

Ruin-mindedness begins with the poet Francesco Petrarch, the subject along with his successors of the fourth chapter. He is the first person we know of who went to Rome with the intention of seeing the ruins. Thanks to his unrivalled knowledge of Latin literature, he viewed the ruins as part of the historical and cultural heritage of the ancient Romans, a material complement to the history of Livy and the poetry of Virgil. His enthusiasm was infectious and it can be claimed that he initiated two new disciplines, urban topography and antiquarianism, the subjects of the next two chapters, 5 and 6.

Petrarch's ruin-mindedness, however, stopped short of an aesthetic response to the ruins; he admired them as vestiges of Roman history and culture, but he didn't find them beautiful. The development of a 'ruin-aesthetic' comes gradually with the Renaissance and is owed to architects like Brunelleschi and to painters like Raphael. The architects wanted to build in the Roman manner, *all'antica*, and the painters introduced Roman ruins into the background of their pictures. Such was their commitment to the study and imitation of the Roman style that they saw the need to conserve the ruins, another core feature of ruin-mindedness: what is beautiful must be preserved for later generations to study and admire and imitate. So the fifth chapter charts the developing sense that the ruins had to be saved in order to serve as models; it also surveys the growth of topographical and antiquarian study, chiefly in the figure of Flavio Biondo.

The sixth chapter continues the topographical theme but adds a new factor in the appreciation of Rome's ruins: tourism. People were now following Petrarch's lead in coming to Rome to see the ruins, and so topographical treatises evolved into guidebooks, many of which focussed solely on the ancient remains to the exclusion of the modern city. These treatises and guides were illustrated with maps and engraved images of the ruins.

The seventh chapter develops the aesthetic theme, tracing the way in which Rome's ruins advanced from the background staffage of Renaissance painting to become the foregrounded subject matter in the Baroque era and the eighteenth century. In short, the ruins had by the 1700s acquired full aesthetic validation when they became the very subject matter of paintings by Claude or in the engravings of Piranesi. The eighth chapter pursues the urge among artists to imagine a reconstruction of the ruins, and not just of individual buildings but of the whole ancient city, as we find in the three-dimensional models of the twentieth century.

Petrarch initiated ruin-tourism, and that flowered in the period of the eighteenth-century Grand Tour. Chapter 9 is devoted to the ruin souvenirs of the grand tourists. Once again the aesthetic validation of ruins was to the fore, since the English in particular decorated the interiors of their houses with scenes of ruination. They brought home models of ruins in cork or marble for display; their porcelain was decorated with ruin motifs. They even built sham Roman ruins in their gardens, the theme of Chapter 10. The eighteenth-century fashion for the English garden swept continental Europe and many gardens, even in Rome itself, have sham Roman ruins after the English fashion.

Conservation is a fundamental feature of true ruin-mindedness, but the early attempts of artists to preserve the ruins of Rome were largely unsuccessful until the tourism of the eighteenth century made it clear that there was an economic benefit to the preservation and attractive presentation of the city's ruins. This is the theme of Chapter 11.

The twelfth and final chapter brings together literary responses to the ruins of Rome. Over the centuries after Petrarch the ruins of Rome had acquired historical, cultural and even aesthetic validation, all the outcome of the development of a sentiment favourable to ruination: ruin-mindedness. For the clear expression of an emotional response we must turn to writers, who can put into plain words how they felt about the ruins they had travelled to see. The feelings are surprisingly various – sometimes elation, sometimes moral disgust or even existential despair. Whatever the reaction, it is always founded, as was Petrarch's, on the fact that the ruins of Rome have an impressive historical and cultural context, thanks to the survival of Latin literature. The physical remains of the ancient city are given meaning by the literary heritage, and it is that which enables writers to respond to them in a way that one cannot respond to a ruin without a secure historical context, such as Stonehenge or Machu Picchu.

Acknowledgements

Most translations are my own, unless a different source is named. I have used the following translations in the Loeb Classical Library (Cambridge, MA and London): Ammianus Marcellinus (1935–9), J. C. Rolfe; *The Greek Anthology* (1916–18), W. R. Paton; Horace, *Odes* (2004), N. Rudd; Pausanias, *Description of Greece* (1918–35), W. H. S. Jones; Pliny, *Natural History* (1949–62), H. Rackham; Procopius, *Gothic Wars* (1919), H. B. Dewing; Strabo, *Geography* (1917–32), H. L. Jones; Tacitus, *Annals* (1931–7), J. Jackson; and Tacitus, *Histories* (1925–31), C. H. Moore.

Many friends and colleagues have offered me valuable specialist information or encouraging support during the years of my work on this book. I am therefore glad to thank Michael Sharp at Cambridge University Press for supporting this undertaking; Ralph Abel Smith for an invitation to visit the print room at Woodhall Park; Lucia Athanassaki, University of Crete, Rethymnon, for an invitation to speak; Julia Bagguley for information on the Royal Collection and the Grand Tour; David Barrie for sustained encouragement; Judy Berringer at Edinburgh University for information on early Greece; Andrew Burnett for numismatic assistance; Giovanna Ceserani at Stanford University for information on grand tourists and the Vasi project; Helen Dorey at the Soane Museum for information about the collection's cork models; Catharine Edwards at Birkbeck University of London for bibliographical information; Sally Evans-Darby for exemplary copyediting; Kirsten Forrest for a chance to see Alan Dodd's decorations in the Alexandra Palace, north London; Luigi Galasso for an invitation to speak at La Cattolica, Milan; Elizabeth Gibson for legal advice on licences and copyright; Mary Gibson for bibliographical information; Woldemar Görler for advice on Potsdam; Hiba Hajaj for showing me Theo Fennell's Colosseum ring and explaining its manufacture to me; Nick Holzberg for an invitation to address The Petronian Society, Munich section; Perilla Kinchin for invaluable assistance with the illustrations; Chris Kraus for an invitation to speak at Yale University, bibliographical information and publication advice and for reading the whole work; Stephen Leach for bringing A. H. Clough's poem to my attention; Susan Miekle for an invitation to speak at Gordon's School, West End, Surrey; Rick Morgan for the photograph of the wallpaper at Boston Manor; David Munro for the photograph of Page-Turner; Isabel Raphael for an invitation to address the Highgate Literary and Scientific Institution; Kate Retford for help securing the photograph of the print room at Woodhall Park and for a steer towards wallpapers; Isabella Sandwell at the University of Bristol for direction to the sham ruins of the Villa Torlonia; Alessandro Schiesaro at Scuola Normale Superiore, Pisa for the invitation to speak at La Sapienza Rome and for information regarding holders of the Chair of Archaeology there; Susan Stephens for an invitation to speak at Stanford University and for sorting out my Greek; and Carolyn Walton for an invitation to address the Burford Art Society and for information about Art UK's website.

I am especially grateful to the Hugh Last Fund, administered by the Society for the Promotion of Roman Studies, for a grant covering the purchase of a number of the images.

Abbreviations

CAH   Cameron, A., B. Ward-Perkins and M. Whitby (eds.), 2000. *The Cambridge Ancient History*, volume xiv: *Late Antiquity: Empire and Successors, A.D. 425–600*, Cambridge.

CIL   1863–. *Corpus Inscriptionum Latinarum*, Berlin.

CTCR   Valentini, R. and G. Zucchetti (eds.), 1940–53. *Codice topografico della città di Roma* (4 volumes), Rome.

DBI   Ghisalberti, A. M. (ed.), 1960–. *Dizionario biografico degli Italiani*, Rome (available online at www.treccani.it/biografico).

DNB   *The Oxford Dictionary of National Biography*, 2004– (available online at www.oxforddnb.com).

ILS   Dessau, H. (ed.), 1892–1916. *Inscriptiones Latinae Selectae*, Berlin.

OCD   Hornblower, S., A. Spawforth and E. Eidinow (eds.), 2012. *The Oxford Classical Dictionary* (4th ed.), Oxford.

ODLA   Nicholson, O. (ed.), 2018. *The Oxford Dictionary of Late Antiquity*, Oxford.

PLRE   Martindale, J. R. (ed.), 1971–92. *Prosopography of the Later Roman Empire*, Cambridge.

1 | Ruins in Antiquity

'My curiosity', said Rasselas, 'does not very strongly lead me to survey piles of stone, or mounds of earth ….'

Samuel Johnson, *The History of Rasselas,*
Prince of Abyssinia, chapter XXX

Greeks and Romans and Ruins

Trouble-free tourism was one of the many blessings conferred upon the elite Roman by imperial control of the Mediterranean basin. Pompey the Great had cleared the seas of pirates in the mid-first century BC, so that travel beyond Italy became less dangerous. A ground-breaking and still indispensable survey of tourism in the early empire is to be found in Ludwig Friedländer's general study of Roman life in that period.[1] Andreas Hartmann's discussion of sightseeing and Robert Turcan provide up-to-date accounts of ancient tourism.[2] We are given a fair notion of what specifically attracted the Roman tourist to venture abroad by an anonymous poet, perhaps writing in the reign of the emperor Nero (AD 54–68), who composed a poem on the wonders of the Sicilian volcano, Etna, which provided the title of his work, *Aetna*. He complained in lines 569–600 that tourists rushed far afield in search of interesting places to visit, whereas they ignored a volcanic marvel which lay virtually on their doorstep (his complaint was in fact baseless, since Romans, including the emperor Hadrian, did visit and even climbed Mount Etna, as Friedländer showed, but it made a good story). The poet claimed they preferred to travel to see wealthy temples and legendary cities, such as Thebes, Sparta, Athens and especially Troy with its heroes' tombs. Paintings and sculptures in Greece were also a draw.

Three categories of tourist site can be recognised in the poem. First, there are the cities famous for the legends attached to them. All of them are in the Greek east, it is worth noting; the tourist was not expected to head for the unsung western Mediterranean. Troy was particularly attractive to the Roman,[3] for reasons that will be set out in a moment. A second object of interest was the tombs of heroes, Hector, Achilles and Paris. Third and last, the poet surveys some outstanding works of art – paintings by Apelles, Timomachus and Timanthes and the life-like bronze sculpture of a cow by Myron. What is missing from his list is ruins. He plainly did not expect that the tourist would seek out a ruined city, with the possible exception of Troy (or, as the Romans knew it, Ilium), to which we may now turn, since it is in its way special.

Another poetic tourist will serve as our guide. In his incomplete epic poem, *On the Civil War*, or, to give it its English title, *Pharsalia*, the Neronian poet Lucan fabricated a visit paid by Julius Caesar to the allegedly ruinous site of Troy (*Pharsalia* 9.961–99). The lure of Troy for the Roman is simply explained: legend consecrated it as the mother-city of Rome, thanks to the escape from the besieged city of the Trojan prince Aeneas with his son Ascanius.[4] This legend had been further sanctioned by the Augustan poet Virgil in an epic, the *Aeneid*, which described Aeneas' wanderings and his final arrival in Latium, the Italian territory watered by the river Tiber, where Rome would be founded in due course, a task reserved for his descendants Romulus and Remus. So Troy was especially attractive to Romans generally as a place to visit; the poet Catullus had been there, but rather for a personal reason, since his brother was buried there. As for Julius Caesar, he had a very personal interest in the Trojan legend. Aeneas' son Ascanius had an alternative name, Iulus. The artful introduction of another letter into his name produced Iulius, and so he became the putative ancestor of the Julian family at Rome (not the only Roman family to advertise alleged descent from Trojan exiles). The historical Julius Caesar had shown favour to the city of Ilium, founded on the site of the legendary Troy, so a visit to the place as imagined by Lucan was not implausible, even though it is a poetic fiction, as Andrew Erskine and Andreas Hartmann rightly insist, despite some scholars' belief in the story.[5] Here anyway is what Caesar is alleged to have seen or tried to find: at Rhoeteum the tomb of Ajax, the walls of Troy built by Apollo, the palace of Assaracus and the temples of the gods, the citadel of Pergama. In vain! In one of his snappiest epigrams, Lucan insisted that 'even the ruins had disappeared' (*etiam periere ruinae*, 969): there was an 'absence of ruins'.[6] Undeterred, Caesar looked for Hesione's rock; the marriage chamber of Anchises (father of Aeneas by the goddess Venus); the place where Paris judged the three goddesses, Juno, Minerva and Venus, in their beauty contest; the spot where Ganymede was carried off by the eagle; and the mountain where Oenone lamented. He crossed the stream Xanthus unawares and almost trod upon the tomb of Hector. His guide chided him for failing to recognise an altar of Zeus in a pile of scattered stones. As Lucan pithily put it, 'a legend clings to every stone' (*nullum est sine nomine saxum*, 973). In Lucan's eyes, Troy/Ilium was so much rubble, its remains unidentifiable except to the professional guide.

Some details of Lucan's account, however fanciful, harmonise with the list of attractions drawn up by the *Aetna*-poet: the tourist is lured to sites with a story and particularly to the tombs of heroes, such as Ajax and Hector; temples too are mentioned by both poets. The serious flaw in Lucan's description of a desolated Troy, however, is that it was unrealistic. After the destruction of Homer's Troy, a new town, Ilium, was built on the site; and though it had its ups and downs, it was a fairly successful settlement, especially after Alexander the Great visited it and initiated a building programme. His visit in 334 BC is described by the second-century AD Greek historian Arrian, *Anabasis* 1.11.7–8, and it is clear that Alexander was not treated to a guided tour of ruins. In due course Romans, for instance the generals Livius Salinator and Lucius Scipio, visited and paid their respects to the city in the 190s BC, according to Livy, *History of Rome* 37.9.7 and 37.37.1–3. Ilium was nonetheless sacked by a rogue Roman general, Gaius Flavius Fimbria, in 85 BC. Erskine has weighed the archaeological evidence for damage against the ancient literary accounts and finds them exaggerated.[7] It seems that the city suffered far less than poets and historians claimed; the historians' accounts were presumably coloured by a desire to blacken further the character of Fimbria. So Ilium appears to have recovered promptly from the assault. Such ruination as there might still have been in Caesar's day was of a prosperous Hellenistic city, not the heroic citadel of Homer. By Lucan's time, the city of Ilium was very prosperous indeed. Never mind: the critical point to bear in mind is that there was a well-known story that could be attached to some legendary sights and material remains in contemporary Ilium, which was rightly reckoned to be the successor of Homer's legendary Troy.

Another kind of attraction for the Roman tourist was omitted from the *Aetna*-poet's list, namely the exotic and unusual. Egypt, to which we now turn, supplied the exceptional in abundance (pyramids, tame crocodiles!). Egypt had become a territory within the Roman empire with the defeat of its last Macedonian monarch Cleopatra in 30 BC. The luxurious modern city of Alexandria was itself a magnet, but Lake Moeris, the pyramids at Memphis (not yet in their present rather ruinous state) and the vocal statue of Memnon at Egyptian Thebes were the chief draws. We have a number of accounts of visits to this latter curiosity.[8] Sometime in the 20s BC the Greek geographical writer Strabo visited Thebes in the company of the Roman general Aelius Gallus. The city had been largely depopulated since the sixth century, so there were indeed ruins to be seen there, but the major attraction was a broken colossus of Amenhotep III (its damage may have been quite recent, the result of an earthquake). Strabo is the first to record in his *Geography* 17.46 that the statue made a noise as the sunlight at dawn touched it. Since the legendary Ethiopian Memnon was the son of the Dawn (Eos in Greek), the statue came to be erroneously identified as a representation of him. It was later visited by the emperor Tiberius' adopted son, Germanicus, in AD 19, after an extensive tour of the Greek east, a tour of which Tacitus provided a full account in his *Annals*, 2.59–61. It is noteworthy that while in Thebes for the sake of the vocal colossus, Germanicus asked a local priest to translate the hieroglyphic records of the extent of the Egyptian empire and the amount of tribute paid to it – a tribute, Tacitus insists, rivalling that of the Parthian or the Roman empires of his own day. Once again we find the Roman visitor looking for historical context into which to set the site visited. There may even be a faint hint that such great prosperity cannot endure. Perhaps one of the last visitors to hear the statue 'speak' was the second-century AD Greek traveller Pausanias, who recorded his amazed experience in his *Description of Greece*, 1.42.3. The lower part of the stone of the Memnon colossus is inscribed with a considerable number of graffiti in both Greek and Latin, which attest to its prolonged popularity as a sight. At some point in the third century, however, someone misguidedly tried to put the colossus back together, thus rendering it mute and so of no further interest to the tourist in antiquity.[9]

This survey of the objects likely to attract the Roman visitor suggests that ruins in and of themselves were pretty much totally neglected. In his account of 'what interested Roman tourists' Friedländer highlighted temples, the tombs of heroes and famous men and battlefields.[10] What engaged the Roman was above all the historical associations of the places he visited. Contemporary Ilium may have had some ruins, but it is not clear that what the tourist was shown was in any way ruinous. Above all, it was the Trojan story attached to the remains that drew the tourist to the place.

We do not have any authentic record of how a Roman viewed a ruin, but the Greek Pausanias, just mentioned, had occasion to visit and describe a number of ruined sites or structures in old Greece, such as Mycenae; they have been conveniently listed by Kendrick Pritchett.[11] Pausanias never hinted that he found ruination itself attractive; rather, he expressed what must have been a common sentiment when in his *Description of Greece* 2.9.7 he dismissed the ruins of a temple of Apollo at Sicyon as 'hardly worth seeing' (ἥκιστα θέας ἄξιον). Nonetheless, he did relate the local legend which accounted for its dedication to Apollo, so once again a ruin is to some extent contextualised for the reader. Pausanias dilated rather more upon the ruins of Megalopolis ('Great City') in Arcadia because its decay was suggestive to him of the malign power of fortune, which brings low what is grand. His often-quoted reflections in the eighth book of his *Description of Greece*, §33, are instructive:

> Megalopolis was founded by the Arcadians with the utmost enthusiasm amidst the highest hopes of the Greeks, but it has lost all its beauty [κόσμον τὸν ἅπαντα] and its old prosperity, being to-day for the most part in ruins [ἐρείπια]. I am not in the least surprised, as I know that heaven is always willing something new, and likewise that all things, strong or weak, increasing or decreasing, are being changed by Fortune, who drives them with imperious necessity according to her whim. For Mycenae, the leader of the Greeks in the Trojan war, and Nineveh, where was the royal palace of the Assyrians, are utterly ruined [πανώλεθροι] and desolate .... These places have been reduced by heaven to nothing. (W. H. S. Jones' Loeb translation)

In Pausanias' opinion, the beauty was lost and the ruins of Megalopolis were a scene of desolation, a point already made by his predecessor Strabo, who quoted a comic poet to the effect that 'the Great City is a great desert' (*Geography* 8.8.1 and 16.1.5).

Pausanias' 'classic reflexions on the grandeur and decadence of human things', as Alain Schnapp judged them,[12] are echoed in a number of Greek epigrams on ruined cities,[13] such as one by Alpheios of Mitylene on Mycenae:

> Few are the birth-places of the heroes that are still to be seen, and those yet left are not much higher than the soil. So, as I passed thee by, did I recognize thee, unhappy Mycenae, more waste than any goat-field. The herdsmen still point thee out, and it was an old man who said to me, 'Here stood once the city, rich in gold, that the Cyclopes built'. (Anthologia Palatina 9.101, W. R. Paton's Loeb translation)

It is significant that the speaker of Alpheios' poem is no more than 'passing by' (παρερχόμενος), a word common in sepulchral or epitaphic verse; a deliberate visit to the ruins of the 'dead' city was never his purpose. Pausanias in the extract from his eighth book on Megalopolis referenced Mycenae, which, like Babylon, was 'utterly ruined and desolate', a description more or less echoing that of Strabo, who claimed that not even a trace of Mycenae was to be found (*Geography* 8.6.10). But the claim is untrue, and it is odd that Pausanias could endorse it, since he had actually visited

the site and mentioned the lion-gate (without comment) and the underground tomb-chambers, among other objects of interest (*Description of
Greece*, 2.16.5–7). Strabo may have written from hearsay, but Pausanias
knew that Mycenae had interesting sights, and yet he could still claim that it
was 'utterly ruined' (it may well have been desolate). So far as they were concerned, such ruins as were to be seen at Mycenae were of slight importance,
and so the city could be written off as destroyed. Ruins as such did not make
any sort of appeal to the imagination or aesthetic sense. They might point
to a moral about the transience of things, but in general they cast no spell.

Another moralising Greek, the sophistic orator Dio Chrysostom, used
the ruins of ancient Greece as a stick with which to beat his degenerate contemporaries in his oration 'To the Rhodians', 31.160, which is perhaps data-
ble within the 70s AD: 'No, it is rather the stones which reveal the grandeur
and greatness of Hellas, and the ruins of her buildings.' James Porter has
repeatedly tried to identify a ruin-aesthetic in antiquity but without providing a single example of anyone, Greek or Roman, who expressed a clearly
aesthetic appreciation of ruins.[14] In an elaborate contextualisation of the
ruin-discourse of Pausanias, Julian Schreyer has constructed 'a spectrum
of eleven semantic aspects assignable to destroyed architecture', but aesthetic appeal is conspicuous by its absence from the proposed spectrum.[15]
In short, it must be admitted that the Romans put no aesthetic value on
ruins.[16] It is also worth pointing out that another absentee from Schreyer's
spectrum is 'conservation', though he does manage to find a few rudimen-
tary examples of ruins which were deliberately left undisturbed.[17]

Why then did ruins cast little or no spell upon the Greeks and the
Romans? The reason is clear enough: ruins were felt to be a defect of material culture.[18] Ruins had no place, especially within still occupied cities and
towns (no more than they have in our own communities: Detroit, Michigan
presumably takes no pride in its current degradation). We find, for instance,
in the charter drawn up between AD 81 and 84 for the Roman town of
Malaca (modern Malaga) in Spain a provision that forbade the unroofing
or destruction of a building within the city limits except with a view to
its replacement.[19] Unroofing would inevitably lead to ruination, and local
councils were at pains to prevent such unsightliness (*deformitas*) within
the town itself. The younger Pliny, for example, presented an appeal to the
emperor Trajan in AD 110 on behalf of the people of Prusa in Bithynia,
where he was the Roman governor, for permission to build a public bath on
the site of a ruinous house (*Letters* 10.71). Massimiliano Papini makes the
valuable point that in addition to inflicting *deformitas* upon the urban environment, ruins were sometimes the product of wars – or worse, internal

skirmishes – with origins so recent they did not possess the romance of more chronologically remote ruins.[20] In other words, a ruin might be an unwelcome reminder of a shameful experience, like modern Berlin's Gedächtniskirche, a memorial of the Second World War.[21] Ancient Rome knew no such physical memorials of the past; indeed, rather the opposite: what risked decay was persistently conserved, as we see in the great care taken of the 'hut' of Romulus (*Casa Romuli*).[22] As Catharine Edwards has said, the hut's authenticity was not the issue, and so a ruin of the genuine article would not have been acceptable.[23] The hut had to be repaired, even completely rebuilt, after fires. It was its symbolic character that mattered. The emperor Augustus took pride in having restored eighty-two temples by 28 BC during his sixth consulship (*Res Gestae* 20), and he established a commission of public works, *cura operum publicorum*, to oversee the main-tenance of civic structures, including temples.[24] Everything in the empire's metropolis had to be splendid. Ruins had no place there.

Ruined cities that had long been abandoned were of course a different mat-ter, but they were pretty cheerless, with no smart lodgings or lively restaurants for the up-market tourist. Let us go back to one of the attractions mentioned by the *Aetna*-poet, 'temples elaborate with human wealth'. The grander ancient temples, especially those in Asia Minor, often boasted park-like precincts with groves and water features. They housed curiosities and important works of art, and so served as the equivalent of modern museums and art galleries (and even sometimes as zoos). Given the choice between visiting a thriving shrine and an abandoned one, there could be no contest. The only possible draw to a (supposedly) ruined city, like Troy or Egyptian Thebes, was the story to be told about the place. As for Ilium/Troy, the Julio-Claudian emperors saw to it that the mother-city was kept in good order. As far as the ancient Greek or Roman tourist was concerned, ruins were never on the 'bucket list'.

A further clue to the attitude of the Roman to ruination is provided by the representational arts of painting and sculpture. Isabella Colpo and Julian Schreyer discuss the presence of ruined structures in Roman land-scape painting and in the plastic arts.[25] Colpo observes that ruins are not found very often in representations of landscape, and that they are neither prominent nor isolated where they are depicted.[26] They generally appear along with other entire structures; that is to say, where the landscape is architectural, ruins are just one feature and not the focus of interest – they are apparently absent from idyllic or sacred scenes. What this suggests is that artists aimed at a realistic portrayal of the contemporary landscape, in which abandoned shrines or habitations were not uncommon. Ruination was a fact of rural life, and an absence of ruins would have been unrealistic.

Contemporary literature confirms the picture. Lovers of Horace's late poems, the Letters (*Epistulae*), will recall that he claimed in one to be writing in the countryside to his friend Aristius Fuscus from 'behind the tumble-down shrine of Vacuna' (*post fanum putre Vacunae, Epistulae* 1.10.49). A pious proprietor might build a shrine to a favoured divinity, but over time it might come to be uncared for and fall into decay, the sort of thing Horace's contemporary Propertius complained of: 'shrines neglected in deserted groves' (*desertis cessant sacraria lucis, Elegies* 3.13.47). Painters who aimed at a recognisable depiction of the countryside would naturally include such untended shrines as a defining feature of the rural landscape. In decorative art no actual ruin need be illustrated; an impressionistic representation of some abandoned structures in the countryside sufficed.

Ruins were also represented in plastic art; for instance, the fallen capital on the Portland vase[27] and, as some argue, the shrine in the lovely sculptural relief in Munich's Glyptothek, which depicts a countryman laden with produce driving an equally burdened ox past the perimeter wall of a rustic sanctuary[28] (Figure 1.1). The 'ruins' on the Portland vase and the Munich

Figure 1.1 *Rustic Sanctuary*, State Collections of Antiquities and Glyptothek Munich, Inv. 455 WAF. Photo: Christa Koppermann.

relief share two characteristic constants, as identified by Colpo: damage to an architectural structure and an invasive tree (perhaps the notorious fig, which is capable of rooting itself in the tiniest crevasse and prising stones apart). The breached perimeter wall in the Munich relief, however, needs more careful inspection: is the shrine really a ruin? It is certainly a somewhat neglected structure, and its wall needs repair. But an offering of fruit has clearly been placed upon a sacrificial table in the interior, and so the shrine has not been abandoned; it is still in use. Such ill-maintained structures, like Horace's shrine to Vacuna, were perhaps not at all uncommon features of the Italian countryside. The depiction is realistic, and it shows what is nowadays rightly called a 'sense of ruination', but it is not exactly an appreciation of it.

Other Cultures and Ruins

The attitude of Greeks and Romans to ruination is unlikely to have been peculiar to them. If we look further afield, we find that enthusiasm for ruins, which some are inclined to regard as a universal sentiment, is scarcely traceable outside the western European cultural tradition. Salvatore Settis, in studies of revivals of the notion of 'the classical', has noted that persistent cyclical revivals of 'the classical' have become one of the defining features of Western cultural memory.[29] For Settis, the sentiments aroused by ruins in particular provide a litmus test of this phenomenon. Ruins, especially those of Rome, denote both a presence and an absence. What is missing from a ruin is obviously 'the absent' – something eroded by time. What is left, the ruin itself, is 'the present', something which has defied time by its very survival. But the ruin is at the same time part of 'the past'; it has somehow defeated time's ravages and survived to tell its story in the present, of which it remains a part. It has acquired a validity just by being itself, a ruin. Settis identified the crucial factor in establishing this validity of the ruin in the West as the absolute discontinuity between the end of the Roman empire and what came after.[30] (He is in effect channelling the Renaissance Italian humanist Flavio Biondo, who first defined the concept of a 'middle age', *media aetas*, between the end of antiquity and his own;[31] his work will be discussed in Chapter 5.) The gradual obliteration of paganism and changes in civic administration, as well as in social and behavioural norms, were over time so complete that only Rome's material remains provided a clue to its culture.

By way of contrast, Settis found no comparable sense of a vast rift or discontinuity in the cultures of India, or China, or Japan; nothing resembling the sense of the 'end of the ancient world' in Europe. Yet even in Europe, the Byzantines insisted upon their cultural continuity with Rome, and so deprived ruins of any pathos as symbols of change from one age to another.[32] In all these cultures, to which that of Islam may be added,[33] there is what Settis calls an 'excess of continuity', which strikes ruins dumb: they have little or nothing of interest to say to later ages, assuming they are allowed to continue in existence at all.

The case of China is particularly significant. Settis' observation of the lack of interest in ruins in older Chinese culture has recently been confirmed by Wu Hung.[34] After a largely futile attempt to find any representation of ruins in older Chinese painting, Hung concluded that 'in premodern Chinese art the sense of decay ... is conveyed by metaphors ... pictorial representations of architectural ruins and actual "ruin architecture" virtually did not exist' in the Chinese artistic tradition until the late nineteenth century.[35] One reason for this is that in early China wood, not stone, was the chief building material, and wood decays completely, leaving little or no trace. That said, Hung draws attention to the way Chinese poets developed imagery for the passage of time in their elegiac *huaigu* poetry.[36] Painters too conveyed their sense of the 'absence' or 'erasure' of what had once been 'present', but in ways far different from the conventional pictorial or illustrative modes of Western art.[37] Hung concluded that the contemporary interest in ruins in China is owed to Western influence thanks to colonisation or globalisation. Apparently unaware of Settis' work, Hung has confirmed his findings.

But as a complement to the excess of continuity in China and Byzantium, Settis also detected an 'excess of discontinuity', particularly in the New World.[38] So comprehensive was the cultural change there after the Spanish conquests that the impressive ruins of Mexico and Mesoamerica were completely robbed of their pathos and symbolism; they formed no part of cultural memory until modern archaeology restored them to notice. (The loss of the native languages and literature, if any existed, is also a factor in the loss of cultural memory.) Comparable to the situation in the New World might be that in Greece, where an excess of discontinuity may also be detected after the destruction of the Bronze Age Minoan and Mycenaean cultures. Later Greeks were fascinated by that 'heroic' period, thanks to their epic poetry, but they did nothing to discover more about it or to conserve its ruins such as Mycenae, as Sir John Boardman has observed.[39] Settis concluded that the sentiment attached to ruins, or what has now become a discourse on ruins, is in its origins a product of Western culture, from which it has been exported across the globe. But it must be borne in mind that even this particular sentiment and discourse about ruination had a beginning and developed only gradually within the western European sensibility. That will be the subject of the third and fourth chapters.

Ruin-Mindedness

François-René de Chateaubriand, who came to Rome in 1803 as a secretary in the French embassy, believed that 'a secret enthusiasm for ruins was a universal passion' ('tous les hommes ont un secret attrait pour les ruines').[40] His opinion becomes especially understandable when we contemplate his portrait by Anne-Louis Girodet in the museum at Saint-Malo in Brittany, his birthplace (Figure 1.2). Chateaubriand is depicted squarely within the tradition of the grand tourist, a tradition that will be discussed in later chapters. His left arm rests upon a fine fragment of Roman stonework, in *opus reticulatum*, and the Colosseum forms the background. Only the

Figure 1.2 *Chateaubriand Meditating upon the Ruins of Rome* by Anne-Louis Girodet de Roussy-Trioson. Photo: Getty Images.

casual dress and the 'wild civility' of his hair betray the romantic, rather than the Enlightenment, enthusiast. And yet Chateaubriand was well read in the classic literatures of Greece and Rome, so that he might have asked himself if Greeks and Romans had been as keen on ruins as he was.

Chateaubriand's successor, Rose Macaulay, who coined the useful word 'ruin-mindedness' in her engaging and deservedly reprinted work *Pleasure of Ruins*, shared his notion that ruination has exerted a universal fascination. Her argument is apparently supported by the considerable extension of interest in ruins during the nineteenth century to such wonders as Petra and Angkor. But it was Europeans, reared in the long tradition of engagement with the ruins of Greece and of Rome, who extended their enthusiasm to those ruins. The same may be said of the British in India. It was the Viceroy Lord Curzon who did so much to conserve and present the great remains of Mughal architecture, for instance, at Fatehpur Sikri.

The first part of this chapter exposed the indifference of the ancient Greeks and Romans to ruination. Modern research, such as that of Salvatore Settis, set out in the second part, suggests that their indifference is a common, perhaps even universal, cultural phenomenon. In that case, we are compelled to ask why the change in attitude to ruins comes about at all. Why, when and how did any ruins, but most especially the ruins of Rome, become interesting, and even beautiful, and certainly worth conserving? Settis provided one necessary pre-condition for the change in attitude, namely a gap or discontinuity in the cultural tradition. But it is hardly inevitable that the gap must at some point be bridged and the thread of the past picked up. There do not have to be cyclical revivals, since cultures can simply move on, indifferent to the physical remains of a remote past, as we see in post-Bronze Age Greece. But once a revival is seen to have taken place, we need to find a reason for its doing so: why then? Why there? Why that?

Settis' focus on material remains, ruins, marginalised at least two powerful strands of cultural continuity in the West. There was discontinuity, to be sure, in material culture, but continuity of a sort with antiquity was maintained in western Europe by the Christian Church and by the conservation of Latin as the official language of the Church. For now, it may simply be noted that in western Europe discontinuity with the Roman past was never absolute or total, thanks on the one hand to the series of bishops of Rome, and on the other to the survival and widespread use of the Latin language among the educated. Rome's political and social importance were in decline, and the physical city was steadily wasting away over the centuries. Few people lived there, fewer still visited, and none of them for the sake of admiring its ancient remains. But the Latin language along with its literature, now expanded and transformed for new purposes by the Christian Church in the West, was still widely understood across the continent. Thanks to the still living and developing language of the Romans and their literary legacy, the memory of Rome, ancient and pagan, among western Europeans was never as obliterated as was the memory of, say, the builders of Stonehenge or Great Zimbabwe.[41]

This brings us back to the ancient tourist. The tourist's chief reason for visiting Troy was that the city featured in literature: its remains, or what passed for its remains, were not dumb; they had a story to tell through Homer's poetry. Once history was developed as a literary form, it too helped to preserve the cultural memory of such once-great cities as Megalopolis. The hieroglyphic inscriptions in Egyptian Thebes, duly interpreted, told Germanicus the story of that proud city. Thanks to literature and writing, the material remains of the past became a significant part of a comprehensible story. By way of contrast, Robert Wood, who brought to Europe's attention the ruins of Baalbek and Palmyra in the mid-eighteenth century, was aware of a considerable defect of literary information about these cities. Susan Stewart has quoted Wood's reflection that while the memory of Troy, the site of which he had visited, and of Babylon and Memphis was preserved in books, Baalbek and Palmyra were 'considerable towns out-living any account of them'. Wood went on to claim that 'our curiosity about these places is rather raised by what we see than what we read, and Balbeck and Palmyra are in great measure left to tell their own story'.[42] Thus Wood could only 'tell the story' of Palmyra, what there was of it, by way of the fifty-seven handsome engravings in his monograph. Only written records, inscriptional or literary, can provide ruins with a human context and a history, and the availability of such records is thus an essential pre-condition for the development of an interest in them. They cannot, simply as ruins, be interesting or comprehensible in themselves. (It should be said that the ruins visited and illustrated by Wood benefited from being Roman in design and from the two centuries of increasing interest in ruination which prompted Wood's own visit to the Near East in the first place.) Once ruins can be set within a narrative and are seen to make their own contribution to a human story, they either continue to live or, in the case of the ruins of Rome, they acquire a dazzling new life. This will be the theme of the third chapter, but beforehand an account of how Rome came to be ruinous will be useful.

Rome was not ruined in a day. This is hardly surprising, since it had for centuries been the largest and most populous city in the Mediterranean basin. Over time it had been adorned with hundreds of temples and other monumental public structures built of dressed stone: racetracks, theatres, public bathing complexes (*thermae*), porticos, libraries. The extant regionary catalogues of the city, works of uncertain purpose originally composed in the fourth century,[1] calculate the number of these impressive buildings and their capacity throughout the fourteen regions into which the emperor Augustus had divided Rome. Even the residential apartment blocks (*insulae*, 'islands') are included, a scarcely credible 46,602 in all. And yet for all that accumulated mass of brick and stone and marble, most of the structures still standing in late antiquity were gone by the Renaissance. Tourists nowadays are bound to be disappointed therefore if they visit the site of ancient Rome's largest racetrack, the Circus Maximus, since all that is left to see of a structure that held 250,000 spectators is a small section of seating[2] (Figure 2.1). But this was not the only venue for such spectacles. The footprint of the track of the stadium of Domitian is still clearly visible as the Piazza Navona; it held 30,000, but what little is visible of the curved substructure at the northern end is now embedded within later structures.[3] The racetrack of Caligula and Nero has completely disappeared beneath St Peter's Basilica in the Vatican City and the parvise in front of it. The fate of that most characteristic of Roman institutions, the public bathing complex (*thermae*), is equally telling. There were seven associated with their imperial builders, but only the ruins of the Baths of Caracalla and of Domitian are left to give us some notion of their gigantic scale (Figure 2.2). This chapter will give an account of how and why Rome became a site of such impressive ruination.

The recurrent and persistent causes of damage to the built environment of Rome were three: fire, flood and earthquake. But in the early fourth century two particular events, the legal sanction of Christianity and the emperor Constantine's removal of the seat of imperial government from

Figure 2.1 Remains of the Circus Maximus. Photo: Luciano Tronati – own work, CC BY-SA 4.0.

Figure 2.2 Panorama of the Baths of Caracalla. Photo: Massimo Baldi – own work, CC BY-SA 3.0.

Rome to the city he founded on the Bosporus, Constantinople, contributed a good deal over time to the decay of the material fabric of Rome.

Fire has always been the chief agent of any city's destruction, and Rome had its fair share of disastrous conflagrations.[4] The roofs of temples were made of timber, and the upper storeys of theatres and amphitheatres had wooden seating, thus providing fire with ample fuel to feed upon. For example, in 217 a lightning strike seriously damaged the wooden upper tier of the Colosseum; repairs took about five years. The building suffered more fires in the early 250s and in 320.[5] The Theatre of Pompey was repeatedly undergoing repairs after fires;[6] extensive repairs were undertaken by the emperor Honorius (395–402). Fires in the jerry-built apartment blocks were 'an all too common accident in the city', according to the late first-century poet Martial (*nimium casus in urbe frequens*, *Epigrams* 3.52.2), among other writers.

In addition to fire, Rome had to put up with a local agent of destruction, the river Tiber, which repeatedly flooded the low-lying regions of the city, chiefly the Campus Martius and the marketplaces (*fora*).[7] (Such flooding was not checked until the river was embanked in the late nineteenth century.) The Janiculum Hill formed something of a barrier to flooding on the west bank of the river but it repelled flood waters towards the east bank, as the poet Horace memorably described in *Odes* 1.2.13–16: 'We have seen the yellow Tiber, its waves hurled back from the Tuscan bank, proceed to wreck the king's monuments including Vesta's shrine' (Loeb translation by Niall Rudd). The effects of flooding on the foundations of buildings cannot be exaggerated.[8] The historian Tacitus described how after a particularly severe flood in AD 69 'the apartment houses had their foundations undermined by the standing water and then collapsed when the flood withdrew' (*Histories* 1.86, Loeb translation by C. H. Moore), and in AD 15 'the Tiber, rising under the incessant rains, had flooded the lower levels of the city, and its subsidence was attended by much destruction of buildings and life' (*Annals* 1.76, Loeb translation by J. Jackson). *Ruina* ('collapse') was one of the peculiar threats to life in the city of Rome, singled out by the satirist Juvenal (*Satire* 3.7–8 and 190–222, where flood and fire are combined as uniquely urban plagues). Rodolfo Lanciani reckoned that the flood of AD 589 brought Rome to the extremity of misfortune: temples, monuments and private dwellings were damaged, and as usual in late antiquity, when resources were severely diminished, in the wake of flood came famine and pestilence.[9]

The Italian peninsula is subject to earthquakes, though Rome itself apparently enjoys a fairly low level of seismicity.[10] If we focus on just one building, the Colosseum, there are records of its repair after earthquakes throughout the fifth and perhaps just into the sixth century.[11] The last inscriptional record of repair is found on a reused statue-base set up by the Prefect of the City (*praefectus urbi*) Decius Marius Venantius Basilius, consul in AD 486,

who paid for the work 'out of his own pocket' (*sumptu proprio*).[12] Thereafter
the records are meagre. There was a major quake in 847, when damage may
have been done to the structure, as many believe; serious damage was certainly done in 1231 by the protracted earthquake recorded by the notary
Riccardo of San Germano.[13] The Italian poet Petrarch mentioned in a letter,
Familiares xi.7, the earthquake of 9 September 1349, now recognised as 'the
strongest seismic shaking Rome ever felt'.[14] Even though there is no record
of which ancient buildings were damaged, it is likely that it was this quake
(rather than that of 847) which brought down the southern perimeter
wall of the Flavian amphitheatre, the debris forming its so-called haunch
(*coxa* or *coscia Colisei*). This immense pile of ready-dressed stone served
for centuries as a handy quarry for new buildings or for repairs to older
ones.[15] Finally, in 1703 an earthquake brought down one of the arcades of
the Colosseum, and its stone too was recycled.[16] Other structures were also
seriously damaged by earthquakes. In the ninth century the much-admired
Basilica Ulpia was so severely damaged that the building was in due course
despoiled.[17] The great quake of 847 devastated a substantial structure at the
end of the Basilica Aemilia, and probably destroyed most of the Basilica
of Maxentius, leaving only the three arcades with coffered vaults we see
today[18] (Figure 2.3).

The product of all this damage was rubble. Rubble could be cleared away;
Tacitus recorded in his *Annals* 15.43.3 that Nero had the rubble produced

Figure 2.3 Basilica of Maxentius. Photo: Wikimedia Commons – public domain.

by the great fire of 64 transported in barges down to Ostia to be dumped in the marshes. But it was always easier to spread the rubble either within the damaged structure, as happened in the Basilica Aemilia,[19] or in open spaces, thus raising the ground level, a practice which had its advantages in the low-lying Campus Martius, which was always liable to flooding (intentional deposition in fact became common in the twelfth century).[20] The result of raising the paving level is best detected in the *area sacra* of the Largo Argentina site.[21] After a fire probably in 111 BC the level was raised about 1.40 metres and paved in tufa. In AD 80 a second disastrous fire destroyed numerous buildings in the Campus. In consequence, the travertine pavement we now see in front of the Republican victory-temple A (so designated because the god to whom it was dedicated is not known) was laid over a metre above the older tufa paving below it.[22] Likewise, the ground around the *Ara Pacis Augustae* (Altar of Augustan Peace), which had of course originally been built at ground level on the Campus Martius, was raised over 1 metre in 80,[23] and by the early second century the complex sat in a pit and needed protection by a brick revetment, since the ground level had risen almost 3 metres.[24] In this way over the centuries, as building after building collapsed as a result of fire or flood or earthquake, the rubble rose higher and higher. In addition, flood waters left a deposit of mud, and alluviation contributed well into the Middle Ages to the rise in the ground level. By late antiquity the level was in places raised by 3–4 or even to 5 metres above the surface of the Augustan period.[25] (By way of comparison, the Mithraeum in London, recently relocated to its original position, now lies 7 metres below street level.) In fact, so elevated had the ground's surface become that even the location of the Roman Forum itself was long unknown, since it had been submerged under rubble and alluvial soil; it became a meadow, called the Cowplain (Campo Vaccino). In the tenth century the Forum of Trajan was covered with crushed pottery, on top of which was spread agricultural soil; streets and houses with gardens were built on top of it.[26] The hillock called Montecitorio, where the Italian Chamber of Deputies now stands, is actually a pile of accumulated rubble.[27]

If Rome's religious life had persisted in paganism or if it had remained the metropolis of the empire, the chances of its buildings surviving would have been stronger. But once the emperor favoured Christianity and settled in distant Constantinople, Rome was marginalised into hardly more than the chief city of Italy. Members of the elite who wished to remain elite adopted the emperor's religion and moved to the new capital. Rome itself was still occupied by wealthy pagans, who were reluctant to renounce the traditional religion of the state, but the tide was set against them. Throughout the fourth century a series of enactments or edicts aimed to reduce the role of paganism. This had an effect on the public structures in which the old gods had been worshipped (the temples) and honoured (the theatres, amphitheatres and racetracks). It must be understood that in Greece and Rome the sort of entertainments we enjoy as secular – going to the races or watching a play – were part of religious festivals, held at fixed times in the course of a year in honour of particular gods. In the Circus Maximus, for instance, the gods had their own box, the *pulvinar*, from which their statues could share in the excitement. So strictly speaking a Christian who was a private citizen ought not to attend the shows – a point driven home in a treatise, *De spectaculis*, by the second-century Christian polemicist Tertullian. A Christian who held public office would find it very hard to bankroll the entertainments of the stage or the racetrack, which in their way did honour to the pagan gods of Rome. (It should also be understood that Christians did not deny the existence of these gods; they held them to be the angels who fell with Lucifer and subsequently set themselves up as divinities on earth to mislead humankind.) Thus the progress of Christianity in due course proved fatal not only to paganism but also to the buildings strongly associated with it. The temples obviously ceased to have any function in a Christian community, and the entertainment venues too suffered when they lost their purpose. It is time to describe the fate of these structures in more detail.

The fate of all the buildings associated with pagan gods was ultimately determined by the policies of the emperors with regard to pagan cult from the fourth century to the sixth.[28] In the course of these two centuries, Christians at last came to outnumber pagans. But the immediate successors of Constantine had had to accommodate a pagan majority, so their attempts to curb pagan practice, for instance by closing temples or banning blood sacrifice, were tentative and often ineffectual.[29] The pace of suppression gradually accelerated, however, as Christianity became ever more dominant. By the late fourth century, Theodosius (Augustus from 379 to 395) and Gratian (reigned in the West 367–83) took more decisive measures against the apparatus of paganism. In 382 Gratian, firmly under the thumb of Bishop Ambrose of Milan, confiscated the endowments of pagan sacrifices and ceremonies.[30] The cult of the Vestal Virgins was abandoned in 394. In 391 the emperors reiterated the ban on blood sacrifice and forbade access to temples (*Theodosian Code* 16.10.10–12). A repetition of the sacrificial ban in the fifth century shows, however, that earlier bans were ignored, but the trend is clear: efforts to eradicate paganism would not cease until success was achieved. During the reign of Justinian, a law of 527, *Codex Iustiniani*

1.5.12, aimed to secure that success by banning pagans from imperial, administrative or judicial employment and by privileging the Christian upbringing of their children. Recalcitrance was punished with a heavy fine or worse. Intolerance had won the day.

Official attempts at repressing the pagan cult did not, however, have as great an impact on the temples and shrines of the gods as might be expected.[31] In 408 the buildings were effectively 'secularised' with the removal of their cult images. Temples lost their religious function. But their destruction was never imperial policy, and as we will see, efforts were made to maintain them, even after they had lost their purpose. Some temples were converted into churches, but Rome was stuffed with them, as we can still see in the *area sacra* of the Largo Argentina. There were far too many temples to be recycled; most of those now visible in the Largo Argentina were absorbed into later secular structures.

The buildings constructed for secular entertainment, on the other hand, fared rather better.[32] Tertullian might attack spectacles generally and deplore the money lavished upon them, but they posed only a moral, not an existential, threat to Christianity. Pagan magistrates, patrons and spectators of all religious persuasions combined to ensure continued support for the shows, especially at the racetrack (*circus*). So long as the shows were popular, their venues were maintained. But mounting the shows was expensive, and by late antiquity lavish outlay no longer helped to secure the sort of rewards that had induced men in the old republic or early empire to spend fortunes on amusing Rome's voters. The Roman Senate of late antiquity was but a shadow of its former self,[33] and the city's grandees preferred to spend their money on themselves rather than on entertaining a much-reduced population. The year 549 is the last-known date at which races, courtesy of the Ostrogothic king Totila, or indeed any other form of shows, were provided in Rome.[34]

Rome exceptionally had three permanent stone theatres: Pompey's, inaugurated in 55 BC; one commissioned to celebrate a victory by Lucius Cornelius Balbus in 13 BC; and the one dedicated to Marcellus of about the same date. They were built chiefly for the performance of 'regular' dramas; that is to say, scripted plays. But in the imperial period the popular forms of staged entertainment were mimes, farces and pantomimes (this last a precursor of ballet). Unfortunately, we have very little information about stage performances in Rome in later antiquity, but it must be assumed that at some point they were given up, and the theatre buildings will have suffered once the *ludi scaenici*, which had traditionally been mounted at the cost of the elite, were abandoned or suppressed.[35] The fine museum of the

Crypta Balbi, itself hardly more than a courtyard of Balbus' theatre, has on display instructive models of the changes to that theatre-complex over the centuries; they vividly depict the decay and repurposing of the buildings from the fifth century to the modern period.[36] The *porticus* of the Theatre of Marcellus was being demolished in 365–70 to provide material with which to repair the nearby Bridge of Cestius, though the stage building was still adorned with statues as late as 421.[37]

Rome's amphitheatres were primarily the venues for two forms of entertainment, gladiatorial combat and beast hunts (*venationes*). These were not part of religious festivals, but in Rome they were closely associated with imperial cult, since only the emperor was entitled to provide them. Both were vastly expensive to mount: gladiators were trained professional fighters and beasts (which only lived to fight once) had to be shipped from remote places (Figure 2.4).

The butchery of the gladiatorial games was obviously anathema to Christians, and there were repeated imperial edicts banning them from the time of Constantine; the last combats were held ca. 400 (not in the Colosseum, oddly enough). The last-known beast hunt was held ca. 500.[38] The upshot was that the huge buildings designed to accommodate vast

Figure 2.4 Loading animals for *Venatio*, Villa Romana del Casale, Sicily. Photo: Getty Images.

audiences lost their primary use and function. There was therefore no point in maintaining them any longer. In the sixth century the Colosseum was sealed off to prevent access.[39]

Finally, the most popular of all Rome's public entertainments were the exciting chariot races, mainly held in the Circus Maximus. As Rome's oldest and largest racetrack, it was always kept in repair, and even in the fourth century senatorial wealth was used to fund races.[40] But after the last-known races held there, king Totila's, of what use was it?[41]

Maintenance of the numerous and huge public structures was the crucial problem. It was noted in Chapter 1 (p. 7) that Augustus recorded with pride the restoration of eighty-two temples, proof that neglect of public structures had a long history. His successors took it upon themselves to ensure the maintenance of public buildings in Rome itself (private citizens could and did build in urban centres beyond Rome). So long as the emperor lived in Rome and saw it daily, the upkeep of the public buildings was his personal concern. But once the emperor had moved away from Rome, maintenance was placed in the hands of an official whose title has already been mentioned, the Prefect of the City (*praefectus urbi*). He was appointed by the emperor and had under him other administrators (also *praefecti*) in charge of different departments, such as the corn and the water supplies; all these posts continued to exist into the sixth century and beyond. One had charge of buildings, the maintenance of which was funded by the *arca vinaria*, a wine tax.[42] The chief obstacle to providing adequate maintenance in the Rome of late antiquity was that its buildings were larger and more numerous than had ever been necessary for its population, and yet building on a colossal scale persisted through the fourth and early fifth centuries.[43] The emperors wanted to leave their personal mark on the city, and a new building served that purpose better than the maintenance of what was already there in abundance.

There was legislation aimed at maintenance, for instance the laws of Valentinian and Valens.[44] One law of 364, *Theodosian Code* 15.1.11, ordered Symmachus, Prefect of the City, to ensure that 'none of the judges shall construct any new building within the Eternal City of Rome if the order therefore of Our Serenity shall be lacking. However, we grant permission to all to restore those buildings which are said to have fallen into unsightly ruins'.[45] This law strongly suggests that finding anyone to undertake maintenance was difficult, since permission given 'to all and sundry' (*universis*) hints that the urban authorities could no longer be required to repair from their own meagre resources. That law was followed up in the next year, 365, by *Theodosian Code* 15.1.14, with one ordering that 'no new structures are to be begun before the old ones are restored'.[46] This only goes to show that maintenance, always less prestigious than building anew, was being neglected. A law of 376, *Theodosian Code* 15.1.19, ordered that

> no one of the prefects of the City or other judges whom power has placed in a high position shall undertake any new structure in the renowned City of Rome, but he shall direct his attention to improving the old. If any person should wish to undertake any new building in the City, he must complete it with his own money and labor, without bringing together old buildings, without digging up the foundations of noble buildings, without obtaining renovated stones from the public, without tearing away pieces of marble of despoiled buildings.[47]

Clearly the now prohibited acts are exactly what was going on. Finally a law of 397, *Theodosian Code* 15.1.36, conceded the destruction of temples, perhaps already ruinous ones, to supply material for repairs:

> Since you have signified that roads and bridges over which journeys are regularly taken and that aqueducts as well as walls ought to be aided by properly provided expenditures, we direct that all material which is said to be thus destined from the demolition of temples shall be assigned to the aforesaid needs, whereby all such constructions may be brought to completion.[48]

That last law, with its focus on roads, bridges, aqueducts and walls, points up the difficulty of maintaining even the city's basic infrastructure in the late fourth century. It cannot be surprising then that maintenance of the vast structures erected for popular amusement proved insupportable. An additional factor which increased the difficulties of the urban authorities tasked with maintenance of the built environment was steady depopulation.[49] Estimations of Rome's population vary, of course, given the lack of reliable data, but no one doubts that it decreased steeply in late antiquity. Conventional wisdom has it that Rome's population was nearing a million by the end of the republic and probably in excess of that in the city's first-/second-century heyday.[50] By the late fourth century, however, it may have been reduced to 500,000. Over the course of the fifth century the population may have dropped by 90 per cent, from 500,000 to 60,000,[51] and by the mid-sixth perhaps it had dwindled to as few as 50,000. By the eighth century there may have been not many more than 10,000 inhabitants.[52]

A significant driver of depopulation was the cost and depletion of the grain supply.[53] The state's provision of free grain (and later on, of free bread) to urban householders and the market sale of it at controlled prices, the *annona*, were seriously compromised after the Vandals occupied the province of Africa from 429 to 534. This deprived the empire of the tax revenue of the province, and so the crucial shipments of grain to Rome were no longer subsidised.[54] Not surprisingly, Rome's population shrank for lack of sustenance.

This shrunken population had no need for buildings designed to accommodate a much larger community, especially the more extravagant ones, like the imperial bathing complexes, the *thermae*, to which we may now turn. Strictly speaking, these well-appointed leisure centres had never been a necessity, since Rome had long had numerous private commercial bathhouses (*balnea*). A citizen who simply wanted to keep themself clean needed no more than that. The imperial structures, with their sculpture gardens, gymnasia and libraries, were therefore a luxury which the city of late antiquity could neither make adequate use of nor financially support. To operate at all, the *thermae* needed constant supplies of water and of wood for heating the water, the floors and the chambers of the complex.

The sources and cost of wood for fuel have been most recently set out by Douglas Underwood, who concluded that it was not all that costly or scarce.[55] In the good times, wood had been supplied from Terracina, down the Latian coast, in exchange for wine,[56] but once the Vandals controlled the sea, shipments in both directions must have become risky. The artificial harbour installations at the mouth of the Tiber at Portus were also no longer well maintained, and so shipment and transport became prohibitively costly. The functioning of the *thermae* was also hampered by the dwindling water supply to the upper reaches of the city. It is arguable that on balance even the aqueducts were something of a luxury, rather than a necessity, since water for everyday use was readily available in the low-lying parts of the city and near the river.[57] Maintenance of the aqueducts had to be incessant, since the flowing water left a deposit on the interior surfaces of the channel which had to be removed regularly. If the deposit was allowed to build up, the flow of water was reduced to a trickle.[58] The official in charge of the aqueducts, the *comes formarum*, is last mentioned in 602,[59] and it is during Pope Gregory I's reign (590–604) that we last hear of a functioning public bath. The *thermae* were soon repurposed as Christian cemeteries, along with other abandoned public areas.[60]

The diminished supply of water by aqueduct also had an impact on settlement within the city. If you lived up on the hills, the aqueducts supplied your water. Once that supply was seriously reduced, tanks, fountains and reservoirs were unfilled, and the hills had to be abandoned for the lower-lying areas of the city. By the time of Theoderic, huge tracts of land within the Aurelian walls were thus gradually disinhabited (*disabitato*).[61] After his reign, warfare and plague caused further depopulation. The many huge structures in the *disabitato*, well outside the now restricted urban centre, were easily ignored and neglected or pillaged.

Money for maintenance became scarcer over time. There is no record of any imperial grant of money for repairs in Rome during the fifth century.[62] An inscription of perhaps 443 attests the scarcity of public funds:[63] the City Prefect, Petronius Perpenna Magnus Quadratianus,[64] recorded that he had repaired the Baths of Constantine 'with the small outlay that the shortage of public money allowed' (*parvo sumptu quantum publicae patiebantur angustiae*).

Although money was scarce for public works, Rome's wealthy Christian elite were happy to spend their fortunes on new churches. Some of the building materials, brick and marble columns, for these often sumptuous structures were taken from older buildings, possibly decayed temples. This brings us to the practice of spoliation.[65] Spoliation is not necessarily destruction. The material, nowadays called *spolia*, may have been removed from unwanted or dangerous structures deemed past repair or restoration. Since public buildings belonged to the state, they were a fiscal asset and the brick and stone of decayed or disused structures could be profitably sold. As an example of this practice, indeed as a justification of it, one need only visit the serene interior of the basilica of S. Sabina, constructed on the Aventine Hill by Peter of Illyria in the period 422–32. The eight columns in its atrium and the twenty-four elegant Corinthian columns of the interior are all clearly recycled from some older, but now unknown, structures.[66] Who would deny the beauty and fitness of this reuse of classical materials? Mrs Charlotte Eaton who stayed in Rome between 1816 and 1818 made a point of visiting the church just to see its columns, not in fact an uncommon draw for tourists of the day, as Rosemary Sweet has demonstrated.[67] Likewise, the twenty uniform Doric columns in cipollino marble in the basilica of S. Pietro in Vincoli, consecrated in 439, contribute much to the harmony of its nave. They too were repurposed from some pagan structure, evidently of considerable status (perhaps the porticus Liviae)[68] (Figure 2.5). This practice of recycling continued well into the Middle Ages. In 1140 Pope Innocent II removed Ionic columns probably from the Baths of Caracalla to rebuild the nave of the church of S. Maria in Trastevere.

So far, focus has been concentrated upon the factors which produced deterioration of the city's material fabric in spite of legislation aimed at keeping up appearances. But there were a few concerted attempts to arrest the decay and repair damage. The emperor Septimius Severus, who reigned from 193 to 211, is credited with a considerable number of restorations: the

Figure 2.5 The nave of San Pietro in Vincoli. Photo: C. Suceveanu, CC BY-SA 4.0.

Temple of Vespasian, the Porticus of Octavia gateway and the Pantheon.[69] The Temple of Peace, which had been damaged in the serious fire of 192, was almost a new construction.[70] The Temple of Vesta was restored by Julia Domna, Severus' wife.[71] The city had been much neglected in the disturbed period before Severus took control of the state. As a military usurper, he was eager to establish his legitimacy, and restoring the splendour of Rome's public buildings was part of his programme to secure popular support.[72] But after the murder of his son and successor Caracalla, Rome descended into a chaos from which it only began to emerge in the later third century under Diocletian.

During this unsettled period the long-standing practice of recycling building material, *spolia*, became more usual.[73] Thanks to the recent archaeological investigations of Simon Barker, it has become clear that the recycling of bricks and especially of costly marbles was a fairly common practice as early as the first century.[74] It made sense thanks to the logistical and economic advantages over production of new building materials.[75] But there were abuses, and legislation in the reign of Claudius, the Senatus Consultum Hosidianum, was passed to prevent purchase of buildings for demolition solely with a view to profit from selling the material.[76] Olivia Robinson plausibly urged that one motive for the Claudian legislation was protection of 'the urban display of the glories of Rome'.[77] But by the third century logistical and economic considerations made demolition and recycling not only more attractive but also necessary. One factor contributing to this practice was the unavailability of the fine white marble of Carrara in Tuscany; the harbour of Luna from which it was shipped had silted up, making its transport prohibitively expensive. By the late third century, exotic coloured marbles too could no longer be imported from remote provinces.[78] A rescript of the emperor Alexander Severus in 222 forbade the removal of marble (*marmora detrahere, Codex Iustiniani* 8.10.2), which shows only that the practice was causing concern, not that anyone could stop it. As an example of this practice, the portico of the highest stage (*summa cavea*) of the Colosseum still shows its third-century repair with stone taken from different sources.[79]

The practice continued in the fourth century. For instance, the emperor Maxentius built a round temple on the upper Sacra via in the Forum, the so-called Temple of Deified Romulus (perhaps Maxentius' son); it became part of the church of Saints Cosmas and Damian in 526 in the reign of Theoderic.[80] The majority of the architectural marbles used in the temple's decoration and even its bronze doors with their marble frame were *spolia* from unknown structures of the Flavian and Severan period[81] (Figure 2.6).

Figure 2.6 Ancient doors of the Temple of Romulus. Photo: Joris, CC BY-SA 3.0.

Recycling persisted under Maxentius' successor, Constantine. His arch, dedicated in 315, is decorated with statues of Dacians dating back to the time of Trajan. Indeed, most of the arch's recycled decorative material was carved in the reigns of Trajan, Hadrian and Marcus Aurelius.[82] The new Christian churches benefited too from the use of *spolia*; the Lateran baptistery, for instance, and the basilica of St John (built in the period 312/13–20) show a wholesale reuse of fine older material.[83] Later in the fourth century, between 360 and 380, the Temple of Saturn in the Forum was restored by the Senate after its destruction by fire. Very little new material was provided, all the rest being recycled, some from the destroyed temple, but a good deal from other sources.[84]

That the appearance of Rome's monumental centre remained nonetheless impressive well into the fourth century is confirmed by the account of the historian Ammianus Marcellinus of the visit, his only one, to the city by the emperor Constantius II (reigned 337–61) in 357:

> So then he entered Rome, the home of empire and of every virtue, and when he had come to the Rostra, the most renowned forum of ancient dominion, he stood amazed; and on every side on which his eyes rested he was dazzled by the array of marvellous sights … he thought that whatever first met his gaze towered above all the rest: the Sanctuaries of Tarpeian Jove [= Temple of Jupiter Optimus Maximus] so far surpassing as things divine excel those of earth; the baths built up in the manner of provinces; the huge bulk of the Amphitheatre [= Colosseum], strengthened by its framework of Tiburtine stone, to whose top human eyesight barely ascends; the Pantheon like a rounded city-district, vaulted over in lofty beauty; and the exalted columns which rise with platforms to which one may mount, and bear the likenesses of former emperors; the Temple of the City [= Temple of Venus and Roma], the Forum of Peace [= Temple of Peace, dedicated by Vespasian in 75], the Theatre of Pompey, the Odeum, the Stadium [both built by Domitian], and in their midst the other adornments of the Eternal City. But when he came to the Forum of Trajan [dedicated in part by Trajan in 113], a construction unique under the heavens, as we believe, and admirable even in the unanimous opinion of the gods, he stood fast in amazement, turning his attention to the gigantic complex about him, beggaring description and never again to be imitated by mortal men. (16.10.13–15, J. C. Rolfe's Loeb translation)

Some fifty years after this formal imperial visit, an *adventus* in Latin, Rome suffered the first of the non-Roman occupations which did much to reduce its prestige. The Visigoths did not, however, deliberately damage the built environment; it is generally agreed that little physical harm was done, since pillage rather than destruction was the price of defeat. Most damage was done by the Romans themselves, not by foreign invaders, who were after portable wealth. The destruction of buildings was just 'collateral damage', not the object of their attack. In 410 the Visigoth Alaric did only limited damage to buildings.[85] It may be that this was when a fierce fire destroyed much of the Basilica Aemilia. It had been one of the grandest buildings on the Roman Forum, but it was only modestly repaired, proof of the declining resources of the city at the time and perhaps of local engineering skills too.[86]

On 11 July 458 the western Roman emperor Julius Valerius Majorian (reigned 457–61) issued a well-known edict, which provides the clearest proof that it was the Romans themselves who did the greatest damage to the city's fabric by stripping or demolishing buildings to get material either for repairs or for new structures. Its terms are clear:

> While we rule the state, it is our will to correct the practice whose commission we have long detested, whereby the appearance of the venerable City is marred. Indeed, it is manifest that the public buildings, in which the adornment [*ornatus*] of the entire City of Rome consists are being destroyed everywhere by the punishable recommendation of the office of the Prefect of the City. While it is pretended that the stones are necessary for public works, the beautiful structures of the ancient buildings are being scattered, and in order that something small may be repaired, great things are being destroyed.[87]

The edict went on to complain that with the connivance of the judges, private persons were removing material from public structures for their own building. The edict therefore orders that ancient temples and other monuments constructed for public use and pleasure must not be destroyed, nor must any material be removed from them. But the third section of the edict hedges by admitting that some public buildings were beyond repair, and that material really was needed for the repair of other structures. The Senate is therefore to consider a claim, and if it is upheld, it is to be referred to the emperor for a decision. Material can be supplied from a public building beyond repair for the repair and adornment of another public work. The despoliation of already ruinous public buildings can thus provide material with which to repair other structures.[88] Two features of the edict deserve particular note. First, the beauty of the old buildings is stressed, and secondly the pagan temples are not to be damaged if at all possible, but conserved.

Despite the spoliation, there was nonetheless some restoration, thanks to the ruler who, after Severus, showed most concern for the care of Rome's buildings, Theoderic the Ostrogoth (454–526).[89] Rome and Italy had slipped from imperial hands, and Theoderic's rule in the West was recognised by Constantinople. His capital was Ravenna, where his splendid tomb monument is still visible. He made his *adventus* to Rome in 500. Rather like Severus', his programme of restoration of public works was a bid for legitimacy and popularity.[90] Theoderic was in effect insinuating himself into the imperial tradition of maintenance of Rome's infrastructure and built environment. He also saw to the restitution of the corn dole, *annona*, a move which ought to have stabilised the population. A valuable record of his works is to be found in the extant diplomatic correspondence of his minister, the *Variae* ('Miscellanies') of Flavius Magnus Aurelius Cassiodorus Senator. Cassiodorus' letters disclose Theoderic's broad aims and reveal what was actually happening in Rome.[91] Aqueducts, *thermae* (tile stamps confirm the restoration of Caracalla's), walls and palaces[92] were all taken in hand. In *Variae* i.25 Theoderic writes to Sabinianus about the annual supply of tiles with which to restore and beautify the city.[93] In *Variae* iii.30, he informs the City Prefect that he is sending to Rome one John to ensure the proper working of Rome's amazing sewer system.[94] In *Variae* iii.31, he expresses his irritation that water is being taken from aqueducts, that the slaves who have care of them have passed into private ownership, that metal is being removed from public buildings and finally that temples marked for restoration are being demolished instead; after all, he is 'striving to bring everything back to its former condition' (*ad statum studeamus pristinum cuncta revocare*).[95] In iv.51, Theoderic encourages Symmachus to repair the Theatre of Pompey.[96] It is surely significant that the king admitted that he 'might have chanced to neglect the matter' (*haec potuissemus forte neglegere*) had he not personally seen the building and been deeply impressed with its scale, hence his concern to have it repaired. He even promised to provide money from his treasury for the works, which were carried out between 507 and 512. He claimed that he wanted 'antiquity to be seen to be more beautifully restored in his times' (*nostris temporibus videatur antiquitas decentius innovata*) – that final appeal to 'beauty' (*decentius*) is rightly stressed by Valérie Fauvinet-Ranson in her translation.[97] But Theoderic's methods nonetheless betray something of the poverty of the times: columns and material were removed from the Temple of Mars Ultor for reuse, as was a pillar from the Colosseum.[98]

At the time of King Theoderic's *adventus* in 500, another visitor had recently arrived in Rome, the north African monk Fulgentius, who was later to be the Catholic bishop of Ruspe in Tunisia. The life of Fulgentius, once attributed to Ferrandus of Carthage, records in § ix.27 that the monk was present at the king's address to the assembled senators and people.[99] The ascetic Fulgentius had put worldly things behind him, but he nonetheless found the spectacle of Rome so dazzling that he exclaimed to his brethren: 'how beautiful can the heavenly Jerusalem be, when earthly Rome is so glittering!' (*quam speciosa potest esse Hierusalem caelestis si sic fulget Roma terrestris*). Even in its reduced condition, the physical aspect of the city still evoked wonder.

The eastern Roman emperor Justinian, after recovering Africa from the Vandals, retrieved Italy as well from the Goths. His successful general Belisarius entered Rome on 9 December 536, and prepared for a siege by the Gothic general Vitigis. This siege, only a part of the wider Graeco-Gothic wars, lasted until March 538. The city was retaken in December 546 by Totila, who was in turn ousted by Belisarius in 547; but Totila then recovered Rome in 550. The wars only drew to a close with the defeat of Totila by the Byzantine general Narses in 552. This prolonged period of warfare naturally had an adverse impact on Rome's built environment. For instance, the Goth Vitigis had cut or at any rate blocked the water supply from the aqueducts (he is unlikely to have done permanent damage, assuming that he intended to keep Rome). Justinian's Pragmatic Sanction of 13 August 554, at the end of the Gothic Wars, regulated Italy's affairs and insisted upon the repair of Rome's public buildings, specifically the infrastructure, the market, the port and the aqueducts.[100] But the fighting up and down the peninsula had devastated communities and agricultural estates, and thus it effectively 'destroyed the very structures it had sought to rescue'.[101] Justinian's measures did little to check Rome's social and physical decline.

The Greek historian of this protracted conflict, Procopius, in his *Gothic Wars* 4.21, noted the abandonment of the Forum of Peace and its temple, which had not been repaired after serious damage by lightning. It had already effectively lost monumental status when utilitarian shops or warehouses were built within it in the early fourth century. And yet Procopius praised the Romans for their love of their buildings:

> The Romans love their city above all the men we know, and they are eager to protect all their ancestral treasures and to preserve them, so that nothing of the ancient glory of Rome may be obliterated. For even though for a

long period they were under barbarian sway, they preserved the buildings
of the city and most of its adornments, such as could through the excellence of their workmanship withstand so long a lapse of time and such
neglect. (*Gothic Wars* 4.22.5–6, H. B. Dewing's Loeb translation)

Recent stratigraphic research indicates that decay in the monumental imperial complexes of Rome was pronounced, thus correcting the rosy picture of
the literary sources.[102]

A century after Justinian's official but ineffective attempts to maintain
Rome's buildings, the Byzantine emperor, Constans II, visited the city in
July 663. It must have presented a fairly shabby appearance by this date,
and that appearance was not enhanced after Constans had pillaged much of
the city's bronze.[103] He is notorious for having stripped the gilt bronze tiles
from the roof of the Pantheon (though it was by now a church), and he took
away many bronze statues, leaving at least that of Marcus Aurelius, which
was thought to be of Constantine.[104] All to no purpose, since he shipped
the loot to Syracuse, where in due course he was murdered by a slave. The
city fell to the 'Saracens', north African Muslims, who bagged the plunder,
which included, it is recorded, the Menorah, brought to Rome in triumph
from the Jewish temple in Jerusalem by Vespasian's son Titus in 70.

In 751 the western exarchate of Ravenna was conquered by the Lombards,
thus ending Byzantine power in Italy and leaving the papacy as the only institution in a position to exercise some control of Rome's government and civil
administration. Under Pope Adrian I (reigned 772–95), necessary repairs
were made to infrastructure, such as the walls and aqueducts.[105] Adrian's
successor, Leo III (reigned 795–816), required military protection from local
insurgents, protection provided by the king of the Franks, Charlemagne,
who was in due course crowned in St Peter's basilica as Roman emperor in
800. During the next two centuries, Rome and the papal territories were
subjected to repeated raids by 'Saracens', who had established themselves
in Sicily and Sardinia. In 1084 the city was sacked by Robert Guiscard, the
Norman duke of Apulia, an event made worse by a fire of terrible extent:
the once populous Caelian hill, next to the Colosseum, was rendered largely
uninhabited by it for centuries.[106] The long-lasting desolation of the city
resulting from the fire is described at length by Ferdinand Gregorovius, who
noted that much ancient marble was removed from the city after the sack
to build or adorn churches in Pisa, Lucca and Salerno.[107] Finally, in the thirteenth century Brancaleone degli Andalò, a Bolognese elected in August
1252 to be the senator in charge of the Roman commune and then restored
to power in 1257, ordered the destruction of more than 140 of the fortified

towers of the city's restive nobility. Gregorovius recognised that many of the towers and fortified residences were embedded within or built upon ancient structures, as confirmed by modern studies.[108] So Brancaleone's systematic slighting of the recent fortifications must also have destroyed a good number of Roman remains, such as the Temple of Quirinus.[109]

At this point, we may leave Rome's pagan structures to moulder on. The city's social and economic decline continues through the following centuries, and its older buildings suffer from the usual physical assaults of fire, flood and earthquake, as well as from lack of maintenance. But poverty is paradoxically a great preservative, as we can see from the almost miraculous condition of imperial Prague. The next serious assault upon the classical remains of Rome would not occur until the city was resurgent in the fifteenth century. But before we turn to an account of the ruins of Rome in the Renaissance, we should first see the extent to which, far from being forgotten, they became the subject of legend and wonder in the city's bleaker ages.

3 | Mediaeval Responses to the Ruins of Rome

In the vast timespan to be surveyed in this chapter, Rome often appeared to be in terminal decline, although there were periods, some quite prolonged, of revival. It was steadily depopulated. What money the elite had, they spent on themselves, rather than on public works or edifices (except for churches). The slave trade diminished once the Mediterranean Sea was no longer policed against piracy by Roman fleets, so the tasks once performed by servile labour, such as cleaning the baths and servicing the aqueducts, went undone; the baths and aqueducts literally dried up. Non-slave skilled labour too was at a premium. There was a risk of invasion by Muslims from North Africa. Substantial public buildings were appropriated either by the elite to be turned into fortified residences (hence the repurposing of the Colosseum by the Frangipane and the Theatre of Marcellus by the Savelli)[1] or by the humble to provide workshops for trades, such as lime-burning, or dwellings (the fate of the Theatre of Balbus). Less fortunate structures were completely dismantled so that the stone and above all the brick could be recycled. The ground level was always rising thanks to the collapse of *insulae* and inundation. The 'ruralisation' of parts of the city produced extensive depopulated zones (*disabitato*) within the Aurelian walls.

And yet, despite this degradation, Rome was never abandoned, thanks to the presence there of the leading bishop of western Christendom, the pope. Papal administrative staff, known as the Curia, gradually replaced imperial officials in the management and maintenance of the urban fabric,[2] but caring for the remnants of pagan Rome (which until about the middle of the eighth century still belonged to the emperor in Constantinople)[3] was for them hardly a priority. Great churches and monasteries were built and maintained, and their materials, both structural and decorative, were often taken from ancient buildings. It was indeed the churches and shrines of martyrs, Peter and Paul in particular, which drew pilgrims to the city. In addition to these pious tourists, high-ranking ecclesiastics came on official business to Rome from all over Europe, especially the western half. Ruins of Rome's pagan past, far more extensive then than at any later time, confronted the visitor at every turn. The function and purpose of these remains of the ancient city were mostly forgotten or at best only dimly recalled, so that legends grew up about them. This chapter will survey the legendary Rome of the Middle Ages.

The Rome of legend was to some extent built upon the Rome of fact, and so a glance at how the Romans of antiquity viewed the city of their own day provides a basis for some of the stories which clustered around its later ruins. Rome was long an object of amazement both to visitors and even to its own citizens.[4] We have only to recall the peasant Tityrus of Virgil's first *Eclogue*, lines 24–5: Tityrus visited Rome to secure a title of ownership for the land where he pastured his flocks, and he told a fellow rustic, Meliboeus, how amazed he was at the scale of the city. He had thought Rome was somewhat like their local market town, but he found that 'she raised her head as far above other cities as cypresses do among pliant osiers'. What is more, by late antiquity that vast city was densely packed with impressive buildings, on a scale not to be seen elsewhere; we may recall the account of Ammianus Marcellinus of the visit to Rome in 357 of Constantius II.[5] But even before late antiquity, the first-century AD polymath Pliny the Elder described Rome's extraordinary extent in his encyclopaedic *Natural History* 3.66–7:[6]

> The area surrounded by its walls at the time of the principate and censorship of the Vespasians … measured thirteen miles and two hundred yards in circumference, embracing seven hills. It is itself divided into fourteen regions, with two hundred and sixty-five crossways with their guardian Lares. If a straight line is drawn from the milestone standing at the head of the Roman Forum to each of the gates, which to-day number thirty-seven … the result is a total of twenty miles 765 yards in a straight line. But the total length of all the ways through the districts from the same milestone to the extreme edge of the buildings, taking in the Praetorians' Camp, amounts to a little more than sixty miles. If one were further to take into account the height of the buildings, a very fair estimate would be formed, that would bring us to admit that there has been no city in the whole world that could be compared to Rome in magnitude. On the east it is bounded by the Dyke [on the Esquiline Hill] of Tarquinius Superbus, a work among the leading wonders of the world. (H. Rackham's Loeb translation)

Later on in the thirty-sixth book of this comprehensive work, Pliny surveyed Rome's most remarkable buildings. Strictly speaking, the book is dedicated to stone and the uses to which it is put. But stone provided a springboard for describing marble sculptures and then impressive buildings constructed in marble or ashlar. After a survey of the then known world's famous buildings, such as the pyramids at Giza and the temple of Diana at Ephesus (both traditional wonders of the world), Pliny turned to 'the wonders of our own city' (*urbis nostrae miracula*, 36.101–25), wonders which were a physical demonstration of Rome's world empire. He proudly claimed that if all the marvellous buildings of Rome were heaped up in one place, you would think it another universe. Then he began his list of specific structures. He seemed to waive the claim to magnificence of the Circus Maximus, but he insisted upon that of the Basilica Aemilia, built on the north side of the Forum in 179 BC, with its columns of Phrygian marble,[7] of the Forum of the Deified Augustus, built in 2 BC,[8] and of the Temple of Peace, built in 75 by Vespasian:[9] the world had seen no more beautiful buildings than these. Pliny added to them the roof of immense span in the Voting Hall (*Diribitorium*) built by Agrippa and completed by Augustus in 7 BC, a building destroyed in the fire of 80.[10] Moving to older structures, he referred in §104 to the substructures of the Capitol, now once again impressively visible in the Capitoline Museums, and especially the sewers. Finally, Pliny praised for their public usefulness the great structures of the aqueducts, initiated by Q. Marcius Rex in 144/3 BC, and the further additions to the water-system made by Agrippa and the emperor Claudius. Pliny claimed that the volume of water, along with its conduits and receptacles, was more marvellous than anything else in the world. In fact, this whole section bristles with the Latin words for 'marvel', the noun *miraculum* and its related verb *miror*. Pliny's enthusiastic cataloguing of Rome's wonders would provide the fifteenth-century antiquarian, Flavio Biondo, with anecdotes about the extraordinary, but by his time vanished, marvels of the ancient city.[11]

It was not just the ancient Romans themselves who were impressed by their city. A third-century rabbi, Hiyya bar Abba, claimed that 'there are three hundred and sixty five thoroughfares in the great city of Rome, and in each there were three hundred and sixty five palaces; and in each palace there were three hundred and sixty five storeys, and each storey contained sufficient to provide the whole world with food'.[12] The rabbi seems to have had some idea of the numerous and extensive warehouses (*horrea*) in which grain was kept to be doled out to the citizens. A Greek historian, Olympiodorus of Egyptian Thebes, described Rome shortly after the sack of the city by Alaric in 410:

> Each of the great houses of Rome contained within itself … everything which a medium-sized city could hold, a hippodrome, fora, temples, fountains and different kinds of baths. At this time the historian emotes: 'one house is a town, the city holds ten thousand towns.' There were also enormous public baths. Those called the Antonine [= Baths of Caracalla] have 1,600 seats of polished marble for the bathers, while the Baths of Diocletian have nearly twice as many.[13]

John Matthews fairly reckoned that the claim that private houses included racetracks was clearly hyperbolical (albeit accurate as regards the imperial palace on the Palatine hill), and yet it is evidence of how readily the non-Roman credited the city with the most extraordinary buildings.[14]

Although many of Rome's buildings staggered the imagination in their scale, it is surprising that none of them secured a place among the traditional Seven Wonders, which were scattered all over the eastern Mediterranean world.[15] This defect was deplored by Cassiodorus, whom we met in the previous chapter. In a letter to the Prefect of Rome, *Variae* 7.15, he referred to the traditional Seven Wonders and not unreasonably asked how anyone could continue to find them outstanding once he had seen so many amazing things in a single city; Rome as a whole was a wonder (*miraculum*). Cassiodorus seems unaware that his view had in fact already been anticipated, when a list of the buildings within Rome itself which rivalled the traditional seven was drawn up.

That list of the Seven Wonders of Rome is preserved in the *Laterculus* ('Register') of Polemius Silvius.[16] Polemius' primary task in the mid-fifth century was to produce a calendar of Christian festivals that would supersede the old Roman (and pagan) *fasti*. But between the calendars of the months he inserted lists of other things, such as the Roman emperors, the provinces of the empire and the correct words to describe the sounds animals make. One list inserted between June and July records Rome's noteworthy buildings: 'Among all these things are seven outstanding marvels [*mira praecipua*]: the Janiculum Hill, the sewers, the aqueducts, the Forum of Trajan, the amphitheatre [= Colosseum], the Odeum [Domitian's] and the Antonian Baths [= Baths of Caracalla].' If the Janiculum Hill is indeed the one referred to, rather than the Capitoline Hill (the text has been queried), it is presumably less for its vistas (albeit praised by the poet Martial, *Epigrams* 4.64.11–13) than for its impressive series of water mills, powered by the *aqua Traiana*, one of which has been recently excavated near the American Academy.[17] The inclusion of the city's remarkable infrastructure of sewers and aqueducts (and possibly water mills) links Polemius to Pliny: the practical Roman admired beneficial public works.

All of this may seem to be just so much civic pride, but we also have apparently more sober documents from late antiquity which confirm by simple arithmetic the incomparable scale of the city. These are the two fourth-century regionary catalogues entitled *Notitia* (catalogue) and *Curiosum* (inventory), mentioned briefly at the beginning of the second chapter.[18] Their true purpose is far from clear, not least because there is no discernible principle underlying the selection of structures mentioned. Why, for instance, was the conspicuous Arch of Septimius Severus not mentioned? They are unlikely to have been administrative documents. Contemporary opinion now inclines therefore to the view that these capricious but impressive lists belong to a category of urban panegyric.[19] Nicholas Purcell saw in them a stage in the development of the marvel-literature of the city, while to Hendrik Dey they present 'an imaginary ... impossible composite, a Calvinoesque "invisible city"'.[20] These catalogues served as important models and sources of information for the writer of the twelfth-century *Mirabilia*, to which we will turn in due course.

Although the traditional list of the Seven Wonders of the known world neglected Rome as a western outlier, the omission was nonetheless made good by an unknown writer of the eighth century. His work, 'The Seven Man-Made Wonders of the World' (*De septem miraculis mundi manu hominum factis*), was generally ascribed to the Venerable Bede.[21] Into this fairly conventional list of marvels the writer inserted one building on the Capitol, known as the *Salvatio Civium*, 'Safeguard of the Citizens'; it would be frequently referred to by later writers.[22] The *Salvatio* is described as follows:

> The first wonder is the Capitol of Rome, the safeguard of its citizens, greater than a city. On it there were statues of the peoples conquered by the Romans, or images of the gods, and on the breasts of the statues the names of the captured peoples were written, and bells were hung about their necks. The priests or guardians day and night by turns kept charge of them and watched them. If any of them moved, the bell promptly made a sound, so that they knew which people was rebelling against the Romans. When this was known they conveyed a message, oral or written, to the Roman emperors so that they would know against which people an army ought to be sent to keep it in check.

Fantastic as this Roman proto-telegraph seems, it may nonetheless have a tenuous link with ancient structures. According to Pliny the Elder, *Natural History* 36.41, the theatre-complex of Pompey was decorated with fourteen allegorical statues of defeated peoples, now Roman provinces. There were similar allegorical figures of cities and provinces of the empire in an Augustan portico known as *ad nationes*,[23] on sculptural panels in the attic storey of the colonnade of the Forum of Nerva,[24] and finally on a portico near the Hadrianeum, the Temple of the Deified Hadrian, some panels of which are now in the National Museum in Naples[25] (Figure 3.1). Reminiscence of any or all of these relief panels may well have contributed

Figure 3.1 Allegorical relief of a Roman province. Photo: Wikimedia
Commons – Carole Raddato, CC BY-SA 2.0.

something to the invention of the fantastic statues of the *Salvatio*. Since this
wonderful device was no longer visible, having been destroyed, perhaps
at the birth of Christ,[26] it is hardly a surprise that the actual Rome of the
eighth century held less appeal to the visitor, as we learn from an English
cleric, Alcuin.

Alcuin, a scholar from York and advisor to the Frankish king
Charlemagne who first went to Rome in 781, described it as ruinous. Since
he visited the city at least twice, he knew what he was talking about. In a
lament for the destruction of Lindisfarne monastery in 793, Alcuin listed
famous cities that had gone to wrack and ruin, and naturally he included
Rome:[27] 'Rome, world capital, world glory, golden Rome, / now all that is
left to you is a cruel ruin.' In a later poem dated 798 to Wizzo (Candidus),
a pupil of his who was on his way to Rome, he described the path amid the

ruins of the *disabitato* which Wizzo would take to reach the church of S. Paolo fuori le mura:[28] 'amid the lofty arches of the walls on the point of collapse'. Alcuin's reference to some unidentified ruins which had to be passed on the way to one of Rome's greatest station churches is perhaps indicative of how travellers navigated the puzzling city at that time. We see this more fully illustrated in a roughly contemporary guide, the so-called Einsiedeln Itineraries.

Einsiedeln is an Alpine village about an hour's attractive rail journey from Zurich. The village boasts one of the finest Baroque monasteries in Switzerland, and its conventual church is the crowning architectural achievement of Kaspar Moosbrugger. A Benedictine monastery is unimaginable without a library, and that of Einsiedeln contains some unusual items, such as the anonymous pastoral poems, known as the Einsiedeln Eclogues, which prudent scholars date to the reign of the emperor Nero (54–68). Another rarity is the codex, numbered 326, containing among a miscellany of items itineraries through Rome. This important text has been edited in the standard collections.[29] There are also up-to-date editions with facsimiles by Gerold Walser, who generously commends Gregorovius' readable account of the Itineraries,[30] and Stefano del Lungo.[31] But it is much more exciting to read the MS itself online.[32] This MS dates to the ninth century, but it is not agreed when and where the Itineraries themselves originated. They begin on folio 79 verso. Their compiler also transcribed a collection of ancient inscriptions to be seen in Rome (they begin on folio 67 recto), so his work is rightly regarded as an early step in the study of epigraphy. The purpose of the Itineraries is debated, but they give every appearance of providing guidance through Rome, presumably for pilgrims. In effect, the Einsiedeln Itineraries are a proto-guidebook, as Anna Blennow has most recently argued.[33]

Each Itinerary lists in columns on facing pages structures and buildings, naming what was to be seen to the left and to the right as the traveller moved towards their destination. (The MS initially confuses right and left, so it would not have been much practical help.) It has been suggested that a map may have accompanied the original text, and Walser's edition provides visual aids.[34] The structures to which the Itineraries drew attention as markers of location are both ancient imperial ones and the contemporary churches and martyr shrines. This juxtaposition of pre-Christian and Christian is already found in the sixth-century *Liber Pontificalis*, a demonstration that 'Rome's antique past, both in physical terms and as an idea, remained a constant factor'.[35] But since the compiler of the Itineraries was a Christian, it is not perhaps surprising that only one pagan temple is cited.

Ancient names are usually provided for many of the old Roman sites and ruined structures (sometimes in error: in the first Itinerary the Stadium of Domitian is misidentified as the Circus Flaminius), but popular names are used as well, such as the 'Palace of Trajan', meaning his *thermae*. We are thus given an idea of what survived into the ninth century and of how it was identified.

One surprise is found in the seventh Itinerary, namely the Palace of Pilate (*palatium Pilati*), located somewhere in the vicinity of the basilica of S. Maria Maggiore. Needless to say, it baffles identification. But there was a long-standing legend that Pontius Pilate was secretly a follower of Jesus and that he left an account, the *Acta Pilati*, of the Saviour's death and resurrection. Now the Einsiedeln MS contains these apocryphal *Acta*, under the commoner name of the Gospel of Nicodemus (*Evangelium Nicodemi*). Pilate's alleged sympathy with Christianity and his recall to Rome by the emperor Tiberius apparently prompted the identification of some building with his Roman residence; another building so identified will be mentioned in the next chapter.

To return to the Itineraries, the ancient remains, both pagan and early Christian, served as a constant resource for the visitor, and a reminder of the city's intricate heritage. Rome was the focus of ecclesiastical business for western Christendom, and also the goal of pilgrimage, since the tombs of the martyrs, especially of the apostles, were much venerated. The remains of pagan antiquity, however, were necessarily encountered at every turn, even if they were not the goal of a visit. Since the Itineraries apparently served no more elaborate purpose than fingerposts, we cannot expect to find in them any sort of response to the presence of the ruins; what is important is that the ruins were ever-present and up to a point still reliably identifiable. For an emotional response we must wait, not for the last time, for a poet.

Hildebert of Lavardin, bishop of Le Mans and then archbishop of Tours, visited Rome on a number of occasions in the early twelfth century, about 250 years after Alcuin. Whereas Alcuin had found the ruin of the city 'cruel', Hildebert was impressed with the ancient remains. Both Rome's ruins and the statuary still to be found there affected him so strongly that he recorded his reaction to them in a famous poem, the first dedicated to Rome itself since antiquity,[36] which was widely circulated and copied; it will be found, for instance, in William of Malmesbury's *Gesta Regum Anglorum* 4.351.[37] The poem's opening words set the tone: 'Nothing matches you, Rome, though you are almost a complete ruin' (*Par tibi, Roma, nihil, cum sis prope tota ruina*). What justified this claim was the sheer scale and magnificence of the remains of the ancient buildings, remains so vast that they could not possibly be repaired by contemporary means (36.23–8):

> So much is still left, so much fallen, that the standing part
>   cannot be matched, nor the fallen repaired.
> Collect resources, new marble and divine favour,
>   let craftsmen's hands be brisk at new works,
> still the crane is no match for the standing wall,
>   nor can the solitary ruin be restored.

Hildebert's conviction that contemporary methods of construction would prove unequal to the task of restoring the ruins of Rome is at first sight strange, since such restoration was hardly envisaged in his day. He may, however, be drawing upon his own experience, since he had himself overseen the continuing construction of the new nave of Le Mans cathedral, which was finally consecrated in 1120. The nave was probably no higher than the 24 metres of its successor, which was under construction after a fire in 1134. Considerable scaffolding and machinery were required to lift masonry to a height of 24 metres. So when Hildebert saw the Colosseum, whose outer ring of wall rises to 48 metres,[38] he must have wondered how the ancient Romans managed to build walls twice as high as those of his cathedral church. Hildebert had personal experience of building on a grand scale, but even the grandest architecture of his own day could not prepare him for the immensity of Roman building. Unexpected, too, is Hildebert's feeling that time and other destructive forces had not utterly deprived Rome's old buildings of all their beauty (36.21–2): 'Still neither the course of years nor fire nor sword / could completely *obliterate this splendour*' (*hoc abolere decus*) (my emphasis). Hildebert is apparently the first to record an aesthetic response to Rome's ruins: for him they still possessed *decus*, an attractive quality more usually found in complete structures. Hildebert's poem on the incomparable impressiveness of the remains of ancient Rome was not meant to stand alone, however. It formed a sort of diptych with a second poem on contemporary Rome, beginning *Dum simulacra mihi* ('while statues pleased me').[39] In that complementary poem the much-degraded Rome of Hildebert's own day nonetheless congratulates itself for now being Christian and the episcopal see of the successor of the apostle Peter (38.11): *plus Caesare Petrus* ('Peter is more important than Caesar').

The pairing of these two poems goes some way towards confirming another of the insights of Salvatore Settis, mentioned in the first chapter, about the pathos of continuity within discontinuity.[40] Hildebert subtly recognised that Rome was somehow the same and yet different. Ancient Rome had been powerful and magnificent, as the ruins attested, while the physical appearance of its modern successor underwhelmed. But spiritually considered, modern Rome surpassed the ancient city, which was after all a ruin. Even so, for Hildebert at least, the ruins still possessed a glamour, not in themselves as ruins but as remnants of a venerated culture.[41] They formed the crucial bridge over the gap between pagan and Christian Rome. So, despite appearances, Rome remained something great and impressive.

The *Mirabilia* Tradition

Given the factual accounts of the scale of the city and of the buildings, civic and private, which filled it, it is hardly surprising that in the early Middle Ages Romans and visitors alike were awestruck by the ruins around them. Peter Burke noted, however, that their amazement was uninformed by historical curiosity: the ruins 'were taken as given. People seem not to have wondered how they got there, when they were built, or why the style of architecture was different from their own. The most they will do is to tell "just so stories" or explanatory myths about the names of places'.[42] Our chief source of these stories is a much-redacted work nowadays titled *Mirabilia Urbis Romae*, 'The Marvels of the City of Rome'.[43]

The earliest version of the *Mirabilia* was composed or rather compiled ca. 1140–3. It is still sometimes attributed to one Benedict as author, but the concept of authorship was pretty indefinite in the twelfth century. This alleged Benedict may or may not also be the author, also named Benedict, a canon of St Peter's, of the contemporary *Ordo Romanus*, an account of the various processional routes taken by the pope to and from either St Peter's or his palace in the Lateran to the important station churches in Rome.[44] The *Ordo* is itself an important document and deserves a brief word before we turn to the other Benedict's more popular work, the *Mirabilia*.

As in the Einsiedeln Itineraries, mentioned earlier, ancient as well as contemporary structures, churches naturally, are named in the *Ordo* to identify the route taken and the stops along the way. The most important of these routes through the city, called the via Papalis, describes the pope's route from his cathedral church of St John Lateran to St Peter's basilica in the Vatican, and a different return journey.[45] Unlike the compiler of the Einsiedeln Itineraries, however, Benedict cited pagan temples by name as way-markers. For instance, on Christmas Day the pope processed from the church of St Anastasia to the Vatican, and according to the *Ordo* he

passed the temples of the Sybil and of Cicero.[46] The oddity of this is that
the so-called Temple of the Sybil was presumably the church of S. Maria in
Cosmedin, and the 'Temple of Cicero' the church of S. Nicola in Carcere:
the ecclesiastical writer has not scrupled to identify contemporary churches
by archaic (and quite imaginary) names. Many other ancient structures
passed in the course of the various processions are named, and some are
even more or less correctly identified. As Chris Wickham remarks, when
Benedict was giving directions, he overwhelmingly thought in classical
terms.[47] The Benedict who compiled the *Ordo* was unlikely to have been
alone in his feeling for the extant remains of Rome's pagan past. They were
a substantial part of the city's structure, and crucially they had their own
individual identities and names, sometimes perhaps mistaken but still
hallowed by tradition and everyday usage. The ruins provided invaluable
orientation through the muddle of the mediaeval city.

We may now turn to the other Benedict (if he is in fact 'other' and
'Benedict'), the author of the *Mirabilia*. The original purpose of his work
is a matter of speculation. It was once generally claimed that the *Mirabilia*
was intended to serve as a guide for pilgrims to the metropolis of western
Christianity. But this seems unlikely, especially when one reads the first
part of the work in its earliest form, §§1–11.[48] This part is clearly modelled upon the fourth-century regionary catalogues. Benedict followed
their model in providing sometimes no more than a bare list of buildings
by name and category, such as the *thermae* and 'palaces' (*palatia*; that is to
say, any vast secular building complexes). None of these structures is clearly
fixed in an identifiable locality. Benedict did, however, fix the locations of
the triumphal arches (§4) and of the theatres (§8). This rather patchy provision of local guidance in the first section of the original *Mirabilia* does little
to support the notion that it was meant to serve as a guide.

A further argument against the notion that the work was a primitive
guidebook is that a considerable number of the buildings mentioned were
no longer extant, such as the alleged Temple of the Sun near the Colosseum,
which will be discussed later in this chapter. In the light of these considerations, the safest course surely is to accept the purpose identified by Benedict
himself. He asserted in the final paragraph, which will be quoted and discussed later in this chapter, that he wrote to preserve the memory of the
city's glorious past. Whatever the work's purpose, it proved a great success
and in its later and expanded redactions it certainly did serve as a guidebook. Arturo Graf and Francis Morgan Nichols provided clear accounts,
based on contemporary scholarship, of the somewhat baffling tradition of
these subsequent redactions.[49] The most significant of them is Peter the

Deacon's *Graphia aureae Urbis Romae*, 'Description of the Golden City of Rome', compiled not long after Benedict's original, ca. 1155;[50] its influence too was considerable, and it was translated into a number of vernaculars.[51]

Just as the purpose of the work is something of an open question, so is the issue of the alleged influence upon it of the contemporary political situation in Rome.[52] In 1143, on the death of Pope Innocent II, a revived Roman Senate and a newly established Commune di Roma made a bid for independence from the papacy and from such of the nobility as supported it – a social and political move to be set in the context of the rise of independent communes in northern Italy, where some communities had already repudiated episcopal authority.[53] The author of the *Mirabilia*, as a cleric, however, is unlikely to have endorsed any diminution of papal power, but his work was clearly welcome nonetheless in the newly patriotic political climate of contemporary Rome.

After the initial list of building types, Benedict selected some of special interest because he had stories to tell about them (§§12–17). We must regretfully ignore his stories about extant statues, such as the marble horses and naked horsemen (philosophers, as he thought them), now on the Quirinal Hill (§13), and focus on the buildings. What strikes us is that most of the buildings were pagan in origin. Our attention can be confined to just two because they are still extant: the Pantheon and the Mausoleum of Augustus.

In §16 Benedict related a long story about the foundation of the Pantheon by Agrippa (he could hardly have failed to identify the founder, given that his name is still visible on the pediment). Agrippa was charged by the Senate to undertake a campaign against Persia, after the bell on its statue in a temple on the Capitol had rung, indicating trouble afoot in that quarter. In a dream the goddess Cybele, mother of the gods, appeared to Agrippa and told him to undertake the campaign, assuring him that he would be successful if he built her a temple. All of this came to pass. Benedict then related how Pope Boniface IV secured the temple for Christian worship from the emperor Phocas.[54] In §19 Benedict claimed that the bronze pine-cone (*pigna*), now in the Belvedere courtyard of the Vatican, had been placed on top of the statue of Cybele to serve as a sort of 'stopper' stuck in the oculus of the dome: a complete fantasy.[55] The important feature of Benedict's account is the link forged between past and present; he was perhaps unconsciously trying to bridge the gap which Salvatore Settis rightly regards as so important for the appreciation of the remains of an antecedent culture.

The Mausoleum of Augustus (§22) is correctly identified by Benedict, and equally correctly it is said to be where the emperor Nerva was buried.[56] Its shape, however, a rotunda surmounted by a domical mound of earth planted (in antiquity) with trees, gave rise to Benedict's fanciful story that the emperor Octavian (i.e. Augustus) had ordered that a parcel of soil be sent from every kingdom in the world. The soil was placed on the top of the mausoleum, forming a sort of hillock, to be remembered by all those coming to Rome.

Impressive as Benedict's coverage of the remains of pagan Rome is, it is something of a surprise that, in the original version of the *Mirabilia*, he never mentioned the aqueducts and touched upon the Colosseum only briefly. In §3 he rightly located the Arch of Constantine 'near the Amphitheatre' (*iuxta Amphitheatrum*, i.e. the Colosseum), and in §14 he gave its height as 108 feet. More revealing is §28 in which Benedict said that in front of the Colosseum there was a Temple of the Sun where ceremonies were held in honour of the statue that stood at the summit of the Colosseum. This meagre coverage was clearly felt to be a defect in the work, so the account of the Colosseum was expanded in a later redaction.

Benedict's 'reviser' mistook the purpose of the Flavian amphitheatre and reckoned that it was itself originally a Temple of the Sun. His error went back to the presence of a 'colossal' statue of Nero, later transformed into a representation of the sun-god Helios, which originally stood at the entrance of Nero's *Domus Aurea* and was later moved when the emperor Hadrian needed space for the Temple of Venus and Roma.[57] The huge statue's proximity to the amphitheatre, which was equally 'colossal' in scale, seems to have led to a loan of the epithet, which, after the statue's destruction, was applied solely to the building, henceforth known as the Colosseum. Since the writer thought the building was a temple, he assumed it had a roof and, given the shape of the structure, he reckoned that the roof was domed, as indeed it appears on some mediaeval maps.[58]

Benedict's work is an entirely fresh departure from the earlier Itineraries, thanks above all to its focus on the legends attached to the ancient structures (either extant or vanished). The final paragraph, §32, is important in that it sets out Benedict's purpose as he saw it, and his personal response to the remains of ancient Rome.

> These and many more temples and palaces of emperors, consuls, senators and prefects were in the time of the heathen within this Roman city, even as we have read in old chronicles, and have seen with our eyes, and have heard tell of ancient men. And moreover, how great was their beauty in gold, and silver, and brass, and ivory, and precious stones we have endeavoured in writing, as well as we could, to bring back to the remembrance of mankind.[59]

First, Benedict lays claim to three sources of information: oral tradition, autopsy and documentary sources. By 'old chronicles', he seems
to refer primarily to the regionary catalogues. But Benedict also made
three express citations from Ovid's 'martyrologion', as the poet's unfinished didactic poem on the ancient Roman calendar, titled *Fasti*, is engagingly styled.[60] The real surprise is the elision of Christian Rome from this
envoi; Benedict's admiration is centred solely on the remains of pagan
Rome. It was the beauty (*pulchritudo*) of the decorative materials with
which that city was built 'in the time of the pagans' that he wanted posterity to remember. With this in mind, if we go back over the text we find
three monuments, all pagan and antique, singled out for their beauty: a
'Temple' of Pompey, generally thought to be his theatre (§23), Trajan's
column (§24) and the Circus Maximus (§29). Their scale too impressed
Benedict, as it had Hildebert of Lavardin: Pompey's 'temple' is 'extraordi-
narily large' (*mirae magnitudinis*), as is the 'temple' (actually the mausoleum) of Hadrian, now the Castel Sant'Angelo (§21). Trajan's column is 'of
extraordinary height' (*mirae altitudinis*); to prove this, Benedict informs
his reader of its exact height, how many steps it has inside and how many
windows, information he derived from the *Notitia*. 'Wonder' is his characteristic response to what can be seen, like the theatre and the column and
the Pantheon (*templum ... mirabile*, §16), but also to what is gone: when
Benedict described the Circus Maximus (§29), his verbs were in the past
tense. Benedict's enthusiasm marks a crucial turning-point in the reception of Rome's pagan remains. Given the wide diffusion of his text – and
it would be among the first to benefit from the new technology of print in
the fifteenth century – Benedict contributed largely to a reassessment of
the value of ruins and to an appreciation of their beauty.[61]

If the author, whether Benedict or not, was a Roman of Rome, as seems
likely, his interest in and enthusiasm for the ancient city was to some extent
engendered by local pride. Two foreign visitors, however, the Spanish
Benjamin of Tudela and the English Magister Gregorius or Master Gregory,
shared his interest in the more amazing remains.

Benjamin of Tudela was a Jew who travelled from northeast Spain via
France and Italy to the Near East; from there he returned to Spain via North
Africa. Why he made this prolonged journey is not known, but for our
purposes his motive is irrelevant. He recorded a stop in Rome ca. 1161,
where he was highly impressed by the scale of the city and by its remaining
buildings.[62] Benjamin reckoned that they were different from all the buildings in the rest of the world. He does not seem to know the *Mirabilia* (perhaps he could not read Latin), so he relied upon his fellow Jews resident in

Rome for his information. He claimed that there were eighty palaces of the eighty emperors from Tarquin to Pippin, father of Charlemagne. He was impressed by the 'palace' of Vespasian, probably the Colosseum, which he described as being 'as big as a citadel'. He identified what may have been the Circus of Maxentius on the via Appia as the suburban palace of Vespasian's son Titus, who, according to Benjamin, was constrained to live outside Rome because he had taken three years, rather than the stipulated two, to conquer Jerusalem.[63] Benjamin's interest in Titus and Vespasian, and in the spoils they brought to Rome from the temple, is understandable,[64] and so it may seem odd that no-one directed him to the Arch of Titus, on which he would have seen depicted Roman soldiers carrying off the seven-branched candelabrum (Figure 3.2). But perhaps Benjamin respected the reluctance of Rome's Jewish community to pass through the arch.[65] He also described an underground burial place, probably the Mausoleum of Augustus, where the emperor and his empress wife were seated on thrones, with about 100 embalmed eminent men standing around them. Benjamin did not claim to have seen all or indeed any of the striking buildings he mentioned.

Our second foreign visitor, Magister Gregorius, or Master Gregory, is so shadowy a figure that he finds no place in the *Oxford Dictionary of National Biography*. He seems to have been an Englishman, who visited Rome at the end of the twelfth or the beginning of the thirteenth century.[66] His title

Figure 3.2 J.-G. Moitte, terracotta sculpture after a relief on the Arch of Titus. Photo: Los Angeles County Museum of Art/public domain.

magister, master, suggests higher education, and his cultural formation is important.[67] His reading provided valuable context for some of the objects or buildings he saw in Rome. Directly quoted are Suetonius and Virgil in §29, Lucan in §25, Ovid in §19; Horace, Seneca and Isidore of Seville are at least alluded to. In his introduction he (mis)quotes the opening lines of Hildebert's poem, *Par tibi*, agreeing with him that though Rome is ruinous, it is incomparable.

Why Master Gregory went to Rome is not made clear in the work he wrote describing what he saw there, the *Narracio de Mirabilibus Urbis Romae*, 'An Account of the Marvellous Things in the City of Rome'.[68] In introducing his work, he used a typical modesty formula in claiming that he had been goaded by the request of his friends to record the admirable things he saw in Rome. But surely Master Gregory composed this record just because he was so profoundly impressed by what he saw there. The *Narracio* had little circulation on its own. There is now only one MS of it, in St Catharine's College, Cambridge, which was discovered and only published early in the twentieth century by M. R. James.[69] But the *Narracio* was known to and cited by the English Benedictine monk Ranulph Higden, who copied some of it into the first book of his *Polychronicon*, a historical work notable for its description of the Roman world. The *Polychronicon's* circulation brought Master Gregory's eyewitness account of the wonderful things he saw in Rome to the attention of an audience which was showing increasing interest in the ancient world.[70]

After describing his first sight of Rome and its bristling towers, he named the gates (§2), and then he described statuary, an object of unexpectedly keen interest, bronze ones first (§§3–9), then marble (§12), especially a statue of Venus, naked, which he went to see three times. (In his account of some of these statues Gregory's model was pseudo-Bede, *De vii miraculis mundi*.) Gregory remarked upon the multiplicity of statues in Rome, and in §8 he focussed on the *Salvatio Civium*, which was once, *quondam*, in the city (he does not specify the Capitol), but was now no longer to be seen. He was told it had collapsed at the birth of Christ. Despite the alleged destruction, Gregory claimed that its walls and 'spooky inaccessible crypts' could still be seen. He is taken to be referring to the remains of the Tabularium, ancient Rome's Record Office, a still imposing structure overlooking the Roman Forum. It so impressed the poet Virgil that he mentioned it in his *Georgics*, 2.502; its tunnels now house Rome's Museo Lapidario[71] (Figure 3.3). At any rate, it is remarkable that he identified some ruin or other as all that was left of the *Salvatio*; he was consciously trying to give a contemporary ruin a specific context

Figure 3.3 Tabularium. Photo: Rita1234 – own work, CC BY-SA 3.0.

and function in antiquity. In this he was not alone: Nikolaus Muffel of Nuremburg, who came to Rome in 1452 for the coronation of the Holy Roman emperor Frederick III, believed the niches in the Pantheon contained the allegorical statues of the provinces, so for Muffel the Pantheon was the site of the *Salvatio*.[72]

After exhausting his enthusiasm for statuary, Master Gregory turned to describing some extant buildings. The *palatium* (= Baths) of Diocletian he described in §15 as vast in size, skilful and admirable in construction. The height of its columns impressed him (he did not seem to recognise that they are actually monoliths) because no-one could throw a stone high enough to reach their top (presumably he tried!). Sensibly he said that he would not invite disbelief by seeming to exaggerate. In §16 he mentioned a ruinous temple of Pallas, one of only two pagan temples named by him (the Pantheon being the second). This is also the only site connected with a Christian martyrdom, that of Hippolytus, the fourth-century bishop of Portus, the harbour of Rome.

In §17 he noted that little remained of the palace of the divine Augustus, probably the Domus Augustana on the Palatine, because the precious materials had been recycled in the construction of churches. (There had indeed been a boom in church construction in the early twelfth century.)[73] In §§19–20 he mentioned various imperial *palatia* too numerous to describe and difficult to identify nowadays. He referred to the Septem Solia, that is to say the Severan Septizodium, and he quoted Ovid, *Metamorphoses* 2.1–2 as if Ovid were describing that very structure. When he visited the Pantheon (§21), he measured its width. In §23 triumphal arches are listed, but Gregory noted acidly that when you've seen one, you've seen 'em all! In §24 he identified an arch of Pompey, completely unknown and historically unlikely, but it would also be mentioned by Petrarch, *Familiares* vi.2.5–14, among other later visitors. Master Gregory's account of triumphal columns (§25) is odd because the columns of Marcus Aurelius and of Trajan had been correctly identified in the Einsiedeln Itinerary and the *Mirabilia*; his error seems to be generated from his reading and his moralising. When he came to Rome's pyramids (§27), he identified one as the tomb of Romulus, not St Peter's grain heap as pious pilgrims mistakenly imagined (this no longer extant structure was the *meta Romuli* of *Mirabilia*, §20). The pyramid of Augustus (§28) was the so-called Tomb of Remus, *sepulchrum Remi*, of *Mirabilia* §2; in fact, it is the still extant Pyramid of Cestius. Finally, there is the 'pyramid' of Julius Caesar (§29), that is to say the Vatican obelisk, mentioned in the *Mirabilia* §18 (*memoria Caesaris id est agulia*), and much later re-erected in the piazza in front of St Peter's Basilica (Petrarch would refer to it in his letter of 1337 to Giovanni Colonna, to be quoted in the next chapter, p. 57). Once again, Master Gregory elaborated his account with recollections, somewhat garbled, of his reading from Suetonius and Virgil. The last building mentioned, but not described, in §31 is the Colosseum, the 'palace' of Vespasian and Titus. Gregory does not seem to know its function, and in a neat rhetorical *praeteritio* he declined to describe it, because 'words were inadequate to indicate its ingenious construction and size' (*quis enim artificiosam constructionem eius et magnitudinem sermone exequi poterit?*).

Although describing in a number of cases structures also mentioned in Benedict's *Mirabilia*, there are few points of contact with that work. The reason for this may be that the mind-set of Master Gregory was largely hostile to fantasy. In the main, he contrasts his information, gleaned on the spot either by observation or what he takes to be reliable report, with the trivial tales of pilgrims. He is not producing a guidebook but a record of Rome's fascinating remains (chiefly statues). The unique and surprising feature of his coverage is the almost exclusively secular and antiquarian nature of his interest. He did not present himself as a pilgrim interested in visiting sacred sites, and he mentioned only two churches. The one church he dealt with most fully was housed in a formerly pagan temple, the Pantheon.

During the period covered in this chapter, the Rome of antiquity was dilapidated and generally dispraised, and yet its ruins were gradually acquiring something of a following. By the end of the period, a widely distributed work with the suggestive title *Mirabilia* shows how far the prestige of the ruins (among other remains of ancient Rome) had risen over time. What was left impressed chiefly by its scale and costly materials. The curious stories attached to the remains provided a kind of context for what visitors saw.

For Alcuin, at the beginning of our period, the ruins of Rome were much like the ruins of Megalopolis for Pausanias: a melancholy warning of the fragility of manmade works. But the great fragments remained significant features of the cityscape, something you had to notice as you walked on your way to one of the great churches on the uninhabited edge of Rome. Ruins served too as landmarks, as we see in the Einsiedeln Itineraries. In a city without street names (except for the most important roads), an impressive structure, however tumbledown, provided orientation. Thus in the tenth century a region of Rome centred on the Theatre of Marcellus was known as the 'regione Marcello'. By such means the Itinerary found a use for the remains of pagan Rome in helping the visitor navigate the Christianised city. Visitors continued to come to Rome, either on ecclesiastical business or as pilgrims. The great churches and shrines ought to have been their priority, but some, like Hildebert of Lavardin, also found an attraction, even perhaps a beauty, in the pagan remains. The ruins benefited from the development of a civic consciousness in the twelfth century, as we see in Benedict's *Mirabilia*, which focussed on secular pagan structures. So successful was this work that it underwent numerous redactions, always with additions of material. In Master Gregory we unexpectedly find a visitor whose sole interest seems to be what is left of pagan Rome (he mentioned only one martyr's shrine).

Once the antique remains had secured sustained interest, they cried out for accurate identification. Identification was to some extent possible, without reliance on what passed for local knowledge, thanks to the existence of pagan authors whose works referred to buildings known to them. Thus a significant link between Benedict and Gregory is their attempt to identify the remains by their use of Roman poetic texts (Ovid's especially) to assist them in this initiative. Benedict and Gregory can therefore be seen as precursors of the poet whose enthusiasm for classical Latin literature put Rome's ruins squarely on the cultural map, Petrarch. He is the subject of the next chapter.

4 | The Watershed

Petrarch and His Successors

The importance of the material to be discussed in this chapter is demonstrated by the sheer bulk of the fourth and final volume of the *Codice Topografico della Città di Roma* (1953), which begins with Petrarch and includes his immediate successors. The period of Rome's history covered is also significant, and it required the division of the sixth volume of Ferdinand Gregorovius' monumental history into in two parts (vi, 1 and 2: 1906). What we will find in the accounts of Rome in the fourteenth century is a more widespread change of sentiment towards the visible ruins, from a casual acceptance of them as an integral part of the cityscape to enthusiastic fascination. That fascination will in turn generate a dissatisfaction with the old fables and a novel desire to replace them with an understanding of the ruins based on a knowledge of Roman history and culture as mediated in classical Latin texts. In fact, the material culture of Rome, especially as seen in the built environment of the city, is for the first time subjected to informed investigation. Petrarch gives the impulse to this new movement, and so persuasive was his advocacy of the ruins that he secured followers who further developed and refined the process of studying the city's material culture. Before turning to Petrarch, however, a résumé of the condition of the city before his visits in the middle of the fourteenth century is necessary.

*

We begin with Rome in 1300, the year of the first ever Jubilee, a holy year instituted by papal decree during which pilgrims to Rome secured forgiveness of their sins and, most invitingly, remission from their penitential time in Purgatory after death. How might the city have looked to those pilgrims? Robert Brentano reckons the population did not exceed 35,000, a number that would fit into the Colosseum; the surface area of the city within the Aurelian walls was about 3,000 acres, and that acreage was not at all densely populated.[1] The reason for the low density was 'ruralisation': farms, gardens and vineyards were all contained within the circuit of the walls, and there was little need to cultivate the ground outside.[2] There were isolated churches, monasteries and the fortress towers of important families scattered about. The main population had settled on the Tiber's flood plain in the Campus Martius. Beyond this inhabited area, the rest of the terrain within the circuit of walls was depopulated, *disabitato*, especially in the southeastern quarter, which had been laid waste by fire in the eleventh century following the Norman Duke Robert's invasion. The hills of the city were also largely abandoned for lack of water, which had once been provided by the system of aqueducts.

Just before the Jubilee of 1300, the great churches at any rate were refurbished. As an example of the smartening-up of the pilgrimage sites, the greatest painter of the day, Giotto di Bondone, was commissioned to adorn the Lateran with frescos. All of this was changed, however, by the time of the next Jubilee in 1350. Gregorovius described the combined effects of the Black Death in the years 1347–9 (further depopulation), of the terrific earthquake of 1349, which probably brought down a flank of the outer wall of the Colosseum (see Chapter 2, p. 17), and of the withdrawal of the papacy to Avignon, a city in the Kingdom of Arles in Provence.[3] Rome's contemporary desolation is recorded by Petrarch himself after his fifth visit to the city in 1366 in his *Seniles*, vii.i, 43, an appeal to Pope Urban V to leave Avignon and settle in Rome: 'the houses are falling down, the walls totter, the churches are collapsing' (*iacent domus, labant menia, templa ruunt*, dated 29 June).

A word must here be said about the self-imposed exile of the bishops of Rome. The removal of the papacy from its diocese was brought about by conflict with the king of France, Philip IV. In 1309 the Gascon Pope Clement V (who had never personally set foot in Rome – his court was at Poitiers) relocated the papacy along with its administration (the Curia) in Avignon, where it remained under a series of French popes until 1374. But because of the subsequent 'western schism', which began in 1378, the papacy did not settle back down in Rome until 1420, after the uncontested election in 1417 of Martin V (a Roman of the Colonna family) at the Council of Constance. The papal and curial absence was catastrophic to Rome's economy.[4] The city's chaotic condition was aggravated by the lack of a strong civic government that could check the conflict of rival families, for example the Colonna and the Orsini factions. Contemporary accounts of attacks on travellers making their way to Rome – not to mention the dangers within the city itself – suggest that fewer pilgrims came to the disordered city, further reducing local revenue. Thus the Rome that Petrarch first visited was poor and perilous, but at least the ruins were left largely to themselves for another century, until the return of the pope in 1420.

Francesco Petrarch and Rome

A short account of Petrarch's life and cultural formation will explain his eagerness to visit Rome and his unexpected reaction to what he saw when he finally got there. Roberto Weiss and Nicholas Mann are reliable guides.[5]

Petrarch's choice of career path must have surprised his contemporaries, given his conventional literary and legal education in the universities of Montpellier and Bologna. Rather than become a notary or a papal secretary, he decided on the then unusual career of literature.[6] He has been called the first 'man of letters' in modern times. His father, a notary, had vainly tried to curb his gifted son's passion for reading Latin literature by burning his favourite books. The reading matter Petrarch most enjoyed is of the first importance. Virgil and Cicero were his earliest loves, and in due course the historian Livy moved into pole position. Thanks to them, Petrarch's imagination was peopled by the ancient Romans, and Roman history, especially as related by Livy, became an obsession. He collected as many books of Livy's history of Rome as he could discover (his copy of them is in the British Library, Ms Harley 2493), and he even wrote a letter to Livy.[7] This obsession took literary shape in a historical work, 'On famous men', *De viris illustribus*, begun in the year 1337 and much developed over time. The figure on whom he became fixated was Scipio Africanus, whose biography was originally the first in the series, but biographies of other eminent Romans from Romulus to Cato the Censor were added. In a letter to Giacomo Colonna, bishop of Lombez in Gascony, *Familiares* ii.9, dated 21 December 1334, Petrarch had stressed how much he wished to see the city in which Scipio Africanus was born and reared; he compared his enthusiasm to Seneca's at the site of Scipio's villa, recorded in one of his letters to Lucilius, 86. Petrarch's devotion to Scipio was then channelled into a Latin epic poem titled *Africa*, which recounted his defeat of the Carthaginian general Hannibal at Zama in the Second Punic War in 202 BC. In the eighth book of the *Africa*, lines 862–951, Petrarch described the visit of Carthaginian ambassadors to Rome and their tour of the city, a passage modelled on the tour of Aeneas in Virgil's *Aeneid* 8.[8] Petrarch's description thus provides an imaginative response to the creative works of antiquity both in literature and, crucially, in material culture, albeit that material culture was by now in ruins. It must be stressed that however imaginative was Petrarch's evocation of the ideal Roman in the person of Scipio, he also respected historical accuracy.[9] This lifelong passion for an idealised Rome, embodied in the figure of Scipio Africanus, explains why Petrarch was so eager to visit Rome. We may now turn to the first of his five visits.

Although Hildebert of Lavardin and Master Gregory had marvelled at Rome's ruins, Petrarch's friend Giovanni Cardinal Colonna di S. Vito – a Roman of Rome – shared the common view that ruins were tiresome. He tried to discourage the poet from visiting Rome on the grounds that, as Petrarch reminded him in a letter written on the Capitoline Hill on the Ides of March (the fifteenth) 1337, 'the ruinous appearance of the city would not equal its reputation or the opinion I had formed of it from reading, and my enthusiasm would grow cold'.[10] In the event, however, Petrarch, ever superior to the common view, overcame any reluctance engendered in him by Colonna's repeated warnings and arrived in Rome in February 1337, where he made a point of gazing at the ruins.[11] He recorded his first impressions of the city in the very short letter just cited: he assured Colonna that he was overwhelmed and stunned, since Rome proved to be greater than he had imagined, and so were its remains. Autopsy did not belie the imagination. Theodor E. Mommsen observed that Petrarch's reduction to almost complete silence at the sight of the remains of the ancient city is the more remarkable when it is compared to his brilliant description of Cologne, which he saw on his travels in Germany.[12] In Germany Petrarch was an alert tourist, but Rome left him, a poet, lost for words. His stupefied reaction when he first saw Rome's ancient buildings is the crucial initial step in the development of a sense of the value of ruins, or ruin-mindedness.

About a dozen years later, in 1352 or 1353, in a letter to Laelius Tosetti Petrarch's enthusiasm for the ruins had not dimmed.[13] Yet again he could not find words to express the value he set upon those glorious fragments of the queen of cities, its magnificent ruins and the many manifest traces of its achievements. In an open letter to the Roman people, known as the *Epistola Hortatoria* (*Variae* 48), which Edward Gibbon cited at length in 1787,[14] he deplored the destruction of the ancient remains and the removal of stone for reuse. Françoise Choay therefore seems rather to underrate Petrarch's emotional response to the ruins when she claims that 'classical buildings still bear an exclusively textual relation to antiquity. The form and appearance of Roman monuments do not appeal to visual sensibility; they give legitimacy to literary memory'.[15] Petrarch's first letter from Rome of 1337, the later one to Tosetti and the *Epistola Hortatoria* all combine to suggest that he did not look upon the ruins in an 'exclusively' textual light. He was almost struck dumb by their sheer scale and he saw in them a physical memorial of Rome's greatness. It can, however, be granted that his response was not aesthetic: the aesthetic sensibility had to evolve over time.

Petrarch followed up his first brief account of his initial reaction in a later, more elaborate letter.[16] The addressee was another Giovanni Colonna, a Dominican friar, not the cardinal. Petrarch reminded him of their walks amid the city's ruination and what they had seen and tried to identify. The dates of the visit and of the letter recorded are debated[17] but immaterial to the present argument. The numerous details in his account of their wandering together among the ruins are too extensive for quotation here, but the point to be stressed is that his imaginative reaction was entirely fuelled by his reading. Petrarch claimed that they saw the palace of the Arcadian king Evander, the shrine of his mother, the nymph Carmentis and the cave of the fire-breathing cattle-rustler Cacus (these are also the first things the Carthaginian ambassadors see on their guided tour in the epic *Africa*, 8.863–75). The figures of Evander, Carmentis and Cacus evoke the eighth book of Virgil's epic, the *Aeneid*, in which the Arcadian king guided the Trojan hero Aeneas around his settlement, Pallanteum, the future site of Rome. This was legendary stuff even in Virgil's day, but the legends came alive for Petrarch once he saw the city Virgil knew. It was thanks to literature that he fancied he could identify many other places and structures.

Petrarch had mentioned in his earlier letter to Cardinal Colonna the 'opinion' of Rome he had already formed from his reading: extensive reading had amply stored his mind with information and impressions drawn from Virgil, Cicero and above all Livy, not to mention the still popular *Mirabilia Urbis Romae*.[18] But it was the ancient Roman writers themselves who had enabled him to imaginatively rebuild and re-people the relics, both legendary and historical, of the ancient city. The influence of Livy's early history of Rome cannot be underestimated, since Livy paid particular attention to the buildings constructed in Rome's early days, such as the Temple of Jupiter Feretrius, founded by Romulus and enlarged by Ancus Martius, whom Petrarch called in his letter the architect king (*rex architector*).[19] Livy also drew attention to the hostility directed against the consul Publius Valerius Poplicola because of the house he was building,[20] a structure Petrarch was confident he had identified (*hic erat Publicolae nequicquam suspecta domus*). Livy's record of Roman building encouraged his devoted reader Petrarch to identify significant structures. And yet much of what he claims to have beheld is either so purely speculative or in some cases so erroneous that we wonder what exactly he was looking at.[21] What structures did he identify as temples dedicated to Jupiter Stator or Feretrius? Where were they located? There are also surprising omissions, such as the Colosseum, not mentioned even as the Temple of the Sun. Failure, however, to mention the Roman Forum is less of a surprise, though some of the incidents that crowded his mind occurred there, since in Petrarch's day the Forum still lay undetected under much soil.[22] As we will see in Chapter 6, locating the

Forum without the aid of excavation and solely on the evidence of ancient texts proved to be a highly contentious issue.

Petrarch's excited account cannot, however, be dismissed as mere gush. His informed sense of history enjoined precision in the identification of at least one structure, and he ventured to correct his friend Colonna when he told him that what he called the Palace of the Sun was really the Septizonium (or more correctly Septizodium), a once gigantic free-standing façade dominating the approach from the Appian Way, built by the emperor Septimius Severus in 203.[23] Petrarch was able to make the correct identification on the basis of his knowledge of St Jerome's Latin version of the Greek *Chronicle* of Eusebius.[24] (The building was dismantled in 1588–9, though enough of it remained before that for drawings to be made and engraved, a reminder that there were more ruins to be seen in Petrarch's day than there are now (Figure 4.1).) Petrarch's exercise of a historical sensibility, which prompted him to identify correctly a still visible structure of ancient Rome, was a first step in the development of the antiquarian study of the ruins that would be taken up by Pier Paulo Vergerio, and then by Flavio Biondo more systematically in the next century.[25]

Petrarch is crucial to the development of ruin-mindedness thanks to his re-evaluation of the ruins of Rome as treasuries of historical memory, not rubble; for him the material remains, still in their proper places, evoked the events of the remote past as vividly as any written text. The Latin writers of antiquity had always had authority among the learned, but Petrarch was the first to find cultural value in material remains, even ruinous ones. Susan Stewart has recently urged that ruins 'call for an active, moving viewer – often a traveller with a consciousness distinct from that of a local inhabitant – who can restore their missing coordinates and names'.[26] That is exactly what Petrarch did when he put Colonna right about the identity of the Septizodium. Stewart went on to make a valuable distinction between 'ruination' and a 'ruin': a ruin is intelligible; sense can be made of it.[27] Petrarch could make some sense of the ruins of Rome because he possessed the crucial key to deriving their 'missing coordinates and names' from the ancient texts, which provided reliable information about their correct names and even their builders – and when you know who commissioned a building, you probably also have a rough idea of its date of construction.

Granted the *Mirabilia* evoked a memory of ancient Rome with its own 'coordinates and names', it was a memory insecurely founded, and the names had become fantastic through corruption. Petrarch's Rome was at least in the specific case of the Septizodium historically anchored. He thus

Figure 4.1 Lafréry, *The Septizodium of Severus*. Photo: Metropolitan Museum of Art/ public domain.

initiated the topographical impulse to describe and resurrect a historical Rome, not a chimera. Just as important was the warmth of his response to the ruins, a warmth he generated in others over time. Nicholas Mann stressed Petrarch's contemporary and posthumous fame, such that there are still over 500 extant Mss of his Latin works, which were among the earliest to be printed.[28] So his feeling for ancient Rome will have been widely disseminated.

What remains fundamental to Petrarch's reaction to the ruins was its source: he drew upon his reading, so that his literary imagination re-peopled the desolate sites, speculatively to be sure, but sufficiently to endow the broken stones with a human dimension they still retain. Alain Schnapp put the matter in a nutshell: 'In Petrarch's view the capital of the ancient world was a site that had to be visited, and with the ancient authors to hand … to read the urban landscape meant also to read the ancient authors.'[29] Petrarch in effect anticipated the requirement identified by William Viney: 'the categorical and explanatory content of the ruin requires a narrative relation between a past no longer in evidence and a present dominated by the presence of this past'.[30] Petrarch could provide the required narrative from his reading of classical Latin texts, and so he endowed the ruins of Rome with their explanatory content. Rosemary Sweet has shown how Petrarch's approach to the ruins was unconsciously replicated in the long eighteenth century by the numerous English visitors to Rome known as grand tourists.[31] The ruins were understood and valued to the extent that they could excite an imaginative association with people known from ancient poetry or history. Reading and ruins were complementary. It was Petrarch who first set this ball rolling, to a degree that Hildebert had not managed to do, and Roman ruin-mindedness developed apace among his immediate successors.[32] But before continuing chronologically with the development of ruin-mindedness, attention may be drawn to an apt pupil of Petrarch's method who lived some centuries later.

Catharine Edwards and Helen Slaney have both emphasised the role of the imagination and feeling in enlivening an appreciation of Roman ruins in Germaine de Staël's novel, *Corinne, ou l'Italie*, published in 1807.[33] De Staël described a situation very similar to Petrarch's, as sketched earlier. One of the heroine Corinne's admirers, the light-minded Frenchman Count d'Erfeuil, regards the ruins of Rome as so much debris, the broken marble being in his eyes of far less interest than any complete building in modern Europe; he feels that the only way to appreciate them is with the aid of learning (*érudition*), something it is clear he is not equal to securing (book 6, chapter 1). On the other hand, the ailing Scottish tourist in whom Corinne is most particularly interested, Oswald Lord Nelvil, is equally mistaken in his feeling that the ruins themselves spontaneously and without 'erudition' reanimate the past (book 4, chapter 5). D'Erfeuil is intellectually lazy, but the enthusiast Nelvil undervalues books as sources of necessary information. It rests with the poet Corinne, like Petrarch, to exercise her imagination on the ruins in combination with legendary and historical knowledge gleaned from ancient literature. As she says (book 6, chapter 5), 'there are plenty of distinguished men in Rome whose sole business it is to find a fresh link between history and the ruins'. Helen Slaney justly observes that it is the 'process of enhancing the skeletal site with factual knowledge already possessed' which enables the viewer to appreciate the ruins.[34] Neither the bare ruins nor bookish erudition suffice on their own; the two only work effectively on the imagination in tandem. De Staël thus unconsciously repeated Petrarch's crucial move, and in doing so she provided a 'philosophy of ruins' for subsequent writers in the romantic age.[35] We may now return to the fourteenth century and to Petrarch's contemporary enthusiasts for ancient Rome.

The most significant of his contemporaries is Cola di Rienzo, born in Rome ca. 1314. His parents were poor, and so he relied upon himself to acquire some knowledge of Latin and its literature, especially historical works. As with Petrarch, so with Rienzo: reading engendered an admiration of the Romans of antiquity, as well as an interest in the city's material remains, especially inscriptions.[36] The rise of the Roman Commune under his leadership as Tribune proved a false dawn of civic independence, but it did revitalise the idea of Rome as an independent self-governing community.

Fazio degli Uberti wrote a poem ca. 1356 titled *Dittamondo*, 'The World's Word', which was designed to complement Dante Alighieri's visit to the world beyond the grave: Fazio described the contemporary world of the living. The narrative is similar to Dante's in that the poet is guided by a pagan, in Fazio's case the third-century Roman geographical writer Gaius Julius Solinus, to interesting places, including Rome.[37] The city appears to the travellers in the person of Roma, a distressed widow, who addresses them and lists her misfortunes as well as her former glories, which she personally points out to them; she is confident 'it will be a wonder if Fazio is not blown away by the greatness on show' ('maraviglia sarà, se riguardando, / la mente in tante cose non abborri'). Some MS copies of the poem provide an illustration of Roma addressing the visitors[38] (Figure 4.2). The top of the map is the south of the city, the bottom is the north, a common orientation which we will encounter again. The Colosseum, by which Roma squats, is depicted as covered with a copper dome because it was then a common notion that it was a temple like the Pantheon, which appears below it.

ne .
ſi
ınto
i .

to .

act̄a

ſno .
ȝ
oı
ı̃ .

ıle
ıoı .

hıle .

Figure 4.2 Roma in Fazio's *Dittamondo*. Photo: Sonia Halliday/Alamy.

The content of Fazio's poem is usually dismissed for merely drawing on Solinus and the *Mirabilia*, among other commonplace sources, 'adding nothing to what was already known'.[39] But this is unfair, at least as regards the Colosseum, which Fazio may have been the first to correctly identify as a place of conflict, not a temple: 'I saw a sort of castle, nearly round / covered in copper and lofty seating / inside for viewing those who fought at the bottom' ('Vedi come un castel, ch' è quasi tondo / coperto fu di rame e d'alti seggi / dentro a guardar chi combattea nel fondo').

Giovanni Dondi dall'Orologio was a close friend of Petrarch and his personal physician after he settled at Arquà near Padua in 1370. He made a pilgrimage to Rome in the spring of 1375, and it is significant that he showed a keen interest in the Roman structures he encountered on his journey south, such as the Arch of Augustus and the bridge of Tiberius, still to be seen in Rimini.[40] His archaeological jottings provided rather hazy measurements of buildings and he made inaccurate transcriptions of inscriptions in Rome; nonetheless, he was in a position to compare the Colosseum to the amphitheatre at Verona.[41] His interest in ancient architecture is confirmed by his copying, ca. 1383, a MS of Vitruvius' treatise *De architectura* acquired and annotated by Petrarch. Dondi dall'Orologio reckoned that the remarkable works of the pagans still to be seen in Rome showed how great they were, and that their like was not to be found elsewhere. Errors notwithstanding, Dondi's work, which does not seem to have had much, if any, circulation, is now credited with being a significant, if faltering, step in the scientific study of Rome's ancient built environment.[42]

Pier Paolo Vergerio was both the biographer of Petrarch and editor of his unfinished *Africa*. He thus naturally shared his friend's attitude to Rome, a city he visited in 1398 and where he later lived. That visit was recorded in a letter, which is really a rhetorical ekphrasis of the city.[43] The most important part of the document, which clearly reveals Vergerio's debt to Petrarch's evaluation of the ruins, expresses his conviction that books and buildings are complementary sources from which a historical, rather than legendary and fantastic, past could be recovered (*cum enim duo sint quibus extare rerum memoria soleat, libris scilicet et aedificiis*).[44] Vergerio naturally deplored the neglect and destruction of buildings, complaining that shrubs growing in the joints of the Pyramid of Cestius obscured its inscription (which he managed to read, however), and that the inscriptions and portraits once on the tombs along the via Appia had been stolen.[45]

Despite this growing enthusiasm for the material remains of ancient Rome, it is worth noting that it was not universally shared. The poet Giannantonio Campano regretted visiting Rome, where he 'saw nothing impressive' in the ruins (*magnitudinem vidi nullam*).[46] Even Giovanni Boccaccio, for all his admiration of Petrarch, had no more than a lukewarm interest in Rome.[47] Not so, however, his teacher of Greek in Florence, Manuel Chrysoloras.

Chrysoloras has the imperishable distinction of re-introducing the study of classical Greek to Italy, where he settled in the late fourteenth century. What concerns us is his path-breaking *Comparison of Old and New Rome*. Written in 1411, it is a rhetorical syncrisis, or comparison, of Rome and Constantinople, his birthplace, presented in epistolary form to the Byzantine emperor Manuel II Palaeologus. As such, it was clearly intended for wider circulation, which indeed it secured in humanist circles, thanks to a Latin translation by Franciscus Aleardus. Christine Smith explained its rhetorical function and provided a full English version.[48] Chrysoloras was enthusiastic about the appearance of Rome, and he had clearly been caught up in the humanist interest in the ruins, evincing a greater interest in pagan than in Christian Rome.[49] He did not aim at an antiquarian's exactness in describing what he saw; rather, he wanted to provide a striking visual image, in the rhetorical tradition of 'enargeia'. What impresses is his imaginative reconstruction of the 'enormous and beautiful' originals from their ruins; he even found the ruin in itself beautiful, since it allowed the viewer to imagine the beautiful whole:

> Yet almost nothing in Rome has come down to us intact: you will not find anything that is undamaged … Rome uses itself as a mine and a quarry. Nonetheless, even these ruins and heaps of stones show what great things once existed, and how enormous and beautiful were the original constructions …. These works were beautiful not only in their original composition and organization; they seem beautiful even in their dismembered state.[50]

Chrysoloras thus sounded a new note in his expressly aesthetic response to the ruination of ancient Rome. He also found in the ruins evidence of 'the practical and economic aspects of Roman culture' and of the moral character of the builders; that is to say, he appreciated their historical and antiquarian value.[51] He referred particularly to relief sculptures depicting the clothing of citizens or the weaponry of troops, which 'make our knowledge of history precise, or rather they grant us eye-witness knowledge of everything that has happened just as if it were present'.[52] Chrysoloras certainly seems to be privileging the visual evidence over the literary here, and he deserves to be seen as a pioneering student of what the Germans call 'Realien', material culture.[53] His assessment of the role ruins had to play in the physical illustration of Roman culture and above all his assertion of their beauty represent a crucial step forward in the development of ruin-mindedness, as Alain Schnapp has stressed.[54]

The humanist Camaldolese monk, Ambrogio Traversari, a pupil of Chrysoloras in Florence, visited Rome for the first time in 1432 upon his appointment as general of his order. In a letter to his brother and fellow monk Jerome, written in February of that year, he recorded his reaction to the ruination of the city: as he wandered about it, 'he was stopped in his tracks by amazement' (*stupore detineor*).[55] Amazement, *stupor*, was the very same word Petrarch had used in his first letter from Rome, describing how he was 'overwhelmed by a vast amazement' (*stuporis mole obrutus*). What amazed Ambrogio was 'the almost unbelievably massive bulk of the ruins' (*ruinarum moles incredibiles ferme*), 'the panels of precious marble veneer lying scattered about' (*proiectas pretiosi marmoris crustas*), the statues and 'the almost endless fragments of columns' (*columnarum fragmenta fere perpetua*). The sight was for him 'proof of human weakness and instability' (*humanae imbecillitatis et inconstantiae documentum*). His moralising reflections upon the sight of the ruins of the ancient city do not diminish, however, his sense of wonder, a sense repeatedly recorded by those who wandered amid the waste of fifteenth-century Rome.

An unknown contemporary of Chrysoloras and Traversari, the so-called Anonymus Magliabecchianus, wrote a treatise on the antiquities and site of Rome.[56] It is a pity that we know next to nothing about the writer, since we are in the dark about his motive for writing such a substantial piece. Its layout is modelled on that of the *Mirabilia* in that structures are listed by category: city gates, main streets, triumphal arches, *thermae*, 'palaces', bridges, obelisks (*aguliae*), including columns and temples. Much of the writer's (mis)information is drawn from the *Mirabilia*, but his use of contemporary names of the remains and his indication of their proximity to a known church suggest that he meant to help the reader locate the structure.[57] For instance, he rightly located the Arch of Septimius Severus (not that he knew it as that) at the base of the Capitoline Hill in front of the church of S. Martina (now rededicated to saints Luke and Martina) and to the side of the church of S. Adriano (now restored as the *Curia Julia*); it goes, he says, by the name of Le Brache, 'the breeches'. He followed Petrarch's lead in the use of Latin authors, but his references are unhelpfully casual. He makes somewhat sketchy appeals to sources, for instance Cassiodorus and particularly Suetonius.[58] Like his mediaeval predecessor Benedict (Chapter 3, p. 47), he referred to Ovid's *Fasti*, in this case to back up his view that the church of S. Croce in Gerusalemme was built near the site of a Temple of Venus and Cupid.[59] Roberto Weiss felt that this vague citation provided 'a useful tip for the humanistic reader'. It would indeed have been a useful tip had Ovid only mentioned a Temple of Venus (with or without Cupid) in that part of Rome. References to Temples of Venus in the *Fasti* occur in the poem's fourth book, which is devoted to the festivals of Venus' own month of April; in it he mentioned only two of her temples, Verticordia on the Capitol (159–60) and Erycina (865–76) near the Porta Collina. The temple referred to by the anonymous writer is in fact a misidentified fragment of the vast Sessorian palace,[60] and so his authenticating reference is entirely bogus (Figure 4.3). Despite his lack of sophistication and his mistakes, the focus of his interest upon what was left of ancient Rome, to the exclusion of the Christian city, and his repudiation of many traditional fables show that

Figure 4.3 Mérigot, *Temple of Venus and Cupid*. Photo: Wikimedia Commons –
Internet Archive Book Images.

the anonymous scholar had imbibed something of the new spirit of interpretation of the remains of antiquity.[61]

The last of Petrarch's younger followers to be considered is Francesco da
Fiano, a humanist and secretary in the papal Curia who acted as guide to the
ruins of Rome; Chrysoloras may have been one of the tourists he assisted.[62]
In 1416 his pupil Cencio de'Rustici, an apostolic secretary who went by
several names – Cinzio or the latinised Cynthius – urged him to write an
invective in defence of the glories of antiquity against 'the destroyers of
outstanding monuments' (*preclarissimorum monimentorum perversores*).[63]
Cencio's language is unbridled; he blames the early and mediaeval papacy
as an institution for the destruction of what was left of ancient Rome: the
amphitheatre, the hippodrome, the colossus, the statues, the walls built with
wondrous art in wondrous stone, all of which displayed the ancient and
almost divine distinction of the Roman people – these were being demolished daily. The proposed invective was never written, but the humanists
were clearly building up a head of steam in defence of the ruins. That will
be the theme of the next chapter.

5 | The Battle for the Ruins

As we saw in the previous chapter, the Rome of the fourteenth century was a mess: underpopulated, misgoverned (insofar as there was any government at all) and poorly resourced. The return of the papacy in 1420 promised well for the recovery of the city. The great churches had been neglected for over a century and needed immediate attention. The influx of courtiers and curial administrators required fitting places in which to live and to work. Infrastructure, such as streets and the water supply, would have to be improved. In short, Rome had to be refurbished and rebuilt. It was this rebuilding and refurbishment, however, which for the next century or so posed the greatest threat to the preservation of the remains of pagan Rome, since the ruins continued to be treated as a ready quarry of dressed stone that had only to be carted to a building site for re-use. There arose in opposition to this destruction two champions in defence of the preservation of the ruins.

New buildings required designers. Architects, who at this time were evolving into a discrete category of artist, were coming so to admire ancient Roman building techniques and the aesthetic of their ornamentation that they insisted on conservation for the purposes of study and inspiration. The enthusiasm of architects for the conservation of the ruins was shared by those members of the curial administration who were increasingly well read in classical Latin literature. Their knowledge of the ancient texts took a practical form in the revival of antiquarianism: the study of the laws, customs, religion and physical monuments of antiquity. The antiquarian directed his knowledge of the texts upon the identification and interpretation of the ruins. It followed that he was loath to let the ruins disappear, since they visibly embodied and projected memory of the past.

In this chapter the struggle to conserve the monumental relics of Rome will be sketched, since conservation is another of the hallmarks of ruin-mindedness. But before focussing on the period of the papal return, a few earlier examples of interest in and care of ancient remains deserve to be highlighted.

The engaging Casa dei Crescenzi, built by one of the most powerful families in Rome at an uncertain date, but probably in the mid-twelfth century, serves as a pre-echo of the Renaissance admiration of Roman architectural ornament in its re-use of ancient materials, *spolia*.[1] It is sited in a prominent position on the Ripa Graeca near the Aemilian bridge, or Ponte Rotto, over the Tiber. What survives nowadays is the lower part of a once grander tower-house (Figure 5.1). An inscription over the entrance claims that the builder's aim was to 'renew the ancient dignity of Rome'. Self-advertisement was certainly also in play, but the desire to reconnect the contemporary urban fabric to a glorious past by the re-use of ancient materials must not be discounted. Some Romans took pride in the antiquity and distinction of their city, and the recycling of architectural elements visibly demonstrated the sentiment. It is no surprise that the name of the family which built the house, Crescenzi, was in due course forgotten and the building was assigned to the patriotic Tribune Cola di Rienzo: it seemed to be the sort of house in which the reviver of the Roman republic ought to have lived, and even as late as 1865 William Forsyth believed the tale.[2] More weirdly still, the house was also once believed to be the residence of Pontius Pilate, and it went under the name of Casa di Pilato well into the eighteenth century.[3] The mediaeval house was not, of course, itself a ruin, nor does the use of *spolia* in its ornamentation evince a desire to look after the ruins. But the

Figure 5.1 The Casa dei Crescenzi. Photo: Wikimedia Commons – Daderot/Creative Commons CCO 1.0, universal public domain dedication.

appropriation of the ornamental stonework and the attempt to reproduce the look of ancient walling, even to the embedding of half-columns in the fabric, clearly acknowledge the high artistic quality and suggestiveness of ancient architecture. It would not take much to enlarge that feeling so as to embrace the ruins of the pagan city.

In 1162 the civic authority, revived in 1143,[4] undertook the protection of Trajan's column from injury.[5] Protection may have been accorded the column less out of a feeling for an ancient monument than thanks to a belief, widely recorded, that Pope Gregory I had resurrected Trajan and baptised him, and so, like Constantine, Trajan was counted a Christian emperor. Whatever the civic administration's motivation, the significance of its measure is that there was now a secular institution which laid claim to guardianship (and in some cases ownership) of the remains of ancient Rome; papal authority had a rival, which would gain power in due course.

Even in the disordered fourteenth century, there was some small feeling for the value of the ancient buildings, perhaps engendered by the enthusiasm of Petrarch and Cola di Rienzo. In Rome's first civic statutes of 1363, which established a code of government under Pope Urban V, the 191st rubric of the second book forbade the destruction of ancient buildings.[6] The purpose of the statute is declared at the outset: 'Lest the city be made unsightly by ruins.' Strictly speaking, the statute did not protect what was already ruinous; it rather aimed to prevent structures being reduced to ruination. Ruins were clearly still deemed a blot upon the city's beauty (a sentiment clearly shared by those who tried to discourage Petrarch from visiting Rome). Protection of ruined structures was not envisaged, but further destruction was expressly deprecated. The first vigorous and sustained challenge to the destruction of the ruins was mounted in the fifteenth century by architects and antiquarians, who valued the ruins for their own sake. To their efforts we may now turn.

Architects

It is curious that while the role of the architect was recognised in northern Europe as a distinct profession by the late twelfth century (we may think, for instance, of William of Sens, who rebuilt the choir of Canterbury Cathedral), this was not the case in Italy. In mediaeval Italy the designers of even such important buildings as cathedrals are often still unknown. Arnolfo di Cambio, a sculptor of renown, certainly did not design the cathedral of Florence, but he was commissioned to produce its façade (now magnificently reimagined in the Museo dell'opera del Duomo). Likewise, the design of its campanile (bell tower) was entrusted to a distinguished painter, Giotto di Bondone, and after his death the sculptor Andrea Pisano continued the work. Thus architectural design in mediaeval Italy was something of a by-product of the established artistic disciplines of painting and especially of sculpture. It is therefore something of a puzzle to explain why the Florentine Filippo Brunelleschi decided to make a career exclusively as an architect and engineer.

Much is uncertain about Brunelleschi's life and work, which makes it difficult and risky for the non-specialist to claim to give a wholly reliable account of him. Details both in the record of his earliest biographers and in architectural histories are nowadays viewed with scepticism.[7] It is, however, agreed that his father, a notary, wanted him to go into the legal profession. But he proved to be an indifferent student, and so his practical parent apprenticed him to a goldsmith (also the first trade of Andrea Pisano). This raises the important question of his competence as a reader of Latin, a language he would certainly have needed for legal practice. But Peter Murray goes so far as to claim that Brunelleschi could not read Latin.[8] Supposing for the sake of argument, however, that he had a smattering of lawyer's Latin, that smattering would still hardly have been sufficient to enable him to read Vitruvius' treatise on architecture or the elder Pliny's enthusiastic catalogue of the wonders of Rome in his *Natural History*, both of which were available in Italy by that time (Petrarch and Boccaccio had copies). The crabbed technical Latin of Vitruvius, which so taxed Raphael that he had to rely upon an Italian translation by his friend Marco Fabio Calvo, and the convoluted style of Pliny require a considerable command of the language. And yet there is nothing to suggest Brunelleschi ever so much as glanced at these works, or indeed at any Latin literature at all.

We are also faced with other unanswerable questions: first, why did Brunelleschi channel his talents into architecture? The traditional story runs that he was so disappointed by his failure to secure the commission for decoration of the doors of the baptistery in Florence – Lorenzo Ghiberti's models were successful – that he resolved to excel in a different craft and chose architecture over sculpture. Whatever his motive, it is a fact that he concentrated on architecture, and that raises a second even more fundamental question: why did he choose the Roman style of design and repudiate the contemporary Gothic?

It cannot be claimed that contemporary Gothic was played out; the magnificent cathedral in Siena is proof enough of that. And yet, whatever Brunelleschi's motivation for repudiating the Gothic style, his own style appears to be strongly influenced by Roman models. The best place to observe such models was obviously Rome, and so Antonio di Tuccio Manetti claimed in the first biography of Brunelleschi, composed ca. 1480, that he had indeed visited the city and made measured drawings of the buildings he saw there. But doubt has been cast on that alleged visit, for instance by Howard Saalman.[9] Marvin Trachtenberg, on the other hand, made out an attractive case for a visit to Rome and for the direct study of ancient remains, especially for the dazzling variety of uses to which the Corinthian order was put in Rome's Pantheon, uses clearly replicated in the Old Sacristy of the church of S. Lorenzo in Florence.[10] Trachtenberg further suggested that Brunelleschi found in classical architectural forms an antidote to the ambiguity and indeterminacy of the mediaeval vocabulary:[11] a Gothic pier can assume any shape, while a classical column is 'quintessentially determinate' in every one of its parts. In other words, Brunelleschi adopted the Roman style because he found it more aesthetically appealing than the Gothic. It was the aesthetic appeal of the Roman manner, the manner *all'antica*, that informed his designs for buildings in Florence (paradoxically, he did not build in Rome). A number of these designs incorporated 'Roman' features, not slavish copies but evocations of the antique Roman style for modern Florentine buildings.

The main features of Brunelleschi's personal 'take' on the *all'antica* style are conveniently listed by Howard Burns:[12] the round, not pointed, arch; columns and pilasters of determinate relations and proportions; the order (usually Corinthian) made up of entablature, capital, column and base; standardised detail; articulated and modelled wall surfaces; interior vistas and centralised compositions. Burns argued that the sources of Brunelleschi's motifs and compositional schemes were not exclusively antique, and that he owed a good deal to local Tuscan models. But it should be borne in mind that one such Tuscan model, the baptistery in Florence, was in Brunelleschi's day believed to be originally an ancient Roman temple of Mars, converted to Christian use,[13] a belief supported perhaps by the presence of *spolia* in its interior decoration. Without literal copying, Brunelleschi looked for and found the underlying principles of the ancient manner of building.[14]

An example may now illustrate Brunelleschi's Roman style: the interior of the church of S. Spirito in Florence (Figure 5.2). The sculptural quality of this structure is seen in the moulding of interior space around the dome. Pre-eminently Roman in character is the grandeur of 'the splendid spatial effect created by the great ring of columns running round the whole church.'[15] Brunelleschi was recognised in his own day and subsequently

Figure 5.2 Brunelleschi, S. Spirito interior. Photo: Wikimedia Commons – Sailko, CC BY-SA 3.0.

as the founder of a new *all'antica* architectural style based on the Roman model,[16] and his successful initiative fired some of his contemporaries with a desire to design and build in this old-new style.

The most important of Brunelleschi's architect contemporaries is Leon Battista Alberti. Unlike Brunelleschi, Alberti had a humanistic education at the University of Padua, and so he not only read Greek and Latin but also wrote in up-to-date Ciceronian Latin (as well as in Italian). He became a member of the Curia, and in the 1440s in Rome he began to study the ruins, particularly the temples and theatres, which, as he said in the first chapter of the sixth book of his ten-book architectural treatise, *On the Art of Building* (*De re aedificatoria*), served 'as the best teachers from which to learn a good deal' (*ex quibus tanquam ex optimis professoribus multa discerentur*). He was 'angry and tearful at their daily destruction' (*nequeo non stomachari ... eadem non sine lachrymis videbam in dies deleri*), a destruction occasioned 'by negligence, not to say greed' (*incuria ... avaritia*). Such was his expert antiquarian knowledge that he acted as guide, *cicerone*, to distinguished tourists, for instance Giovanni Rucellai of Florence. Rucellai visited Rome in the year of Jubilee 1450 and later wrote in Italian a somewhat dry account of his sightseeing of the ruins, many of which he praised for the size and beauty of their materials.[17] Again in 1471 Alberti guided a trio of visitors, Giovanni Rucellai's son Bernardo (an accomplished humanist and independent-minded antiquarian), Donato Acciaiuoli and Lorenzo de' Medici, Bernardo's brother-in-law.[18] Alberti marshalled the fruits of his humanist reading and of his antiquarian researches in the architectural treatise just cited, *De re aedificatoria*, a work in progress until his death in 1472, which was printed in 1485.[19]

Alberti's focus in this treatise was less on the engineering involved in the construction of large-scale buildings (a matter of considerable interest to Brunelleschi) than in devising a set of theories about buildings, their makers and their functions; the work's target audience was not the professional builder but the patron of architecture, be he priest or prince.[20] Alberti's theoretical approach was pragmatically founded upon autopsy, thanks to his systematic study of the ancient monuments and his not uncritical debt to Vitruvius, each in the light of the other.[21] He encouraged careful and extensive observation, and bade the architect record in his sketchbooks the orders, the locations of buildings and the kinds of as many ancient works as possible; measurements were to be taken and proportions noted.[22] His injunction was followed, for example, by Bernardo della Volpaia in the Codex Coner, conserved in the Soane Museum, London and in the sketchbooks of the Sangallo family, 'perhaps the most extensive body of drawings of ruins before the mid-sixteenth century'.[23]

In his practice as an architect, Alberti's deployment of *all'antica* design is manifestly indebted to specific Roman models. In Florence, for example, the Palazzo Rucellai, designed for Giovanni Rucellai, evoked the tiers of pilasters and architraves on the outer surface of the Colosseum[24] (Figure 5.3).

Alberti's influence both as theorist of architecture and as practitioner of design on Roman lines was decisive for centuries. His designs *all'antica* marked an alternative to Brunelleschi's, in that Alberti demonstrated how such peculiarly Roman structures as the triumphal arch and the amphitheatre could be repurposed to serve as models for the façades of very different contemporary buildings, churches and urban palaces.

Giuliano da Sangallo is the most important successor of Brunelleschi and Alberti. For our present purpose his fine Brunelleschian church of 1485 in Prato, S. Maria delle Carceri,[25] is of less significance than are his drawings of Roman ruins (among other buildings), now preserved in the so-called Sienese Sketchbook (*Taccuino senese*), in the Codice Barberiniano 4424 in the Vatican Library and in the recently discovered *Libro Capponi* in Florence's Biblioteca Nazionale Centrale. In the Codice Barberiniano, his drawing of a then-surviving portion of the portico of the Basilica Aemilia in

Figure 5.3 Alberti, Palazzo Rucellai, Florence. Photo: Wikimedia Commons –
Benjamin Núñez González – own work/CC BY-SA 4.0.

the Forum, later destroyed by the architect Donato Bramante, is especially
valuable.[26] From it we discover the model for the rosettes on the necking
bands of the Doric columns and pilasters in the sumptuous church of the
Madonna di S. Biagio in Montepulciano, Tuscany, designed by his younger
brother Antonio da Sangallo the Elder and built between 1518 and 1545
(David Watkin inadvertently attributed the church to Giuliano).[27] This is
another object lesson in the aesthetic value with which the ruins were now
endowed and the service they provided as models to be adopted in contemporary buildings.

In the course of the fifteenth century, fledgling architects flocked to Rome
to view, measure and draw the ruins, which they not only studied but also
wrote about and emulated in their own designs. (Briggs draws on Vasari for
a list of them.)[28] In this way, the ruins came to acquire a strong, aesthetic
value, something in addition to the historical value previously conferred

on them by Petrarch. This aesthetic value nourished a feeling that the ruins should not just be studied but also preserved from damage or destruction. This feeling was actively promoted by humanists and more especially by antiquarians, to whom we may now turn.

Humanists and Antiquarians

We saw in the previous chapter that Petrarch's enthusiasm for the ruins of Rome was founded on his wide reading of ancient literature, especially the historian Livy. He sensed that the material remains of Roman culture were complementary to the surviving texts. Later humanists who shared this feeling actively opposed the destruction of the relics of ancient Rome, and Cencio de'Rustici was mentioned in Chapter 4 (p. 66) as an example. Appeals for conservation and interpretation in the light of ancient texts were more methodically developed by subsequent humanists, especially Poggio Bracciolini, Cyriac of Ancona and most significantly Flavio Biondo and his followers.

Poggio Bracciolini, a papal secretary in the first half of the fifteenth century, is now chiefly remembered for his extraordinary vigour and resourcefulness in seeking out the manuscripts of classical Roman writings which lay disregarded in the monastic libraries of Europe. He announced his finds to his circle of fellow humanists and ensured that copies of the new texts were made available. Once in Rome with the restored papacy, he was able to complement his literary studies with careful inspection of the city's material remains, especially its inscriptions.[29] But it was the visible ruins of Rome that most attracted him. He recorded his researches upon them in a work written between 1431 and 1448 and entitled *The Changeableness of Fortune* (*De varietate Fortunae*).[30] After all, what could better illustrate Fortune's instability than the shattered ruins of a once great metropolis of empire? His elegiac sentiment was finely paraphrased by Edward Gibbon at the beginning of chapter 71 of the *Decline and Fall of the Roman Empire*:

> The sacred ground is again disfigured with thorns and brambles. The hill of the Capitol … how is it fallen! how changed! how defaced! …. Cast your eyes on the Palatine hill, and seek among the shapeless and enormous fragments the marble theatre, the obelisks, the colossal statues, the porticos of Nero's palace …. The public and private edifices, that were founded for eternity, lie prostrate, naked, and broken, like the limbs of a mighty giant; and the ruin is the more visible, from the stupendous relics that have survived the injuries of time and fortune.

This extract echoes unconsciously the musing of Pausanias (a writer unknown to Poggio) on the site of Megalopolis in Arcadia with its sense of disfigurement and defacement cited in the first chapter. But the language – both Poggio's and Gibbon's – is now emotive and sympathetic. We note the pathos of the sheer scale of the ruination: 'enormous fragments, colossal statues, limbs of a mighty giant, stupendous relics'.

But Poggio was no sentimentalist. It is generally acknowledged that he set archaeology on a firm foundation thanks to his careful study of the actual materials of the ruins and to the use he made of inscriptions which supplemented and sometimes confirmed the writings of Greek and Latin authors. For instance, he castigated Petrarch for failing to read the inscription on the Pyramid tomb of Caius Cestius – Petrarch had followed popular legend and identified it as the Tomb of Romulus' brother Remus. Poggio also paid no attention to the mediaeval notion that the Colosseum was a temple; he knew it was an amphitheatre designed for public games (*ad ludos populo edendos*). Ancient sources, such as the historians Livy and Ammianus Marcellinus and the author of a treatise on aqueducts, Frontinus, which Poggio had himself discovered in 1429, were of course especially rewarding guides. But Poggio also appreciated the occasional value of mediaeval texts, the acts of martyrs, the lives of popes in the *Liber Pontificalis* and even popular names. Given his dedication to what was left of ancient Rome, he naturally deplored the persistent demolition of its structures. For example, he wrote that the Temple of Concord (in reality the Temple of Saturn, a common error) and its portico, 'a very handsome marble building' (*opere marmoreo admodum specioso*), were nearly complete when he first saw them, but the temple and much of the portico had been destroyed subsequently to produce lime. Likewise, the Tomb of Caecilia Metella, 'an exceptional work' (*opus egregium*) on the via Appia, had suffered considerable damage during his time in Rome.

The growing enthusiasm for Rome's ruins was infectious, and an interest in local ruins as well was being rapidly generated throughout the rest of Italy.[31] Nor would it take long for that enthusiasm to be extended to the Roman remains across the Adriatic Sea in the eastern Mediterranean, where of course Greek buildings would also be encountered. Since this cultural history must confine its focus to the ruins of Rome, the contribution of Cyriac of Ancona to the discovery of the Greek world can only be mentioned; it is more fully sketched by Roberto Weiss.[32] For our present purposes, the importance of Cyriac's visits to the ruins of the Greek East and of Egypt is the emerging ripple-effect of ruin-mindedness: it starts with Rome, spreads to Italy and then moves to neighbouring lands within the vanished Roman empire.

Cyriac had a mercantile rather than humanist upbringing, and his working knowledge of Latin was acquired largely through his own efforts. His
enthusiasm for Roman ruins was thus unmediated by any thorough engagement with Latin literature; rather it was direct, thanks to the presence on
the harbourside of his native city of Ancona of the elegant Arch of Trajan
(Figure 5.4). The story is engagingly told by his friend and biographer
Francesco Scalamonti in §§53–6 of his *Life of Cyriac of Ancona*.[33] About
the time that Gabriele Cardinal Condulmer, who in due course became
Pope Eugenius IV, was the papal legate in Ancona, Cyriac boldly resolved
to master Latin by reading Virgil's *Aeneid*. In 1410 Condulmer instigated
repair work on the port of Ancona. Scaffolding was erected around the
arch, which enabled the nineteen-year-old Cyriac to study the fine structure at close range. Even though the bronze letters of the inscription had
been carried off centuries before by north African raiders, Cyriac, whose
Latin had clearly improved by now, was able to make out the words from
the traces of the letters incised in the marble. Scalamonti claimed that it
was this remarkable work of architecture and its vanished inscription which
gave Cyriac his vocation, as he himself put it, 'to search out and examine
all the other noble memorials of antiquity in the world'. In 1423 Cyriac

Figure 5.4 Arch of Trajan, Ancona. Photo: Wikimedia Commons – Claudio.stanco,
CC BY-SA 4.0.

visited Rome, where he stayed with Cardinal Condulmer and rode round the city on his white horse (Scalamonti specifies the colour of the nag) carefully inspecting the ruins. It was there apparently that he began compiling inscriptional material for his *Commentaria*. It was his belief, according to Scalamonti, that material remains provided more trustworthy information about the past than books, and so he resolved to travel and to make a record of the monuments he saw to preserve their memory for posterity.

Cyriac's improved linguistic skills now enabled him to use the elder Pliny's *Natural History*, a manuscript of which he carried with him as his guide to the architectural and other wonders of the Graeco-Roman East.[34] Once he reached Constantinople, he began to learn Greek. Buildings and inscriptions were not his sole interest. He also sought out ancient manuscripts, particularly of historical and geographical writers, both in Latin and ancient Greek,[35] and coins; he transcribed inscriptions, again in both languages. He wrote reports in diaries and letters of his travels in Greece, Egypt and Asia Minor, where he sought out the ruined remains of Hellenic culture, which he drew and described. Some elaborate reimaginations of Roman sites and structures have also been occasionally ascribed to him; they are discussed and illustrated by Richard Brilliant, who felt that the sketches were an attempt 'to repossess ... the historical reality behind the present ruin', perhaps the motive of whoever in fact drew them.[36] In 1433, as recorded in §99 of Scalamonti's biography, he acted as guide for the Holy Roman emperor Sigismund of Luxembourg, who had just celebrated his coronation, on a tour of the ruins of Rome.[37] This may well be the earliest guided tour of Rome's ancient remains, seventeen years before Alberti's, mentioned earlier. On that occasion Cyriac deplored the destruction of the elegant marble buildings, sculptures and columns for lime. The emperor joined him in criticising the lazy indifference of men and praised Cyriac's concern for the ruins.[38]

Cyriac gathered the fruits of his life-long researches into a six-volume collection entitled *Antiquarum Rerum Commentaria*. Extracts from it were copied by some of its earliest readers in the 1460s, but unfortunately the collection was never printed. His Mss were destroyed in fires in the sixteenth century, but some fragments were published in the eighteenth century. His later influence was therefore relatively slight, but his example had already fired others to pursue his lines of research and enquiry.

Flavio Biondo is generally regarded as the father of modern antiquarianism and scientific topography, thanks to a more systematic and historically based attempt than Poggio's to locate and identify correctly Rome's ancient structures, even some no longer extant. After a humanist literary training in northern Italy, he joined the Curia in 1433 under Pope Eugenius IV (formerly Gabriele Cardinal Condulmer). In early 1446 he finished a treatise on the renewal of the city of Rome, entitled *Rome Revived* (*Roma instaurata*).[39] The two-volume edition of the Latin text with an ample introduction, French translation and commentary by Anne Raffarin[-Dupuis] is an indispensable guide to the work.[40]

Biondo's title, *Roma instaurata*, 'Rome Revived', deserves attention. In classical Latin the verb *instauro* means to restart or renew an activity after an interruption or interval. Biondo's choice of the verb indicates his belief that there was just such a hiatus in the city's history, a sort of abyss between antiquity and his own times.[41] This is in effect the very gap in continuity that Salvatore Settis, cited in the first chapter, believes to be of fundamental importance to the development of a new attitude to the revival of the classical and the validity of ruins.

Biondo's treatise is divided into three books, each of which is miscellaneous in content. Buildings are grouped and described by type: the first book treats of the city gates, hills and churches (among other things); the second of baths, temples, aqueducts and theatres; and the third of amphitheatres and games, with a variety of other structures, especially the Pantheon. Biondo integrated his antiquarian knowledge with his topographical interest in ancient Rome. The account of a particular type of building provided a platform for an antiquarian disquisition on Roman customs connected with it. This is seen, for example, towards the end of the second book in the account of the Theatre of Pompey, §§CIII–CXXIV.[42] Biondo begins with antiquarian material on the origin of the theatre, the *scaena* and the *orchestra*; that is to say, the parts of any theatre building. He then cites the elder Pliny for information on some theatres no longer extant (even in Pliny's day!). After this general exordium he gets round to collating the ancient sources of information about the Theatre of Pompey, remains of which he was the first to identify and locate, thanks to his noticing a vast curved wall near the monastery 'of the Rose' (§CIX). Once he has exhausted that topic, he reverts to antiquarian matter, with some observations on actors in ancient Rome. This blending of the antiquarian and topographical will be taken up in later guides to the city, to be discussed in the next chapter.

Biondo also interspersed his survey of ancient Rome with accounts of Christian churches. Indeed, the final part of the third book is given up entirely to a description of the modern 'revived' city, which Biondo found no whit inferior to its ancient predecessor (§LXXXIV). For Biondo Rome's, real greatness was to be seen in both the visible remains of its glorious past and in the restoration of its modern buildings, particularly in the Vatican, by the returned papacy. Biondo's chief aim nonetheless, as stated in the opening words of his dedicatory letter to the Holy Father, was 'to renew to the best of his ability a knowledge of Rome through her ruins rather than contemporary buildings' (*Urbis Romae ... ruinarum potius quam aedificiorum, quae nunc cernuntur, notitiam pro uiribus innovare*).[43] To do so entailed accurate identification of the remains of antiquity and of their exact functions. To secure accuracy and comprehensive coverage, Biondo took aim against the legends and guess-work which characterised the *Mirabilia* tradition, deploying the blast power of humanist artillery, marshalled from Latin authors (Biondo, unlike Poggio, could not read Greek),[44] from inscriptions and from coinage. On-the-spot autopsy was equally crucial to his campaign, evidenced, for instance, in his successful location of the remains of the Theatre of Pompey in the second book.[45]

Biondo also repeatedly deplored the damage done to ancient monuments by the persistent pillaging of their stonework. In the last section of the first book (§104), he expressed amazement that the 'marvellous structure' (*mirabile ... aedificium*) of the Baths of Diocletian on the Esquiline Hill had survived both barbarian conquerors and the 'unconscionable hand' (*improba manus*) of those who were plundering its ashlar; he reckoned that there were not four 'palaces' in contemporary Italy to match it for 'scale and magnificence' (*magnitudine et ... sumptuositate*). In §101 of the second book he claimed that the majestic aqueducts were ruined not by lapse of time but by the unholy hands (*manus improbae* again) of men who took the stone to build their own 'very nasty houses' (*sordidissima ... aedificia*, an expression used in i.104 as well), and in §7 of the third book he even complained that the daily sight of stone being carried away made him 'sometimes regret living in Rome' (*nos aliquando Romae fastidiat habitatio*).[46] His work therefore aimed both to preserve as much of the memory of ancient Rome as possible and to offer his readers a vision of just what classical Rome had been. In this it was largely successful; his treatise achieved the unusual distinction of early printing in 1471 and then of translation into Italian in the next century, when from a technical point of view it was finally superseded by Bartolomeo Marliani's handbook of Roman topography.[47]

Biondo's work was not illustrated,[48] but it nonetheless bore cartographic fruit in a famous bird's-eye view of the city drawn in Venice by the noble Florentine antiquarian Alessandro Strozzi in 1474.[49] Strozzi's map is based on a conjectured archetype (also used at about the same time by Piero del Massaio), but now no longer extant; it might have been sketched by Biondo himself. Strozzi's map is bound up with a collection of Cyriac of Ancona's ancient inscriptions; it is the product of personal interest and initiative,

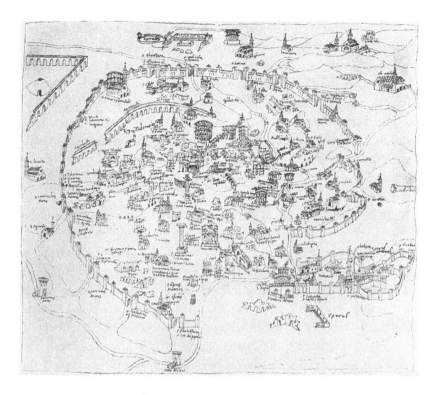

Figure 5.5 Strozzi, *Map of Ancient Rome*, 1474. Photo: Wikimedia Commons – public domain.

never intended for circulation (Figure 5.5). As was usual at the time, north is at the bottom of the page. The city's monuments and earliest churches are very carefully drawn and labelled. Some of the ancient structures are given both their Latin and contemporary Italian names, for example, the *sepulcrum Adriani* and Castel Sant' Angelo, but other ruinous ancient piles are unidentified. Many of the structures illustrated went unrecorded in earlier maps or in the *Mirabilia* tradition. Their presence, their location and their identification are all plainly owed to Biondo's recent work.[50] A later hand has added some further identifications or corrections, showing that this private map was an antiquarian's 'work in progress'. Strozzi's personal map, based upon the most up-to-date information drawn from Biondo's text and supplemented by a collection of Cyriac's inscriptions, combines several contemporary humanist initiatives in order to provide an accurate reconstruction and visualisation of Rome.

Biondo found a worthy successor in Pomponio Leto, a passionate and learned student of the remains of ancient Rome, who unfortunately never organised the results of his research or published them. All that has come down to us is a Ms record, imperfectly preserved in the so-called *Excerpta* of 1484, of Leto's observations as delivered on a guided tour of the ruins when he conducted a visitor from north of the Alps around the city.[51] Leto's tour started at the Colosseum and ended on the Campidoglio. He took in all the hills and drew attention to particularly interesting sights. The colonnades of the Forum of Trajan, for instance, he described as 'so wonderful that the viewer could scarcely believe they were made by the hands of men rather than by giants' (*adeo mirabile opus fuit ut qui intuerentur non poterant adduci ut crederent illud esse factum manibus hominum, sed manibus gigantum*).[52]

A pupil of Pomponio Leto's, Andrea Fulvio, also served as a tour guide to the ruins, but this time we know exactly whom he conducted around them, namely his friend, the painter Raphael Sanzio. Raphael was sufficiently impressed with what he saw that he began to incorporate ruinous structures in some of the landscapes which formed the background of his paintings, a matter to be more fully described in Chapter 7 (p. 126). In 1513 Fulvio dedicated to Giovanni de' Medici, Pope Leo X, a two-book Latin poem on the ruins, to be discussed in Chapter 12 (pp. 278–9). The pope urged him to produce a more extensive work in prose, and so in 1527, just before the sack of Rome, he published his long-awaited *Antiquitates Urbis*.[53] In the preface, dedicated to another Medici pope, Clement VII, Fulvio expressed his desire for the preservation of the ruins of Rome. The five books of the work surveyed comprehensively what remained of the ancient city, without, however, neglecting the fine new buildings arising, such as the basilica of St Peter in the Vatican. Fulvio looked at the ruins 'not as an architect, but rather as an historian and antiquarian' in the tradition of Flavio Biondo, as he claimed in the preface,[54] and he often deplored their destruction and the export of antiquities to other parts of Italy. The success of Fulvio's work is proven by its publication in an Italian translation in Venice in 1543 and a second edition of the Latin text in 1545. Thanks to its expansion and the inclusion of illustrations of the ruins, either in their actual state or reconstructed, in a later Venice edition of 1588, it became something of a guide-book, at least until it was superseded by more up-to-date works.[55]

Papal Measures to Preserve the Ruins

During the fifteenth century two distinct strands of interest in Rome's ruins were being developed. We have just noticed the interest of the antiquarians, who can be said to continue the literary and historical study of the ruins initiated by Petrarch in the previous century. Their focus is very much on the past and they seek to correctly identify and locate the ruins as a part of the ancient city's splendour. The architects, on the other hand, found in the ruins inspiration and models for contemporary building, so their focus was on the present day, an important shift of emphasis. The ruins were to be studied, drawn and measured, so that the results of this study could be applied in the design and construction of new churches, palaces and public buildings. The ruins in effect now spoke directly to the artist as raw material for appropriation. And that engendered a new way of looking at the ruins: henceforth their powerful aesthetic appeal is a given, not to be questioned. In a letter to Giovanni de' Medici dated 22 March 1443, Alberto degli Alberti made the usual complaint that the daily burning of marble for lime was a disgrace (*villania*), but he also unexpectedly remarked that contemporary building was sorry stuff (*triste*), and that Rome's beauty was its ruins.[56] Such a response to decay must be recognised as a striking development in aesthetic sensibility; it is a response that would grow considerably over time.

The developing interest in the ruins provoked outrage among humanists at their wanton destruction, as we have seen, and a concern to preserve them from further damage. Since many of the ruins belonged to the papacy, a number of measures were adopted by the popes from the fifteenth century on which reflect this concern, although Ronald Ridley provides a depressing survey of their infringement.[57] The root of the problem was that the owners of ruins, even the popes, regarded them as an asset; measures for their conservation diminished the asset's value and so they were circumvented for profit.

Not long after his return to Rome in 1420 Pope Martin V (himself a native of Rome, reigned 1417–31) issued a bull in 1425 which reinstated the originally civic officials known as the *maestri di strade e degli edifici*. As their title implies, they were charged with the maintenance of streets and structures. Martin in effect appropriated these once civic officials for the papal administration of Rome when he renewed their duty to monitor, regulate and restore infrastructure.[58] It is clear that the *maestri* were not so much concerned with the less useful structures, such as temples and baths, as with necessary civic amenities like bridges, fountains and aqueducts.[59] Their maintenance of at least one ancient monument, the Arch of Constantine, can in part be explained by the fact that Constantine was the first Christian emperor. That consideration had likewise ensured the preservation of the equestrian Statue of Marcus Aurelius, since the horse's rider was long believed to be Constantine.

Martin's attitude to the conservation of ruins becomes clear from his licence to excavate stone from what was believed to be a temple, called at the time Canapare or Cannapara, in 1426. David Karmon is at pains to emphasise the apparent restrictions laid down in the licence, pointing out that it allowed excavation of 'the travertine stone that was not exposed to view' (*lapides Tiburtinos non apparentes*).[60] This sounds conscientious, but the licence did not expressly forbid tampering with the visible stone, and indeed it went on to recognise that excavation might destabilise the temple's structure, causing it to collapse into ruin; in that case, all the stone could be burnt for lime. It would surely be naïve to imagine that the owners of the lime kilns did not take the hint and ensure at least some damage to the visible structure. Karmon recognises that the licence was also designed to prevent the lime-burners from taking more than their stipulated share; the structure's stone was deemed an asset and the owner was preserving anything left of it for future exploitation. The 'temple' was not being conserved expressly for its historical or aesthetic value, and whatever the Templum Canapare was, it has completely disappeared. The papacy did not yet see itself as the guardian of the ruins.

A brief issued in 1439 by Pope Eugenius IV (reigned 1431–47), to whom Biondo dedicated his treatise *Roma instaurata*, forbade destruction of 'even the smallest stone' (*et minimus … lapis*) of the Colosseum and other ancient buildings. Eugenius, in exile in Florence at this time, had heard that travertine stone was being removed from the *coscia* or southwestern 'flank' of the Colosseum, which had been thrown down by an earthquake.[61] His language in the brief, however, clearly refers to demolition (he used the Latin verbs *demolior* and *deicio*), not to the removal of stone already fallen, so it remains somewhat unclear whether the removal of debris was specifically forbidden.[62] The ban was at any rate a first step on the road to more comprehensive preservation. One sentence in the brief is particularly striking: Eugenius asserts that 'demolishing the city's monuments is nothing less than degrading the *outstanding quality* of the city itself and of the whole world' (*nam demoliri Urbis monumenta nihil aliud est quam ipsius Urbis et totius orbis excellentiam diminuere*). It is almost as if Eugenius regarded Rome as what we should now call a UNESCO World Heritage Site, which it indeed became in 1980.

Eugenius' brief had no effect, however, on his successor Nicholas V (reigned 1447–55). Nicholas, the founder of the Vatican Library, was an enlightened humanist,[63] and he was also the most ambitious of papal builders, though few of his schemes were fulfilled. It was appropriate that in 1452 Alberti presented him with a copy of his work in progress on architecture,

De re aedificatoria, which the pope read.[64] To facilitate his construction projects, Nicholas had removed 2,300 wagon-loads of travertine from the Colosseum (but again it is likely that the stone came from the already collapsed southwestern perimeter wall). A number of other structures were plundered for the reconstruction of the Vatican and of the Lateran palaces. Nicholas' aspiration was clear: Rome must be modernised so as to look like the centre of Western Christendom – or rather of Christendom as a whole, now that Constantinople had fallen to the Ottomans in 1453. Gregorovius enumerated his colossal projects, which were commemorated with a medal showing the refurbished city and inscribed 'Roma Felix'.[65]

Nicholas' destruction of the ancient remains is generally deplored, but a practical question must now be raised: what use were they in a modern city? They had not yet become major tourist attractions in their own right, nor was there any prospect of, or indeed point in, reconstructing such ruined structures as the baths (*thermae*) and temples which happened to have survived a lapse of, by now, nearly 1,000 years. Some baths and temples, the Pantheon or the Thermae of Diocletian, could usefully be recycled as churches. The Pantheon had already been converted into the church of S. Maria ad Martyres in the early seventh century;[66] the recycling of the baths will be discussed later. But other monumental structures, for instance the Colosseum, had no conceivable function in the Christian Rome of the fifteenth century. Modern Rome needed stone for its new bridges, walls, aqueducts, churches and palaces. The pragmatic mind could see no point in going to the trouble and expense of quarrying and transporting fresh stone to the city (though in fact new stone was brought down the Anio from Tivoli).[67] Considerable quantities of fine travertine ashlar lay in heaps within the very walls of the city, much of it at the base of the Colosseum. Recycling that stone for the construction of the first bridge over the Tiber to be built since antiquity by Pope Sixtus IV made far more sense than conservation, a policy urged by only a handful of architects, topographers, antiquarians and humanist poets.[68]

Aeneas Silvius Piccolomini, who became Pope Pius II (reigned 1458–64), recorded the personal pleasure he took in looking at the city's ruins and his distress at their gradual destruction:[69]

> I delight in gazing on your ruins, Rome;
>   from their fall your former glory is plain.
> But your present population digs out the ancient walls
>   and bakes the hard marble to produce quicklime.
> If the unholy crew go on this way for three hundred years,
>   there'll be no sign here of your renown.

(Hartmann Schedel quoted this poem at the conclusion of his account of Rome, illustrated by Michael Wolgemut's famous view of the contemporary city, in the Nuremberg Chronicle of 1493.) Pius was himself a humanist and so he shared the concern of the learned at the wholesale destruction of what had survived, however fragmentary, of the built environment of the past. He therefore issued a bull on 28 April 1462, entitled 'Cum almam nostram urbem', which forbade destruction, exploitation or removal of antique stones and marble. Before turning to some details in this papal bull, it is worthwhile to recognise how similarly slow has been the development in more recent times of a sense of the need for legally enforced preservation of the material culture of the past.

In the United Kingdom, for instance, the ruins of Gothic ecclesiastical buildings enjoyed enthusiastic appreciation from the eighteenth century on, but they were not legally protected from spoliation or even destruction. The first legal safeguard, the Ancient Monuments Protection Act, had a tortuous history. A bill was initially proposed by Sir John Lubbock in 1873 and supported by John Ruskin. Rejected seven times by Parliament, it only became law in 1882. Simon Thurley witheringly assessed the whole process: 'the mountain of debate produced the molehill of an act'.[70] Most of the monuments listed for protection were prehistoric, not Roman, or mediaeval, or later.[71] The 1882 act was revised in 1900 and again in 1913.[72] The revision of 1913, the Ancient Monuments Consolidation and Amendment Act, deserves special notice in the present context because the Chief Inspector of Ancient Monuments, Charles Reed Peers, had in his evidence drawn attention to the damage done to the Roman Wall constructed across Northumberland under the emperor Hadrian by the quarrying of the basalt upon which the wall was built.[73] Since the value of the quarried stone was considerable and compensation would have had to be paid for the loss of income to the owners of the sites, no provision was made in the 1913 act for the protection of the wall. But in 1928 the wall, along with other Roman remains, was scheduled in a list of monuments of national importance. It still required a further special act, the Ancient Monuments Act of 1931, to ensure the preservation of the wall and of its spectacular landscape for posterity, though even then some problems in the logistics of its conservation took time to resolve. Hadrian's Wall is of course now a UNESCO World Heritage Site. In the light of such modern foot-dragging by the state, the Renaissance papacy hardly deserves the criticism usually heaped upon it for maltreatment of the ruins of Rome.

To return now to Pius' bull of 1462, its prefatory remarks are highly significant in that the ruins are claimed to add to the beauty of the city: 'let

the ancient structures of former days and their remains survive for posterity, since the same structures confer upon the afore-mentioned City
ornament and the greatest splendour' (*antiqua et prisca aedificia, et illorum
reliquiae ad posteros maneant, cum eadem aedificia ornamentum et decorem
maximum afferant dictae Vrbi*). The Latin word *decorem* carries us back to
Hildebert of Lavardin's use of the related word *decus*.[74] The aesthetic value
of the ruins is now so clearly foregrounded that it provided henceforth a
strong argument for their preservation. The responsibility for preservation
was conferred upon civic officials, the Conservators.[75] This inadvertently
produced a problem: care of the antiquities belonged now both to the civic
Conservators and to the papal *maestri*, a recipe for demarcation disputes.
So in 1494 the Conservators had to be confirmed in the civic statutes as
the principal guardians of 'ancient things'.[76] In 1588/9 the Conservators
appealed to their officially recognised role, especially in its original enunci-
ation in the bull of 1462, when they made a U-turn and rescinded permission they had only just granted for the destruction of the handsome Tomb
of Caecilia Metella on the Appian Way. Pope Sixtus V wanted the structure
to serve as a quarry and he had already destroyed some of the Caetani fortress that had been attached to it in the early fourteenth century. He initially
secured the Conservators' agreement to this, but after a month they recalled
their duty and repudiated their previous consent.[77] So occasionally, at any
rate, the Conservators did their job.

Despite Pius' personal sense of the beauty of the ruins, he nonetheless
notoriously flouted his own ban when he set about removing columns from
the Porticus of Octavia to serve as a handsome new loggia for the old St
Peter's Basilica.[78] But as Ruth Rubinstein stressed, he was to some degree
conscientious in importing new marble from Carrara and in retrieving
unused ancient stonework buried in silt at the mouth of the Tiber at Ostia.[79]
Even the material taken from ruins in Rome itself was effectively conserved
in the recycling.

In 1515 Pope Leo X (reigned 1513–22) issued a papal brief authorising
collection of building material within 10 miles of Rome to supply stone
for the new St Peter's Basilica; the brief allowed that stone with letters or
other carving on it might not be suitable and indeed should be preserved.[80]
At some point, perhaps in 1519 (the precise date is debated), the scholar
Baldassare Castiglione and the artist Raphael Sanzio, who had settled in
Rome in 1509 and been appointed architect of St Peter's in 1514, wrote
a now famous letter or rather report to Leo urging the preservation and
measurement of ruins, as well as their reconstruction in drawings.[81]

The memorialists deplored the endless destruction of the fine monuments: 'so many beautiful things have been destroyed' ('sono state ruinate tante cose belle').[82] Once again, their aesthetic appreciation of the ruins is noteworthy and indeed it is becoming normative. The report strongly advocated the conservation of the ruins as evidence of the great achievements of the Italian past. Raphael also encouraged the production of a graphic record in drawings to be produced with the aid of the most up-to-date instruments of measurement; these would serve to reconstruct on paper at least the ruins of ancient Rome.[83] Whether that reconstruction would take the form of a map or of views is unclear, since the painter's initiative was cut short by his death in 1520. Up to a point, his scheme was realised by his friends Andrea Fulvio and Marco Fabio Calvo (his reconstructions will be described in the next chapter).

In 1534 the humanist Pope Paul III (reigned 1534–49) appointed the diplomatist Latino Giovenale Manetti to be the first Commissioner of Roman Antiquities (*Commissario Generale alle Antichità Romane*), a post that endured until 1870.[84] The bull which instituted this new office described the then precarious state of Rome's ruins and the pope's sense of a personal obligation to preserve the memory of its old monuments.[85] It was recognised that keeping the ruins cleared of vegetation, especially ivy, would check the damage done to stonework by plants,[86] but it is also clear that not much was done about it. One of Manetti's early tasks was to prepare the Forum for the triumphal visit (*adventus*) of the Holy Roman emperor Charles V, an event to be discussed in Chapter 11 (pp. 241–2).

Despite the pope's expression of personal concern for the preservation of the ruins and the establishment of an official to protect them, in the decade 1540–9 Paul, like his predecessors, allowed excavation (but not dismantling of visible stonework) in the Forum to provide material for St Peter's Basilica.[87] Excavation there and of the upper Sacra via exposed the Temple of deified Julius to destruction,[88] and uncovered the marble steps of the Temple of Antoninus and Faustina, which were removed. All of this was done without protest from the new Commissioner for Antiquities, Manetti. Thus the appointment of a Commissioner in reality only showed that a problem was recognised to exist, not that anything much was going to be done about it. And yet Paul's permits of excavation make sense of a sort.

Let us consider the case of the stairs on the podium of the Temple of Antoninus and Faustina. In the sixteenth century they, along with the lower part of the portico's columns, were deeply buried, unseen, unused and unnecessary, under 8 metres of soil and accumulated rubbish. The contemporary main door of the church of S. Lorenzo in Miranda, still encased

Figure 5.6 Temple of Antoninus and Faustina. Photo: Wikimedia Commons – ThePhotografer – own work, CC BY-SA 4.0 International; the staircase is modern.

within the ancient temple, is now visible several metres above the top level of the temple's podium. That gives us an idea of how much soil had to be removed to disclose the buried stairs (Figure 5.6). No one could have foreseen a time when the whole of the Forum would be excavated to its ancient pavement level, an excavation that might reveal in front of this particular temple a flight of fine marble stairs to be admired by tourists. (Excavation down to the original street level of the Sacra via was finally carried out by the French in the early nineteenth century.)[89] A buried stair only had value when recycled. Since no visible structure was destroyed or removed, there was no obvious hypocrisy in Paul's project.

Concern for the conservation of Rome's ruins at this time even took pictorial form. In 1983 a painting was rediscovered (now in the Liechtenstein Princely Collections) which is apparently the first entirely devoted to a ruinous landscape[90] (Figure 5.7). It was painted in 1536 by Herman Posthumus, who accompanied the emperor Charles V on his visit to Rome in that year.

Figure 5.7 Herman Posthumus (1512–66), *Landscape with Roman Ruins*, 1536, Liechtenstein, The Princely Collections – Vaduz-Vienna. Photo: 2024 © Liechtenstein, The Princely Collections – Vaduz-Vienna/Scala, Florence

Within a fabulous landscape, Posthumus has scattered a fair number of objects that were actually visible in contemporary Rome, some in private collections. Ruth Rubinstein plausibly suggested that the painting was in effect a plea for the conservation of the ruins of Rome.[91] The first three words, 'Tempus Edax Rerum', of the inscription, drawn from Ovid's *Metamorphoses* 15.234–6 and inscribed on a prominent stone tablet in the lower register, enunciate the painting's theme: ravenous time destroys everything. But time does not gobble up everything; there are scraps from its table and the leavings can be saved, so as to be measured and imitated (as the little figure in the lowest register to the lower right of the inscription is doing). Rubinstein regarded all this as an appeal to the cognoscenti to collect and to artists to study what time had not devoured. The force of the Ovidian motto could after all be mitigated.

Nonetheless, conservation of the ancient ruins was fitful at best,[92] and their reconstruction was impractical, with one exception: it became something of a competition among the popes to re-erect the fallen obelisks,[93] or in the case of the Vatican obelisk to relocate it in the square in front of St Peter's Basilica.[94] The ruinous Colosseum was also a special case, and its preservation was in due course assured by the pious, if erroneous, belief that large numbers of Christians had been martyred there (there were attested martyrdoms in the amphitheatre, but not as numerous as was believed). Two popes, Sixtus V and Clement XI, had wanted to turn the lower range of the encircling arcade into manufactories and the upper arcades into dwellings, but these commercial activities aimed at urban regeneration foundered on the high cost of adapting the structure.[95] It was thanks to Clement X that in the Jubilee year of 1675 the whole building was used as a shrine to those believed to have been martyred in the arena. In the 1740s the saintly friar, Leonard of Port Maurice, erected in the Colosseum the fourteen Stations or Way of the Cross (*Via Crucis*), a devotional practice which he, as a Franciscan, specially promoted. In 1742 Benedict XIV, who had a very high regard for Leonard, reconsecrated the Colosseum and made it a church in 1744. The building's denizens, chiefly prostitutes and robbers, were obliged to shift. From that time on the building was under direct papal care and it was scrupulously maintained. By this time in the mid-eighteenth century there was also an additional and compelling motive for the preservation of such an imposing structure as the Colosseum: tourism.

Nowadays, a determining factor in the conservation of ruins, wherever they exist in the world, is mass tourism. And tourism, where Rome is concerned, must be seen as something distinct from pilgrimage. The interest of the tourist is secular, of the pilgrim religious. We have seen in the third chapter that some mediaeval pilgrims to Rome did evince an interest in the secular pagan remains, but that interest was incidental to their primary reason for visiting Rome. But in the account in this chapter we have encountered genuine tourists, such as the emperors Sigismund and Charles, whose interest was different: they regarded themselves as successors of the Roman emperors, and so the remains of imperial Rome had a particular resonance for them. Over time less exalted tourists, especially from Protestant northern Europe, visited Rome specifically to satisfy their interest in classical antiquity, an interest first acknowledged as a reason for repairing a ruin by Pope Alexander VII (reigned 1655–67). He justified the repair of the Pyramid of Cestius on the grounds that if it were destroyed, fewer *virtuosi forestieri* would come to Rome to study antiquity as part of their education.[96] The importance to the tourist of conserved antiquities is also cited in an edict of the great art collector Alessandro Cardinal Albani in 1733:

> of the highest importance is the conservation in the city of the famous works of sculpture and painting, and especially of those things made the more estimable and rare by their antiquity; their conservation not only contributes much to learning, both sacred and profane, but it also

encourages strangers [*Forastieri*] to come to the City to see and admire them; it also provides a sure standard of study to those who work in these noble arts, with great advantage to public and to private welfare.[97]

The date of the edict and the final phrases translated above tell us just what classes of *Forastieri* or foreign tourists Albani had in mind. On the one hand, there were the artists who came to Rome to study architecture, sculpture and painting, for instance at the prestigious Académie de France, founded in 1666 at the instigation of Jean-Baptiste Colbert, the finance minister of King Louis XIV. Young French painters and architects were awarded prizes and scholarships to enable them to study the fine arts at their source. On their return they were to deploy their skills to improve the quality of artworks on home soil. On the other hand, and far more economically significant, there were the northern European and predominantly British gentlemen, the grand tourists, who proved to be of the greatest advantage to public and private welfare. More will be said about them in subsequent chapters, but it is certainly worth drawing attention now to a damning judgement passed upon the condition of the antiquities by one of England's grandest grand tourists, Horace Walpole. Just seven years after Albani's edict, Walpole wrote a letter from Rome on 7 May 1740 to his friend Richard West: 'I am persuaded that in a hundred years Rome will not be worth seeing: 'tis less so now than one could believe … the few ruins cannot last long.'[98] Walpole may have exaggerated, but Albani's anxiety was nonetheless well founded.

*

Throughout the fifteenth century the humanist successors of Petrarch followed up his hint, made explicit by Vergerio, that the ruins of ancient Rome are complementary to the transmitted texts of poets and historians. In combination the two, ruins and texts, provided a more complete image of Roman culture. Buildings, even in ruins, come to be seen as having no less validity than literature. The humanists discovered more texts than Petrarch ever knew, such as Frontinus' treatise on the aqueducts, and in their effort to identify and understand the remains of ancient buildings they made use of hitherto somewhat neglected texts, such as the late antique regionary catalogues. Images of buildings on coinage and inscriptions added to their knowledge, understanding and appreciation of the built environment of antiquity. The humanists gradually developed new and specialised categories of research in topography, antiquities (including numismatics and epigraphy) and archaeology. That the humanists in question were also members of the Curia, which was now re-established in Rome itself, only sharpened their appetite for viewing and preserving the ruins.

A second and unexpected cause for reassessing the value of the ruins was a change in architectural style from Gothic to *all'antica*. This stylistic change is unexpected because it was effected initially by a man who was not a Roman but a Florentine, and who could not be described as a humanist. Whatever his motive, and his aesthetic sense seems to be at the root of the matter, Brunelleschi changed the course of Italian architecture by adopting the Roman manner of design. Architecture was then brought within the humanist range of interest by his successor Alberti, whose treatise in Latin was based upon classical precedent in Vitruvius. Architecture in the Roman style thus becomes a humanist study, and the ruins were observed and drawn by the Sangalli, among others, to provide models for the contemporary *all'antica* style of building.

Architecture is a practical art, and it was especially needed in the Rome of the fifteenth and sixteenth centuries, once the city was again the seat of the papacy after a century of exile. Old buildings needed restoration or even replacement, and new buildings had to be constructed to accommodate ecclesiastical dignitaries and papal administrators. A fine example of such a modern building is Raffaele Cardinal Riario's Palazzo della Cancelleria nuova, the design of the exterior of which is now attributed to Baccio Pontelli.[99] It was built between 1489 and 1513 (Figure 5.8). The Cancelleria

Figure 5.8 Cancelleria nuova, Rome. Photo: Wikimedia Commons – Lalupa/public domain.

Figure 5.9 Cancelleria nuova, courtyard. Photo: I, Sailko, CC BY-SA 3.0.

is the first Renaissance palace to be built in Rome in the *all'antica* style promoted by Alberti. Its excellent stonework was fetched from the nearby ruins
of the Theatre of Pompey and from another source, the so-called Arch of
Gordian, as we are told in the little guidebook published in 1510 by Francesco
Albertini, a work to be discussed in the next chapter.[100] The Egyptian granite
columns of its serene courtyard, perhaps designed by Antonio Sangallo the
Elder, had also adorned the upper tier of the theatre (Figure 5.9).

It was the pressing need to rebuild the city in a modern style that posed
the greatest danger to the ruins. Fine ashlar and columns were to be found
in abundance in Rome itself. Why open new quarries and lay down roads to
bring the stone to the building sites when every material that was needed,
even the humblest brick, lay ready to hand in the city itself? The humanists, as we have seen, protested at this recycling and even destruction to
provide building material. Some popes showed a measure of sympathy for
their pleas and took measures, easily evaded, to check the destruction. After
all, the humanists were few and their writings had no extensive circulation.
Rome had to be rebuilt and the more economically, the better. The next
chapter will continue the story of humanist engagement with the ruins into
the sixteenth century, when that mighty engine of enlightenment, the printing press, materially benefitted their efforts.

6 | From Topographical Treatise to Guidebook

The target audience of the humanist antiquarian and topographical treatises described in the previous chapter was an educated and well-to-do elite. The treatises were written in Latin and available to readers only in manuscript format. Flavio Biondo's scientific topography of the ancient city made no appeal to the eye, as it lacked illustrations; he did not present his findings in graphic form, something that would have made manuscript reproduction difficult and costly. Neither did Alberti illustrate his architectural treatise.[1] The map of Rome produced by Strozzi was a one-off, drawn for private use. Pomponio Leto's knowledge of the ruins was only preserved by hearsay. The Florentine scholar Bernardo Rucellai produced an independent-minded treatise entitled *De urbe Roma*. Despite its merits, it seems to have had almost no contemporary circulation at all; it was published in an eighteenth-century work, corrected against just two manuscripts in Florence.[2] Restricted dissemination was therefore an obstacle to the propagation and exchange of knowledge. This obstacle was triumphantly overcome in the mid-fifteenth century with the invention of printing with movable type. This method of printing widened a readership hitherto restricted by the reproduction of manuscript. Printing also facilitated the inexpensive inclusion in treatises of replicable images and maps, either woodcut or engraved, which could easily be combined with the letterpress. Elizabeth Eisenstein described this innovation in the diffusion of technical literature as a 'communications revolution in itself'.[3] The printed and illustrated book vastly enlarged the potential readership of this learned material and, as we have seen, both Biondo's and Alberti's treatises were early beneficiaries of the print medium, in 1471 and 1486, respectively. But once the potential readership had been enlarged, there were fresh issues to confront. What of the Latinless reader? Translation of the learned treatise could put the results of up-to-date scholarship into their hands. The format of the volume had also to be taken into account. The press could easily produce cheap and handy volumes for the less well off; their compact size would appeal to the traveller and tourist. In this chapter the review of scholarly topographical works focussed upon Rome's ruins will be continued, but it should be understood that the ample production of printed volumes which both explained and illustrated the ruins of Rome engaged an altogether wider readership than the first humanists could have imagined.

Before surveying the printed accounts of the remains of ancient Rome, it will be helpful to distinguish three strands of interest in the ruins. The theatre may serve as an example. The student of topography knew that there were three theatres in ancient Rome, those of Pompey, Balbus and Marcellus; he aimed to pinpoint their exact location within the city. The student of antiquities gathered information on theatrical culture: how were plays commissioned and performed, who were the actors, what did masks look like; these and many other questions relating to drama and its performance were answered by the antiquarian. Finally, what did a Roman theatre look like? That is the concern of the artist and architect, and it is no surprise that they attempted to reconstruct the look of the original building from the clues provided by the ruins. Of course, these three interests, the topographical, the antiquarian and the architectural, were often blended, but it is well to bear in mind that one or the other may preponderate in any particular treatise.

The topographical treatises of the sixteenth and seventeenth centuries drew mainly on ancient texts for information about buildings and their location, so attention must here be drawn to the existence of a rogue work which misled topographers for centuries. The story of this work is conveniently told in English by Edward Bunbury, in Latin by Urlichs and in Italian in the *Codice Topografico*.[4] In 1503 Janus Parrhasius published a work on the regions into which the city was anciently divided, the *Libellus de regionibus urbis Romae*; he named the author as P. Victor, and even went so far as to advertise the volume as a golden booklet (*libellus aureus*). It was certainly mined as such, given the numerous reprints it enjoyed for the next three centuries and for the material extracted from it by the topographers. The only problem is that the name P. Victor was apparently an invention of Parrhasius, and the contents of the book, far from being ancient, are now seen to be the work of a contemporary humanist scholar. This unknown student of Rome's built environment took the ancient regionary catalogues as a framework on which to hang additional material from his own reading. So no fraud was intended, and indeed it is even possible that Parrhasius himself was duped by a manuscript into believing the whole work ancient. Anyway, for ancient it passed until the early nineteenth century, and the phantom authority P. Victor (with variations of that name) was frequently cited in the earliest printed works of topography, to which we may now turn.

Francesco Albertini's *Opusculum de mirabilibus novae et veteris urbis Romae* was first published in Rome in 1510.[5] There were further Roman editions in 1515 and 1523. An illustrated edition was published in Basel in 1519 and another edition in Lyons in 1520. These latter publications deserve particular note. Thanks to the proliferation of presses beyond the Alps (and to the lack of protective copyright legislation), descriptions of contemporary Rome could quickly and easily be republished and disseminated far more widely than the manuscript treatises of the early humanists.

Albertini said in his dedicatory epistle that he had been commended for an earlier work and encouraged to provide a correct account of the wonders of Rome, since earlier ones were 'incomplete and full of trifling legends' (*imperfecta fabularumque nugis plena*). His chief sources of information were the recent humanist researches.[6] For instance, he visited the house of Pomponio Leto on the Quirinal Hill in order to view an inscribed stone there, and he cited, but not consistently, his debts to Flavio Biondo.[7] The first two books of the treatise focus on structures and on antiquities. The ancient buildings are listed by category: baths, theatres, temples and so on, and they are located with reference to easily identified contemporary structures, such as churches or city gates. For example, the Baths of Diocletian are 'not far from the church of S. Susanna' and the Theatre of Marcellus is 'not far from the church of S. Nicola in Carcere'. Interspersed among the articles on the ruins, Albertini, following Biondo's practice, provided antiquarian essays on such matters as the tribes among which the Roman citizens were distributed and the city's fourteen regions or wards. Since the second book comprised the temples of ancient Rome, Albertini kicked off with an antiquarian disquisition on Rome's priesthoods and magistracies. The third book left antiquity behind for a description of the wonders of the modern city, such as the palaces of the cardinals and the Vatican. By thus separating more completely than Biondo had done the ancient from the modern city and the pagan from the Christian, Albertini provided a template to be followed by later writers of guides to Rome.[8]

Albertini strove to provide reliable information for a wide audience; the small format of the booklet was presumably designed to make it handy and inexpensive, like the contemporary printed editions of classic texts by Aldus in Venice. The book's prompt success is shown by the use made of it by the Franciscan friar Mariano da Firenze, who compiled an *Itinerarium urbis Romae* from it in 1518.[9] Albertini transcribed recently discovered inscriptions that identified ancient builders and he laid claim to first-hand observations, for instance of collapsed columns or inscribed bronze tablets.[10] It perhaps goes too far to regard him with Amy Marshall as a scientific topographer,[11] but he is trying to offer trustworthy guidance to what remained to be seen of ancient Rome. The numerous reprints of his book, even outside Italy, demonstrate the success of his undertaking: there was an eager European market for an up-to-date account of the ruins.

Albertini's opusculum was originally issued without illustrations or a map. The first attempt at a graphic reconstruction of ancient Rome was Marco Fabio Calvo's *Antiquae urbis Romae cum regionibus simulachrum*, first published in 1527, just before the notorious sack of the city by the troops of the emperor Charles V, and reprinted in 1532. Calvo was the friend of Raphael, who as mentioned in the previous chapter had translated Vitruvius' architectural treatise from difficult Latin into Italian for the painter. Their interest in ancient Rome's architecture and topography was intended to take shape in a visual reconstruction of the city. What Calvo in his old age finally produced was this, at first sight, rather odd treatise. (It may even have struck contemporaries as odd, if it was a copy of Calvo's archaeological plan of ancient Rome which was burnt when skylarking papal courtiers let burning candle wax fall on it.)[12]

Calvo's treatise began with a sort of historical overview in fanciful woodcut reconstructions of the city's growth in four epochs: the Romulan, the Servian, the Augustan and finally Rome in the time of the elder Pliny.[13] There is little explanatory text, probably because Calvo's maps were intended to illustrate Andrea Fulvio's *Antiquitates*, published at Rome in the same year.[14] Calvo designed ideogrammatic pictures of Rome, that is to say that the city is viewed from above, enclosed within its circuit of walls, and the prominent structures are unconnected by streets, a traditional way of depicting cityscapes, found in antiquity and in a well-known fifteenth-century bird's-eye view of Rome in Taddeo di Bartolo's fresco of 1414 in the Palazzo Pubblico of Siena. The peculiarity of Calvo's maps, however, is that they depicted only structures appropriate to the chosen historical period, and they are not ruinous, thus realising Raphael's scheme to reconstruct the evolving appearance of ancient Rome. Figure 6.1 shows the representation of the early Rome of Romulus.

The maps are followed by schematic plans of the fourteen regions: avenues cross the page with rows of houses stacked on either side of them; between the rows are depicted imaginative reconstructions of local buildings such as storehouses and flour mills (Figure 6.2). What makes the treatise significant is Calvo's desire to reconstruct the ancient city without reference to its post-classical additions, an initiative that will be followed by a good number of map-makers, as we will see.

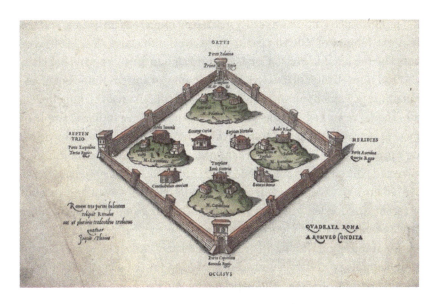

Figure 6.1 Romulan Rome in Calvo's *Simulachrum*, 1532. Photo: Metropolitan Museum of Art/public domain.

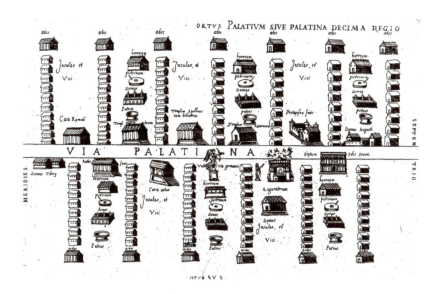

Figure 6.2 The Tenth Region of ancient Rome in Calvo's *Simulachrum*. Photo: Wikimedia Commons/public domain.

In 1534 Bartolomeo Marliani published his *Antiquae Romae Topographia*.[15] Philip Jacks and Pamela Long provide expert guidance to the publishing history of this work in its various editions and revisions.[16] This first unillustrated edition was sadly marred by numerous misprints, and the Beinecke Library of Yale University has a copy of the book (1972.790) corrected by the hand of Pietro Corsi. The French humanist François Rabelais, who had himself intended to write a topography of ancient Rome but abandoned the scheme upon the publication of Marliani's treatise, nonetheless published a reworked version of it in Lyons in 1534,[17] another example of the ease of transmitting and transforming information thanks to the printing press. Only in 1544 did Marliani himself get round to republishing a corrected edition under a modified title, *Urbis Romae Topographia.*

Marliani's aim was to supersede Biondo in reliability by taking account of recent discoveries. His own reliability did not go unchallenged, however, notably by Pirro Ligorio, a challenge he sought to meet in a 1553 reprint of the work, which will be discussed later.[18] Advantage was taken of print technology in the second edition of 1544 for the inclusion of woodcut illustrations of some of the ancient remains and of a map indicating their location. The remains are not, however, represented only as ruinous. They are also shown in architectural plan, in section and elevation as they might have appeared when new. This revised and illustrated version was a considerable success and was often reprinted, even beyond Italy.[19] Epitomised versions were also published. In 1548, Hercole Barbarasa produced an Italian translation of the work, which of course made the work accessible to the Latinless.[20] The date of publication, 1548, is itself telling, just two years before the Jubilee of 1550 (a year in which Marliani's Latin version was republished in Basle). The Jubilee of 1525 had been a disaster for a variety of reasons, and that of 1550 was to prove fairly subdued,[21] but the publisher's hopes for a success can be assumed. The translation was certainly reprinted in 1622.[22] Barbarasa's dedication of the work to Giovan' Battista Grimaldi included enthusiastic gush about the ruins: they are 'marvels which have escaped the damage of Time and the whole world gazes upon them in utter astonishment' ('le miracolose ruine, scampate da l'ingiuria del Tempo, con estremo stupore di tutto il mondo, vi si contemplano'). At this point, two centuries after Petrarch first visited Rome in 1337 and expressed his enthusiasm for its ruins, we ourselves might pause to marvel at the heightened evaluation of them thanks to the industry of architects, antiquarians and topographers. The ruins have been insensibly transformed from shapeless heaps of rubble, as Petrarch's friends saw them, into wonders of the world.

Marliani's second edition of 1544 provided a double-sheet map of the location of the remains of ancient Rome.[23] The map's viewpoint is neither pictorial nor in perspective, but ichnographic; that is to say, it depicts the plan or footprint of buildings, and some roads are sketched in. It is not a reconstruction of the totality of ancient Rome but of the city minus all contemporary structures and with only a few of the extant remains, such as the Colosseum and Baths of Caracalla, included in the uncluttered layout.

This sort of map, the ichnographic rather than the pictorial, was important to students of topography, but since the present work is concerned with the culture of the ruins as ruins, and since orthogonal ichnographic maps cannot by their nature represent a ruin, they will for the most part have reluctantly to be neglected. Even Leonardo Bufalini's impressive woodcut map of Rome of 1551, which included plans of ancient structures, some of them no longer extant, has to be no more than mentioned, since it too is ichnographic.[24] In fact, pictorial mapping was the generally preferred mode of representation, since it appealed to vision rather than to the imagination.[25] The pictorial also seems more natural; the orthogonal and ichnographic image is too abstract for most viewers.

'Lucio Fauno', a pseudonym of the humanist Giovanni Tarcagnota, is our first true populariser. His work of 'vulgarisation' was dismissed as worthless ('wertlos') by Ludwig Schudt,[26] but that assessment missed the point of his initiative. His Italian translation of Biondo's *Roma instaurata* under the title *Roma ristaurata* was first published in 1542 and then reprinted three times. It clearly met a need, first and foremost for the Latinless reader, and secondly for the visitor, thanks to its handy duodecimo format. Fauno designed his work to be user-friendly by simplifying Biondo's Latin in his translation and by removing the citations of ancient authorities, an advantage for the non-professional reader, since Biondo's scholarly presentation is austere – a work one consults rather than reads. Fauno also provided an index to the monuments. In 1548, he produced a five-book guide of his own, *Delle antichità della città di Roma*, which appeared in Latin dress as *De antiquitatibus urbis Romae* in the following year; it is a compilation based primarily on Biondo and Marliani's first edition. Like Barbarasa's translation of Marliani, Fauno's two guides were clearly produced in time for the Jubilee of 1550. It was a successful publication, often reprinted. The most convenient part is the *Compendio di Roma antica*, a précis of the preceding material at the end of the volume; this brief section was separately published in 1552. It satisfied publishers and readers, presumably tourists, even though none of the editions was ever illustrated.

Pirro Ligorio is something of a maverick among antiquarians and topographers, not least because his chief attainments were in the fields of architecture and painting. David Coffin provides comprehensive guidance based on a lifetime's research into Ligorio's life and work.[27] As an antiquarian,

Ligorio produced during the decade of the 1550s ten manuscript volumes in Italian on the antiquities of Rome, and these he reworked later in life until they amounted to thirty volumes, a veritable encyclopaedia of antiquarianism. (The volumes, now conserved in the National Library in Naples and the Italian State Archive in Turin, respectively, are gradually being edited and published.) The only fruit of these extensive researches ever to see the light of day in Ligorio's own lifetime were two small works, the first on Rome's racetracks (*circi*), theatres and amphitheatres, published in 1553 in Venice;[28] the second on the Baths of Diocletian, published in Rome in 1558. In an appendix to the earlier work, entitled *Paradosse*, Ligorio set out to correct what he believed to be mistaken opinions about the identity and location of ruins and sites.[29]

Ligorio's vaunted corrections sometimes misfired. For instance, he took a backward step in claiming that the Septizodium at the foot of the Palatine hill was not built by Septimius Severus, an issue Petrarch had correctly cleared up two centuries before him.[30] That blunder notwithstanding, his laudable aim, stated on folio 18 left of the little treatise (*trattarello*), was 'to the best of his ability to refresh and preserve the memory of ancient things' ('desiderando à tutto mio potere di rinfrescare e di conservare la memoria delle cose antiche'). On that same page he indicated just how he intended to go about 'refreshing' the memory of ancient things: in effect he would, as an artist, visualise them, by means of the reconstructions he drew for engravings of the major buildings and of maps. The engravings were not after all published contemporaneously with the booklet, as was plainly intended, but they did appear subsequently, and will be discussed in due course. He also had a second means of visualising ancient Rome, namely in a series of maps of the city. They remain his most interesting contribution to the increasing allure of Rome's ruins.

The first map, a copperplate engraving published in 1552, was a traditional bird's-eye view of the contemporary city, in which the extant ancient remains (some in fanciful reconstructions) were highlighted, but modern buildings also figured along with some no longer extant ancient ones[31] (Figure 6.3).

The second, archaeological map of 1553 was clearly designed to accompany the little treatises, especially the *Paradosse*, published in the same year.[32] From this map Ligorio had removed practically all modern structures and located only the ancient remains, some of which he imaginatively completed. In doing so, he followed Calvo's lead to some extent. But Ligorio showed originality too: where no trace was left of an ancient structure, its conjectured location, based on the bogus authority

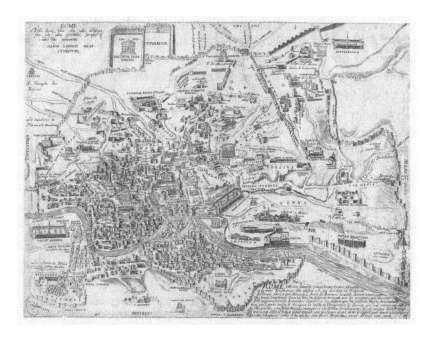

Figure 6.3 Pirro Ligorio, map of ancient Rome, 1552. Photo: Metropolitan Museum of Art/public domain.

of 'P. Victor', was indicated by a label printed in the hopefully appropriate spot.[33] A further innovation was the inclusion of the names of the fourteen Augustan regions.

Ligorio's conjectures shot sometimes wide of the mark. For instance, he placed the *Scalae Gemoniae*, Stairs of Groaning, on the Aventine Hill, whereas they still lead, as they have always done, up from the Forum to the citadel on the Capitoline.[34] Far and away his most serious lapse was his mislocation of the Roman Forum, which he placed in the valley between the Capitoline and the Palatine hills, a location for which he had argued in the first of his *Paradosse*. It must be recalled that the Forum was still buried under many metres of soil and rubbish, so its whereabouts was fair matter for conjecture, though, as Frances Muecke has shown, there was surprisingly little interest among earlier topographical writers in pinpointing its exact location.[35] Marliani, however, had already got the location more or less right (he extended it a bit too far east, right up to the Arch of Titus), but Ligorio, whose command of the ancient languages was not that secure, insisted that Marliani was wrong. They engaged in heated polemic over the issue.[36] A learned third party, Benedetto Egio, joined the fray in support of Ligorio.[37] The upshot of this unedifying dispute was that Ligorio's proposal,

rather than Marliani's, won the day and was adopted by a number of subsequent topographers (and by the engraver Piranesi),[38] until the matter was
satisfactorily resolved only well into the nineteenth century.

These two early maps were but dry runs for Ligorio's *magnum opus*, the
third and best-known map, a spectacular topographical reinvention of
ancient Rome, the *Anteiquae Vrbis Imago*, printed in 1561:[39] any physical
trace of the modern city is erased in favour of a phantasmagoric vision of the
past. The original fifteen engraved sheets of this huge map measure 1.26 m
by 1.49 m or 5 by 4 feet, a scale commensurate with Ligorio's ambition to
create an image that might do justice to the late imperial metropolis of
empire. The whole of Rome is depicted in razor-sharp detail, all of its many
buildings intact, not ruinous. Such a free-wheeling vision for a long time
diminished the value of the map in the eyes of scholars, but Howard Burns
turned the tide of adverse criticism in a sympathetic re-evaluation.[40] Burns
urged that the word *imago* in the titling of the map be taken literally: it is an
'image', not an ichnographic plan, and the imagistic character excuses the
adjustments made for the sake of prominence; the Pantheon, for instance, is
skewed so as to make its portico visible to the viewer. The 'blurb' provided by
the publishers in the cartouche assured the user that Ligorio's reconstruction
was based not just on direct investigation of the physical remains but also on
ancient texts, like the regionary catalogues, and especially on coins.

Coinage provided an invaluable resource for establishing the appearance
of some of Rome's public buildings, since the emperors had been keen to
depict what they either restored or constructed for public benefit, as testimony of their benevolent care of the citizenry. A good example, taken up by
Ligorio, is Nero's Great Market Hall, the *Macellum Magnum* (Figure 6.4).[41]

Figure 6.4 Coin depicting Nero's *Macellum Magnum*. Photo: Dirk
Sonnenwald, Berlin, Münzkabinett der Staatlichen Museen, 18204470, public
domain mark 1.0.

Ligorio was a real innovator, especially in his depiction of the everyday buildings such as the apartment blocks (*insulae*). Burns demonstrated that Ligorio's buildings were not modelled on those of his own day (some of which he did not like), but on representations of what he had seen on ancient reliefs, and perhaps other material, all of which gave Ligorio's 'image' a look of authenticity, elaborated in his infatuation with the splendour of the city in its prime.[42] Ligorio's evocation of Rome's magnificence fired imitators such as Étienne Dupérac and especially Mario Cartaro.[43]

Ligorio was offered a yet more substantial opportunity to 'refresh the memory of ancient things' by one of his patrons, Cardinal Ippolito II d'Este (1509–72), for whom he worked on the Villa d'Este and its enchanting gardens in Tivoli to the east of Rome in the Sabine Hills. In the late 1560s, after the publication of his three maps, now in his capacity as architect he designed and had constructed in the gardens a small-scale three-dimensional model of Rome, named the Rometta or Fountain of Rome. What exactly was represented is a matter for debate, not least because it is now little more than a ruin itself, thanks to the subsidence of a portion of the hill on which it is built (Figure 6.5). Some maintain that it is a model exclusively of ancient Rome (like the 1561 *imago*), while others point to the evidence of

Figure 6.5 Ligorio, *Rometta Fountain*, Villa d'Este, Tivoli. Photo: Palickap – own work, CC BY-SA 4.0.

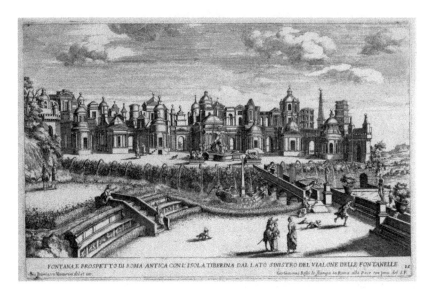

FONTANA E PROSPETTO DI ROMA ANTICA CON L'ISOLA TIBERINA DAL LATO SINISTRO DEL VIALONE DELLE FONTANELLE

Figure 6.6 Venturini, *Ligorio's Rometta*. Photo: Metropolitan Museum of Art/public domain.

contemporaries that modern structures appear to have been introduced.[44] It seems fair to say that the overall impression, both from what remains and from engraved views, such as Giovanni Francesco Venturini's of the late seventeenth century, is that the imagined appearance of the ancient city predominated, not least because no building appears in a ruinous state[45] (Figure 6.6). What is more, John Evelyn, who visited the garden on 7 May 1645, described it as 'the Cittie of Rome, as it was in its beauty, all built of small models, representing that Citie with its Amphitheaters, Naumachia, Thermae, Temples, Arches, Aquaeducts, streetes & other magnificences, with a little streame running through it for the River Tyber, gushing out of the Urne next the statue of that river.' It represented in Evelyn's eyes nothing of the contemporary city which he assiduously, if sometimes erroneously, described in his diary.

A reason for building the Rometta was recorded by a young French tourist, Nicolas Audebert, who visited the garden in 1576/7. Cardinal d'Este, often disappointed in his attempts to ascend the throne of St Peter, was building so grand and fortified a palace in Rome that the pope, Pius V, told him to desist. He did so by exiling himself to his villa at Tivoli. He commissioned Ligorio's Rometta, according to Audebert, with the remark that 'since he couldn't have a palace in Rome, he'd have Rome in his palace' ('puis qu'il ne luy estoit permis auoir un chasteau en Rome, qu'il vouloit auoir Rome en son chasteau').[46] Indeed, the fountain is so placed that the viewer on the terrace sees both a model of Rome and in the remote western distance the real Rome, a charming conceit.

Ligorio's scheme of mapping only the ancient remains was continued rather more modestly by Onofrio Panvinio, dubbed by Paulo Manuzio that 'glutton for antiquity' ('antiquitatis helluo'). Panvinio's extensive antiquarian studies were never published but remained in manuscript, although he did publish an edition of the regionary catalogues which passed under the names of 'P. Victor' and 'Sex. Rufus' in 1558.[47] His map of 1565, entitled *Anteiquae Vrbis Imago*, was engraved in 1573 by Dupérac and printed,[48] and there were reprints of it in 1580 and 1698. From this map every trace of the Christian and the modern has been removed,[49] and the ruins, but only the extant ones, are reconstructed. Philip Jacks pointed out that Panvinio aimed to remedy a defect of previous maps, including Ligorio's, namely their illogical street patterns. He used dotted lines to indicate major streets or routes,[50] and made no attempt even to conjecture where the lesser roads were.

The last reconstructive map in perspective to be considered is that of the Frenchman Étienne Dupérac, who has just been briefly mentioned.[51] Dupérac came to Rome in 1559, having learned to engrave in Venice; his engraved views of the city's ruins will be discussed in the next chapter. In 1574 (as usual just before a Jubilee year, that of 1575) he published a very large bird's-eye view map of a reconstructed Rome, entitled *Urbis Romae Sciographia*, which owed something to Ligorio's 'imago' and to Panvinio.[52] But unlike his predecessors, Dupérac was able to make use of the newly discovered fragments of the Severan marble plan, *forma*,[53] about which something may now be said.

In a large hall belonging to Vespasian's Temple of Peace a huge map of Rome was attached to one of the walls, now part of the church of Saints Cosmas and Damian.[54] A replacement of the map made in the time of Vespasian, now known as the *Forma Urbis*, was incised on marble ca. AD 203–11 in the reign of Septimius Severus. Its fragments were first discovered in 1562, just after Ligorio published his map, and fragments continue to turn up. The map is ichnographic, but not only the footprint of buildings; their names too were incised, and the network of streets is made clear. Amanda Claridge provides an illustration of the fragments of the map itself, from which it is clear how the missing parts can sometimes be reconstructed.[55] Thanks to the marble plan's fragmentary remains, Dupérac, unlike Ligorio, was able to introduce clear streets and roads (but presumably much was still guesswork).

Dupérac's work shows that topographical studies of Rome were not the exclusive preserve of Italians. At the end of the sixteenth century another

Frenchman, Jean-Jacques Boissard, published in Frankfurt a sumptuously illustrated series of volumes entitled *Romanae urbis topographia et antiquitates* (1597–1602). The title page announced that the topographical material was drawn from Onofrio Panvinio, Bartolomeo Marliani and bogus 'P. Victor', whose first name, Publius, is accidentally Christianised to Petrus. Boissard said in his introduction that when he arrived in Rome he found that topographical guides were sold out, and that anyway their information was too ample to be taken in by the tourist with little time. Once he was settled in the city, he found himself undertaking to guide visitors from Italy, France and Germany among the ancient remains. On these tours he observed his troops laboriously copying his remarks into notebooks, and so he decided to save them the trouble by compiling himself some brief notes for a three-day visit. But that proved too short, since there was also much to be seen in the private collections and palaces of the city, and so a fourth day was added to include these. Boissard was by no means blind to the beauty of contemporary buildings like the Cancelleria and the Palazzo Farnese, and equally he admired the paintings of Raphael and Michelangelo. The reason for drawing attention to this avowedly derivative work is that it is expressly intended to serve as a guidebook, setting out crisply (if optimistically) what the pilgrim or tourist should make a point of seeing 'in the space of four days' (*dierum quatuor spatio*). In the second edition of 1627–8, the first fifty-eight pages comprise the four-day guide, written in Latin; Boissard clearly expected to serve an educated international readership. Since the book's format, however, is a small folio, it is unlikely that it could have been used at all comfortably by a tourist on the hoof. The guide is followed by Panvinio's account of the fourteen regions of the city, based upon 'P. Victor'. The second part of the work begins with nine chapters drawn expressly from Marliani. There is a pause in the topographical material for the unexpected and unexplained introduction of Calvo's *Simulachrum* and some engravings of famous ancient sculptures. Then the thread of topography is picked up again with the rest of Marliani. Three more volumes followed, but these contained hardly any text, mainly comprising illustrations of inscribed stones and sepulchral monuments. A German-language edition of just the four-day visit was published in 1681. It is hard to know if the bulky volume was of any practical use to the tourist, but it deserves to be mentioned here because it is clearly designed to serve as a guide for those whose interest is almost solely classical; the contemporary city is largely neglected. One reason for that is that both the author Boissard and his famous engraver Theodor de Bry were northern European Protestants for whom Counter-Reformation Rome was presumably uncongenial.

Pompilio Totti was the first to publish separate but complementary guides to Rome. The first to appear was the *Ritratto di Roma antica* (1627), followed in 1638 by the *Ritratto di Roma moderna* (it covered modern Rome in six days). The use of Italian is significant, as is the handy format; this was a book designed to appeal to the averagely educated student or tourist, such as John Evelyn, who used both volumes when writing up the account of his visits to Rome in 1644 and 1645. Totti's *ritratto* or portrait of ancient Rome was as much antiquarian as topographical; it included, for instance, disquisitions on Roman marriage with illustrations. Where Totti engages with the buildings of the ancient city, he deals with them by category: temples, *thermae*, racetracks. Although the work is focussed upon ancient Rome, Totti happily included some information about the contemporary city, for instance the fountain on the Janiculum Hill erected by Pope Paul V. Alberto Caldana reassesses the value of the work, especially the inclusion of illustrations engraved on copper, a technical improvement on the use of woodcuts in earlier guides.[56] But as Tschudi explains, the small dimensions of the printed page prompted the reduction of distances and the aggregation into a single image of buildings that in reality were further apart: 'Rome itself was refounded as visual fiction.'[57] What is more, the illustrations are predominantly of fanciful (and borrowed) reconstructions with only occasional representations of ruins, for instance of the Colosseum and the 'Temple of Peace'. As a guidebook, it hardly illustrates the reality of the actual city, but it invites the user instead to wonder at the lost magnificence of the ancient city.

Totti's portrait of ancient Rome, for all its inadequacies, was republished in an enlarged edition in 1633 and 1638. The pair of guides were taken over in 1654 by Filippo de' Rossi. In 1697 a further revised and enlarged edition appeared under a new title, *Descrizione di Roma antica*, again a compilation of various authorities (named on the title page); there were four subsequent printings. In 1739, Gregorio Roisecco took over the printing, and in 1745 revised the work, integrating ancient and modern, *Roma antica, e moderna*; the antiquarian material is printed separately in a third volume, a tidier arrangement than that of Biondo and Albertini. This was perhaps the most sumptuous of the eighteenth-century guidebooks.[58]

The priest Alessandro Donati was a poet and professor of rhetoric in Rome's Jesuit Collegio romano. In 1638, he published *Roma vetus ac recens*. It proved a success and enjoyed numerous reprints; the Amsterdam reprint of 1695 demonstrates that the work had secured a European readership. Donati wrote in Latin, ensuring an erudite target audience rather than the average tourist. This is borne out by the original scheme adopted by Donati in describing Rome's built environment. He explained in the first sentence of the dedication to the Jesuit-educated Pope Urban VIII that his work was to be a historical survey of building activity in 'Rome ... from its first beginning through the different periods of construction right down to the present day' (*Romam ... a prima origine per varias aedificandi aetates ad nostra usque tempora deductam*).

Between the table of contents and the beginning of the first book there is a fine map, depicting only the ancient remains, but with the addition of only two churches, St Peter's in the Vatican and St Paul 'outside the walls'. It is based on Ligorio's map of 1553, and so it preserves the misguided location of the Forum, as well as the misplacement of the *Scalae Gemoniae* on the Aventine Hill. Donati regrettably endorsed Ligorio's theory of the location of the Forum in book II, chapter XVI, but he dithered over the location of the *Scalae* in book II, chapter XIII: he was inclined to place them on the Aventine Hill, but was well aware of the evidence for the Capitoline. He concluded rather lamely that there was authoritative evidence for either view (*qui utrumque tueri velit, auctores habet, quibus id tueatur*). At least he managed to part company with Ligorio regarding the Septizodium at the head of the Appian Way. He was clear that it was built by Septimius Severus, and yet the preliminary map retains the faulty identification of it as 'Septizonium vetus'. In a way this hardly mattered since, as Donati noted, the structure had completely disappeared by his time, as Pope Sixtus V had recycled all of its stonework in 1588–9.[59]

It is really only Donati's first book which offers a chronological account of who built what and when in the city of Rome in antiquity. The second book is dedicated to the buildings of the Capitol and its adjacent *fora*, and the third to those on the Palatine and the other hills of the city. Thus far Donati followed the now usual pattern of segregating the ancient remains from the modern city. The fourth and concluding book resumed the chronological scheme in providing an account of Christian Rome, starting with Constantine and then tracing the development of the papal city down to his own day in the papacy of Urban VIII. With chapter 9, for instance, he begins the story of modern Rome's buildings from the return of the papacy from Avignon.

The illustrations also show another instance of Donati's novel approach: he offers 'then' and 'now' paired views, 'then' being imaginative reconstructions and 'now' the actual state of the ruin. The engravings of the Temple of Antoninus and Faustina are good examples of the scheme. This impressive survey is equipped with helpfully comprehensive indexes both of the illustrations and of the matter. Donati's unusual and imaginative approach to presenting a historical survey of the building of ancient and contemporary Rome deserved its success.

Famiano Nardini's *Roma antica*, first published in 1665,[60] was not especially original, and like Donati he was ensnared by Ligorio's notion of the location of the Forum. Still, the work secured a considerable reputation, thanks to numerous reprints and revisions. Once again, the use of Italian strongly suggests a wish for wide readership. Nardini has one secure claim to fame because he was the first to correctly identify the Temple of Venus and Roma in book III, chapter XIII. This impressive and original double-fronted temple with back-to-back *cellae* had been designed by the emperor Hadrian and rebuilt by Maxentius,[61] but it had long been incorrectly identified under a number of names, chiefly as a temple to the Sun and the Moon. Nardini finally got it right, and so perhaps it is not surprising that his work was chosen for augmentation in 1818–20, and the identification of the temple more fully documented thanks to recent excavations.

The last two works, by Donati and Nardini, bring us well into the seventeenth century, and that prompts stocktaking to this point, because topographical treatises have clearly reached something of an impasse. Donati, for all his learning, either mistakenly heeded the siren song of Ligorio or could not make up his mind in the light of apparently conflicting textual evidence. Nardini, on the other hand, did make a signal advance, but for the most part his work was derivative. In the final footnote, 86, of the final chapter, LXXI, of his history of the decline and fall of Rome, Edward Gibbon noted that their books were recent but imperfect. Such limitations also characterise works which have not been given separate treatment in the survey above. The handy guidebook of the great architect Andrea Palladio, *Le Antichità di Roma* of 1554;[62] Bernardo Gamucci's fully illustrated guide, *Libri quattro dell'antichità della città di Roma, raccolte sotto brevità da diversi antichi et moderni scrittori* (Venice, 1565);[63] and Girolamo Franzini's guide, *Le cose maravigliose dell'alma città di Roma* of 1588 all proved serviceable, since they were frequently reprinted and reworked. None of them added to knowledge, but, to be fair to them, they did not aspire or claim to do so. The limitation which the topographers seem scarcely to have grasped is that their approach was purely philological and text-based. Ancient texts were either faulty or vague about locations and, in the case of 'P. Victor', a good deal less authoritative than they were cracked up to be. Inscriptions proved helpful, but their evidence too needed interpretation.

So by the mid-seventeenth century not much more could be done than to argue about the correct interpretation of texts. As Lawrence Richardson has said in his survey of topographical studies of this period, 'new information of real value could only come from the physical remains themselves, and those to a very large extent lay buried'.[64] The only way forward therefore would be to 'unbury' them. Disinterment, however, required the development of an altogether new discipline, archaeology, but none of the topographers discussed so far suggested this solution, even assuming they recognised that there was a basic defect in their own approach. Indeed, Gibbon himself, in the footnote just referred to, listed three methods for making good the deficiencies of topographical accounts of ancient Rome, but excavation is not one of them. Excavations had been carried out in Rome, but they were not motivated by topographical research. The excavator was looking for fine statuary or coloured marble, or worse, stone for conversion into lime. Increasing the knowledge of the remains of ancient Rome was not on the agenda. This is understandable: excavation was and still is very costly and time-consuming. Pure research will not justify the outlay. On the other hand, once tourism came to be recognised as a factor, as it was in the eighteenth century, excavation became more attractive. To anticipate briefly the theme of a later chapter, it was the work done in disclosing the wonders of Pompeii and Herculaneum which provided a spur to excavation in Rome. For that, we must wait until the nineteenth century and the French occupation of the city. But for now we may agree with the nineteenth-century English student of Roman topography Edward Bunbury that 'the shovel of the excavator has done more than all the labours of the learned'.[65]

A number of the topographical works reviewed above were designed to serve equally as guidebooks, most clearly the four-day excursion outlined by Boissard. To enhance their appeal many of them were equipped with illustrations, one of the capital benefits conferred by the printing press. But in the main the early illustrations of the ruins were sketchy and their reconstructions, if provided, overly fanciful. A view of the Forum of Nerva, for instance, reproduced in a 1725 Amsterdam reprint of Donati's *Roma vetus ac recens*, copied a drawing made in the 1560s by Giovanni Antonio Dosio, of which there are a number of versions.[66] An etching based on the drawing was used earlier, in the third, 1665 edition of Donati (this followed its use a century earlier in Gamucci's work, mentioned earlier). The promenading figures are decorative enough, but no attempt was made to represent the structure to scale, since that was not a matter of concern to the target audience. The details, moreover, of the carving of capitals and entablatures or friezes were likewise neglected. But there are two serious defects. First, Dosio's drawing was made on site and reliably represented the ruin as it was. The engraver, however, has rotated the image through 180 degrees (at least he got the inscription round the right way!). Secondly, in 1606 Pope

Paul V had the ruin demolished so as to recycle its stone in his fountain on the Janiculum Hill. So, foisted upon the unwitting purchasers of those 1665 and 1725 reprints was an inaccurate illustration of a vanished structure.

It is now feasible to consider what might be called the progeny of the topographical treatise, the dedicated guidebook. A number of the treatises so far mentioned, particularly those written in Italian, were clearly intended to direct the visitor to places of interest. What is somewhat surprising is that the earliest writers of guides assumed that the interest of visitors could be confined to either ancient or modern Rome. Pompilio Totti's guides exemplified this separation by confining the old and the new Rome to separate volumes. Even if a single guidebook dealt with Rome in both periods, they were not usually integrated. Given the huge number of guides to the city, selection is necessary, and so two of the most successful will have to serve as exemplary.[67]

In 1763, Ridolfino Venuti published in Rome his *Accurata e succinta descrizione topografica delle antichità di Roma*, the success of which is proved by its republication in 1803 and in 1824. Venuti was a respected student of antiquities, and Pope Benedict XIV appointed him commissioner of antiquities in Rome and superintendent of the papal collections in the Vatican museum.[68] Like Totti's guides to Rome, which separated ancient from modern, Venuti's ancient volumes comprising the antiquities were complemented by one published posthumously on the modern city (Rome, 1766). The topographical tradition dominated the layout of Venuti's text, but he also equipped the volume with a map sketching out a 'methodical route' or 'systematic itinerary' (*giro metodico*) to guide the user among and around the ruins of the city. At the end of the second part (or volume), there is a folding map of the remains of the city which depicts only the ruins (with a few modern structures to serve as fixed points). They are joined one to another by a single spaghetti-like strand marking the *giro metodico*, with numbers indicating sites of interest identified at the margins of the map.[69] There are curious features in this map. The third item, for instance, just after the start of the itinerary, indicates the site of the 'Ruminal Fig Tree'; but the location of this famous but long-defunct plant is entirely conjectural, as are a number of the others. Venuti was visualising a Rome shorn of almost everything modern and supplemented by historical fantasy. This takes us back to Petrarch's first visit to the city, when he claimed to discern what was no longer visible there, including the Ruminal Fig.[70] So the 'methodical route' is designed to appeal to the student of Rome's remote past, a student with little or no interest in the modern city, who must use the 'mind's eye' as well as the physical ones as the journey proceeds.

Lady Miller used the book during her stay in Rome in 1770–1 and she assured her correspondent that she found it 'serviceable',[71] though the 'cuts', as she called the engravings, were 'unfortunately ... but poorly executed'. (Some of the views were drawn by Piranesi, whose engravings she would collect.)[72] One wonders, however, given the absence of any indication of the modern network of streets, just how serviceable the 'giro' might prove. But of course the English visitor did not need the map and tended to rely upon the local guide or 'cicerone'. Venuti's 'giro' really does seem to be designed to appeal to the imagination rather than to guide the foot-slogging tourist.[73] Nonetheless, the success of Venuti's work is also demonstrated at the end of the second part, where on three pages are listed the English 'associates' (we would call them subscribers) in the publication of the work.[74] A number of them were grand tourists, like Lady Miller and her husband, and Lord Brownlow.[75] We cannot leave the engaging Lady Miller without drawing attention to her reaction to the Colosseum, which she found 'a *definition* of the *sublime* in *architecture*' (her italics).[76] Now, since the publication of Edmund Burke's *Philosophical enquiry into the origin of our ideas of the sublime and beautiful* in 1757, 'the sublime' had become a fashionable concept. For Burke, sublimity was the aesthetic effect of the process of viewing upon the viewer. Lady Miller had no hesitation in perceiving the shattered Colosseum as sublime, and that is a step up in the aesthetic appreciation of ruins, an appreciation encouraged in the guidebooks of Giuseppe Agostino Vasi.[77]

Vasi was an engraver of views, whose work as a *vedutista* will figure in the next chapter.[78] Here we are concerned with him as the initiator of an influential series of guidebooks that were revised and reprinted for well over a century. In 1763, he published in a very handy sextodecimo format an *Itinerario istruttivo per ritrovare con facilità tutte le antiche e moderne magnificenze di Roma*. The convenience for the tourist of the combination of ancient and modern, rather than their separation, even if bound between the same covers, is obvious. Vasi provided itineraries for an eight-day stay in Rome. He also provided illustrations, which in the early editions of the guides were reductions of the engraved views published previously. The high quality of these miniature views is rightly praised.[79] In 1773, Vasi brought out the first edition of the guidebook in French, the *Itinèraire instructif de Rome*. Giuseppe produced three editions up to 1777. After his death in 1782 his son Mariano took over the enterprise, producing his first revision (possibly his father's work), in French, in 1786, and then numerous reprints and revisions in both French and Italian followed up to his death, ca. 1820. The Italian edition of 1794 has been reprinted with notes.[80] In the final editions of his lifetime Mariano Vasi prudently called upon the assistance of a rising young Roman archaeologist, Antonio Nibby, about whom more will be said later.

The younger Vasi brought to his account of the grandest of all Rome's ruins, the Colosseum, a sensibility that is the high-water mark of ruin-mindedness. He found it so picturesque in its ruination that he had no desire for it to be restored: this was a task to be left entirely to the imagination.[81] This assessment of the picturesque quality of the ruin is found in some earlier editions (e.g. that of 1794), but not in all. Christopher Woodward claims that the discovery that a ruin may be found more beautiful than its intact original design belongs to the Welsh painter-poet John Dyer, who visited Rome in 1724 and found 'the triumphal arches more beautiful than ever they were', thanks to the softening effects of decay and vegetation.[82] Dyer's romantic view of the ruins betrays an entirely modern sensibility, like Lady Miller's later perception of 'the sublime'.[83] Such responses to ruination were unexampled in antiquity, and perhaps were not generally common even in the eighteenth century. The picturesque or the sublime fragment surpassed the intact original thanks to its suggestiveness and the pathos of its appeal. The sentiment was echoed by the French writer Stendhal, who used Nibby's revision of Vasi's guide, in his account of a visit to the Colosseum dated 16 August 1827 in *Promenades dans Rome* (1829): in his eyes the structure was 'perhaps lovelier nowadays that it is fallen into ruin, than it ever was in all its magnificence ... to-day it is the finest relic of the Roman people' ('plus beau peut-être aujourd'hui qu'il tombe en ruine, qu'il ne le fut jamais dans toute sa splendeur ... aujourd'hui c'est le plus beau vestige du peuple romain'). In fine, we have reached peak ruin-mindedness, now that the ruin is deemed an aesthetic improvement on an undamaged original.

The edition of the Vasi guide used earlier, that of 1820, was, as mentioned, passed for revision to Antonio Nibby, an important figure in the production of guides to the Roman ruins and in the continuation of the Vasi series.[84] In his youth Nibby had followed a course on archaeology under Lorenzo Re, since 1810 the first professor of archaeology in the University of Rome, La Sapienza. Re insisted that his students not only acquaint themselves with the textual sources but also study the remains in their actual state: autopsy was essential, and Nibby had personally witnessed the archaeological activities in Rome of the occupying French (1809–14).[85] This fired his enthusiasm for study of the ancient remains of the city. In 1818–20 he published a revision of Nardini's *Roma antica* of 1665, reusing too Nardini's engravings, to which were added new ones based on drawings by Antonio de Romanis. His revision took the form of annotations which brought the work up to date in the light of recent excavations. He also produced in 1818 the *Raccolta de' monumenti più celebri di Roma antica*, with a bilingual text in French and Italian. He was thus the right man for the job of carrying on the work of the Vasis, at least regarding the remains of ancient Rome, and his first revision of the guide appeared with his name on the title page in 1818.[86] Guides under his own name started in 1824; one innovation was that the illustrated buildings and views now occupied a full page. Nibby's guides were long the most favoured by the educated tourist, and rightly so, since Nibby was a professional archaeologist, who in 1820 became Re's successor as professor of archaeology in the 'Archiginnasio romano', La Sapienza. He excavated much of the area between the Colosseum and the Arch of Constantine, and within the Roman Forum. It was he who first correctly identified what had been known up to his day as the Temple of Peace as the Basilica of Maxentius. In short, he made available in his guides and other writings the most accurate and up-to-date information on the ancient remains of Rome. It is testimony to the value of his work that in 1831, a year after the publication of the third edition of his guide, his companion Richard Burgess published *The Topography and Antiquities of Rome: including the recent discoveries made about the Forum and the Via Sacra*. Burgess was well aware that the names attached to the buildings were often wrong,[87] and in his first volume, p. 293, he hailed Nibby's correct identification of the Basilica of Maxentius.

The Vasi–Nibby guides can be regarded as the first modern guidebooks, since they treated the city as an integrated complex of ancient and modern, pagan and Christian. The buildings could conveniently be visited by following itineraries; they were not grouped, as in the old antiquarian studies, generically (theatres, temples, triumphal arches) or by historical chronology. This all made for a user-friendly layout for the contemporary tourist. The visitor standing in the Forum wants information on both the Arch of Septimius Severus and the nearby church of S. Luca (now recently conserved and well worth a visit). The tourist does not want the information on the ancient arch and the modern church to be confined to separate volumes, or to be found in sections that described structures by type. The information needed to be provided topically, in the same section of the guide. The success of the guides was ensured by frequent revision of the textual information, though the engraved illustrations were often seriously out of date. For instance, in the 1839 edition the Arch of Titus is still enmeshed in the later structures removed by Giuseppe Valadier in the early 1820s. The guides at last secured an anonymous English version in 1841, entitled *New guide of Rome, Naples and their environs*, with attractive engravings by Pernié. Needless to say, this guide too was often revised and reprinted. In 1844 Agostino Valentini took over publication of the 'Nibby' guides, with very superior illustrations by Gaetano Cottafavi (he also produced engraved views of the city)[88] and Domenico Amici. The only serious defect in the guides was the lack of useful maps. In the older versions there were just two maps – one of the ancient city, highlighting the extant remains, and another of the modern city. But they hardly provided adequate guidance through the network of contemporary streets. Perhaps the lack of maps was intentional, so as to compel the tourist to hire a personal guide.

Just as the Vasi guides found a continuator in Nibby, his guides were given a prolonged life by Filippo Porena, starting in 1882 and ending in 1894. The need for revision was sharpened once Rome had become the capital of a unified Italy. The city's infrastructure was undergoing a complete overhaul, and new buildings, residential and governmental, were under construction, especially on the Quirinal and Esquiline Hills. Naturally these works disclosed remains of the ancient city, and so a sort of rescue archaeology was set in train, the results of which were incorporated in revisions of Nibby's authoritative work. New material meant that the original eight-day visit had to be extended to ten.[89]

∗

These Renaissance and later topographical studies have as their descendants our modern archaeological guides to Rome: Henri Jordan's *Topographie der Stadt Rom im Altertum*, Berlin 1871–1906; Claridge (2010); Coarelli (in Italian in the Laterza series, frequently revised and reprinted, translated into French in 1994, and into English 2014); and most recently Carandini's impressive *Atlas* (English version 2017).

All such studies are testimony to one of Rome's unique qualities among the great cities of the world, namely the intimate coexistence of the monuments of a remote and alien past with a lively present. The physical appearance of the city is extraordinary, and nothing matches it. Not even Athens rivals it for the range and scale of ancient structures still visible in the modern cityscape. But the coexistence of the material structures is deceptive just because it masks the major lacuna in the continuity of Rome. The existence of such a gap bolsters the view of Salvatore Settis, described in the first chapter, that a gap in continuity is a necessary precondition for an appreciation of ruins. In fact, the lacuna to be found in the deceptive continuity of Rome overdetermines the apprehension of difference. There are two gaps in the city's continuity, the first between antiquity and the varied modern presents – the Renaissance, Baroque, the Kingdom of Italy and the Fascist period – and the second between the pagan and the Christian buildings in the city: the Pantheon was a temple and is now a church, but it had a fallow period between its lapsed pagan function and its re-dedication to the Virgin Mary.

The differences are crucial for our sense of Rome and of the city's unique character. In essence, the difference, the gap, the lacuna, the hiatus, or whatever we choose to call it, was divined, if not enunciated, by Petrarch in the letter to Colonna (*Familiares* 6.2), described in the fourth chapter. It will be recalled that Petrarch gave an account only of the ancient and pagan structures they wandered among; no Christian or contemporary sites were named. In §16 of the letter he defined the ancient as pagan and the recent as dating from the Edict of Milan in 313. For Petrarch, pagan Rome was something distinct from Christian, and that distinction was kept up by the humanist topographers and mappers: they charted only the ancient city as best they could. Their researches into a discrete Rome – classical, pagan and ancient – were followed up in the popularisations in the vernacular languages: works with titles like *Antichità* are concerned solely with the Rome of the ancient Romans, to the exclusion of the modern city. To be sure, Biondo had dedicated the last book of his three-book *Roma instaurata* to the revived modern city, but that only corroborated a tendency to keep the past separate from the present; there was to be no intermingling such as we expect from our own guides to the city. Alberto degli Alberti was right: Rome's ruins are its allure – 'il bello di Roma son le cose disfatte'.

7 | The Ruins Visualised

Paintings and *Vedute*, Drawings and Engravings, Photographs

An important contribution to the developing sensibility of ruin-minded-ness was neglected in the previous chapter, which focussed upon archi-tects, humanist topographers and antiquarians as the agents of change in the appreciation of the visible remains of ancient Rome. That neglected contribution was initially made by fifteenth-century Italian painters, who somehow or other also developed an enthusiasm for Rome's ruins and the Roman style of building, which they began to incorporate into their reli-gious works. This chapter will first trace the curious development of the appearance of Roman ruins in paintings (and one illustrated book). The development is curious because the ruins originally appear somewhat inci-dentally (albeit significantly), as background or 'staffage' (the accessories of a picture), but then they gradually move forward and finally become the chief subject of a painting. This starring role is obviously a tribute to their newly found aesthetic value.

The pictorial value of the ruins of Rome was not limited to paintings, however. As we saw in the previous chapter, thanks to the printing press, woodcut or engraved views of the ruins and some imaginative reconstruc-tions could be included as illustrations in architectural and topographical treatises and in guidebooks, where they served an explanatory or purely illustrative function. In the following narrative, attention will be drawn to related *vedute*, 'views', which were sold in sheets to tourists or published in volumes. Once Rome became a training-ground for artists, the ruins were drawn in pencil or depicted in watercolour by amateurs and by professional artists and architects. Photography then took over the job of providing images of the remains in the nineteenth century.

From an early stage, artists and architects, challenged by the fragments of structures, liked to imagine what the ruin had looked like before its decay, and their attempts at reconstruction not only of individual struc-tures but also of the cityscape as a whole became popular exercises of their imagination, as we have already seen in maps of the city and in the illus-trated topographical works and guidebooks. Since a good deal of European architecture was based on classical models, it made sense for budding architects to practise design in the Roman style by imaginatively reconstructing the now fragmentary original. More recently, the availability of digital and computer-generated imagery (CGI) has prompted archaeologists to try their hands at reconstructing the original appearance of buildings and complexes, such as the Forum of Trajan and the Roman Forum. All these and a number of other visual apprehensions of the ruins are the subject of this and of the next chapter.

*

Painting

The growing appeal of ruins so far charted also gathered strength in the Renaissance thanks to their visual representation, another crucial stage in the development of an enthusiasm for ruination. Once again, we are confronted with a shift in sentiment. Just as Petrarch's friend Cardinal Colonna thought that the actual sight of the ruins of Rome would disappoint the poet, so too it might be felt that visual representations of them would leave a viewer unimpressed. It was noted in the first chapter that Chinese painters developed no tradition of depicting ruins in their scenes of melancholy desolation. Partly this may be due to an absence of substantial ruins in ashlar, thanks to the less monumental style of building in ancient China. But the lack of any aesthetic appeal in the fragmentary must also be a factor in the neglect of ruination. Neither in the Western artistic tradition do ruins figure in Byzantine or mediaeval painting. It is therefore somewhat surprising that around Colonna's time (perhaps in the late 1330s) the first representation of Rome in ruins was painted by Maso di Banco in the Chapel of S. Silvestro, which belonged to the Bardi family, in the church of S. Croce in Florence (Figure 7.1).[1]

The scene depicts a story found in Iacopo da Varagine's (or de Voragine's or da Varazze's) *Legenda Aurea* ('The Golden Legend'), chapter 12. On the left of the fresco, Pope Sylvester, who reigned from 314 to 335, is compressing the snout of a noxious dragon, whose putrid breath had slain hundreds (including the two magicians lying on the ground). What makes Maso's scene remarkable is its anachronism. Sylvester was the bishop of Rome during the reign of the emperor Constantine, who is depicted with his courtiers on the right. Of course, the Rome of Sylvester's day was no ruin, but Maso has depicted the ruinous city of his own day. Art historians reckon that the red buildings are contemporary brick, while the white are

Figure 7.1 Maso di Banco, *Pope Sylvester and the Dragon*. Photo: Wikimedia Commons – Sailko, CCA 3.0.

broken ancient marble; it is clear from the foliage growing in the cracks that the ruins are not to be imagined as recent. The single standing column of the Corinthian order and the broken round arch may serve as hallmarks of the Roman architectural style, *all'antica*. Now since the legendary dragon's lair lay in the Forum (under the now vanished church of S. Maria Liberatrice), that single column is arguably the Column of Phocas, which has always stood solitary since its erection in the seventh century. Maso's fresco, executed perhaps little more than a decade before Petrarch visited the city, heralds an unprecedented interest in the look of the contemporary city.

Before looking at paintings which depict specifically Roman ruins, it is important to recognise how quickly Brunelleschi's adoption of the *all'antica* style in architecture was taken up by a contemporary Florentine painter. In about 1527 Masaccio painted on the wall of S. Maria Novella in Florence an image of the Holy Trinity. One extraordinary feature of this recently conserved work is the setting of the Trinity within a purely *all'antica* framework, with pilasters of the Corinthian order and a coffered barrel-vaulted ceiling in perspective behind the sacred figures (Figure 7.2).

Rome's ruins benefitted from the triumph of the *all'antica* style in contemporary architecture and became commoner in painting of the fifteenth century. Andrea Mantegna, for example, twice depicted the martyrdom of

Figure 7.2 Masaccio, *Holy Trinity*. Photo: Wikimedia Commons – Web Gallery of Art 14208/public domain.

Sebastian, the first time in 1457 and the second in 1480, a version now in the Louvre (Figure 7.3).[2] Hitherto the soldier-saint had been shown tied to a tree for execution by the Roman equivalent of a firing squad, but in both cases Mantegna has him tethered to a ruinous classical arcade, the Corinthian order of which is a hallmark of Roman architecture. The ruin, which is 'generic' Roman and not of any known structure, is in some

Figure 7.3 Mantegna, *S. Sebastian*. Photo: Wikimedia Commons – public domain.

measure symbolic: the soldier-saint's death heralds the eventual Christian triumph over paganism.[3] But Mantegna's choice of a ruined arcade over a tree is consistent with the artist's addiction to ancient Roman architecture. In the 1460s he went with friends on archaeological expeditions because, as Sir Kenneth Clark put it, he was searching for visual evidence that life had once been lived on the heroic plane.[4] It is the 'generic' Roman ruin which provides that 'heroic plane'. It may even be the case that, as Andrew Hui suggests, the presence of a ruin in the background of the painting is an index of the rise of historical consciousness about the period's ruptured relationship to the antique past.[5]

What is altogether unexpected is the presence of *all'antica* ruins in scenes depicting the Nativity of Christ, a feature to which Jacob Burckhardt drew particular attention at the very end of his pioneering account of the ruins of Rome in the Renaissance.[6] The presence of classical ruins is downright unscriptural, since the second chapter of the Gospel according to Mark makes it clear that Jesus was born in a stable, and that is how the scene was represented in Byzantine and in Western mediaeval paintings; indeed, the Byzantine tradition remained rooted in scripture. But Italian painters of the latter half of the fifteenth century, while sometimes depicting a stable-like setting, also introduced Roman ruins.[7] Usually they too are generic ruins of *all'antica* architecture, with round arches and capitals of the Corinthian order. They evoke no identifiable ruin, as in a representation of the adoration of the three Magi in a panel painting of 1478/82 by Sandro Botticelli in Washington's National Gallery of Art (Figure 7.4).[8]

In at least one work, however, the lovely 'Ruskin' Madonna, now in the National Gallery of Scotland in Edinburgh, the ruin in the background is reckoned to represent a structure still visible in Rome. The painting is dated to about 1470, but its ascription is contested. It used to be assigned, with reservations, to Andrea del Verrocchio,[9] but in the recent exhibition of his work at the Palazzo Strozzi in Florence it was confidently ascribed to one of his pupils, Domenico Ghirlandaio. Whoever painted it, the ruins behind the Virgin are reckoned to evoke a legend, found once again in da

Figure 7.4 Botticelli, *Nativity*. Photo: Wikimedia Commons – public domain.

Varagine's *Legenda Aurea*, chapter 6, and referred to by Petrarch, among
many others. The Romans had a temple full of idols which they claimed
would endure until a Virgin gave birth. So on the night of Jesus' birth, this
temple was split and ruined. The tale identified the temple as dedicated
to Peace, an unfortunate blunder since the real Temple of Peace was built
under Vespasian. Be that as it may, what was commonly identified as the
Temple of Peace in the Renaissance we now know as the New Basilica of
Maxentius/Constantine, as noted in the previous chapter.[10] Verrocchio or
Ghirlandaio, both of whom visited Rome, arguably attempted a fairish representation of what was still left of that magnificent building.

At this point it is appropriate, for a purely chronological reason, to
diverge momentarily from painting in order to offer a brief account of
that most beautiful of Renaissance printed books, Francesco Colonna's
Hypnerotomachia Poliphili. The daunting title means 'Poliphilo's dream-
strife of love', which is about as illuminating as the narrative itself. Poliphilo,
the narrator of the first of the two books, describes how after Insomnia left
him he fell asleep and had a dream, in which again he fell asleep and had
another dream. In this dream-within-a-dream he found himself in a mysterious land where he strove to secure the love of the chaste Polia. Ultimately
he met with success, at least in his dream. The action of the first book of the
fable, such as it is, takes place in a landscape littered with ruins and other
structures. Now the great renown of the original book, published by Aldus
Manutius in Venice in 1499, rests not so much on the story and the artifi-
cially Latinate vocabulary of the Italian prose as on the wonderful woodcut
illustrations, which understandably prompt considerable discussion.[11]

The designer of the illustrations is not certainly known, but the Paduan
artist Benedetto Bordone is currently in pole position. Since Poliphilo makes
it clear that the ruined structures he gazed on in rapture in his dream were
those of antiquity, the illustrator, who was working in the northern Italian
tradition of Andrea Mantegna and Giovanni Bellini, rightly chose to design
them along *all'antica* lines. They are not to be identified with the actual
ruins of Rome, but the pyramids and obelisks which Poliphilo admired are
clear enough evocations of what could be seen in Rome. The warmth of
Poliphilo's lyrical description of architectural fragments and the charm of
the illustrations cannot be overestimated: ruins are at last endowed with full
aesthetic force. Indeed, given the theme of the narrative, the ruins are even
eroticised. Joscelyn Godwin fairly claims that when Poliphilo stands agape
before the stupendous buildings of antiquity, he seems to enjoy the same
state of arousal as when he voyages to Cytherea in the company of Cupid,
Polia and six exquisitely seductive sailor-nymphs.[12]

Colonna's prose, however weird, found an adapter at least in Jean Martin, whose French version, *Discours du songe de Poliphile*, first published in 1546, crucially included reworked illustrations based on the original woodcuts. The translation's success is proven by two reprints and later adaptations. Margaret McGowan has drawn attention to the varied impact of these images in sixteenth-century France, at a time when French artists and architects were streaming to Rome in ever greater numbers to study antiquity on its home ground.[13]

To return now to painting: in the early sixteenth century, ruins, again often only generically 'Roman' in appearance, began to figure in the landscape backgrounds of paintings made by artists resident in Rome. A. Richard Turner, in a pioneering essay entitled 'In ruinous perfection', traced the introduction of ruinous landscapes to Raphael, an insight more fully developed and illustrated by Arnold Nesselrath.[14] It will be recalled from Chapter 5 that Raphael along with Baldassare Castiglione composed an appeal to Pope Leo X to rescue Rome's ruins from further destruction. So taken with ruination was Raphael personally that he set broken structures, some now identifiably Roman, into the background of a number of his religious paintings. We discern, for instance, the remains of the Forum of Nerva in the Esterhazy Madonna of 1508 in Budapest,[15] of the Temple of Minerva Medica in 'The Holy Family under an oak tree' in the Prado (a work generally agreed to have been completed by Giulio Romano)[16] and in 'The Madonna of the Blue Diadem' in the Louvre (attributed to him and Gianfrancesco Penni, ca. 1512).

Turner also focussed particularly upon the engaging landscapes with antique Roman buildings by a pupil of Raphael's, Polidoro da Caravaggio. These frescoes, dated to 1524/5, may be seen (if you are persistent) in the Fra Mariano Fetti chapel of the church of S. Silvestro al Quirinale in Rome.[17] Another artist active in Rome at this time, Giulio Romano, incorporated ruins into the background landscape of his 'Raising of Lazarus' of 1517 in London's National Gallery. In Turner's words, Romano's reaction to ruins in a landscape was unabashedly emotional, since he had grasped their aesthetic possibilities in the play of mass and void, and of light and dark: 'he has caught the age-old gravity of ruins as they emerge from the earth. Brick and mortar slowly crumble, while organic life clings to any available foothold'.[18] The painter and architect Baldassare Peruzzi, also an associate of Raphael's, used a ruin for clever self-advertisement. In a nocturnal nativity scene, recently acquired by National Museums, Northern Ireland, there is a piece of antique architecture behind the figure of St Joseph. It is manifestly the Theatre of Marcellus, with a modern, but also ruinous, storey set atop

Figure 7.5 Parmigianino, *Madonna and Child*. Photo: Wikimedia Commons – public domain.

the ancient arcade. That storey had been added by none other than Peruzzi himself (he actually added two), who had been commissioned by the Savelli family to turn the theatre into a palazzo. The work was done in 1523–7, so the dating of the picture to ca. 1515 is out by a decade. Contemporaneously (1527–8), Francesco Mazzola, better known as Parmigianino, started but did not finish a painting of the Madonna and Child, now in London's Courtauld Gallery (Figure 7.5). Parmigianino was in Rome from 1524 to 1527, where he came to admire the paintings of Raphael, from which he learned to include identifiably ancient Roman buildings in his own work. The structure in the upper-left corner is reckoned to be an evocation of the much-admired (and still undismantled) Septizodium.

Such was the fascination of the ruins of Rome that even artists who never crossed the Alps were inspired to represent them, for example the Frenchman, Antoine Caron, whose only signed and dated painting, *Massacres under the Roman Triumvirs* of 1566, is now in the Louvre (Figure 7.6). The subtext of this macabre vision seems to be the contemporary religious wars and dynastic politics in France.[19] The French 'triumvirate' prefigured by the Romans of the late Republic, Mark Antony, Octavius and Lepidus, were Anne de Montmorency, Jacques d'Albon de Saint-André and

Figure 7.6 Caron, *Massacres*. Photo: author.

François Duke of Guise. It is the background, stuffed with an anachronistic melange of ruins (some reconstructed) and modern buildings (for instance, Michelangelo's recent redesign of the piazza on the Capitol), which locates for the viewer the slaughter in ancient Rome. Since he never visited the city, Caron relied on the engraved views of the *Speculum* of Antoine Lafréry, a collection to be discussed later.

Vedute

Steadily through the sixteenth and seventeenth centuries, engraved illustrations of the ruins and of their imagined originals became a regular feature of books on topography or architecture. What was less to be expected was that the ruins moved from the background of paintings like Caron's to occupy the front of the stage and become the principal subject of 'stand-alone' works of art. Human figures are no longer the chief actors and their presence seems designed only to provide a sense of scale and local colour. The ruins are now the protagonists and their assumption of that role demonstrates their achievement of full aesthetic validity. There were several ways of presenting the ruins. The most straightforward was an accurate topographical depiction of the structure in its current condition, the *vedute esatte* or *dal vero*. Imagination, however, was given free rein in fanciful representations, the *vedute ideate* or *di fantasia*. These might group together recognisable structures in Rome which were in fact scattered far apart from one another. Finally there are the *capricci*, completely invented ruinous landscapes, which gave the artists the chance to create wildly picturesque visions of ruination, not unlike the work of the unknown illustrator of the *Hypnerotomachia Polifili*.

A number of factors in what is now called the Baroque period of artistic production promoted the development of ruin paintings. The factors are related to one another because they all combine in interior decoration. The walls of rooms in grander residences were still being frescoed, but owners were also commissioning or buying easel paintings in oils to hang on them. The format of the paintings was variable and they were framed. They were not usually displayed as individual works of art but arranged attractively over the wall surface, the different shapes and sizes of the works, along with their different subject matter, producing an aesthetically pleasing display. The subject matter was very various: portraits, floral paintings, religious or genre scenes, 'marines' (pictures of ports or of storms at sea), histories, mythologies, still lifes, battles, landscapes and topographical or architectural views, real or imagined. Since the works chosen for display were so varied, few were to be singled out by the viewer for particular attention: it was the ensemble that mattered. Of course, large works by important artists took pride of place, at eye level (or 'on the line'), leaving to the lesser fry high or low or marginal spaces. So in terms of the quality of artistic production or originality of invention, competence in the artist was all that was required for inclusion in a decorative scheme, since some works were never meant to stand out. The artists knew their place and concentrated on their strong points. Specialisation prompted collaboration in the production of works. A painter of architecture, for instance, had only to master what was known in the trade as *quadratura*, and he might turn to a figure-painter for the inclusion of human beings and animals. A flower painter would produce an oval wreath of exotic blooms into which an artist competent in figures would insert a portrait or a saint's face. Finally, during this period purchasers would not have to be commissioners of the paintings that were intended to fill spaces: they bought what they found in the artist's studio because they wanted the sort of thing he painted for their décor.

To appreciate how a ruin view functioned in baroque interior decoration, we need only visit the first room of the gallery in the Palazzo Spada in Rome (now a faithful reconstruction of the original hang of the seventeenth

Figure 7.7 Palazzo Spada, picture gallery. Photo: Wikimedia Commons – Kent Wang, CC BY-SA 2.0.

century) (Figure 7.7): the portraits of the family's cardinals, the *porporati*, naturally take pride of place against an appropriately 'purple' silk wall covering; Cardinal Bernardino by Guido Reni holds court. To fill some of the space left below the cornice, two ruin paintings, among others, are inserted. Some paintings are artistically important; others serve merely to occupy blank space. It is the overall look of the loaded wall that matters, not the quality of the ancillary works. For that reason we need not focus long on any particular early practitioner of the art of the *veduta*.

The ruin-piece became a distinct pictorial genre largely thanks to northern European artists like Matthijs Bril and his younger brother Paul (Figure 7.8). A. Richard Turner had little time for their work, which he dismissed as 'superficial anecdote' with its 'stock pictorial stunts', lacking any 'deeply felt aesthetic expression'.[20] Censure, however, misses the point of their work. Landscapes with ruins had become an attractive decorative convention, subordinate to loftier subject matter, and the artists who produced these works were well aware of their status in the hierarchy of painting, which is not to say that their skill was underrated. The work of the Dutchman Cornelis van Poelenburgh, who continued the tradition of the northern *vedutista* working in Rome, achieved international recognition,

Figure 7.8 Matthijs Bril the Younger, *Forum of Nerva 1570–80*. Photo: Metropolitan Museum of Art/public domain.

and in 1637 he made a visit to London at the invitation of King Charles I. In the next century a grand tourist like Horace Walpole collected his works, which were also to be found in the collections at Holkham Hall, where seven of his works still hang in the Landscape Room, and in Felbrigg Hall in Norfolk. The Art UK website lists and illustrates forty-nine of his works that can be seen in public collections in Britain. Poelenburgh's 'Roman' ruins tend to be generic, as in the scene of dancers near a ruin in Figure 7.9.

One another seventeenth-century Dutch artist who exploited the depiction of ruins was Jan Baptist Weenix. He went to Rome in 1643 and stayed for four years, securing the patronage of Pope Innocent X. His works, which commonly feature readily recognisable Roman ruins, are to be found in numerous collections. The Wallace Collection in London has an attractive 'hunting party on a seacoast amid ruins', among which the Pyramid of Cestius figures prominently, thus bringing together three popular subjects of the day.[21]

One of the earliest Italian artists to make ruins the principal subject of his paintings was Viviano Codazzi, an 'architectural painter' who moved from Naples to Rome in 1647/8, where he began to make the city's ruins the subject of his paintings. Initially his work followed on from van Poelenburgh's in that his ruins tend to the generic, set in undefined landscapes.[22] But he also designed *capricci* – 'old favourites in new situations'[23] – of the Colosseum

Figure 7.9 Van Poelenburgh, *Figures Dancing Near a Ruin*. Photo: Detroit Institute of Arts – public domain.

with the Arch of Constantine,[24] or the Arch of Titus, the buried 'Colonacce' in the Forum of Nerva and the so-called Temple of Peace.[25]

One of the most successful devisers of *capricci* and *vedute ideate* was the Milanese Giovanni Ghisolfi.[26] The Liechtenstein Museum in Vienna possesses two of his views of Rome's ruins (which may, however, be either replicas or copies). Horace Walpole owned paintings by him, and the National Trust in the UK boasts five of his works. David Marshall has demonstrated that in an important respect Ghisolfi broke with the earlier tradition of ruin-painting in that he painted what he had seen, for instance the actual features of a ruined column in the Forum.[27] Earlier painters tended to depict homogenised images of architecture as found in illustrated treatises by the likes of Palladio. Ghisolfi's depictions of architectural details, however, were based on autopsy, and so his paintings often reproduce such precise particulars as the varied colours of the different stones used for a column's shaft and capital. Such realism was to become the norm.

The foregoing sketch of the work of some of the many *vedutisti* who specialised in illustrating the ruins of Rome (or of 'Roman' ruins) makes no claim for the artistic merit of such works. Their role was complementary within a larger scheme of interior decoration, *arredamento*, and the artists who were commissioned to provide them were clearly comfortable with the requirements of the genre. Its importance for our project is that it demonstrates the now firmly established aesthetic appeal of ruination in itself, an appeal almost certainly unknown to other cultures or other ages. That the aesthetic quality of ruins might transcend the merely decorative, however, is owed to Claude Lorrain, who not only refined the painterly aesthetic of ruin-mindedness but also ensured its wide dissemination, a crucial factor.

Claude settled in Rome in 1627, where he particularly cultivated landscape painting. Although it was not regarded as the highest genre of art, there was a ready market for landscape painting in Rome, especially if the terrain was ornamented with the local ruins which evoked the past splendour of the ancient city. Claude's landscape of choice was the desolate Roman campagna, into which he insinuated ruins that were not to be found there in reality. What set his work far apart from that of the run-of-the-mill *vedutista* was his poetic economy of vision. His ruins, and only ever a few of them, are carefully placed in a glowing pastoral landscape that is never as cluttered as that of a Ghisolfi. An example of his manner of depicting the ruins of Rome is seen in the engraving of a landscape with the Arch of Titus in Figure 7.10, the original of which is in the collection of the earl

Figure 7.10 Claude Lorrain, *Landscape with the Arch of Titus*. Photo: National Gallery of Victoria, Melbourne – public domain.

of Radnor at Longford Castle in Wiltshire. The shattered arch is set on the edge of a pond on a hill-top; in the middle distance the shaggy remains of an aqueduct stride across the scene. A triumphal arch, reflected in the still waters of the pool, has no business outside a city, but its pastoral setting and its marginal position on the canvas evoke the pathos of man's doomed ambition to aeternise worldly success.

Perhaps the supreme example of Claude's poetic ruin-scapes is his silvery final work of 1682 in the Ashmolean Museum in Oxford:[28] the painting depicts Ascanius shooting Silvia's stag, an episode drawn from Virgil's *Aeneid*, book 7, lines 483–502 (Figure 7.11). The painting was commissioned by a member of the Colonna family, which traced back its origin to the Trojan Ascanius, son of Aeneas. Claude offered another hint at the family name by means of the prominent columned portico on the left margin of the painting. It is entirely anachronistic that Ascanius, who had just arrived in Latium, should appear in a landscape already littered with Roman ruins. Equally implausible is the presence of such a massive urban structure, a temple, in a sylvan scene. It is instructive to compare the painting with one of the preliminary drawings, also in the Ashmolean Museum[29] (Figure 7.12). The ruined portico in the sketch is smaller and slightly

Figure 7.11 Lorrain, *Ascanius Shooting a Stag*. Photo: Getty Images.

Figure 7.12 Lorrain, *Drawing of Ascanius*. Photo: Getty Images.

obscured by a tree, but the human figures are larger and more prominent. Claude altered their relation in the finished work, in which the ruins are further enhanced in scale and number. He added a section to the left where columns are tumbled on the ground. Visually considered, the ruins have taken control of the viewer's eye, at least on the left-hand side of the painting. If interpretation might be hazarded, Claude has 'totalised' something of the Roman experience from its origins with the arrival of the exiled Trojans in Italy, to its decline and fall, symbolised by the ruin of a pagan temple. However that may be, the charm of the composition is undeniable, and Claude's landscapes were to have a profound influence on English garden design, as we will see in Chapter 10.

That influence was diffused abroad in two ways. First, English collectors bought Claude's works in considerable numbers. The Art UK website lists and illustrates sixty-nine works in British public collections, but of course not all of them are landscapes with ruins and there are paintings still in private collections. Secondly, Claude himself kept drawings of his genuine works, now preserved in the British Museum. These drawings were engraved and published in London between 1774 and 1777 as a book entitled *Liber Veritatis*, which carried Claude's romantic vision of a ruin-infested landscape across educated Europe. This fuelled an enthusiasm for viewing ruination on classic ground and even for reproducing it in English parkland. A further sign of Claude's considerable influence is seen in the work of his less distinguished contemporary in the depiction of ruins, Pierre Patel, whose *Rest on the Flight into Egypt* in the National Gallery, London clearly owes a good deal to Claude's manner, without the hazy shimmer. A later *vedutista*, Hendrik Frans van Lint, actually provided numerous copies of Claude's work for those who could not find or afford originals.[30] In addition to his work as a copyist of Claude, van Lint produced accurate views of standard sites (the Forum and Colosseum), but he also chose to depict some unusual ruins, for instance the Baths of Caracalla and of Diocletian. He tried his hand at least once at a *capriccio*.[31]

The most productive 'ruinist' artist was Giovanni Paolo Panini. What distinguishes Panini's management of ruins from that of his predecessors were his scenographic skills, which are apparent in his earliest paintings in Rome in the second decade of the eighteenth century.[32] Scene-painting for the theatre required mastery of perspective: what appeared large at the front of the stage must diminish in proportional scale as the scenery retreats to the back of the performance area. This use of perspective was a skill transferrable to the flat canvas or wall, and thanks to it what was flat could seem to have depth. This skill Panini fully exploited and his architectural painting is enlivened by the impression of the recession of the structures from the surface into the background. Equally enlivening was his figure-painting, which owed something to the style of Ghisolfi: angels, nymphs and cupids dance or play amid and even upon the towering ruins, and the overall effect proved highly successful in Rome.[33] Finally, his command of colour harmonies recommended his work to contemporary commissioners and buyers. David Mayernik has drawn attention to his 'juicy' painterly technique and to the exclusion of brick ruins such as the Basilica of Maxentius from his assemblages: it was the special beauty of weathered stone which he delighted in representing.[34] As a seminarist in his native Piacenza, Panini had learned French, and his ability to speak the language brought him into contact with ranking members of the French community in Rome. It was thus that the French ambassador in Rome, Melchior Cardinal de Polignac, commissioned two views of contemporary Rome from him in 1729 to commemorate the birth of the Dauphin. (His commissions from British grand tourists will be noted in Chapter 9.) At some time in the 1720s Panini also became an instructor in perspective at the Académie de France in Rome, so that his influence on the young painters sent to Rome, above all on Hubert Robert, was considerable.[35]

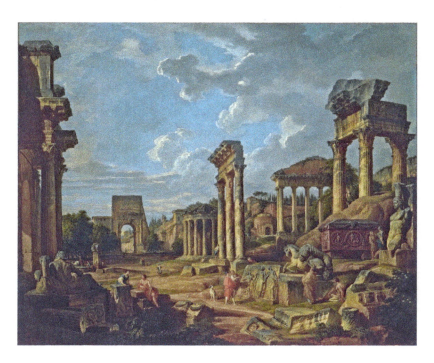

Figure 7.13 Panini, *Capriccio* of ruins and sculpture. Photo: Yale University Art Gallery/public domain.

As an exponent of ruin-painting – a *rovinista*, as the Italian art historian Roberto Longhi denominated the type – Panini depicted ruins either in their actual state, *vedute reali*,[36] or jumbled together in *capricci* (his most popular form), or in entirely imaginary constructions. David Watkin summed up his achievement: he 'played a leading role in inventing a pictorial language expressive of the obsession with a half-real, half-imaginary world of vanished Roman grandeur'.[37] Rudolf Wittkower assessed him as the 'one great master who raised both the *veduta esatta* and *ideata* to the level of great art'.[38] It is not therefore surprising that he influenced the young Piranesi, among others. Panini's *capriccio* of ruins and sculpture gives an idea of his attractive and highly marketable manner (Figure 7.13).

The original of the next work illustrated hangs in the Louvre (replicas of it will be found in other collections). Commissioned by the abbé de Canillac in 1758–9, it depicts the extant monuments of ancient Rome and is clearly a tour de force, as is its complementary painting of the grand buildings of modern Rome (the prominent cleric is assumed to be de Canillac). (There is a helpful 'key' to the structures represented accompanying the illustration in David 2002: 24.) We will return to this painting in the final chapter, since it has a role to play in Michel Butor's novel, *La modification* (Figure 7.14).

Figure 7.14 Panini, *Ancient Rome*. Photo: Metropolitan Museum of Art/public domain.

Panini's most gifted French student in Rome was Hubert Robert, whose work was so heavily invested in the depiction of ruins, both Roman and other, that he was known as 'Robert des ruines'.[39] On his arrival in Rome in 1754 he probably became an assistant as well as a student of Panini's. During his extended stay (1754–65), he also enjoyed the friendship of Piranesi, whose influence is seen in the theatrical qualities of his exhibition pictures,[40] for instance in the monumental architecture and deep perspective of *A Hermit Praying in the Ruins of a Roman Temple* (Figure 7.15). In 1766 he was officially recognised as a painter of ruins on his admission to the Académie des Beaux-Arts.

Robert exhibited ruin scenes for the first time when he made his début at the Académie's Salon in 1767. The 'philosophe' Denis Diderot regularly reviewed the exhibited works of art, and his enthusiasm for Robert's pieces (some unfortunately now lost) was unbounded.[41] In fact, Diderot went off at score on a multifaceted meditation on what he called 'the poetics of ruins' ('la poétique des ruines')[42] – a slogan which provided the theme of Roland Mortier's important study.[43] Diderot's critique is a fundamental document for 'ruinologists', since it substantially widened the appreciation of ruins to include sentiment (chiefly the increasingly fashionable melancholy)[44] and

Figure 7.15 Robert, *A Hermit Praying in the Ruins of a Roman Temple*. Photo: Getty Open Content Program.

dreamy reflection. It is also significant in that Diderot's enthusiasm was not restricted to the ruins of Rome. He enlarged the geographical scope so as to embrace ruination in other cultures.[45] He even had the nerve to criticise Robert for failing to grasp and exploit the full potential of the 'poetics of ruins' as Diderot himself conceived it – he suggested, for instance, removing from one painting three-quarters of the human figures since he felt they were destructive of the air of silence and solitude.[46] Of a sketch he complained that the lack of Latin inscriptions on the ruined monuments deprived them of communicative power.[47] Clearly there was often a considerable gulf between the artist's imagination and the philosopher's expectations.[48] Robert was at bottom a worldly fellow who knocked off versions of the Temple of the Vesta at Tivoli in order to pay for his wife's silk dresses.[49] He could not be expected to share Diderot's intellectualist position. Diderot's authority and prestige, however, along with the wide circulation throughout educated Europe of the periodical which published his review, did much to valorise and advance the cult of ruins generally. Diderot's enthusiasm for Robert was made the more understandable by an impressive exhibition in the Louvre in 2016. One of the paintings on display, a prevision of the 'ruins of the Louvre' (1796), illustrates a fashion for depicting modern buildings as ruins, the ruins of the future. It is a fashion worth a brief diversionary account.

The Ruins of the Future

Once the ruin had achieved sufficient aesthetic status to occupy the foreground of paintings and to become their very theme and subject matter, architects and painters exercised their imaginations on contemporary buildings to illustrate how they might look if overtaken by a decay like Rome's.[50] For instance, the first architectural project of William Chambers in 1752 was a design for a mausoleum, never built, for Frederick Lewis, prince of Wales, who had died the previous year. One of the collection of eight designs depicted the proposed mausoleum as a ruin, a somewhat puzzling conceit. David Watkin rightly recognised that the drawing of a ruined tomb was quintessentially picturesque,[51] although it may just have been an unexpected way of showing the structure in section. Christopher Woodward also drew attention to a contemporary tendency to attach moral virtue to ruins, so that even a decayed mausoleum suggested defiance of time's destructive power. Such an interpretation is supported in this case by the addition of cypress trees growing around the dome of the ruin, trees not included in Chambers' perspective view of the undamaged structure in a landscape.[52] The cypresses referenced the description of the Mausoleum of Augustus in Rome by the Greek writer Strabo, *Geographia* 5.3.8, C 236, who said that the imperial family's tomb was a mound planted with trees on a high platform.[53] The ruins of the Mausoleum were and are still extant, so Chambers will have gained some idea of the structure's scale. He may also have been honing the courtly skills that would see him become the favourite architect of King George III: Prince Frederick did not bear the name Augustus, but many of the males and females of the Hanoverian dynasty did, so the choice of the English mausoleum's Roman model was flattering.

This ruin-conceit became something of a fashion, at least among the architectural draftsmen at the Académie de France, where Chambers was at the time.[54] In 1796 Hubert Robert depicted the Louvre as a sort of gypsy encampment, with an artist sketching amid its ruins (Figure 7.16). The date of the painting is significant since the revolution that had convulsed France prompted the destruction of buildings associated with the aristocracy, like the Bastille, which Robert had painted as it was being torn down.[55] Robert

Figure 7.16 Robert, *Ruins of the Grande Galerie*. Photo: Web Gallery of Art/public domain.

was himself imprisoned from November 1793 to August of the following year, a time during which he cannot have been certain of release. In 1795, upon his rehabilitation, he was included in a committee charged with turning the Louvre into a public art gallery.[56] His vision of the future ruins of the Grande Galerie of the museum served as a meditation upon the endurance of art despite the worst men can do. The Belvedere Apollo with the bust of Raphael at its feet, before which a young artist sits sketching, and one of Michelangelo's Slaves (still to be seen in the Louvre) survive and confirm the continuity of artistic creation, the only stable thing in an unstable world.[57]

Robert's fantasy of Paris in ruins proved grimly prophetic. Less than a century later, much of mediaeval Paris was swept away by Baron Haussmann, prefect of the Seine, with a view to modernising the city. But worse was to follow with the bombardment of Paris during the rule of the Commune in 1870; this left real ruins aplenty. The English travel firm Thomas Cook & Son organised excursions to Paris to view the ruins,[58] and illustrated guidebooks were published to direct the tourist to the most interesting of them. By that date ruination readily evoked an aesthetic response.[59] Hans and

Blanc in their guide to the Paris ruins, for instance, unconsciously echoed Mariano Vasi's appraisal of the ruined Colosseum (cf. Chapter 6, p. 115) when they drew particular attention to the Ministry of Finance in the rue de Luxembourg; in their opinion, 'what had formerly been a dreary office block had now been transformed into a superb ruin' ('Le ministère des finances, qui n'avait jamais été qu'un monument médiocre, est devenu une ruine superbe').[60] Anne Green provides impressive literary context as well for their appraisal in her final chapter, entitled 'Ruins'.[61] We may now leave the real ruins of late nineteenth-century Paris and return to the fashion for architectural fantasies of ruination.

In two watercolours preserved in the Soane Museum, Joseph Michael Gandy imagined Soane's masterpiece, the Bank of England, as a ruin: *Architectural Ruins – A Vision* (1798) and *A Bird's-Eye View of the Bank of England* (1830) (Figure 7.17). Once again, alas, this anticipation of ruin proved all too prophetic of that noble building's sorry fate: it was pulled down in the mid-1920s and Sir Herbert Baker's crass replacement now squats within its curtain of walls.[62]

Soane's personal fascination with imagined or imaginary ruins also deserves a moment's attention here, and we will return to it in the tenth chapter where the sham Roman ruins in his villa garden will be described.

Figure 7.17 Gandy, *A Bird's-Eye View of the Bank of England*. Photo: © Sir John Soane's Museum, London.

During a period of great mental distress he composed a bizarre account, published in full by Helen Dorey, of his own house in Lincoln's Inn Fields as a ruin puzzling to visitors.[63] In the persona of an antiquary, Soane offered varied speculations about the ruin's origin and purpose: was it a Roman temple, a burial site, a religious house or even the abode of a magician? So strange and disturbed is the work that its neglect is understandable, but as an addition to our appreciation of England's most ruin-minded of architects, it is an invaluable and, as Brian Lukacher described it, 'tragicomical'[64] manifesto of anticipatory ruination.

The point of these *capricci* of imagined modern ruins was presumably to show that contemporary Paris and London had appropriated the high Roman tradition of dignified monumental design, and so, if some catastrophe overtook them, the very ruins of the Louvre and the Bank would bear witness to French and British architectural culture, and perhaps have the same allure for posterity as the Colosseum. The message, if any, was that art and virtue survive. Such patriotic sentiment took a nasty turn, however, in the mid-twentieth century. The German architect Albert Speer and his patron, Adolf Hitler, also appreciated the attraction of Rome's ruins. Hitler had visited the city in 1938 and found the ruins impressive,[65] while Speer enunciated a 'theory of the value of ruins' ('Theorie vom Ruinenwert'). In accordance with this notion, German state buildings were to have the durability and aesthetic appeal of imperial Rome's public works, so that if they too should ever fall into ruin, they would leave an impressive testimony of the Third – and 'Thousand-Year' – Reich.[66] To this end, the use of modern structural materials, steel and ferro-concrete, was to be repudiated in favour of granite, preferably German.[67]

*

Drawings

In Chapter 5 it was noted that fifteenth-century antiquarians and architects filled their sketchbooks with illustrations of Rome's ruins; Arnold Nesselrath has provided a comprehensive study of their work.[68] These drawings generally served practical purposes, either for the design of contemporary buildings or as staffage in paintings, and as such they were not intended for reproduction, though in the event some were published as engravings.[69] Printing, however, encouraged both the illustrations for books and the single-sheet view, so drawing served as a natural preliminary to a more worked-up depiction of a structure or view.

Maarten van Heemskerck arrived in Rome from Harlem in 1532, where he stayed for four or five years. He made topographical drawings of the ruinous sites of the city, in which the aesthetic impulse and the accuracy of objective representation are in lively tension. These superb drawings were scarcely known until their acquisition by the Kupferstichkabinett in Berlin in 1879, when they were subjected to antiquarian rather than art-historical analysis.[70] Van Heemskerck arguably made them for his own pleasure and for the delight he took in what he saw. He recycled the images he had made of ruined buildings in Rome in his later biblical engravings,[71] and in 1535/6 he produced a vast oil-painting of the *Panorama with the Abduction of Helen amidst the Wonders of the World*, now in the Walters Art Museum in Baltimore. The 'grandiose and archaeologically unrestrained' landscape is littered with 'ruins and reconstruction', some of which at least is recognisably Roman[72] (Figure 7.18). On the other hand, his self-portrait of 1553 in the Fitzwilliam Museum in Cambridge, UK, in which he depicted himself twice – as he was at the time of the self-portrait, aged fifty-five, and as a young man in Rome drawing the ruined Colosseum – is, to use an overworked word, iconic.[73]

One of the most significant 'ruinists' in mid-eighteenth-century Rome was the long-lived Charles Louis Clérisseau, yet another pupil of Panini's at the Académie de France in 1749. David Watkin provides a crisp and informative account of his work and considerable influence:[74] the English architects Robert Adam and William Chambers owed their 'Roman' neoclassical style to him,[75] Catherine the Great acquired over a thousand of his drawings[76] and he assisted Thomas Jefferson in the design of the Capitol building in Richmond, Virginia. The bulk of his output was in

Figure 7.18 Heemskerck, *Panorama with the Abduction of Helen amidst the Wonders of the World.* Photo: Walters Art Museum/Creative Commons Licence.

watercolours or gouache, since he liked to work quickly. He depicted both actual remains, and more importantly imaginary buildings, which fired the imaginations of his architect companions. Seventy-four sheets of his watercolours were presented to the Fitzwilliam Museum in 1821 by the Revd. J. W. Whittaker, and Sir John Soane collected some twenty of his paintings.[77] Lindsay Stainton reckoned that Clérisseau excelled in arch-aeological accuracy and that he achieved greater picturesque effects than Panini, possibly thanks to the influence of Piranesi. His use of gouache – a bright, flat, opaque medium – facilitated the depiction of detail and gave an air of reality to the imaginary scenes.[78] In Rome, Clérisseau's career was securely founded on producing for grand tourists depictions of the ruins of Rome, either in their actual state or in *vedute di fantasia*. Such was his success that when he settled in London for a few years in the 1770s, he continued to produce, exhibit and sell his fanciful views. He executed ca. 1766 a most engaging piece of fantastic ruinosity in the convent of S. Maria della Trinità dei Monti in Rome, a monk's cell embedded within the ruin of a Roman temple, seemingly open to the sky; Thomas McCormick provides the fullest account with illustrations both of the watercolour sketches and of the actual room.[79]

*

Engraved Views

Painted *vedute* found a monochrome complement in engravings, a cheaper medium and easier to transport. They had already appeared as illustrations to treatises on architecture and topography, but from the second quarter of the sixteenth century they began to be printed for acquisition as single sheets by collectors. After about 1540, Antoine Lafréry, or Antonio Lafreri as he called himself after he settled in Rome, published for the tourist trade and collectors a great number of such single-sheet engravings, which comprised a wide variety of art objects: religious paintings, sculpture, architecture and, of course, Roman antiquities, buildings and sculpture. What is known of his life and of the vast output of his own team of engravers is comprehensively described by Birte Rubach and more briefly by Pamela Long.[80] Since the individual sheets were selected, arranged and gathered into an album by the tourist-collector as a do-it-yourself repertoire of engravings, Lafréry printed special title pages for the different home-made volumes. One such specific title, *Speculum Romanae Magnificentiae*, 'The Mirror of Roman Grandeur', was intended for a collection of engraved views, maps,

Figure 7.19 Lafréry, title page for the *Speculum*. Photo: Metropolitan Museum of Art/ public domain.

statues and antiquities in general (Figure 7.19). The exact date of its production is not known but it is likely to have been designed and printed before the year of Jubilee, 1575, so as to be ready for the expected influx of pilgrims and penitents.[81] The handsome architectural frame was designed by Étienne Dupérac, whose work will be discussed later.

The engravings that made up the volume could of course be by any artist or publisher, not just the work of Lafréry's team. The subject matter of the engravings too was not standardised, but reflected the taste and interests of the purchaser of the engravings which the volume comprised. So, bibliographically speaking, there is no such book as Lafréry's *Speculum*. Rebecca Zorach offers brisk guidance through the complexities of the formation and dispersal of the volumes which carry the *Speculum* title in her introduction to the University of Chicago exhibition catalogue, for which there is also a handy website.[82] Birte Rubach provides illustrated catalogues of Lafréry's maps of Rome and of the images of ancient monuments both in the actual state (*ad vivum*) and in fanciful reconstructions, a numerous category.[83] The importance of such collective volumes is that they were taken home by the tourists who put them together, and thus views of Roman architecture (among other things) were made available to those who had not the advantage of visiting Rome. The prints were acquired for what they recorded (however inaccurately) and not as works of art, so that the collections served as reference works to be stored in a library.[84] But artistic quality as well as accuracy of representation will come thanks to Piranesi.

Volumes of ruin views were produced by other publishers, for instance the Antwerp artist and engraver Hieronymus Cock. He had perhaps spent two years in Rome, 1546–8; the visit is doubted, but whether he ever visited Rome or not, he was clearly enthralled by the architectural remains. In 1551 he published twenty-four etched views of the ruins, *Praecipua aliquot Romanae antiquitatis ruinarum monimenta*. Cock is reckoned to have drawn some of the views which he himself etched, but he may have relied upon drawings of other artists in addition to his own.[85] His ruin scenes could be dramatic, for instance one in which the Baths of Diocletian are the site of a violent attack[86] (Figure 7.20). An original and personal feature of Cock's depiction of the ruins was their setting in an invented landscape, its skies filled with clouds and light. Rebecca Zorach has rightly identified this new quality as picturesque,[87] so picturesque indeed that Cock's designs appealed strongly to Paolo Veronese, who appropriated some of them, including the Septizodium, in his enchanting landscape frescoes, painted in the 1560s in the Villa Barbaro at Maser in the Veneto.[88] Such attractive images aimed to please rather than to inform, and Cock's collection of views pleased a good deal, as is clearly shown by the plagiarism or revision of the series by Jacques Androuet du Cerceau and Battista Pittoni.[89] A number of Pittoni's versions of the views were then taken over by the architect Vincenzo Scamozzi for his hastily produced *Discorsi sopra l'antichità di Roma* (Venice, 1582).[90]

EX RVINIS THERMARVM IMP DIOCLITIANI, PROSPECTVS VNVS,

Figure 7.20 Cock, *Baths of Diocletian*. Photo: Los Angeles County Museum of Art/ public domain.

Another Netherlandish artist whose imagination was fired by the remains of ancient Rome, Hendrick van Cleve, visited the city, perhaps in the early 1550s, where he made numerous drawings of the ruins. He published ca. 1560/80 a series of thirty-eight plates entitled *Ruinarum varii prospectus ruriumque aliquot delineationes* – inventoried in Flemish as a 'runenboeck', 'Book of Ruins' (Figure 7.21).

An associate of Lafréry's, Étienne Dupérac, whose reconstructive map of ancient Rome was described in the previous chapter, also produced engraved views of the individual ruins. In 1575 he published *I vestigi dell'antichità di Roma*, a series of *vedute*.[91] This was a year of Jubilee, as noted earlier, so the timely publication was clearly aimed at the tourist trade. Dupérac's ruins are engagingly depicted as part of a living city, not as architectural models (his view of the Septizodium is reproduced in Chapter 4, p. 59). In his view of the Campidoglio from the Forum, for instance, laden donkeys are being driven across the plain (Figure 7.22).

Dupérac's views were shamelessly copied by Aegidius Sadeler, who republished them in 1606 in Prague with the title *Vestigi delle antichita di Roma Tivoli Pozzi et altri luochi*. Mention must also be made of an album of fine drawings on vellum ascribed to Dupérac and dated 1574/5, a 'little jewel … in a class of its own', according to Rudolf Wittkower.[92] The

Figure 7.21 Hendrick van Cleve III, *Interior of the Colosseum*, Colisei prospectus. Harvard Art Museums/Fogg Museum, Light-Outerbridge Collection, Richard Norton Memorial Fund. Photo © President and Fellows of Harvard College, M24480.16.

Figure 7.22 Dupérac, *View of the Campidoglio from the Forum*, 1584. Photo: Metropolitan Museum of Art/public domain.

drawings are enclosed within elaborately designed frames and there was usually room at the bottom of the image for descriptive matter. Some of the drawings are paired with one another, the contemporary ruin with an imagined reconstruction of the original, the reconstruction generally preceding the ruin.

The most sumptuous survey of engraved views of the ruins of Rome was first published posthumously in 1709 by Bonaventura van Overbeke; there was a second publication in 1763 and the work also appeared in French and Italian translations. The three volumes, dedicated to Britain's Queen Anne, were entitled *Reliquiae antiquae urbis Romae*. Ernest Nash claimed that the series of 146 plates provided the first systematic pictorial documentation of ancient Rome, something Nash's own fine volumes brought up to date thanks to photography.[93] The material is arranged according to building type: city gates, temples, triumphal arches and so on. The first volume provided a map of the city in which only the visible ancient remains were located; there was one exception, however, since the Casa dei Crescenzi (Chapter 5, p. 68) was still identified as the House of Pilate (vol. iii: 41, with figure 23). An anachronistic charm of the engravings is the figures of men gazing or gesticulating at the ruins: they are all clad in togas, *all'antica*, as if ancient Romans had risen from the dead to view what was left of their once splendid metropolis.

The views of the ruins produced up to this point have made scant claim to be seen as works of art, with the possible exception of Cock's. This modest tradition was radically overturned by the panache of Giovanni Battista Piranesi, whose series of magnificent engravings revolutionised the craft and transformed forever the way the ruins of Rome would be viewed or imagined. The most comprehensive English-language guide to Piranesi's multifaceted activities is John Wilton-Ely's study.[94] Marcello Barbanera provides a crisp, up-to-date account of his significance, both artistic and scientific, in Italian.[95] Susan Stewart offers a warm and substantial appreciation of his art in her recent study, which is less concerned, however, with his images of Rome's ruins than with his unrestrained imaginative works.[96] The University of South Carolina's online Digital Piranesi project provides images of the engravings and a good bibliography.[97]

In his birthplace, Venice, Piranesi was taught Latin by his brother, and – shades of Petrarch! – he developed an enduring passion for Livy, whose history he was reading even on his deathbed. He was apprenticed to an architect, and so throughout his life he identified himself as an architect, though he designed very few works. Nonetheless, his architectural training promoted an accuracy of representation, best seen in his pioneering archaeological work, *Le antichità romane* of 1756, and above all it engendered in him an informed admiration of Roman building techniques, which are often illustrated in his collections of views.[98] It was also crucial for Piranesi's artistic development that, like Marco Ricci and Panini, he had formal training from theatrical scene-painters. From them he would have learned how to exploit linear perspective, especially in the use of diagonal axes, so as to give illusionistic depth to his illustrations.[99]

In 1740, when Piranesi arrived in Rome, he immediately fell in with the *vedutisti* Panini and Vasi. Vasi, whose guides were discussed in Chapter 6, pp. 114–15, was also a notable engraver of views, who published between 1747 and 1761 a ten-volume series, *Delle magnificenze di Roma antica e moderna*.[100] From Vasi Piranesi learned the engraver's craft, but he surpassed his master in 'his sensitivity to the qualities of mass and volume as well as a more painterly technique'.[101]

The reason why Piranesi surpassed not only Vasi but even all previous and subsequent engravers of views is that the ruins made a more powerful appeal to him, as they had done centuries before to Petrarch. The ruins of Rome were not simply subject matter for *vedute*, the sale of which would provide him with an income and perhaps even prestige. The ruins mattered greatly as the material remains of an ancient civilisation, evoking in Piranesi a conviction of Rome's cultural destiny.[102] In order to realise fully his 'view' of the ruins, he had to overhaul the traditional craft of the *vedutista* so as to turn it into a worthy vehicle by which to convey to the viewer the true splendour of the monuments. In an often-cited passage he recorded that the 'speaking ruins' (*parlanti ruine*) had filled his spirit with images that even the most accurate drawings could not convey.[103] In that case, accurate drawing would have to be reformed if it was to do justice to the representation of the ruins.

Piranesi's earliest engraved views in the 1740s were frequently re-used topographical vignettes for guidebooks, for instance a supposed Temple of Venus.[104] From the late 1740s until his death, Piranesi issued separately 135 large-format plates of *Vedute di Roma*. Giovanni Bouchard published thirty-four of the early plates in *Le Magnificenze di Roma* in 1751. In 1756 Piranesi published the four-volume treatise entitled *Le antichità romane*, a turning-point in the history of Roman archaeology thanks to the combination of his understanding of architectural design and engineering with a visual artist's imagination.[105] Piranesi's fresh approach to what had hitherto been a restricted field of study was an international success, crowned in 1757 by his election to an Honorary Fellowship of London's Society of Antiquaries: he was taken seriously as an expounder of Rome's antiquities.

In 1761 his artistic skills secured him admission to Rome's Accademia di S. Luca, a venerable Roman association of painters and sculptors.

In 1761 he published *Della magnificenza ed architettura de' Romani*, a polemical work of 200 pages with 38 plates, in which he advanced the claims of the Italian, which is to say Etruscan and Roman, creative genius, strongly urging the superiority of native Italian architecture over that of Greece. Rudolf Wittkower provided a masterly sketch of the origins and conduct of the Greece versus Rome debate.[106] In the mid-eighteenth century, counterclaims had been made, chiefly by French aesthetic theorists, in favour of the simpler Greek style of building, which, they maintained, had the intrinsic merit of originality. Interest in the architecture of ancient Greece was successfully fuelled by the publication in Paris in 1758 of Julien-David Le Roy's *Les ruines des plus beaux monuments de la Grèce*, whose engraved views were criticised by Piranesi. Roman architecture by contrast was elaborately ornamental and, like Latin literature, considered to be largely derivative, which was as much as to say degenerate. In *Della magnificenza* Piranesi launched a counter attack, described by Peter Murray and John Wilton-Ely.[107] The theoretical opinions put forward on either side of the debate are for our purposes of little importance, not least because of their tendentious foundations. What matters is Piranesi's ardent commitment to Roman culture, especially its building tradition, and the best weapon he had in his armoury was his artistic skill. Thus his later views of Roman ruins aimed so to amaze the viewer that the continuance of the Roman style of building by contemporary architects would be ensured. Lesley Lawrence argued that in the latter half of the century, among British architects at least such as Sir William Chambers, Piranesi's advocacy of the Roman style had pretty much driven the Grecians from the field.[108] But the threat to Rome's pre-eminence was real enough, and it gained traction in the early nineteenth century in the writings of a number of visitors, particularly in Joseph Forsyth's *Remarks on antiquities, arts, and letters, during an excursion in Italy, in the years 1802 and 1803* (London, 1813, 2nd ed. 1816) and Edward Burton's *Description of the antiquities and other curiosities of Rome* (Oxford, 1821); they persistently belittled the remains of ancient Rome as violations of the chaste simplicity of Grecian architecture.[109]

It is now time to see how the mature Piranesi presented the ruins of Rome in what he regarded as a proper light. Thanks to his early work in the design of stage scenery, he brought theatrical perspective to the representation of the ruins, for instance in this view of the 'Temple of Peace', really the Basilica of Maxentius, in the collection of *vedute* (Figure 7.23). This is ruin-mindedness in spades. The averagely competent *vedutista*, a Vasi for

Figure 7.23 Piranesi, *The 'Temple of Peace'*. Photo: Yale University Art Gallery – The Arthur Ross Collection/public domain.

instance, would have confined the entirety of this massive structure within the straightjacket of the compositional frame. Piranesi's ruin, however, is far too sublime to be restricted by the bounds of a sheet of paper (even when it is a large sheet of paper), and so the image is cropped, its top and one flank thrusting out of the picture plane and over the plate edge. The clever choice of viewpoint (as if from an elevated box in a theatre), the pronounced diagonal recession of the huge masonry, the tonal contrast of the bright light admitted through the windows upon the shadowed stonework and the small gesticulating figures all create an impression of grandeur and vitality. But the image is not mere pictorial rhetoric. As John Wilton-Ely observed, the light searches out the structural patterns of concrete and the brick reinforcement, which makes the plate a demonstration of Roman building science.[110] Finally, the presentation is made picturesque thanks to the vegetation on the stonework and the pale glimpse of contemporary Roman dwellings through the lower arcade. The ruins of Rome are now firmly planted centre-stage, upon which they perform a heroic role.

There was, however, a downside to this thrilling exaggeration: the ruins never looked like that in reality, since the viewpoints and above all the scale of the ruins were Piranesi's own invention.[111] Inevitably some visitors raised on his impressions felt rather let down on their first encounter with the actual ruins – George Eliot was perhaps one such disappointed tourist.[112]

But leaving such disappointment to one side, Piranesi's passion for ruination is clear: it fired his imagination, and so his views of ruins are probably
more popular than those he made of the complete buildings of contemporary Rome. The reason for this is that views of complete modern buildings
make less of an appeal to the imagination. Denis Diderot in his critique of
one of Robert's paintings exhibited in the Salon of 1767 had remarked that
for a palace to be an object of interest (in a painting), it had to be ruined.[113]
In the following century, John Ruskin recognised a sort of hierarchy in the
subject matter of representative art when he claimed that 'a ruined building
is a noble subject, just as far as man's work has been subdued by nature's',
whereas the depiction of an undamaged building was art merely redu-
plicating art and so necessarily second-rate (in Ruskin's personal view, of
course).[114] A ruin prompts meditation on Time's or Fate's conquest of man's
work. Piranesi's images suggest, however, that he regarded ruination on the
scale of Rome's as defiance of Fate and Time and Decay. The ruins spoke to
him and thanks to him they speak to us.

Piranesi's technique exerted a strong influence on Luigi Rossini. Rossini
had initially aspired to be an architect, but finding employment in that line
blocked, he took up engraving. He published a large collection of folio plates
of Rome's antiquities in 1823, a highly successful and remunerative venture.
His views have been found mechanical, faithful but lifeless records.[115] But
while he was a professed follower of Piranesi, he was independent-minded
and set himself a different goal, namely to record accurately exactly what he
saw, for instance those monuments newly released from attached structures
and accumulated soil.[116] His view of the Arch of Severus, reproduced in
Chapter 11, p. 246, is a good example of his manner. The human staffage in
this view are ordinary Romans, not the wildly gesticulating mannikins of
Piranesi. Rossini also showed considerable imagination in his viewpoints,
often aerial. Like other *vedutisti*, he engaged in speculative reconstructions
of what ancient Rome might have looked like, especially in *I sette Colli di
Roma antica e moderna* (Rome, 1827–9), which included a partial panorama, a novel format to be discussed in the next chapter.

*

Photography

In the middle of the nineteenth century, the venerable media for the representation of Rome's ruins in paintings, engravings, etchings and lithographs were joined by and in due course gave way to the new technology

of the photograph, a story traced for the papal period by Piero Becchetti and Stephen Dyson, and for the early period of the Italian state by Karin Bull-Simonsen Einaudi.[117] Photography secured an enthusiastic early following by the French and Italian members of the *Scuola romana di fotografia*, which met in the Caffè Greco. Among the first Italian practitioners of the craft, pride of place goes to Giacomo Caneva and Gioacchino Altobelli, who opened his studio in 1858.[118] He experimented with colouring the *prove* or 'proofs' and his work won prizes at the Paris Universal Exposition of 1867. He also introduced figures into his scenes (of course, they had to stand still for a considerable time). His capture of the monument of Janus Quadrifrons is reproduced in Carrandini's *Atlas*.[119]

Among the earliest exponents of the new craft were two Scots, Robert Macpherson and James Anderson. Macpherson settled in Rome around 1841 as a painter, but he was never to prove a successful one. Poor eyesight drove him instead to photographic work in 1851, without, in his own words, his forfeiting his claim to the title of artist.[120] One factor that set him apart from others at the time was his successful commercial activity: though his prints were large and expensive, they still sold, at least for a while.[121] His contemporaries generally acknowledged the quality and originality of his work, thanks especially to the surpassing grandeur of his *vedute*, which owed something to Piranesi and secured him the palm among architectural photographers.[122] The American sculptor long resident in Rome, William Wetmore Story, reckoned that of all Macpherson's admirable photographs, that of the Theatre of Marcellus was the finest[123] (Figure 7.24). The Luminous-Lint website offers an online portfolio of eighteen of Macpherson's photographs of Rome's ruins,[124] and the British School at Rome houses a Robert Macpherson collection in its archive (reference number: PA-RMP).

James Anderson opened his photography studio in Rome in 1853, and his son and grandsons continued the business up to 1963.[125] The pictorial quality and historic value of his views are confirmed by their reproduction in even the most up-to-date works on Roman antiquities, for instance Carrandini's *Atlas*.[126]

It is significant that a number of the earliest photographers, British and Italian, began their careers as artists and they brought their representational skills to the composition and lighting of their views. The still experimental factors in early photography also contributed a good deal to the charm of these pioneering views. Different sizes of print, types of negative (e.g. calotype or glass), processing agents (e.g. albumen) and the paper which received the print produced a varied range of effects in the image, either soft grained or sharp edged, which made the work of individual practitioners

Figure 7.24 Macpherson, *Theatre of Marcellus*, 1858. Photo: Metropolitan Museum of Art/public domain.

distinctive and appealing. Only later in the century when the technique was standardised and prints became a cheap commodity for mass tourism was there a decline in the artistic quality of the views.[127] Unsurprisingly, these lovely early photographic *vedute* by *pittori-fotografi* nowadays command fancy prices, for instance at the auction of the Orsola and Filippo Maggia collection.[128]

John Henry Parker, an Oxford book publisher and in due course the first Keeper of the Ashmolean Museum, compiled a thirteen-volume series, *The Archaeology of Rome*, between 1874 and 1883, that broke with the picturesque tradition of the *veduta*. As the title indicates, Parker aimed to provide an up-to-date survey of what contemporary archaeological activity had revealed of ancient Rome. His innovation was to use photography, rather than drawing, as a medium of illustration (though he also used engraved drawings). Parker shared John Ruskin's enthusiasm for the photographic medium, which they appreciated provided unrivalled precision of detail, what Ruskin would have called objective 'truth', undistorted by the artist's subjective approach.[129] Parker did not in the event use all that many photographs in the volumes of the *Archaeology*, but he supervised the production of *A catalogue of 3391 historical photographs of antiquities in Rome and Italy* (1867–79), which was revised and enlarged in 1883.[130] The aim of that collection was primarily to provide accurate illustration of architectural categories, such as walls and aqueducts, with close-ups of ornament and detail. Parker did not initially offer attractive *vedute* to tourists, but so successful were his archaeological photographs that he began to commission views of the remains of Rome that belonged more to the old tradition of *vedute*, to be sold separately. The value of Parker's early objective photographs is confirmed by the inclusion of a number of those taken in 1875 to illustrate the recently excavated Tomb of the Statilii in Nash's *Pictorial Dictionary*, itself a splendid photographic document.[131]

A popular photographic device of the mid-nineteenth century was the stereoscope, which enabled two-dimensional images imprinted on glass or card, called stereograms, to appear as if three-dimensional. A number of practitioners and firms, such as the French photographers Claude Marie Ferrier and Charles Soulier[132] and the Americans Underwood and Underwood, produced stereoviews of Roman scenes for tourists. The stereogram of the Column of Phocas by Ernest Lamy, dated between 1861 and 1878, is good example of the type (Figure 7.25). More examples may be seen in the exhibition catalogue, with essays, inspired by Francesco Sicilia.[133]

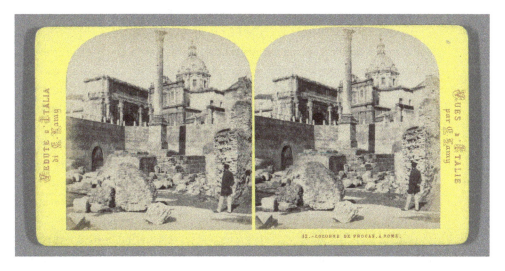

Figure 7.25 Lamy, stereogram of the Column of Phocas, 1861–78. Photo: Rijksmuseum – CC0/public domain.

8 | 'Virtual' Rome

Rome Reconstructed – Visionary Archaeology

Textual critics of classical literature are occasionally confronted by manifest defects in the manuscript tradition. There are words or phrases missing which spoil the coherence and meaning of a line of verse or of a sentence in prose. It is part of the critic's task to propose restoration of the missing elements by conjecture. It should come as no surprise, then, that students of the material remains of Rome also turned to conjectural restoration of the fragments of classical architecture. Ruins provided a clue, or one might even say they issued a challenge, to the architectural imagination for a conjectural completion of the original design. Given the often vaulting ambition of architects, they have naturally been inspired by the ruins to complete not just individual structures but even the whole cityscape of ancient Rome.

Rome was one of the largest and most populous cities in antiquity. Emperors with unlimited resources of gold and slave labour had over the centuries studded the city with structures of unparalleled scale and decorative magnificence, thanks especially to the development of the use of concrete, which made possible the airy spans of vaulting we see in the dome of the Pantheon and the remains of the Basilica of Maxentius. But equally appealing to the architect was the harmony of the Roman decorative style, something Brunelleschi was the first to appreciate, as we saw in Chapter 5. From the smallest shrine to the grandest basilica or bathing establishment, columns of imported marble, crowned usually with Corinthian capitals, were consistently employed. So the first enthusiasts for the *all'antica* style not only made accurate drawings of the fragments of Roman buildings but also imagined what the original structure might have looked like.

It seems, however, that the earliest imaginary representation of the look of the ancient monuments of the city is not to be found in Italy but in Germany. Ludwig IV the Bavarian became Holy Roman emperor in 1328, and to celebrate his coronation in Rome on 17 January a seal was designed, known as the *Bulla Aurea*, the Golden Bull (from the Latin *bulla*, 'seal')[1] (Figure 8.1). The image depicts a selective representation of what is predominantly imperial Rome. There are only two churches (S. Maria Maggiore and St Peter's), and they are close to the rim, as indeed they do lie outside

Figure 8.1 Golden Bull of Ludwig IV the Bavarian.
Photo: Lutz-Jürgen Lübke, Münzkabinett, Staatliche
Museen zu Berlin – public domain mark.

the historic centre of the city. The central field is occupied by secular structures: Trajan's Column, the Pantheon, Hadrian's Mausoleum, a triumphal
arch (perhaps Constantine's) and the Pyramid of Cestius. Of course, the
Colosseum is also depicted, and significantly it is complete but not 'roofed',
as it is shown in some images and described in the account of the building
in the *Mirabilia*. The very centre is occupied by the ancient Tabularium,
which served as the contemporary Palace of the Senators on the Capitol.
The structures depicted on the seal were plainly chosen to validate Ludwig's
claim to the empire. Ferdinand Gregorovius once again tells the story.[2] It
will be recalled that the papacy had taken itself off to Avignon, so there
was a power vacuum of sorts in Rome. The pope, John XXII, had fallen out
with Ludwig, who seized the opportunity to march on Rome, occupy it and
accept at the hands of the secular arm, the people and the Roman Senate,
the imperial diadem. Ludwig lodged in the palace of S. Maria Maggiore
and crossed the city to S. Peter's where he was crowned, not by the pope of
course, but by a Roman nobleman, Sciarra Colonna. The seal tells the story
visually and propagandistically: the churches are on the margin, the Palace
of the Senators is now central and the prominent corona of antique buildings stresses the Roman aspect of Ludwig's title, *Romanorum imperator*.

It was noted in Chapter 5 that fifteenth-century architects commonly
made sketches of the ruins of Rome to provide them with motifs to
be adopted in their own buildings. It was but a step, perhaps taken by
Cyriac of Ancona, to attempt a fanciful completion of the ruins (Chapter
5, p. 78). Since Cyriac, or whoever made the drawings, was not an

architect, he failed to appreciate the regularity of the ancient orders, and it was left to later illustrators of topographical treatises to propose more correct reconstructions of ruined or even of vanished buildings. We have already seen (Chapter 5, p. 87) that Raphael and Castiglione composed a memorandum in 1519 to Pope Leo X, in which it was proposed to make drawings of the ruins and even to sketch reconstructions of their original forms, where possible. Drawings served a private purpose, and their more public complement was the printed woodcut or engraving, which enabled those who had never visited the city to visualise its ancient remains either in their actual state of decay or in the imaginative reconstructions we have already encountered in the work of Lafréry in the mid-sixteenth century (Chapter 7, pp. 145–7 and Chapter 6).

Drawings and engravings are two-dimensional, 'flat art'. The eighteenth century saw the introduction of three-dimensional models of the buildings of Rome, both in their ruined state and in conjectural reconstructions (these will be described in the next chapter). Some hardy spirits were not content with modelling single structures and ventured to reconstruct the whole of the city as it might have looked in late antiquity. In the twentieth century, the newer technologies of cinema and television have encouraged physical recreations of a pseudo-Rome. These are generally fantastic and make a strong appeal to the eye. The most up-to-date medium, often used by scholars, is digital and computer-generated imagery (CGI). So flexible is this that all sorts of buildings and cityscapes can now be configured, with a greater attempt than in the cinema at historical and architectural authenticity. These reconstructions, in their varied formats and media, are the subject of the rest of this chapter.

*

Engravings and Watercolours

In 1504 Benedetto Bordone (mentioned in Chapter 7) had printed in Venice twelve sheets of woodcuts, made by Jacob of Strasbourg (his name takes varied forms). The sheets depict the triumph of Julius Caesar, in the narrative form of a frieze, which owed something to Mantegna's cycle at Mantua, and now at Hampton Court Palace. An anachronistic feature of the engraved series is the goal of the triumphal procession, the Colosseum (Figure 8.2). Benedetto had obviously never seen the ruin itself, since the orders of the columns in his depiction are all the same. But reasonably

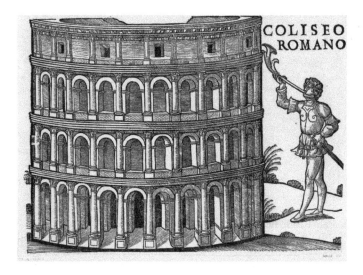

Figure 8.2 Bordone, *Colosseum in the Triumph of Caesar*, 1504. Photo: Berlin State Museums, Kupferstichkabinett/Volker-H. Schneider – public domain mark 1.0.

enough he reconstructed the building as undamaged (though there is a small piece missing from the outer rim at the back), topped by its fourth storey. The series of woodcuts was republished in differing versions, and its images were widely reproduced in various media.[3] The Colosseum is most splendidly reproduced in a wooden frieze installed in the Castillo de Vélez Blanco in Andalusia, Spain, in the early years of the sixteenth century (Figure 8.3). (The frieze is now in the Goya Museum, Castres, France.) The builder of the castle was Pedro Fajardo, a soldier recently ennobled for his military success; the triumph of Caesar was an obvious subject to celebrate and commemorate Fajardo's fame.

The architectural treatise was an obvious vehicle for the imaginative reconstruction of classical architecture. In 1540 Sebastiano Serlio published in Venice the *Terzo Libro* of his general architectural treatise; it was devoted to 'antiquities', that is to say the architecture of Rome.[4] Since the book and its illustrations were intended to inform practising architects, the buildings were not depicted as ruinous but in tidied-up reconstructions, like that of the Temple of Vesta at Tivoli (Figure 8.4). Obviously this was not an exercise in unrestrained fantasy, and sometimes only well-preserved portions of structures were illustrated.

The most celebrated engraved depictions of fancifully reconstructed ruins of Rome were produced by Giacomo Lauro. Twenty-eight years in the making, his first volumes, entitled *Antiquae Urbis Splendor*, were published

Figure 8.3 Frieze from Castillo de Vélez Blanco. Photo: author.

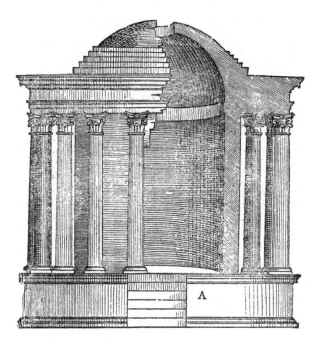

Figure 8.4 Serlio, Temple of Vesta, Tivoli. Photo: Wikimedia Commons – public domain.

in Rome between 1610 and 1614, followed thereafter by two more. In the first volume there is a map illustrating only the position of the ancient remains, to the exclusion of the modern city, a pictorial practice we have encountered before.

Only the third volume of the initial series, the *Complementum* of 1615, showed a single structure, the Colosseum, in its actual ruinous state, all the other ruins being represented as completely 'rebuilt'. The final volume of 1628, however, provided views of ruins, often in their actual setting, along with contemporary basilicas and palaces. Each plate was equipped with a textual description in Latin at the bottom of the page, so the images staked a claim to be something more than mere *vedute* (though Fane-Saunders is dismissive of the scholarship in the annotations).[5]

Lauro's undertaking was highly successful and there were several later reprints, even one as recently as 1996.[6] The reprint of 1625 provided on the verso of each plate translations of the original Latin text into Italian, French and German. The reason for this was that 1625 was designated a Jubilee Year, so the publisher, Andrea Fei, was expecting to sell copies to ultramontane pilgrims and tourists. The work reappeared in an Italian-language version, *Splendore dell'antica e moderna Roma*, in 1637,[7] and in its Latin version, *Romanae magnitudinis monumenta*, it was further revised and published in Rome in 1699 by Domenico de' Rossi, with the addition of new engravings by Pietro Santo Bartoli.[8] In this re-edition the material was divided into two parts, the first for ancient remains, the second for the building of the modern city, a separation we have already encountered.

The sources of Lauro's views of the ancient remains have been charted by Victor Plahte Tschudi, who devotes the valuable first chapter of his book, *The Archaeology of Prints*, to Lauro's game-changing 'redefinition of Roman antiquity', a redefinition which replaced archaeology with allegory.[9] Many of Lauro's images are no more than reworkings, sometimes slovenly, of the superior prints of previous engravers. As Laura Di Calisto points out, Lauro, like some of his predecessors, never aimed at plausibility in his reconstructions.[10] Indeed, a good number of the structures illustrated are complete inventions, such as the House of Cicero and the Gardens of Ovid. The clue to his aim is in the very title of the work, *Splendor*: the ruins were fully reconstituted so as to dazzle potential buyers of the volumes with the impressive grandeur of ancient Rome. His 'reconstruction' of the Circus Flaminius is characteristic of his licence (Figure 8.5). The Circus Flaminius was not actually a racetrack for chariots, nor was it shaped like other race-tracks, nor had it seating.[11] The antiquarians of Lauro's day were unaware of the true nature of this so-called circus, and the artist was deluded into imag-ining it to be like standard racecourses. Quite apart nonetheless from the enduring popularity of the prints themselves, they provided contemporary artists with a repertoire of images to serve as models for their own works. The architect Francesco Borromini found in Lauro's reconstructions both inspiration and challenge.[12] The sculptor Alessandro Algardi decorated a

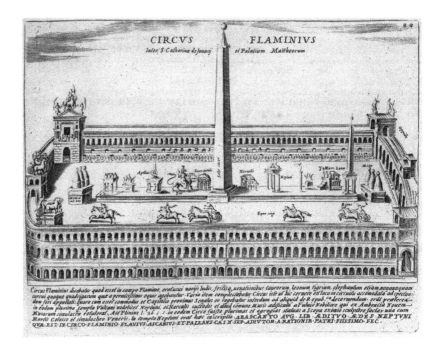

Figure 8.5 Giacomo Lauro, *The Circus Flaminius*, Harvard Art Museums/Fogg Museum, Gift of Max Falk. Photo © President and Fellows of Harvard College, M24967.78.

vaulted passage in the Villa Belrespiro, now known as Doria-Pamphilj, with reproductions in moulded stucco of some of Lauro's reconstructions.[13]

In 1721 the Austrian architect Johann Bernhard Fischer von Erlach finally published in Vienna his long-meditated historical sketch of architecture, *Entwurff einer historischen Architektur*; the text was in both German and French, so as to secure an international readership. Of that first edition there were very few copies, but the work was often reprinted and appeared in an English translation in 1730 (it too was reprinted). The second book of Fischer's treatise was dedicated to Roman architecture. Hans Aurenhammer stressed that Fischer was 'fully acquainted with the findings of contemporary archaeology', and that he relied as well for his reconstructions on written sources, coinage, drawings and of course the ruins themselves, which he had seen on his stay in Rome in 1671.[14] Nevertheless, as a practising architect devoted to the baroque style, Fischer could not help turning out reconstructions that looked very much like the urban schemes of his own day. For instance, his Forum of Trajan, with its symmetrically arranged fountains, equestrian statues and the central column, all encircled by uniform colonnades, looks more like contemporary Rome or Paris than ancient Rome (Figure 8.6).[15] The plates of his own designs were frequently

Figure 8.6 Fischer von Erlach, *The Forum of Trajan*. Photo: Wikimedia Commons – public domain.

reproduced in later architectural treatises, and by this means Fischer had an influence even on Piranesi.[16]

In 1738, a treatise entitled *Del Palazzo de' Cesari* by the Veronese scientist and antiquary Francesco Bianchini F. R. S. was posthumously published. This work was generated by the recent excavations made on the Palatine hill by the Farnese family.[17] In the handsome engraved elevations Bianchini proposed a speculative reconstruction of the imperial palace, which over time engulfed the hill. The views numbered XII–XVII had considerable and long-lasting influence, for instance on Piranesi.[18] Much of the reconstruction of the Palatine in Gismondi's *Plastico*, to be described later, was also owed to Bianchini's images.[19] Bianchini also proposed a reconstruction of Nero's *Macellum Magnum*, Great Market, on the basis of its image on coins.[20] Although not a physical trace of the market remained in Rome, the German architect Georg Christian Unger was inspired by Bianchini's model to base his design on it for that of the Belvedere on the Klausberg in the park of Sanssouci in Potsdam (1770–2)[21] (Figure 8.7).

It would be surprising if Piranesi too had not ventured upon imaginative reconstructions, and in *Il Campo Marzio dell'antica Roma* of 1762 he offered his vision, unusually in aerial perspective, of the completed Mausoleum of Hadrian, of the Theatres of Balbus and Marcellus and of the Pantheon.[22] Such 'optimisation' of the traces formed by the ruins formed part of his

Figure 8.7 Unger, Belvedere, Potsdam. Photo: Wikimedia Commons – Krückstock, CC BY-SA 3.0.

polemical defence of Roman building and urban planning mentioned in the account of his *vedute* in the previous chapter.

The young architect Luigi Canina went to Rome in 1818 and allegedly worked on illustrations for the revised edition of Vasi's guidebook, though its reviser Antonio Nibby continued to use the old ones. In 1822 Canina produced a treatise on the Colosseum, including a reconstruction, with fifteen designs, a project perhaps influenced by Luigi Valadier. He also did some architectural work and archaeological excavations for the Borghese family, but when commissions dried up, he turned himself into an architectural historian. In the years 1830–40 he published (with types designed by himself) the *Architettura romana*, itself only part of an historical series. On the death of Nibby in 1839 he became 'commissario delle antichità'. The third edition of his *Indicazione topografica di Roma antica* appeared in 1841 (the first edition was in folio (1830), the second in octavo (1831)). In it he described the ancient city region by region, and he illustrated them with eerily unpeopled engravings of the reconstructed buildings, paradigms of the neoclassical movement (Figure 8.8). Finally in 1845 he produced in folio his second edition of an *Esposizione storica e topograpfica del Foro romano e sue adiacenze* (reprinted in 1974). It provided ichnographic maps

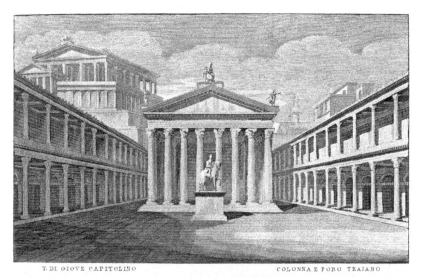

Figure 8.8 Canina, *Forum of Julius Caesar*. Photo: © Royal Academy of Arts, London; photographer: Prudence Cuming Associates Limited.

of the Forum and, in plates V–VI, Canina's own imaginative reconstruction of the appearance of the building flanking the central open space. Plates VIII and X represent contemporary views of the ruined Forum, which are complemented in plates IX and XI by Canina's reconstructions.

Imaginative reconstructions of the Roman Forum became something of a commonplace among early nineteenth-century British architects: Charles Robert Cockerell and James Pennethorne both produced a number of versions.[23] Cockerell's design lies behind some later popularisations, for instance that of George Scharf in an edition of Macaulay's *Lays of Ancient Rome* and the frontispiece, ascribed to Mr P. W. Justyne, of William Smith's often reprinted *Smaller History of Rome*. Pennethorne produced a pen-and-wash drawing in 1825, which he elaborated on a grander scale in watercolour.[24] The latter secured him election to Rome's Accademia di S. Luca in 1826. Geoffrey Tyack observed that Pennethorne's view of an amply spacious Forum was unrealistic, given what contemporary archaeology had disclosed of its actual extent: 'the true subject is the idea of ancient Rome'.[25] That idea was subsequently proposed (but not realised) by Pennethorne for contemporary London in his 1838 design for the Royal Exchange in the City: the superb octostyle portico and the Corinthian order evoke the 'Temple of Jupiter Stator' in his drawings of the Forum.[26] The popular diffusion of such complete reconstructions (especially those of Giuseppe Gatteschi, to be described later) would in due course provide the models for the visions of ancient Rome to be seen later in films and on television. The cityscape is vastly imposing, thanks especially to the stacking up of buildings on the slopes and the tops of the Palatine and Capitoline hills. The architectural style is agreeably harmonious: fluted columns of the Corinthian order, pediments and broad staircases.

The early nineteenth century saw a growing battle of styles among architectural students. As we have already seen, the Roman style had been challenged by the Greek in the mid-eighteenth century, and that challenge was growing louder, even in Rome itself. And coming up on the inside, at least in northern Europe, was a fresh threat from the Gothic. The Roman style thus needed champions, and the Académie de France in Rome picked up the gauntlet, or at least tried to do so. The Prix de Rome for students of architecture had been revived after the French Revolution. The Académie's *pensionnaires*, 'students' or 'residents', were required to provide in their third year careful architectural drawings of the ruin of a designated monument in or near Rome, and in their fourth and final year a conjectured reconstruction of it.[27] These drawings, called *envois*, 'missives', were then sent to Paris to show what the student had accomplished in his time at Rome and to serve as models for those who aspired to secure the Rome prize themselves. Of course, it was also assumed that once the student had returned to France and was launched in private or public practice, he would continue to design in the Roman style. A handsome selection of some of the work of these students was published by Massimiliano David in 2002. The drawings are often impressive, especially the reconstructions, which allowed the students some play of imagination. It is doubtful, however, that they ever served much practical purpose, and by mid-century some students were openly challenging the value of the exercise. That said, American architects working in the late nineteenth-century beaux-arts tradition did not hesitate to design a railway station along the lines of Roman *thermae* (Figure 8.9).

Imaginative reconstructions on paper continue to be produced chiefly for illustrating books. In Britain, Alan Sorrell and Peter Connolly were indefatigable archaeological artists. Sorrell was a neo-romantic painter who studied at the British School at Rome. Most of his atmospheric archaeological illustration was of sites in Roman Britain, such as Hadrian's Wall, but with Alan Birley he produced a fine book with reconstructed views of Rome in the time of Constantine.[28] Connolly drew perspective views of Rome in the early third century;[29] representative of his manner are the frontispiece and pp. 104–5 (Colosseum), 116–17 (*Domus Aurea*), 184 (three theatres)

Figure 8.9 Warren and Wetmore, Grand Central Terminal, New York City. Photo: Metropolitan Transportation Authority of the State of New York, CCBY-SA 2.0.

and 231 (imperial *fora*). His handsome original gouache of the entire city, in which the network of streets is largely speculative, is displayed in the Hellenic and Roman Library in the Institute of Classical Studies in the Senate House, London. The French architect and archaeologist Jean-Claude Golvin has since 1989 produced many fine watercolours of reconstructed buildings and cityscapes, most notably in and of Rome.[30]

*

The Panorama

One of the late eighteenth century's most engaging and popular amusements was the panorama, invented and developed by the Irishman Robert Barker. Bernard Comment has surveyed the medium's history and Valentin Kockel has focussed on those depicting Rome in the nineteenth century.[31]

Ludovico Caracciolo designed a modest panorama of contemporary Rome in 1824. Comment reckons that it was 'poetic licence [that] allowed [Caracciolo] to condense and group together buildings that would not actually have been visible from a single vantage-point'.[32] This engaging panorama is now unfortunately in storage in London's Victoria and Albert Museum, but it can be viewed online.[33]

Luigi Rossini produced a three-page partial panorama from the Colosseum to the Basilica of Maxentius in *I sette Colli di Roma antica e moderna* in 1827–9;[34] the high viewpoint is from the tower of the church of S. Francesca Romana (= S. Maria Nova) overlooking the Forum Romanum.

The Swiss architect Josef Bühlmann and the painter Alexander von Wagner began their panorama of Rome (Rundbild in German) in 1886 and exhibited it first in Munich in 1888 and then in Berlin. Unlike the earlier panoramas just mentioned, this one depicted a reconstruction of Constantine's triumphal entry into Rome after his defeat of Maxentius at the Milvian Bridge in AD 312. In effect, it was a 'history' painting in the round. An explanatory booklet was produced to accompany the painting by Franz von Reber, himself a professor of art history in Munich who specialised in ancient art. Reproductions, large and small, were also published. The designers of the panorama based their reconstructions on the latest archaeological information. Although the work met with some criticism, Ferdinand Gregorovius liked it. In due course Bühlmann's panorama was to influence Gismondi,[35] and it inspired a recent 'vision' of Rome in AD 312, serving as the springboard for the book *Das antike Rom und sein Bild*.[36] Bühlmann went on to publish a work on ancient architecture, illustrated with reconstructions, for instance a view of Rome in the time of the emperor Aurelian.[37]

*

Postcards

Since the nineteenth century, one of the most enduring media for the representation of the ruins of Rome has been the photographic postcard. Its attractions are obvious: a postcard is small and cheap. Sometime in the late 1950s Romolo Augusto Staccioli produced a still-popular collection of postcard-sized views of the ruins entitled *Rome Past and Present*.[38] The cards are colour photographs of the extant ruins, and over each card can be laid an acetate page that shows a fanciful reconstruction of the original. The acetate cover leaves clear patches so that the actual ruins on the postcard show through as part of the reconstruction. Figure 8.10 shows the Forum of Julius Caesar, in 'now' (b) and 'then' (a) versions. The tourist is thus presented with the actual state of the ruins and a 'virtual' original, a topic to which we may now turn.

*

Figure 8.10 (a) Staccioli, reconstruction of the Forum of Julius Caesar. Photo: author; (b) Staccioli, ruins of the Forum of Julius Caesar. Photo: author.

Digital and Computer-Generated Imagery (CGI)

The representation of Rome's ruins has been persistently promoted by technological innovation; first the printing press, and then the photographic camera. Nowadays the wonders of digital and computer-generated imagery have facilitated the imaginative reconstruction of Rome's ancient monuments and even of the city as a whole.[39] The grandest building complex in ancient Rome was the Forum of Trajan and the Basilica Ulpia; Ammianus

Marcellinus' impression of its scale may be recalled (Chapter 2, p. 28). James Packer gathered decades of research and speculation about the appearance of the complex into a sumptuous trio of volumes, handily reduced in scale for popular consumption.[40] One of the important features of his monograph is a thorough overview of previous imaginative reconstructions, though Fischer von Erlach's was omitted.[41] They all try to give some idea of how imposing this building complex was. Packer's historical survey is also of interest, since he dates the stirring of an interest in the original look of this Forum to the French excavations of 1811–14, the subject of a later chapter. That interest took visible form in the *envoi* of a student of the Académie de France, Jean Baptiste Cicéron Lesueur, who produced an illustrated monograph on the site. After Lesueur, a considerable number of budding architects – Angelo Uggeri, Prosper-Mathieu Morey, Fjodor Richter, the formidable Luigi Canina (who made two attempts at it), Julien Guadet, the archaeologist Giuseppe Gatteschi and of course the builder of the *Plastico*, Italo Gismondi – all tried their hands at reconstructing the original of the stunning complex. Packer is generous in admitting the cumulative value of these speculative views in the formation of his own reconstruction, which was produced digitally. The capital advantage of this medium is that it allows for corrections to be introduced in the light of fresh evidence or a rethinking of the problems.[42]

Probably more interesting to the average student of the remains of ancient Rome, however, is the Forum Romanum, and it is no surprise that there have been projects for its digital reconstruction. Between 1997 and 2002 the Cultural Virtual Reality Laboratory at the University of California, Los Angeles created a digital model of the Roman Forum; the project has been resumed but it does not seem to be possible to view the models online, which rather defeats the purpose of the exercise. Print still seems to be a more reliable medium. Most recently, Gilbert Gorski and James Packer have provided a totalised account of the site as it might have appeared in the mid-fourth century.[43] Like their Renaissance predecessors, they rely heavily on the ancient coins on which structures were represented, and they are well illustrated (though their evidence can be hard to interpret). The proposed reconstructions avowedly owe a good deal to the specula-tions of earlier architects, and once again praise is lavished on the *envois* of the students at the Académie de France in Rome.[44] Such fine watercolours, however, are too expensive and time-consuming to produce nowadays, so digital images illustrate their volume, unfortunately without the fanciful colouring of the stone surfaces that is one of the charms of the later *envois*.

The dazzling coloured reconstructions produced by Inklink of Florence for the Electa guidebook to the Forum and Markets of Trajan are prohibitively expensive.[45]

*

Models of the Ancient City

Digital imagery, for all its flexibility, remains two-dimensional, unless it is modified into three-dimensional 'virtual reality' (VR). But before note is taken of that modern marvel, the pioneering, single-handed attempts to build three-dimensional 'replicas' of ancient Rome deserve attention, starting with the models of Giuseppe Marcelliani and the *maquette* of Paul Bigot.

Not a great deal is known about the sculptor Giuseppe Marcelliani and his partial reconstruction of central Rome. A well-illustrated volume of essays entitled *Restitutio Urbis* offers a brief account of Marcelliani's model,[46] which was first exhibited in 1904 and continued to be displayed for about twenty years. The remains of this decorative model are apparently still stored in the cellar of the Museo della Civiltà Romana in EUR in Rome.[47]

The work of the architect Paul Bigot is better preserved, more ambitious and more scientifically researched than Marcelliani's. It was designed and built for exhibition at the Mostra Archeologica of 1911 in the Baths of Diocletian and it is now conserved in the University of Caen in Normandy.[48] An impressive website tells and illustrates its story.[49]

Bigot, a student at the Académie de France in Rome from 1901 to 1904, decided that his final-year project, the traditional *envoi*, would be the Circus Maximus.[50] The *envoi* consisted of drawings,[51] but to assist his visualisation of the racecourse, Bigot began to build a plaster model of it, which he extended to include parts of the Palatine and Capitoline hills, to serve as background. The project grew literally under his hands as he undertook to model the central portion of the ancient city at the height of its development in the fourth century. His model was subject to constant revision as new information became available.[52] Indeed, such was its fame that three copies of it were made, of which apparently only one survives, now in the Brussels Museum of Art and History;[53] that copy, which alone benefits from being coloured, has been recently conserved (Figure 8.11).

Figure 8.11 Bigot, *maquette* of Rome. Photo: Q. Keysers, CCBY-SA 3.0.

Two problems that Bigot inherited from the cartographers of the Renaissance and had to get over were ignorance of the street-plan of the ancient city and of the architecture of the private residences, especially the blocks of flats (*insulae*). Bigot decided to design the houses along the lines of what was known from other towns, such as the recently excavated port city of Ostia;[54] in this regard, he was following in the footsteps of Pirro Ligorio.

The most famous reconstruction of ancient Rome in plaster, popularly known as the *Plastico*, was designed by the architect Italo Gismondi, the head of the Sopraintendenza di Roma (Figure 8.12). It was begun in 1933 for the 1937 Mostra Augustea, but from time to time it was 'corrected' and enlarged until 1973, so as to comprise the whole of the city in the time of Constantine. It is housed, but at the time of writing not yet on display, in the Museo della civiltà romana; it does, however, figure on the museum's website.[55]

Gismondi conscientiously relied upon the latest archaeological findings, especially those of Guglielmo Gatti,[56] but he also appropriated the fanci-ful reconstructions of Étienne Dupérac's private houses and of Francesco Bianchini's imperial palaces on the Palatine hill, as well as the *envois* of the architectural students of the Académie de France and Bühlmann's panorama. The structures were coloured to create a lively and realistic

Figure 8.12 Gismondi, *Plastico*. Photo: J.-P. Dalbéra, CCA 2.0.

appearance. Termites subsequently damaged the wooden armatures upon which the plaster was moulded, so this impressive three-dimensional tribute to the grandeur of Rome has needed considerable conservation, still underway. The *Plastico* has proved a boon for the cinema.[57] It was, for instance, used in a scene of Mervyn LeRoy's *Quo Vadis* (1951) in which Nero showed his courtiers how he wanted Rome to be rebuilt after the great fire of AD 64.[58] Ridley Scott's aerial view of Rome in *Gladiator* (2000) was inspired by his gazing down upon Gismondi's model.[59]

The most recent model of the entire city in antiquity is, as might be expected, virtual rather than material, thanks to CGI. Matthew Nicholls, of Reading University, has constructed the model, which can be viewed on its own website.[60]

*

Cinema and Television

The modern attention focussed upon Rome and its history in cinema and television owes a good deal to the older tradition of European drama. Playwrights and players (always deemed a rackety bunch) elevated their craft when they donned the buskin to evoke the Roman past: Shakespeare's *Antony and Cleopatra*, *Coriolanus* and *Julius Caesar*; Jonson's *Sejanus*; Addison's

Cato; Corneille's *Pompée* and *Sertorius*; and Racine's *Bérénice* all attest to the allure of Roman history. A historical play might also be expected to make an appeal to a more learned audience (at least Ben Jonson thought so). Given that long tradition of drawing on Rome's past for the stage, it is no surprise that early cinema sought to validate its own claims to cultural status by choosing Roman themes as subject matter. But setting the action in the physical city of Rome, either among its extant ruins or within reconstructions of its ancient glory, had the further advantage of providing spectacular scenographic images. The physical city of Rome thus became one of the hallmarks of visual extravagance on screen, as Monica Cyrino has helpfully charted.[61]

Visual spectacle was amply provided by the monumental architecture of amphitheatres and racetracks. The Forum Romanum was obviously a site of major pictorial value in the cinema. The centre of Italian film production, Cinecittà, founded in 1936 to further the Fascist programme, had a set representing the reconstructed Forum, which led the way in setting a standard of impressive display. Hollywood gratefully exploited Cinecittà's facilities for LeRoy's *Quo Vadis* with its Great Fire sequence, and for Wolf Mankiewicz's *Cleopatra* (1963) with Elizabeth Taylor's anachronistic entry into the Forum via the Arch of Constantine.[62]

The extant ruins of Rome also have a role to play when the modern city is the location,[63] sometimes to forge a link between past and present, sometimes to make the contrastive point that the contemporary world falls short of a past it is incapable of comprehending. In Federico Fellini's *La Dolce Vita* (1959), the vast remains of the Baths of Caracalla served as a nightclub in which the sex-goddess Sylvia (played by Anita Ekberg) performs lasciviously, a scene illustrating the vulgar superficiality of contemporary life amid the ruined splendour of a superior civilisation.[64] In his later films, *Fellini Satyricon* (1969) and *Fellini's Roma* (1972), he remythologised ancient Rome. In *Satyricon* the Rome of the emperors is chaotic and (again anachronistically) crumbling into ruin.[65] One scene in *Roma* takes place in the city's underground railway system. A borer knocks through a wall to reveal a series of rooms or passages decorated with undamaged Roman frescoes, which evaporate upon exposure to modern technology.[66] In the movie's final scene, a horde of motorcycle 'barbarians' converges on the Colosseum at night before driving away into their own obscure future; the amphitheatre has been trivialised as a traffic roundabout.[67]

It is the reconstructions of ancient Rome for the screen, however, which most impress audiences, and the most impressive of all time was the reconstruction of the Forum in Las Matas, Spain for the scene of Commodus' triumph in Anthony Mann's *The Fall of the Roman Empire* (1964). The

American souvenir programme set out the statistics for the construction of this immense set:[68] 170,000 cement blocks for the paving of the Forum, 610 columns, 22,000 feet of steps and stairways, 230,000 tiles for roofing. Not unreasonably, Lloyd Llewellyn-Jones deemed it an 'exaggerated realism' of an 'over-Romanised Rome'.[69] The set was re-used for educational films,[70] but at some stage it was bulldozed to make way for luxury accommodation, so 'Rome' was reduced to ruination once again.

Inspiration for the designs, made by John Moore and Veniero Colasanti, was provided to some degree by the reconstructions of Giuseppe Gatteschi, published in *Restauri della Roma imperiale*, Rome, 1924 (reprinted in 1931).[71] James Packer noted Gatteschi's reliance on earlier designs and found his 'compilations' inaccurate,[72] though that did little to impair their popularity, especially with designers of film sets. Chiara Piccoli has written sympathetically about Gatteschi's aims and method.[73] He had studied the ruins for some twenty years before embarking on his visual restorations and he aimed above all to excite popular interest in what Rome might actually have looked like. To that end, his cityscapes are thronged with people going about their everyday activities. He also suggested the reliability of his reconstructions by providing a photograph of the contemporary condition of the monuments reconstructed on the facing page, a 'then' and 'now' juxtaposition, such as we have encountered before.

Less costly were the reconstructions in Ridley Scott's *Gladiator* (2000), which benefitted from the use, for the first time, of computer imaging technologies to create a vision of Rome on 'an unprecedented scale and a stunning level of detail'.[74] Nonetheless, a partial sham Colosseum, indispensable to the conclusion of the film, had to be constructed in Malta.[75] The two lower tiers of the amphitheatre were built at full scale, while the upper two tiers were added with CGI. The spectators in those upper tiers were also computer-generated.[76]

Television was at first necessarily restrained in its depiction of ancient Rome, since elaborate sets would prove too expensive and perhaps not look very impressive on the small screen in the family home. With the HBO TV series *Rome* (2005–7), however, there was something of a return to reconstructions on a considerable scale in Cinecittà of the spectacular public spaces of the ancient city.[77] These sets as usual served the eye-appeal of scenes of triumph – Caesar's over Gaul, Octavian's over Cleopatra – but the viewpoint was that of the groundling, the Rome of the poor, a subversive avoidance of the usual magnificence of the big screen that owed a good deal to *Fellini Satyricon*.[78]

*

Visualising ancient Rome, either what actually remained of it in the form of an ever-diminishing number of ruins or what it might have looked like in speculative reconstructions, has been the single theme of this and the preceding chapters. We have ranged over nearly 700 years of looking at and representing pictorially Rome's ruins, starting with Maso di Banco's fresco in Florence and ending with the virtual visions produced with the aid of the computer. Over the centuries, pretty much every conceivable form of image-making has been employed in the exercise of recording or imagining the appearance of ancient Rome: painting and drawing, engraving on wood or metal, photography and plastic modelling in three dimensions. What ought to astound us is that this prolonged, varied and widespread focus of visual attention has centred upon hardly more than a handful of ruins in a single city. Most of those who have produced the images are moreover not even native to that city – the initiatives to represent and to reconstruct ancient Rome have long been conducted on an international scale. Perhaps the most important inference to be drawn from this survey is that the ruins have at last attained unchallengeable aesthetic validity, thanks to their gradual move to the foreground of graphic art and their dominance of pictorial space. Rome's ruins have become a subject in their own right because they are found beautiful.

9 | Remembering the Grand Tour

Paintings, Models and Other Souvenirs

The pace of ruin-illustration became something of a gallop in the eighteenth century with the arrival of the British grand tourists. In fact, there were earlier 'grand tourists' in the seventeenth century. In the Soane Museum there is a sketch by the Englishman Henry Stone of fashionable men gazing at ruined columns in what seems to be the Roman Forum.[1] The sketch is dated 1638, the year in which the poet John Milton also arrived in Rome. Mention has already been made of John Evelyn's tour in 1644–5 (Chapter 6, p. 106). But such visitors were few, since travel licences to Catholic Rome, the enemy of Protestant England, were hard to come by. The cultural phenomenon of eighteenth-century grand tourism is accessibly documented by Christopher Hibbert, Rosemary Sweet and Andrew Wilton; Michel Makarius provides an overview of artists of the period.[2] Most recently, Giovanna Ceserani of Stanford University has produced an online database of the tourists and an illuminating study of the influence of the Grand Tour on the professionalising of British architects.[3]

The typical grand tourist was for the most part, but not exclusively, a wealthy British youth of a burgeoning imperial nation. The foundation of his education was classical literature. He was sent at an appropriate age to continental Europe, which now served as a sort of vast finishing school. France refined the manners and Italy satisfied the artistic appetite. The cultural interest of the British grand tourist was rather more restricted than that of earlier visitors to Rome. Francis Haskell reckoned it broadly true that after about 1720 British visitors came primarily to admire the classical past; their interest in contemporary Italian culture was minimal, except when living talents could be hired to satisfy their tastes.[4] Those tastes are best seen in the souvenirs they brought back to the British Isles and in the decoration of the public rooms of their homes. Collecting souvenirs of one's travels was as common then as now, and the grand tourist had an impressive range of knick-knacks to choose from in Italy, where paintings and sculptures and antiquities (up to a point) were all for sale. Andrew Wilton provided a comprehensive survey of such souvenirs in his essay 'Memories of Italy', published in the catalogue of the Victoria and Albert Museum's exhibition of the Grand Tour.[5]

The seriously wealthy tourist would have his portrait painted locally, crucial proof of his visit to Italy. If he waited to do so in Rome, he would probably turn to the 'uncommonly dear' Pompeo Batoni, and have himself depicted against a backdrop of ruinosity.[6] The portrait of Sir Gregory [Page-]Turner now in the Manchester City Art Galleries is a typical stunner (Figure 9.1).[7] Turner, who made the Grand Tour in 1768–9, dressed for his three-quarter-length portrait in fashionable red silk; his pose evokes the Apollo Belvedere on display in the Vatican and his left hand rests on a map of Rome, with the Colosseum glimpsed in the background.

The grand tourist of middling wealth was unlikely to commission portraits or drawings, but could certainly put together a collection of engravings of the ruins, as we have already seen in the previous chapter. Our old friend, Lady Miller, who appeared in Chapter 6, p. 114, rejected the work of 'Sadler' (i.e. Marco Sadeler) as inaccurate and she even ventured a measure of disapproval of Piranesi's prints (Figure 9.2):[8]

Figure 9.1 Batoni, *Portrait of Sir Gregory Turner*. Photo: David Munro.

Figure 9.2 Piranesi, *Pantheon*. Photo: Metropolitan Museum of Art/public domain.

> Piranese's [sic] are too confused to give a clear idea of [the ruins]; he is
> so ridiculously exact in trifles, as to have injured the fine proportions of
> the columns of the portico to the pantheon, by inserting, in his gravings,
> the papers stuck on them, such as advertisements, etc. … yet they are
> esteemed the best here; and we have made an ample collection of the most
> valuable of them.

If the tourist intended to record his travels by decorating his house back
in the United Kingdom, he would also acquire painted *vedute*, such as have
also been discussed in Chapter 7, though there were by now Italian artists
in England who could do the job locally, as we will soon see.

Ruin Views as Decoration in English Houses (and Elsewhere)

Vedute were designed above all to be decorative, so it is not surprising that
the grand tourist eagerly purchased them with a view to displaying them
on the walls of his house(s). Paintings, engravings and drawings served
as advertisements of the owner's cultural attainments, but they were also
attractive souvenirs. Once on show in England, they formed part of the
interior decorative schemes in the houses of the well-to-do.

Thomas Coke, who made the Grand Tour in 1712–18, bought five paintings and some drawings of topographical views by Gaspar van Wittel, or, as

Italianised, Gaspare Vanvitelli.[9] The five canvases are still to be seen in the Green State Dressing Room at Holkham Hall in Norfolk.

Italian artists had long sought their fortunes in England, so the owner of a country estate did not have to commission paintings in Italy if he could find a suitable executant on home ground. The poetical *vedute* of the Venetian scenery-painter and artist Marco Ricci proved popular in England, where he worked for aristocratic patrons.[10] In London in 1725, with his uncle Sebastiano, he contributed to a famous collection of imaginary funeral monuments commissioned by Owen McSwiny. He painted the landscape and ruins for two of the allegorical tombs, one for William Cavendish, first duke of Devonshire, now in the Barber Institute of Fine Arts in Birmingham, UK, the other for Admiral of the Fleet Sir Cloudesley Shovell, now in the National Gallery of Art in Washington, DC (Figure 9.3).

Figure 9.3 Ricci, *Monument to Sir Clowdisley Shovell*. Photo: The National Gallery of Art, Washington, DC, Samuel H. Cress Collection/public domain.

Both of them were originally acquired by the duke of Richmond and displayed in his country seat, Goodwood, in Sussex.[11]

Ricci's *vedute* of ruins were all fanciful (*ideate* and *capricci*), and their composition owed much to his work as a stage designer.[12] Lucy Whitaker has recognised his greatest contribution as a *vedutista* in the transforming light which subtly modulates the architectural forms.[13] His posthumously published engravings in the *Experimenta* of 1730 are as attractive as his paintings, and they are reckoned to have had an influence on the work of Piranesi[14] (Figure 9.4). His *capricci*, examples of which are to be found in the Royal Collection, bring together in decorative proximity more or less recognisable ruins (Ricci did not aim to be exact), such as an obelisk, the Pyramid of Cestius and the round temple by the Tiber.[15]

Most impressive is the decoration of the former drawing room (now the dining room) at Shugborough Hall, Staffordshire (National Trust). Its

Figure 9.4 Ricci, *Classical Ruins with Equestrian Statue and Round Temple.* Photo: Los Angeles County Museum of Art/public domain.

walls are adorned by large canvases in tempera, set in gilded stucco frames. Ascription is contested, but the likeliest candidate is now Pietro Paltronieri, a Bolognese 'rovinista' – that is to say, a specialist in scenes of ruination – who had contributed the fanciful architecture to a number of the imaginary tombs referred to earlier.[16] The paintings at Shugborough were commissioned by Thomas Anson, a grand tourist in 1724–5 (Figure 9.5). The ruins depicted are only generically Roman save for the Pyramid of Cestius; they are certainly not to be found in or near Bologna, as is claimed in the National Trust's guidebook. Paltronieri painted a cycle of ruin views for the palazzo Caprara in Bologna in the early 1730s, and that is perhaps what the author of the guidebook had in mind.

The work of Giovanni Battista Busiri was particularly admired by Englishmen. Two grand tourists, Henry Fiennes Pelham-Clinton and Robert Price, were keen to acquire examples. Price, a gentleman artist taught by Busiri, concealed the precious watercolours in his fiddle case to avoid customs duty on his return to England![17] But the most significant collector of Busiri's work was William Windham II of Felbrigg Hall in Norfolk (National Trust). He remodelled a room in his ancestral home, now the Cabinet Room, specially for the display of twenty-six gouaches by Busiri which he had acquired during his stay in Italy in 1739–40 and had framed

Figure 9.5 Shugborough Hall, former drawing room. Photo: Tony Hisgett, CCBY-SA 2.0.

in finely carved and gilded woodwork.[18] The subject matter of Windham's collection is various, but many of the paintings depict Rome's ruins, such as the Temple of Minerva Medica. The original scheme for the disposition of the Felbrigg collection is extant.[19] Windham was assisted with the drawing of the plans by his architect James Paine, but the balanced arrangement in three tiers is clearly his own. The plans are drawn to scale and carefully labelled; superimposed slips indicate alternative arrangements or changes in the overall scheme. It is a charming room in which to experience a comprehensive decorative scheme still largely intact as planned, altogether an astonishing survival.

The indefatigable collector Horace Walpole, who made the Grand Tour in 1739–41, decorated the walls of the Green Room in his house at Strawberry Hill, Twickenham, with many Roman landscapes with ruins by Andrea Lucatelli (or Locatelli). Lucatelli painted *vedute*, though less often than *capricci*, and enjoyed a European reputation until his untimely death.[20] His vast output followed the tradition of 'rovinismo romano', especially the work of Ghisolfi (mentioned in the previous chapter), and his own work, like Ghisolfi's, was often confused with Panini's. But Walpole's collection was dispersed in a sale in the nineteenth century, so we can only guess at the look of the room as decorated with the paintings.

Contemporaneously with Windham and Walpole, Henry Howard, fourth earl of Carlisle, made his second visit to Rome in 1738–9, where he commissioned Panini to produce six views of the city's ruins. The artist needed a bit of goading to complete the commission, and the paintings, all of them *capricci* of the ruins, reached Castle Howard in Yorkshire in 1741, where they may still be admired in the Long Gallery. Panini painted five ruin *capricci* also in 1738, which have been restored to their original place in the Great Room of Marble Hill in southwest London. They were either bought or commissioned by the builder of the house, Henrietta Howard, countess of Suffolk. She did not make the Grand Tour, but was nonetheless able to instal ancient Rome in Twickenham.

King George III was never a grand tourist, much as he might have liked to be. As a second best, in 1762 he bought some of the art collection of the British Consul in Venice, Joseph Smith. In 1742 Smith had commissioned Giovanni Antonio Canaletto to paint five grand upright views of Rome's three triumphal arches, the Forum and the Pantheon. (Canaletto had made drawings of ruins on a visit to Rome in 1719/20; it is not clear that he ever visited the city again.) Francis Haskell noted that this exclusive focus on the grand monuments of antiquity was 'like some signal to show that Rome and Roman values were once more about to resume the leading rôle in Italian art'.[21] The unusual format (for Canaletto) further suggests that they were destined for a special place in Smith's palace on the Grand Canal, where 'they must have made a great impact' (Haskell again).[22] Once in Buckingham House (now Palace), they were hung in the entrance hall, along with Canaletto's more characteristic views of Venice.[23]

At Stourhead in Wiltshire (National Trust) may still be seen the romantic views painted in watercolour by the Swiss artist Abraham Louis Ducros. They were purchased in Rome by Sir Richard Colt Hoare, who made a somewhat belated Grand Tour for six years, 1785–91.[24] Ducros himself had travelled to Rome in 1776, where he established a business with the engraver Giovanni Volpato in 1779. Together they produced numerous souvenir views of Rome for tourists. A work of that period is Ducros' *Temple of Peace* (Figure 9.6).

In the following year Ducros and Volpato published their first series of prints, *Vues de Rome et de ses environs* (Rome, 1780). Their collaboration continued until 1789, but by 1782 Ducros was beginning to take on commissions for his own paintings. His first important commissions were for oil paintings, such as those commemorating the visit to Italy in 1782 of the Russian grand duke Paul Romanov: the *Grand Duke Paul and the Grand Duchess Maria at Tivoli* and the *Grand Duke Paul and His Suite at the Forum* (both now in St Petersburg, Peter and Paul Fortress). By 1783

Figure 9.6 Ducros, *Temple of Peace*. Photo: Yale Center for British Art/public domain.

Ducros had probably already begun to paint the large-scale watercolours that made his name. In 1786 he met Sir Richard Colt Hoare, who became his most important patron and bought thirteen landscapes between 1786 and 1793. Hoare was himself an accomplished draughtsman and he highly rated Ducros' watercolour technique, which in his opinion rivalled painting in oils.[25] The views at Stourhead include the arches of Constantine and of Titus.

The 'rovinista' whose work is most extensively represented in English houses is the Venetian Antonio Pietro Francesco Zucchi (Art UK catalogues ninety-four of his works).[26] He was much employed by the architect Robert Adam as a pupil of Clérisseau's in Rome, where Adam was himself on a Grand Tour at the time (1754) (cf. Chapter 7, p. 144). On his return to Britain, Adam designed some of the most outstanding neoclassical houses and their interior decoration in the country. Harewood House, in Yorkshire, is one of his finest and still most complete achievements. Its Music Room was decorated ca. 1765–71 with paintings of ruins by Zucchi, who became an indispensable part of the Adam design machine, as David Watkin put it[27] (Figure 9.7).

Adam's decorative scheme for the Music Room at Harewood is piquant. The arrangement of the parts is symmetrical and harmonious: the pattern of the carpet, for instance, reflects that of the plasterwork on the ceiling. The furniture, original to the room, would have been arranged in an equally

Figure 9.7 Harewood House, Music Room. Photo: Daderot/public domain.

symmetrical fashion against the walls. The paintings are anchored in a balanced array on the walls by their gilded frames. Everything is in perfect order, except for the subject matter of the paintings, in which ruin and decay hold sway, in contrast to the bright integrity of the room, with its fashionable pink, silver and pale-green chromaticism.

Ruin scenes had become common decorations from the mid-1760s and were projected by Adam for Hatchlands in Surrey (National Trust), Lansdowne (Shelburne) House in Berkeley Square, London and Castle Ashby in Northamptonshire.[28] In 1767 Zucchi also painted two decorative ruin scenes in the 'eating' room of another Adam house, Osterley Park, now in west London (National Trust); they are unusual in that the figures are dressed in 'Turkish' costume.[29] Zucchi worked as a *vedutista* in the tradition of the architectural *capriccio*, so the ruins are mostly generic Roman. But since Adam had made his name initially in 1764 with the publication of the ruins of the palace of the emperor Diocletian (reigned 284–305) at Spalatro in Dalmatia (the modern Split in Croatia), one of the scenes in the Music Room at Harewood depicts the ruins of that structure; that may also account for the 'Turkish' costume on the figures at Osterley. What we are seeing then is another example of the 'ripple-effect' of enthusiasm for the ruins of Rome: the enthusiasm extends to embrace structures further afield, as it had done since the days of Cyriac of Ancona.

Adam's liking for contained disorder in a decorative scheme is replicated in the entrance to the Saloon of Kedleston Hall in Derbyshire (National Trust) (Figure 9.8).[30] The design of the room is all symmetry and order. The niches with the diamond coffering evoke the apse of Hadrian's Temple of Venus and Roma. But the paintings of ruins above the doors by William Hamilton, a pupil of Zucchi's, tell a different story from that of the room they adorn.[31] And yet it was ruins which were the source of the decorative motifs of the Pantheon-like room.

Less costly than paintings as interior decoration were engravings pasted on the walls to form 'print rooms', of which only a dozen or so still survive in English and Irish country houses, such as Blickling, Petworth and Uppark. A miscellany of engravings, not unlike the miscellany of paintings displayed on the walls of Rome's Palazzo Spada illustrated in Chapter 7, were symmetrically arranged on the walls. Decorative engraved paper frames enclosed them, and engraved swags or festoons joined them to each other. The views of Rome's ruins by Piranesi might figure in the overall design, as they do at Blickling Hall, Norfolk (National Trust) and especially in the Engravings Room (intended originally for billiards) at Woodhall Park, Hertfordshire, designed in 1782 by R. Parker.[32] Among the twenty

Figure 9.8 Kedleston Hall, the Saloon. Photo: The Roaming Picture Taker, CC BY-SA 2.0.

Roman views by Piranesi attached to the walls, the Pantheon takes pride of place over the fireplace on the south wall and elsewhere in the overall design (Figure 9.9).

Another medium of interior decoration that found favour particularly with the modestly affluent was wallpaper depicting Roman ruins in land-scapes.[33] John Baptist Jackson was the first to produce large sheets of paper bearing engraved ruinous scenes, showing the influence of Sebastiano Ricci; his sheets reproduced the look of the walls of print rooms.[34] The paper of subsequent designers was usually in quite large panels, so that it was hung on staircases or in halls, as may be seen in the recently conserved Boston Manor House, Middlesex. The original mid-eighteenth-century paper is at the top of the staircase, which has been fully covered with a modern repro-duction (Figure 9.10). A particularly splendid example is to be seen in the Jeremiah Lee Mansion, Marblehead, MA. These ruins scenes were based on paintings by Panini, among others.

The fashion for Roman ruin décor continued into the early nineteenth and even the twentieth centuries. In 1811–14 Sir Jeffry Wyatville added a

Figure 9.9 South Wall, Print Room, Woodhall Park, Hertfordshire. Photo: Matthew Hollow, Courtesy of Paul Mellon Centre for Studies in British Art.

Figure 9.10 Wallpaper, Boston Manor, Hounslow. Photo: Rick Morgan.

staircase to Bretton Hall in West Yorkshire which is believed to have been decorated by the Cremonese artist, Agostino Aglio, with spectacular ruin *capricci* in the tradition of Marco Ricci and Panini.[35] The fashion was revived by the English mural artist Alan Dodd, who in 1988 drew upon the engravings of Piranesi for six decorative ruin scenes on panels in the Roman Bar of the Alexandra Palace in north London (Figure 9.11).

The charm of Rome's ruins was also felt by the British in their remote colonies, even in the howling wilderness of eighteenth-century Connecticut. In the Wadsworth Athéneum in Hartford there is a reconstructed interior of the parlour taken from the Seth Wetmore House, built in 1746. The painted overmantel of the drawing room's fireplace depicts an imaginary pastoral landscape, dominated most unexpectedly by the famous trio of columns of the Temple of Castor and Pollux in the Roman Forum.[36]

The artist as grand tourist was not an exclusively European phenomenon. Thomas Cole, though born in England, was an American citizen when he went to Italy in 1832. The views of Roman ruins he painted there, for instance the fragment of an aqueduct and arch near Tivoli (Figure 9.12),

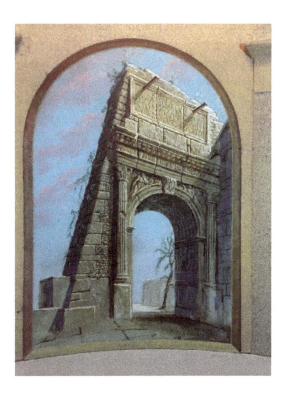

Figure 9.11 Dodd, *Arch of Titus*. Photo: author.

Figure 9.12 Cole, *A View Near Tivoli (Morning)*. Photo: Metropolitan Museum of Art/ public domain.

enjoyed considerable success back in the United States. Cole's exposure to the ruins of the once great imperial power of Rome inspired a series of five paintings entitled 'The Course of Empire'.[37] The series read a moral lesson to the young American republic of the threat of degeneracy upon the acquisition of empire. In the final painting, the once sumptuous material culture of the imaginary but evocatively 'imperial Roman' city has been reduced to ruins, and Nature is recovering the terrain with vegetation – no human presence, only wild animals.

*

Drawings

Before the invention of photography and especially of the personal box-camera, the grand tourist might well rely upon his own skill, or that of others, as a draughtsman to record what he saw. Charles Townley was a repeat grand tourist who resided in Rome for several years (he was a Catholic). He is chiefly remembered as a serious collector of statuary, most of which entered the British Museum in the early nineteenth century as the so-called Townley Marbles. But he also commissioned the architect

Vincenzo Brenna early in his career (ca. 1769) to produce a series of careful drawings of reconstructions of ancient remains, such as the Aula Regia of Domitian's palace on the Palatine hill. Townley's collection of drawings is now in the Victoria and Albert Museum.[38]

Drawing was a gentlemanly accomplishment, and it had for some time an advantage over early photography in that colour could be employed to represent more accurately or more attractively what was observed. The English grand tourist in particular took his watercolours with him when he travelled abroad, and filled a portfolio with views to take home as souvenirs of his visit. Francis Hawcroft's catalogue for an exhibition of the works of John Robert Cozens, Thomas Jones, William Pars and Francis Towne held in 1988 at Manchester's Whitworth Art Gallery provides a survey of dedicated artists' views of Rome's ruins.[39] Towne is generally reckoned to take the palm, as an exhibition of his Roman watercolours in 2016 in the British Museum, to which he bequeathed them, fully demonstrated. He earned his living by his work and so he sold replicas of the drawings he made on his personal Grand Tour in the years 1780–1. It is worth noting that Towne concentrated exclusively on the remains of ancient Rome, as if the modern city held no attractions for him at all. Richard Stephens makes out a good case that the ruins had a moral message for the provincial Englishman (Towne lived in Exeter), out of sympathy with government in remote London: 'the downfall of ancient Rome represented a moral warning about the risks to liberty and prosperity of abandoning a civic-minded lifestyle for luxury and corruption … to draw Roman ruins was to articulate the warning visually'.[40]

*

Micromosaics and Fans

Paintings, engravings and drawings were the commonest media for recording views. A new medium of pictorial representation of the ruins of Rome started to be produced in mosaic in the late 1750s in the Vatican Mosaic Studio.[41] This workshop was initially set up in the sixteenth century to reproduce in durable mosaics of stone and smalt (vitrified glass) the oil paintings commissioned for display over the altars in St Peter's Basilica (the original paintings copied in mosaic are displayed in one of the Vatican's museums). As the production of mosaic copies of the basilica's paintings was drawing to a close, the mosaicists, fearful of losing their livelihood, took to producing mosaics in miniature, *mosaici in piccolo*, or micromosaics. These wonderfully wrought scenes served as decorative pictures, such as Domenico Moglia's view of the Pantheon ca. 1850 (Figure 9.13).

Jewellery, snuff boxes and tabletops also provided surfaces for micromosaics. Mrs Eaton was sufficiently impressed with the objects that she described the process and noted that the shops selling the productions were to be found in the streets leading up to the Spanish Steps.[42] Cesare Roccheggiani's shop, for instance, was in via Condotti 14–15 from 1874.[43] The views of the ruins reproduced by the mosaicists were sometimes based upon contemporary engravings made for the tourist market, such as Domenico Pronti's *Nuova raccolta di 100 vedutine antiche della città di Roma*, published in 1795.

Giacomo Raffaelli was one of the most talented of these *mosaicisti in piccolo*. His late eighteenth-century view of the Arch of Janus Quadrifrons, part of the Rosalinde and Arthur Gilbert Collection now housed in the Victoria and Albert Museum, demonstrates an early stage in the development of the craft: the glass pieces (not marble) are larger than those used in the

Figure 9.13 Moglia, micromosaic view of the Pantheon. Photo: Wikimedia Commons/public domain.

nineteenth century and their colours are more varied and bright[44] (Figure 9.14). Examples of the work of Michelangelo Barberi will also be found in the Gilbert Collection, along with Moglia's. The quality of the workmanship varied, the best and costliest examples being made of very tiny tesserae so closely joined that the seams are almost invisible. Ilaria Bignamini calculated that as many as 1,400 tesserae per square inch of mosaic surface were possible.[45] Cheaper work, made of large tesserae set widely apart in the mastic bond, was coarser in appearance.

We found in Lady Miller a grand tourist who was not male, and Emma Gleadhill has recently brought the female visitor to Rome out of the shadows. Souvenirs to suit her were of course produced. In 1784 Mary Berry bought two fans decorated with the ruins of Rome.[46] The Royal Collection possesses just such a fan, which belonged to Princess Augusta, a daughter of King George III (Figure 9.15).

*

Figure 9.14 Raffaelli, micromosaic view of the Arch of Janus Quadrifrons. Photo: © Victoria and Albert Museum, London.

Figure 9.15 Princess Augusta's fan. Photo: Royal Collection Trust/© His Majesty King Charles III 2023.

Architectural Models

The grand tourist went to Rome chiefly to gaze upon and study the antiquities. Flat art – paintings, engravings, drawings or watercolours, micromosaics and fans – would provide him or her with convenient mementos of their visit, but ingenious Italian artisans also devised a three-dimensional and yet still portable souvenir, namely the architectural model of ruins. These proved highly desirable not only to the wealthier tourist and collector but also to the professional architect. In 1769, for instance, Charles Townley commissioned a large-scale cork model of the Temple of Vesta in Tivoli from the young engraver and architect Vincenzo Brenna (both mentioned earlier).[47] The models represented the buildings either in their present ruined state or in conjectural reconstructions of the original. The media in which the models were made varied: cork, pumice, wood, bronze, plaster, marble and alabaster all served. Broken marble was especially easy to find amid the city's rubble, and it was worked by carvers in miniature, *scalpellini*, to represent columns, arches and temples. Story suggests that hawkers sold the models in the streets of Rome.[48] The gentleman collector, like John Stuart, third earl of Bute, would most probably put the models on display in his library, where other antiquities, such as busts and small tomb chests (*cineraria*), were exhibited.[49] The German poet Johann Wolfgang von Goethe recorded in his *Italian Journey* that on his arrival in Rome in

November 1786 the dreams of his youth, formed by 'paintings, drawings, etchings, woodcuts, plaster casts and cork models', he now saw in reality.[50] In 2017 there was an exhibition of such engaging architectural souvenirs in San Francisco's international airport; David Weingarten and Lucia Howard's fine accompanying catalogue, *All Roads Lead to Rome: 17th–19th Century Architectural Souvenirs from the Collection of Piraneseum*, is well worth tracking down.[51]

The earliest three-dimensional models were made from cork, an attractive medium because its warm colour and pock-marked surface admirably reproduce the look of the ruins themselves. Cork is not as fragile as marble or plaster, and its lightness made it easy to transport. It is also largely resistant to decay and insect damage. Valentin Kockel, Gianluca Schingo, Françoise Lecocq and Richard Gillespie all provide guidance to the origins and early masters of the technique known as phelloplasty, 'phellos' being the ancient Greek word for cork (Lecocq also lists the principal European collections of architectural models).[52]

One of the earliest practitioners of this skill was Augusto Rosa, whose Arch of Constantine can be seen in the Hessisches Landesmuseum in Darmstadt, Germany, where a number of his other models are attractively displayed (Figure 9.16).

Figure 9.16 Rosa, cork model of the Arch of Constantine. Photo: Wolfgang Fuhrmannek, © Hessisches Landesmuseum Darmstadt, CC BY-SA 4.0.

The prince of cork-modellers is reckoned to be Antonio Chichi, thanks in part to the possibility that he was a member of Piranesi's workshop.[53] The most numerous examples of Chichi's models, originally thirty-six in number, are to be found in German collections: Darmstadt has twenty-six and Kassel thirty-three.[54] The Herzogliches Museum in Gotha, Germany has twelve models, including a reconstruction of the Temple of Portunus, once known as Fortuna Virilis. Chichi here secured a more authentically antique look by releasing the structure from the later convent in which one flank was embedded. In other cases he removed modern accretions; for example, the seventeenth-century 'ass's ears' bell towers do not appear on his models of the Pantheon, the finest of which has recently been scrupulously conserved for the Ghent University Museum collection.[55]

Italians, however, did not monopolise the modelling of ruins in cork. The Schloss Johannisburg Museum in Aschaffenburg has fifty-four models, most of them the work of the German Carl Joseph May. May was by trade a Hofkonditor or court pastry-cook, and so he was adept at making architectural models in sugar, *pièces montées*, a skill useful in his new line of business, which began in about 1790.[56] May's models were competent, as can be seen in one of his versions of the Arch of the Argentarii (the right-hand pier is May's restoration), now in the Los Angeles County Museum[57] (Figure 9.17). One of the chief advantages of May's work was that it was a good deal cheaper than Chichi's, whose models he copied, as he never visited Rome.[58] Carl's son Georg continued in his father's footsteps, with the advantage of an extended visit to Rome in 1827, thanks to the patronage of King Ludwig I of Bavaria. Georg's models displayed the ruins as they were to be seen in their excavated or newly restored state[59] (Figure 9.18). His 1835 model of the Arch of Titus in Aschaffenburg, for instance, includes the supplementary flanks added by Giuseppe Valadier about fifteen years earlier.[60]

The young John Soane spent twenty-seven months in Rome in the years 1778–80, and the experience 'coloured his entire career, culturally and emotionally', as David Watkin illustrated.[61] The museum he established in his London townhouse on Lincoln's Inn Fields conserves the impressive collection of cork models he put together over the years.[62] In 1804 Soane acquired his first model, of the Temple of Vesta in Tivoli, made by Giovanni Altieri in the 1770s, for £16 (= £1,650 in today's money).[63] He then bought a model of the Temple of Fortuna Virilis, possibly made by the Londoner Richard Dubourg (Figure 9.19).

By 1829 Soane had a sufficient number of items to justify construction of a dedicated Model Room in the attic of his house; in 1834 the models were moved to another room, on the second floor, which has been recently

Figure 9.17 Carl May, cork model of the Arch of the Argentarii. Photo: Los Angeles County Museum of Art/public domain.

Figure 9.18 Georg May, cork model of the restored Arch of Titus. Photo: Lutz Hartmann, CC BY-SA 3.0.

Figure 9.19 Soane's cork model of the Temple of Fortuna Virilis. Photo: © Sir John Soane's Museum, London.

reinstated.[64] That an architect of Soane's standing collected models in cork demonstrates their value to a professional, who had lectures to illustrate and articled pupils to train.

Cork models were not cheap knick-knacks, since considerable time (three to four months) and care went into their production. The master craftsman who ensured an accurately scaled representation of the ancient structures kept no stock of the models, which were produced only as required.[65] Chichi styled himself architect, a claim substantiated by the quality of his work. Ercole Silva, the late eighteenth-century champion of the English-style garden in Italy, highly praised the accuracy of Roman cork models and their usefulness for study, and presumably for imitation.[66] It is no surprise then that they were usually acquired only by the wealthy. Hence their presence in the princely collections of Germany, the Royal Collection of King Gustavus III in Stockholm and the imperial collection in the Hermitage in St Petersburg.[67]

In London, Richard Dubourg (or Du Bourg) mounted a long-popular 'Classical Exhibition' of cork models from 1775, which contained items he himself and others had made over a period of twenty years. Richard Gillespie's well-researched articles on Dubourg and his models have superseded earlier accounts of the artist and his exhibitions and so his expert guidance is followed here.[68] Dubourg's models, unlike those mentioned earlier, were not souvenirs. They were necessarily constructed on a larger scale with a view to public exhibition. One visitor to the exhibition on 11

March 1785 was Soane,[69] who as noted earlier purchased what may be one of Dubourg's own models, a reconstruction, based on an engraving of Piranesi's, of the Temple of Fortuna Virilis in the Forum Boarium.[70]

Dubourg personally described the characteristics and functions of the original buildings: for instance, it had to be explained to the visitors that the Colosseum was not a theatre. Thus instruction was combined with entertainment, as numerous contemporary accolades attested. In 1785 a number of Dubourg's exhibits were destroyed by fire; that the fire was started when an exhibition of the eruption of Vesuvius got out of hand was denied by the exhibitor.[71] Dubourg then set up a second enlarged exhibition in 1799. The exhibition room was illustrated in a handbill advertisement of ca. 1808–9. A large model of the amphitheatre at Verona was the centre-piece,[72] with the Temple of the Vesta on its precipice at Tivoli behind it. Some of the models on stands at the left of the handbill are readily identifiable as sepulchral monuments along the Appian Way, for instance the Tomb of Caecilia Metella. Since Italy was inaccessible to the British traveller during the Napoleonic wars, the exhibition served a valuable function in providing a vicarious, inexpensive and accelerated visit to the ancient ruins of France, Italy and Rome. One such visitor was Mrs Eaton. Once she finally got to Rome, illness postponed the start of her sightseeing. In her delirious state she could only visualise the Colosseum 'as [she] had seen it in the cork model' in London.[73]

Cork models of ruins, like plaster casts of ancient sculpture, were disregarded and neglected during much of the twentieth century, and many were discarded (or in museological cant 'deaccessioned') from collections as so much useless lumber.[74] Dubourg's cork model of the Colosseum, now his only securely known extant work, is a sorry example of this depreciation. It was sold at auction on his retirement in 1819 and in due course given to the South Kensington (now Victoria and Albert) Museum. It then found its way to the Science Museum in 1909, and in 1929 it was shipped to Melbourne, where it was lodged but still neglected in Museums Victoria. It was very nearly deaccessioned even from that collection, until Richard Gillespie took an interest in it. His account of the model's fate is fascinating, and it is a relief to know that this important physical document of eighteenth-century learning and taste is once again duly appreciated[75] (Figure 9.20).

The renewed appreciation of the aesthetic charm and historical value of cork models has generated a revival of the craft, most notably by the German cork-modeller Dieter Cöllen.[76] His skill is in demand for the conservation of historical collections and he has also produced an imaginative

Figure 9.20 Dubourg, cork model of the Colosseum. Photo: Jon Augier, © Museums Victoria, CC BY. Licensed as Attribution 4.0 International.

reconstruction of the monumental Roman temple that stood in the praetorium of Cologne, where it is on display in the Jüdisches Museum.

An obvious material with which to construct architectural models is wood, and without doubt the most impressive wooden model imaginable is Carlo Lucangeli's of the fully reconstructed Colosseum, a model twenty-two years in the making between 1790 and 1812. After a very hard time throughout the nineteenth century, it is now once again on display in the Parco Archeologico del Colosseo.[77] Conservation has revealed the original colouring of the wood, and the use of pencilled lines to define exactly the blocks of ashlar. Lucangeli was intimately acquainted with the structure, having supervised the clearing of the Colosseum of rubble, a task directed by Carlo Fea.[78] Between 1792 and 1805 he also produced a cork model of the building in its contemporary ruined state, which was purchased in 1809 and sent to the École des Beaux-Arts in Paris[79] (Figure 9.21).

A new medium for the construction of architectural models, plaster of Paris, was introduced in the early nineteenth century by Jean-Pierre Fouquet and his son François, who crafted exquisite (and hence very costly) reconstructions, not ruins, of ancient buildings.[80] As usual, the architects John Nash and Sir John Soane bought a good number of them for display in their collections; Soane's joined the cork models in the dedicated Model Room in 1834.[81] Nash's model of the Arch of Constantine is now on display in Room 128 of the Victoria and Albert Museum.

Figure 9.21 Lucangeli, model of the Colosseum. Photo: Wikimedia Commons – Jean-Pierre Dalbéra from Paris, France, CC BY-SA 2.0.

In the nineteenth century, alabaster or marbleised plaster or bronze were also used to fashion models of ruins or their reconstructions. The Royal Collection possesses three marble and gilt bronze models of triumphal arches by Giovacchino and Pietro Belli, made in the years 1808–15[82] (Figure 9.22). These luxury items are unique and were never meant to be reproduced for general purchase. The Belli arches are not depicted as ruins but as they might have been in their original state, as the added figures show. The three models were brought to London by a dealer and offered to the prince regent for 3,000 guineas; eventually he bought them in 1816 for 500 guineas, and displayed them in his London residence, Carlton House. There is an element of pathos to his purchase, since, as prince of Wales and heir to the throne, he was forbidden by his father, King George III, to travel abroad. Unlike his younger brothers, therefore, he never enjoyed making the Grand Tour of continental Europe. The best he could manage was the purchase of books, engravings and models representing things he would never see.

More accessible for the budget tourist were models in marble, tinted alabaster or marbleised plaster of the remaining columns of the Temple of Vespasian and of the Temple of 'Jupiter Stator' (really of Castor and Pollux) in the Forum.[83] The later nineteenth-century models, which still turn up

Figure 9.22 The Bellis, Arch of Constantine. Photo: Royal Collection Trust/© His Majesty King Charles III 2023.

fairly regularly at auction, were clearly produced after the French excavations in the early part of the century exposed the high podiums of the temples. A model in the Soane Museum, however, was made before the podium of the temple of 'Jupiter Stator' was made visible.[84]

The Sarcophagus of Lucius Cornelius Scipio Barbatus, consul in 298 BC, is strictly speaking not itself a ruin, but it was found in the ruinous tomb-complex of the family of the Scipios on the via di Porta San Sebastiano in 1782.[85] It is now in the Vatican Museums (Figure 9.23). Such a striking object was carefully modelled on a portable scale for the tourist trade in a variety of materials and colour-ways (ivory or ox-blood or black)[86] (Figure 9.24). What is not obvious from most illustrations of these models is that some of them had a practical use. After a hard day's sightseeing, let us suppose, the tourist would relax by writing up their diary or enthusiastic letters home from Italy after dipping their pen into an inkwell shaped like the sarcophagus of Scipio. The lid of these sepulchral models can be lifted off and the interior has two reservoirs for inks, between which is a shallow depression, perhaps intended for pen nibs. William Forsyth reckoned that 'of all the monuments of ancient Rome this was the one that was more frequently

Figure 9.23 The Sarcophagus of Scipio. Photo: Getty Images.

Figure 9.24 Model of the Sarcophagus in *rosso antico* marble, ca. 1810. Photo: author.

produced in miniature in marble or bronze than any other, except perhaps the Temple of Vesta.'[87]

For some, however, miniature scale was unsatisfactory, and in the nineteenth and twentieth centuries Scipio's sarcophagus often served as the model for tomb chests. Five at least can be found in London cemeteries.

The monument of Mrs Henry Wood in Highgate impresses (the cemetery is one of the Magnificent Seven burial grounds established on the outskirts of the metropolis in the 1830s). There are two more or less faithful replicas in the Kensal Green Cemetery. Presumably one of the local monumental masons had this design in his repertoire. The more faithful of the two versions reproduces the varied modelling of the rosettes in the metopes, as in the original. A second is less imaginative, with the rosettes all the same. The Marylebone Cemetery, in East Finchley, London, also has two replicas, one being a rather svelte version, 'Scipio-lite', but the other it hosts is the most imposing of all the replicas, the tomb of an 'Australian colonist', the banker Thomas Skarratt Hall, which has understandably secured listed status (Figure 9.25). The cemetery's website claims mistakenly that the design is derived from the tomb of Napoleon in Les Invalides, Paris; that tomb is similar, but definitely not the model.

London is not the only place in which these reproductions are to be found. There are also a fair number in American cemeteries, some illustrated in Douglas M. Rife's 'Gravely Speaking' blogsite;[88] he cites a trade publication of 1928 which provided guidance for stonemasons in the execution of the tomb. Probably the most distinguished occupant of such a tomb is Eli Whitney, in the Grove Street Cemetery, New Haven, Connecticut (Figure 9.26).

Figure 9.25 Tomb of Thomas Skarratt Hall. Photo: No Swan So Fine – own work, CC BY-SA 4.0.

Figure 9.26 Eli Whitney's sarcophagus in New Haven. Photo: Wikimedia Commons – Noroton/public domain.

Bronze was a favoured medium for architectural modellers, and a model of Trajan's column by one 'Hopmartin a remarkably ingenious German' was regarded by Mrs Eaton as 'an extraordinary work', thanks to the accurate reproduction of the whole of the bas-reliefs. The artisan's name was actually Wilhelm Hopfgarten, who with a fellow Prussian, Benjamin Ludwig Jollage, made models in bronze of Rome's triumphal arches, columns and ruins so skilfully executed that they were often commissioned by the papacy as diplomatic presents. The models represented the structures not as they were at the time but as they might have looked in antiquity.[89] So the columns of Trajan and of Marcus Aurelius, for instance, are surmounted by their respective emperors, not saints, as nowadays.

It is worth mentioning, by the way, that moulds of Trajan's column were made to be cast in plaster for the Victoria and Albert Museum. Like the cork models described earlier, the purpose of this gigantic undertaking was to provide a model for study by artists. The two towering halves of the column may still be seen in the Cast Room of the museum. Frank Salmon provides a brief account of the making of such casts in the eighteenth century: it was difficult and expensive, so not many were made.[90] Soane acquired some, which can still be seen in his museum. The casts, like his cork models, served an instructive purpose, since Soane's drawing office was right next to the cast gallery; his students had this 'grammar of antiquity' constantly before their eyes.

To return to bronze-casting: unknown artisans produced rather less impressive and less expensive models than Hopfgarten which, like those of Scipio's sarcophagus, were designed for other than purely decorative or study purposes: models of the Tomb of Caecilia Metella on the Appian Way, of the Pantheon and of the Temple of Vesta by the Tiber were all designed with removable tops so as to serve as an inkwell. Forsyth claimed that the models of the inkwell-temple were 'one of the commonest objects in the shops of Rome'.[91] Such inkwells were the stock in trade of a Florentine firm, Fratelli Pisani. Still further down the economic scale were inkwell-ruins in marble or alabaster.

*

Ruin Scenes on Ceramics

Once back in England, the grand tourist might extend his passion for Roman ruins to local productions by purchasing ceramics decorated with scenes of ruination. Robert Hancock was an engraver of plates used for the decoration of porcelain at the Worcester manufactory between ca. 1756 and 1774. As Anne Puetz says, he 'exploited grand tour nostalgia in transfer-printed Worcester pieces featuring scenes of Roman ruins derived from engravings after Gianpaolo Pannini', as can be seen on a punch-bowl from the 1760s[92] (Figure 9.27). The ruins in these *capricci* are often generic, and the designs are given names like 'The Temple Ruins' and 'The Amphitheatre', but in

Figure 9.27 Robert Hancock, transfer print on Worcester Porcelain Punch-bowl. Photo: © Victoria and Albert Museum, London.

Figure 9.28 Prattware dish with ruins *capriccio*. Photo: author.

the examples illustrated the tell-tale Pyramid of Cestius, or the three columns of the Temple of 'Jupiter Stator' (i.e. Castor and Pollux), identify the site as Rome. The fashion continued into the nineteenth century, though in a somewhat debased form, as can be seen in a mid-century Prattware dish (Figure 9.28). Even twentieth-century porcelain has been decorated with Rome's ruins. In the 1950s Piero Fornasetti produced a series of plates, named simply enough 'Rovine' on the reverse, two of which were decorated with views of the ruins of the Forum taken from older engravings or lithographs.

Alternative Models

Alternative models, particularly of the iconic Colosseum, continue to be produced to serve a range of functions. The décor of an aquarium, for instance, can be enhanced for the delight of the fancy fish with a model of the truncated Colosseum. At the luxury end of knick-knacks, the London jeweller Theo Fennell designed and constructed a 'slain gladiator opening ring', the micro-sculpture of which was made by Willard Wigan (Figure 9.29). The ring is surmounted by an exquisitely modelled miniature Colosseum. The building is represented as entire and its cavity is

Figure 9.29 Theo Fennell, Colosseum ring. Photo: author.

covered by a rock-crystal dome. Inside the arena a dying gladiator lies on the ground. The ring comes equipped with a magnifying glass and the ensemble is packaged in a box shaped like the Pantheon. Needless to say, the ring's price is provided only 'on application'. Finally, it is now possible to channel one's inner child with a model of the Colosseum devised by Lego. With over 9,000 plastic 'bricks', it is surely a bargain at £449.99.

It would perhaps be fair to object at this point that the foregoing account of souvenirs has been enlarged to include objects that do not qualify as such. A souvenir, strictly defined, is a keepsake secured at the site whose memory it is designed to evoke. But replicas of the sarcophagus of Scipio in London and New Haven, the fanciful designs on English crockery and plastic models in Lego can hardly be called souvenirs. The only justification for their inclusion here is that, like genuine souvenirs, they are replicas or evocations of Roman ruins, thus confirming the hold those ruins have long had on the Western imagination, whether or not we have actually visited Rome. Sarah Benson has persuasively argued that the major work of broadcasting

Roman monuments was done by mass-produced souvenirs, which brought Rome to the rest of Europe and the world.[93] Reproducing the antiquities in a range of media – engraved and printed images, plaster casts and cork or bronze architectural models of buildings – began in Rome. The ruins created an appetite for their replication in the form of the portable and sometimes not-so-portable 'souvenir'.

10 | Ruins in the Landscape Garden

> RUINS: Prompt dreaming and give a poetic cast to landscape.
>
> Gustave Flaubert, Dictionary of *Received Ideas*

The previous chapter surveyed some of the souvenirs the grand tourist of the eighteenth century (and later tourists) brought back to England to remind him (or her) of the ruins of ancient Rome. His library contained topographical treatises on the city and volumes of engraved views of the ruins, either of his own choosing with a Lafréry 'title page' or in the sumptuous volumes of Piranesi. It might also be decorated with architectural models in cork, marble or bronze of the most famous remains. The walls of the public rooms of his (or her) country seat were hung with paintings or engravings of ruins, and dessert might be taken off crockery adorned with ruinous scenes. But that was not enough: the truly ruin-minded of the day were not to be confined to the interior, since the exterior too, the landscaped parkland, provided scope for ruination, in the form of three-dimensional structures, sham ruins. The most engaging manifestation of ruin-mania is thus to be found in the English garden of the eighteenth century. Such was the charm of this fantasy (and such, for a change, was the fashion for things English on the continent of Europe) that the sham ruin was exported to the gardens of France, Germany, Poland, Russia and even Italy, a well-documented cultural exchange.[1] Our tour of garden ruins necessarily starts in its place of origin, England.

Landscape Gardens in England

The eighteenth-century English garden was peculiarly well adapted to accommodate sham ruins, which were only one form of ornamental structure in a varied scheme. The ground plan of these revolutionary gardens was artfully informal, 'arti-natural', superseding the rigidly geometrical gardens of Holland and France. Informality was supposed to be more natural and 'picturesque', a descriptor which became a technical term for the style later in the century. Informality banished rectilinear canals or rectangular water tanks in favour of lakes constructed with irregularly curved shore-lines. Garden walks were no longer straight alleys but sinuous paths (an advantage if the garden was small and lacked extensive vistas). Trees were planted in groves or clumps rather than ranks and files (another advantage, since trees in ranks needed pruning, and pruning required trained staff). As you strolled along one of these winding wooded walks, your gaze was arrested by buildings of various kinds, dairies or tea houses or hermitages, and these would usually be designed in styles exotic at that time, Turkish or Chinese, say, so as to please the eye. For those who had made the Grand Tour to Italy, ruins that evoked those of Rome clearly now gave an aesthetic pleasure to the eye, as the paintings and engravings we have already considered demonstrate, so it seemed perfectly in order to decorate 'picturesque' gardens with sham antique ruins.

The initiator of this fashion for sham ruins was Batty Langley, whose impressive publishing activity is surveyed by Eileen Harris.[2] Langley was the son of a gardener in Twickenham, to the west of London, and in his early years garden design was his own occupation. But he also aspired to the role of theorist, and in 1728 he published a couple of works in which he set out his views on 'irregular' gardening. In the introduction to the first treatise, entitled *New Principles of Gardening* (London, 1728: xv),[3] he recommended Roman-style ruins as terminal decoration for 'such Walks that end in *disagreeable Objects*'. His four engraved illustrations, plates XIX–XXII, of which XXII is actually the volume's frontispiece, provided 'views of ruins after the old Roman manner for the termination of walks, avenues, &c'. Günter Hartmann noted of this particular 'view' that Langley broke decisively with the Baroque tradition of terminating a formal alley with a symmetrical structure by substituting a picturesque ruin.[4] Yet it is curious that Langley did not recommend Gothic as a suitable style for a ruin in England, since later in his career as a professed architect he whole-heartedly embraced the native Gothic and vilified Burlingtonian classicism; but in this early work on garden design only the Roman is proposed and illustrated. The triumphal arch depicted on plate XX is clearly modelled on the then still partially buried Arch of Constantine in Rome (Figure 10.1). In the event, however, the sham ruins erected in gardens were almost never copies of structures to be seen in Rome, which were apparently felt to be too 'site-specific' and so unsuited to replication elsewhere. (The ruins of Athens, on the other hand, would prove to be a different matter.) If constructed in stone, Langley's sham ruins might have proved prohibitively expensive, but

Figure 10.1 Batty Langley, plate XX of *New Principles of Gardening*, 1728. Photo: author.

again on p. xv of his introduction he recommended either that they be economically constructed out of painted canvas or that they be 'actually built in that manner with *Brick*, and *cover'd with Plaistering* in Imitation of Stone'. It is recognised that Langley's encouragement for the construction of ruins in gardens comes well before any actual known ruins were built, so he anticipated or even created the fashion; he did not follow it.

Now in England, as has just been suggested, the most obvious architectural style to adopt for a ruin was the Gothic; indeed, some gardens, notably the one at Duncombe Park in Yorkshire, were blessed with genuine Gothic remains that became the centre-piece of their design. The theorist of contemporary gardening, William Mason, in his poem *The English Garden* (1772–81), strongly deprecated the sham Roman ruin on English ground:

> … though classic rules to modern piles
> Should give the just arrangement, shun we here
> By those to form our ruins; much we own
> They please, when, by Panini's pencil drawn,

Or darkly grav'd by Piranesi's hand,
And fitly might some Tuscan garden grace;
But Time's rude mace has here all Roman piles
Levell'd so low, that who, on British ground
Attempts the task, builds but a splendid lie
Which mocks historic credence. Hence the cause
Why Saxon piles or Norman here prevail:
Form they a rude, 'tis yet an English whole.

Mason's critique was endorsed and indeed extended to all fake ruins by the Abbé Jacques Delille in his poem *Les jardins ou L'art d'embellir les paysages* (1782), chant 4.

A different critique of the classical ruin was advanced by Henry Home, Lord Kames, in chapter XXIV of his *Elements of Criticism* (1762: iii.313), on the subject of 'Gardening and Architecture'. He argued that a Gothic ruin 'exhibits the triumph of time over strength, a melancholy but not unpleasant thought', whereas a classical (or, as Home put it, 'Grecian') ruin suggested rather 'the triumph of barbarity over taste, a gloomy and discouraging thought'.

Despite such critiques, Roman ruins had nonetheless already secured a following. The garden at Stowe in Buckinghamshire, now in the care of the National Trust, was one of the first to be equipped in 1737 with a ruin of a temple in the Roman manner (as regards its pediment at least), designed by the architect William Kent. The commissioner of the structure, Richard Temple, first viscount Cobham, was a Whig who had had a spectacular falling-out over the excise bill with the prime minister, Sir Robert Walpole. His sham ruin (removed in the 1770s) was called the Temple of Modern Virtue, and the headless statue is said to represent Walpole. The ruin of the temple of 'modern virtue' was making a political critique; the complementary Temple of Ancient Virtue, evoking the Temple of Vesta at Tivoli, was not a ruin at all. Contemporary morality, allegedly undermined by Walpole, was being pilloried.[5]

More clearly decorative, and more clearly Roman in style, is the now genuine ruin of an originally ruinous triumphal arch, erected sometime between 1758 and 1762 by the Hon. Charles Hamilton in his 'pleasure ground' at Painshill in Surrey, a county unexpectedly rich in sham Roman ruins[6] (Figure 10.2). Hamilton made the Grand Tour twice, for the first time in 1725 (a Jubilee year) until 1727, and again in 1732. In 1738 he acquired land at Cobham and started to design one of the most complete English landscaped gardens in existence. (It is now in the care of a trust which is conserving and even gradually rebuilding the various structures.) The

Figure 10.2 The Mausoleum, Painshill Park, Surrey. Photo: author.

beautiful hilly landscape is dotted with attractive follies, such as a Turkish tent and a Gothic summer-house. Of course, Hamilton the grand tourist had brought back from Italy many sculptural souvenirs, and to house the marble boxes, *cineraria*, which contained the ashes of the Roman dead, he constructed a triumphal arch, enhanced by an unusual feature, namely niches in its walls, as if the arch had been repurposed at some later date as a columbarium, or dove-cote, for the reception of the *cineraria*.[7] This hybrid architectural fantasy was approached along a path planted with dark yews, an ensemble designed to awaken melancholy reflections on the transience even of memorials of human achievement. The mausoleum is in sad condition now, but restoration is envisaged. In its original form, however, as recorded in a number of contemporary illustrations, especially a painting ascribed to William Hannan, ca. 1773, the flanking pylons supported a complete vault, as shaggy with vegetation as the genuine ruins of Rome, thus providing a frame for a picturesque view across the river Mole to a meadow. Hannan's painting also validates the folly's aesthetic: the ruin is decorative and it takes centre stage just because it is an attractive object of interest in its own right. Indeed, so acceptable to contemporary taste was Hamilton's arch-mausoleum that Josiah Wedgwood included an image of it on one of the cream-ware plates in the famous 'green frog' service supplied to Catherine the Great, empress of Russia, in 1773, thus perhaps opening Russian eyes to the charms of the folly (see later for a possible result).[8]

One visitor, however, was unimpressed by the arch. Horace Walpole came to 'Payne's Hill' on 22 August 1761 and in his journal he caustically condemned, among other defects, the combination of a triumphal arch with a columbarium:[9]

> The ruin is much better imagined [sc. than the even more severely criti-cised Gothic summer-house], but has great faults. It represents a triumphal arch, and yet never could have had a column, which would certainly have accompanied so rich a soffite [the soffit has disappeared]. Then this arch is made to have been a columbarium. You may as well suppose an Alderman's family buried *in* Temple Bar [Christopher Wren's impressive gate straddling the Strand at the western entrance to the City of London].

The waspish Walpole arguably missed the point. Hamilton's hybrid ruin is not unlike a *capriccio* by Panini or Ricci in its combination of diverse elem-ents, never found together in antiquity, to create a new, modern structure, cheekily 'post-classical' as we might call it nowadays. But the combination of triumphal arch and columbarium might also have conveyed a sobering moral message: in the famous words of Walpole's friend the poet Thomas Gray, 'the paths of glory lead but to the grave'.

Another ruined triumphal arch, designed in 1759 by Sir William Chambers (whom we first encountered in Chapter 7, p. 140), can still be seen at Kew Gardens in Richmond, Surrey.[10] In fact, this arch was not the decorative folly it might appear to be, since it was originally constructed as a viaduct to provide along its top a cattle drove and carriage road straddling one of the principal walks of the garden (Figure 10.3). Once again, a con-temporary painting (illustrated here by the preliminary sketch) was made of the 'ruin' ca. 1762 by Richard Wilson, famous for his views of the Italian landscape (Figure 10.4). Elizabeth Einberg observed that Wilson entered into the spirit of the 'deception' by creating an Italianate landscape (there are cypresses, seen to the left in the sketch) and by inserting in the fore-ground an artist sketching the ruin, just as he might if it were the genuine article.[11] Indeed, the deception was surprisingly successful: Christopher Woodward records that an early nineteenth-century engraving of Wilson's painting was entitled 'Villa Borghese' and its true subject was not identified until 1948.[12]

It would be a shame to exclude from our tour the Temple of Harmony in Halswell Park, Goathurst, Somerset. Strictly speaking it is disqualified by not being a ruin, but rather a handsome reconstruction of the Temple of

Figure 10.3 Chambers, arch at Kew. Photo: Patche99z, CC BY-SA 3.0.

Figure 10.4 Wilson, sketch of Kew Arch. Photo: Getty Images.

Fortuna Virilis (Figure 10.5). Halswell Park was landscaped for Sir Charles Kemeys Tynte, and the replica, ascribed to the gentleman amateur architect Thomas Prowse, was erected in 1764–5. Roy Bolton's illustrated blog-post of 2016 tells the full story of the building's design.[13] Robert Adam later added an aedicule to the west wall within which a statue of 'Harmony' (actually Terpsichore) was placed. To Adam and ruins we may now properly turn.

Robert Adam lived in Rome as a grand tourist in the 1750s, where he passed much time with Charles Louis Clérisseau drawing and designing, as mentioned in Chapter 7. The local ruins were one of his subjects, and there is a ruin *capriccio* after the manner of Panini ascribed to him. He also sketched designs for gardens, in which picturesque Roman ruins naturally figure.[14] He was confident that his designs surpassed those of William Kent, whose ruins he deemed 'good for nothing'. It used to be believed that his chance to realise his designs came on his return to England in 1758, when he was introduced to Sir Nathaniel Curzon of Kedleston Hall in Derbyshire, the hall of which has been described (Chapter 8, p. 188). Initially, Adam was charged only with the management of the grounds, and his design of a very imposing ruined structure, which was apparently to be occupied by a

Figure 10.5 Goathurst, Temple of Harmony. Photo: by Stronach at English Wikipedia – transferred from en.wikipedia to Commons, CC0 1.0 universal public domain dedication, https://commons.wikimedia.org/w/index.php?curid=32927719.

pretend hermit, was thought to be intended for the park[15] (Figure 10.6). If, however, that drawing was executed in Rome, under Clérisseau's influence, it is perhaps only an exercise of the fancy, a *capriccio*, like Adam's other designs for garden ruins.[16] The domical covering owes something to the Temple of Minerva Medica.

Sir John Soane, an admirer of Adam's work, has already been frequently mentioned, and he must once again step forth, now as a designer and builder of sham ruins. In 1802 he wrote up an account of the remnants of a Roman colonnaded precinct which he claimed to have discovered in the grounds of his recently built country house, Pitzhanger Manor, in Ealing, Middlesex, but now part of Greater London.[17] Further clearance of the site led him to conjecture, as he claimed, that there had been a temple of Jupiter Ammon there.[18] As an architect, Soane easily outdid most commissioners of fake garden ruins.[19] Soane's pupil George Basevi made a watercolour sketch of the 'excavated' complex on 20 December 1810, in which only the top half of two columns supposedly buried is visible, a conceit to be encountered again in Potsdam and Vienna[20] (Figure 10.7). The numerous plans of the ruins may be accessed in an illustrated online article.[21] In 1832, when Soane sold the house, he commissioned Charles Richardson to make a trio of 'views', one of the ruins 'as they are', one of them 'as if excavated' and finally one of them restored.[22] The elaborate complex of the folly was swept away in the later nineteenth century, though fragments remain.

Figure 10.6 Adam, design for a *capriccio* of a Roman ruin. Photo: © Victoria and Albert Museum.

Figure 10.7 Basevi, *Garden Ruins at Pitzhanger Manor*. Photo: © Sir John Soane's
Museum, London.

Back in the county of Surrey, near Virginia Water, we may still visit what
ought perhaps to be called a 'pseudo-sham' ruin, since it is constructed
of genuine Roman columns and architraves.[23] Jane Roberts tells the full
story of the acquisition of the raw material, which was brought from Leptis
Magna in North Africa in 1816, a gift to the prince regent from the Bashaw
of Tripoli:[24] twenty-two granite and fifteen marble columns, ten capitals,
twenty-five pedestals, ten pieces of cornice, and a variety of inscribed or figured slabs. Initially the stones were stored in the quadrangle of the British
Museum in London, but between 1827 and 1828 the favourite architect
of the regent (by now the king), Sir Jeffry Wyatville, devised a two-part
plan for their erection in Windsor Great Park as a 'Temple of Augustus',
the largest artificial ruin ever constructed in the British isles, according
to Sir Roy Strong[25] (Figure 10.8). The entrance to the complex from the
lakeshore of Windsor Great Park is a colonnaded avenue, suggestive less
a temple than rows of shops. Fallen fragments are left lying about to form
a pleasing Roman ruin. The A329 Blacknest Road from Virginia Water to
Ascot divides the colonnaded avenue from a semi-circular exedra-like area
enclosing the rest of the complex. The total cost of the folly was £12,000.

Figure 10.8 Wyatville, Roman ruins at Virginia Water: The Avenue. Photo: US Library of Congress/public domain.

This most elaborate of English landscaped ruins was in a dangerous state even by the end of the nineteenth century, and by the mid-twentieth it had fallen into serious disrepair.[26] In 2008 conservation and restoration of the monument with traditional materials were taken in hand, and it is now most attractively presented. An account of the recent works is provided on the website of the Crown Estate, *The Ruins, Virginia Water, Past and Present [The Royal Landscape]*.[27]

The British fondness for garden follies and eye-catchers fell off somewhat in the nineteenth century, but it has recently blossomed again. In 1970 a ruined portico was erected at Hodnet Hall in Shropshire with columns and a fragment of a pediment taken from a country house demolished in 1955, Joseph Bromfield's Apley Castle (1794–7).[28] The Folly Flaneuse blogsite provides an account with illustrations of its construction.[29]

About the same time, Sir Frederick Gibberd, the abstract modernist architect-planner of Harlow New Town, Essex, was designing his own garden nearby, and he ornamented it with a pair of Roman-style Corinthian columns, which support an entablature (Figure 10.9). Since the elaborate leafage of the Corinthian capital was modelled upon acanthus leaves, the acanthus is cleverly planted at the base of the columns. Gibberd had salvaged the handsome stonework from his reconstruction of Coutt's Bank in

Figure 10.9 Gibberd, ruins of a Roman temple. Photo: author.

the Strand, London. The plans of this folly are displayed in the garden's tea house and they are clearly labelled as the 'ruins of a Roman temple'.[30]

Before crossing the English Channel to the continent, one last eighteenth-century garden deserves to be mentioned because it realises the threat to the primacy of Rome's monumental ruins anticipated by Piranesi (a threat mentioned in Chapter 7). The garden is that laid out for Thomas Anson at Shugborough Hall in Staffordshire (the hall's interior decoration was illustrated in Chapter 8).

This garden contained a most varied collection of ruins and follies. There is, for instance, still to be seen a bizarre 'Gothick' ruin (much reduced from the original in extent) on the bank of the river Sow. Up until 1795, on the opposite bank there was what seems from contemporary paintings and watercolours to have been the portico of a ruined Roman temple;[31] it was undermined and washed away when the river flooded. The remaining follies of the parkland are the 'ruins of Athens', numbering three: the 'Lanthorn of Demosthenes' (now identified as the choragic monument of Lysicrates), the Tower of the Winds (minus the bas reliefs of the winds themselves) and the Arch of Hadrian (which might at a pinch be deemed 'Roman'), impressively sited on a hilltop. This enthusiastic import of Hellenic ruination is easily explained: the owner of Shugborough, Thomas Anson, a member of the Society of Dilettanti, was a subscriber to Stuart and Revett's *Antiquities of Athens*, and he commissioned Stuart to provide the ornamental replicas for his grounds. (Replicas of the ruins of Rome were uncommon, as noted earlier.)

Landscape Gardens in Continental Europe

The fashion for English garden design was exported to continental Europe, and in its baggage came the sham classical ruin. Here are some examples. First comes La Naumachie (1772/3) in the Parc Monceau, Paris; columns from the basilica of Saint Denys were recycled by its designer, the multi-talented Louis Carogis Carmontelle, who perhaps had in mind the Maritime Theatre at Hadrian's Villa, Tivoli (Figure 10.10). The original, far more extensive garden of the duc de Chartres boasted a number of other structures which were meant to illustrate a world history of architectural design.

Figure 10.10 La Naumachie, Parc Monceau. Photo: patrick janicek, CC BY-SA 2.0 generic.

In what is now Belgium, the prince de Ligne had what looks like the ruin of the pronaos of a Roman temple constructed in his garden at the Château de Beloeil near Mons ca. 1775.[32]

A few years later, 1778–85, Arkadia Park in Poland was landscaped at the instigation of Helena Radziwill to designs by the German Szymon Bogumil Zug.[33] Among the garden's decorative structures there is a fragmentary aqueduct, evoking the broken ranges of aqueducts snaking across the Campagna (Figure 10.11).

Also in Poland in the royal gardens of Lazienki Park in Warsaw, a summer theatre was erected in the lake in 1790–3, designed by the German Johann Chrystian Kammsetzer, and fully described by Günter Hartmann[34] (Figure 10.12). The restored auditorium (*cavea*) is built on the lakeshore, and it is separated from the unexpectedly ruinous stage building by a canal, so that the *scaena* is placed on an island. The illusion of antiquity was sustained at the inauguration of the theatre with a ballet entitled 'Cleopatra'. The garden's official website provides a fine series of illustrations.[35]

In Russia, the neoclassical architect Giacomo Quarenghi designed a Kitchen Ruin pavilion which was built with genuine Roman architectural *spolia* in the Catherine Park, Pushkin (Tsarskoye Selo) in the 1780s. Other decorations were suitably 'distressed' so as to sustain the illusion of

Figure 10.11 Arkadia Park, aqueduct. Photo: Jolanta Dyr – own work, CC BY-SA 3.0.

Figure 10.12 Theatre ruin, Lazienki Park, Warsaw. Photo: Ken Eckert – own work, CC BY-SA 4.0.

ruination. The kitchen pavilion, which some regard as one of Quarenghi's finest works, was sited near the Concert Hall, also designed by him, so as to provide meals for concert-goers.[36]

In the states of Germany, too, the English landscape garden had become highly fashionable, and as usual along with landscape came ruination. One of the earliest ruin complexes was built on the Höneberg, subsequently dubbed Ruinenberg, in the park of Sans Souci at Potsdam.[37] In 1748, King Friedrich II, aka Frederick the Great, had a reservoir built to supply the fountains of the garden. His architect Georg Wenzeslaus von Knobelsdorff and the stage-designer Innocente Bellavite placed round its margin screens of sham antique ruins, comprising a Doric monopteros (round temple), three high Ionic columns with entablature, a small pyramid and a ruined wall, designed as if from a Roman theatre[38] (Figure 10.13).

A second apparently ruinous structure in the royal parks of Potsdam is an adjunct of the Marmorpalais, built by King Friedrich Wilhelm II in the Neuer Garten. To minimise the risk of fire, the palace's kitchen, Schlossküche or Küchengebäude, was prudently detached from the main building and joined to it by an underground passage.[39] The humble kitchen was given a frontispiece which takes the form of a half-sunken temple ruin (Figure 10.14). It was built in 1788–90 to the design of Carl Philipp Christian von Gontard. The structure was kept low so as not to intrude upon the view of the lakeside summer palace, but economy may also have been a consideration: half-columns are cheaper than complete ones and require less substantial underground supports. Equally, the truncation of the columns

Figure 10.13 Knobelsdorff, Ruinenberg, Potsdam. Photo: DerFotogfraf – own work, CC BY-SA 4.0.

Figure 10.14 Schlossküche, Marmorpalais. Photo: Oursana/public domain.

evokes the contemporary appearance of a number of structures in Rome itself, for instance the two so-called Colonnacce in the Forum of Nerva, always visible though half-buried,[40] and what was then known as the Temple of Jupiter Tonans 'The Thunderer' (actually the Temple of Vespasian) in the Roman Forum. In the eighteenth century its columns were still buried, as we see in one of Piranesi's engravings of the building (Figure 10.15).

There is a humbler cluster of ruination across the lake from the Marmorpalais in Schloss Klein-Glienicke, in a pleasure garden designed ca. 1816 by Peter Joseph Lenné for Karl August Fürst von Hardenberg. The collection is made up of genuine *spolia* and comprises two column sections of the temple of Poseidon at Cape Sounion, a capital from the Pantheon and another one from the basilica of St Paul Outside the Walls[41] (Figure 10.16).

The half-buried trio of columns, cited earlier, was reproduced for Duke Karl Eugen of Württemberg in his English landscape garden at Schloss Hohenheim near Stuttgart as the 'Three Columns of the Temple of Jupiter Tonans' in 1778 by the court architect Reinhard Heinrich Ferdinand Fischer. Fischer originally designed a 'village' Rome, with a bath, an aqueduct and a still extant pub. What remains of the 'temple' today is a genuine ruin with only one of its three columns left standing (Figure 10.17). Contemporary engraved views of the buried columns, however, exist, for

Figure 10.15 Piranesi, Temple of Jupiter Tonans, Jupiter the Thunderer, actually the Temple of Vespasian and Titus. Photo: Harvard Art Museums/Fogg Museum, permanent transfer from the Fine Arts Library, Harvard University, gift of Thomas Palmer, Esq., of Boston, 1772. Photo © President and Fellows of Harvard College, 2008.312.44.

Figure 10.16 Ruin cluster at Schloss Klein-Glienicke. Photo: Andreas F. E. Bernhard, CC BY-SA 3.0.

Figure 10.17 Three columns of Jupiter Tonans, Hohenheim. Photo: Weltenspringerin – own work, CC BY-SA 4.0.

Figure 10.18 Sham ruin at Schloss Hohenheim. Photo: Creazilla/public domain.

instance one by the painter Victor Heideloff, published in 1795 in *Ansichten des Herzoglich Württembergischen Landsitzes Hohenheim* (the Roman pub is in the background) (Figure 10.18).

In Germany, pride of place must go to the famous Gartenreich ('garden realm') at Wörlitz.[42] This was the project of the Enlightenment prince, Leopold Friedrich Franz von Dessau-Anhalt. As a grand tourist he had travelled in England (among other places), accompanied by his friend the architect Friedrich Wilhelm von Erdmannsdorff, who was yet another pupil in Rome of Clérisseau's . After their return to Germany, the ideal garden realm began to be planned along English lines and laid out upon the banks of the Elbe from 1768 to 1794. Among the numerous buildings in the park is a small schloss built in honour of the prince's wife, Luise, and so it is known as the Luisium. In its garden there is a folly, a 'Ruinenbogen', or ruined triumphal arch, dating to the early 1770s, and possibly designed by Erdmannsdorff. In 1780 Erdmannsdorff designed a villa for Leopold's younger brother, Georg, and in the estate's grounds, the Georgium, erected a ruined Ionic temple, known as 'Roman ruins' (Römische Ruine) or the 'seven columns' (Sieben Saülen) (Figure 10.19).

Figure 10.19 'Roman Ruin' in the Georgium, Dessau. Photo MH.DE – own work, CC BY-SA 3.0.

At Wilhelmshöhe near Kassel there is a 'ruined' Roman aqueduct[43] (Figure 10.20). It was built 1788–92 to a design by Heinrich Christoph Jussow and it proved something of model for similar structures.[44]

At Schloss Schwetzingen in the Rhinepfalz there is also an aqueduct, built in 1776–9, but it is not as picturesquely integrated with its landscape as the one at Wilhelmshöhe. The garden does, however, boast a most curious structure, built in the wild, or 'English', garden in 1787 to a design by Nicolas de Pigage, another artist from Lorraine, like Claude, and later dedicated to Mercury[45] (Figure 10.21). While most garden ruins are simply ornamental, a few invite reflection and interpretation, as we saw in the case of one of the earliest, the tumble-down 'Temple of Modern Virtue' at Stowe. The interpretation of the Schwetzingen ruin is unsurprisingly controversial: if the Mercury to whom it was dedicated is Hermes Trismegistos, then the temple represents the ruin of Superstition. The temple has something of a look of the tomb, so Superstition is arguably buried there. On the other hand, Mercury was also deemed 'rational' thanks to his invention of language, so the structure might be Masonic and a shrine to Reason.

Grandest of all these follies is a vast ruin, recently conserved, in the grounds of the Schönbrunn Palace in Vienna.[46] The ruin was designed in

Figure 10.20 Ruined aqueduct, Wilhemshöhe. Photo: A. Savin, WikiCommons.

Figure 10.21 Shrine to Mercury, Schloss Schwetzingen. Photo: Dguendel – own work, CC BY 4.0.

1778 by Johann Ferdinand Hetzendorf von Hohenberg to serve as an eye-catcher at the end of a formal *allée*, as recommended by Batty Langley.[47] It was originally intended that the ruins represent those of Carthage, and that they should be flooded by a cascade, another way of suggesting the fall and rise of empires – Rome's empire, which appropriated Carthage's, was after all continued by the Habsburg Holy Roman empire. Once again, the Corinthian columns are half-sunk in the ground, like the ones of the Schlossküche in Potsdam (Figure 10.22). But somewhat prophetically, by about 1800 the ruins were themselves called 'Roman', and in 1806 the Holy Roman empire joined its progenitor in the history books, courtesy of Napoleon.

Adoption of the English landscape garden by designers across continental Europe even involved carrying coals to Newcastle, as it were, for sham Roman ruins were introduced even into Italian gardens of the eighteenth century. In the ducal gardens of Parma, for instance, there is the now really ruinous ruin of a Tempietto d'Arcadia, briefly described by Carlo Mambriani.[48] It was designed in 1769 by Ennemond Alexandre Petitot, a student at the Académie de France in Rome and much influenced there by Panini. It is one of the earliest examples of an artificial Roman ruin in an Italian garden. A photograph gives a stark impression of what is left (Figure 10.23). But Petitot's own drawing of the grove *en fête*, engraved by Giovanni Volpato, suggests what the ruin, softened by vegetation as at Painshill, was intended to look like (Figure 10.24). As an architect, Petitot,

Figure 10.22 Karthago, Vienna. Photo: Jorge Valenzuela A, CC BY-SA 3.0.

Figure 10.23 Petitot, Tempietto d'Arcadia, Parma. Photo: Lex2/public domain.

Figure 10.24 Petitot's drawing of the *tempietto*. Photo: Metropolitan Museum of Art/ public domain.

like Piranesi, strongly promoted the Roman style of building design, and he is also remembered for a set of engravings satirising the growing fashion for Greek architecture, published in Parma in 1771, *Mascarade à la grecque*.

At Caserta, outside Naples, there is a sham temple on an island in the royal garden. In 1786 Queen Maria Carolina (sister of Marie-Antoinette) commissioned an English-style garden designed by the German botanist Johann Andreas Graefer, who was recommended by Sir Joseph Banks and came over from England to supervise the work. A ruin was clearly an essential element in the concept, but the garden was not a success with the Neapolitans (Figure 10.25).

'What a strange idea – what a needless labor – to construct artificial ruins in Rome, the native soil of ruin!': so exclaimed Nathaniel Hawthorne in his last novel, *The Marble Faun* (a work to be discussed in the final chapter). Nonetheless, Rome can boast some fine sham ruins, indeed one of the earliest of them, possibly designed by Gian Lorenzo Bernini, no less. Bernini took over from Carlo Maderno the design of the Palazzo Barberini in the late seventeenth century. Thanks to its extensive garden, the palace revived the example of Nero's *Domus Aurea* in the creation of a country estate in a city centre. The palace is separated from its garden by a sort of moated courtyard, which had to be bridged so as to connect the *piano nobile* to

Figure 10.25 Island temple at Caserta. Photo: Marcok, CC BY-SA 3.0.

the garden proper. The bridge was designed as a crumbling ruin, hence its Italian name, *ponte ruinante*. It consists of two arches, the one nearer the palace being broken in half, the gap being covered by a drawbridge. To enhance the ruinous effect, a voussoir of the complete arch was 'dropped' as well. The material of which the bridge was constructed is ancient *spolia*, probably found on the site of the palace-garden complex. (The use of *spolia* argues against the notion of Claudia Conforti that the bridge was not intended to be a counterfeit ruin but a dramatic enactment of the moment of collapse.)[49] Although the bridge is not actually in the garden, nor at this date was (or, indeed, is) the garden designed in the English style, still the credit for the fancy of constructing a sham Roman ruin in Rome must go to the designer of this bridge, very possibly Bernini.

It was not until the following century that something of a fashion for sham Roman ruins sited within Roman gardens took hold.[50] The earliest example is a crumbling temple in the garden (once again, not strictly speaking designed along English lines) of the Villa Albani (now Albani Torlonia) on the via Salaria.[51] Its construction is dated to the 1760s, and its design is sometimes attributed to Carlo Marchionni, but without concrete evidence; recently, Alessandro Spila has plausibly suggested Clérisseau as the designer.[52] Paul Zucker regarded the structure as Greek in style, thanks to the influence of J. J. Winckelmann, one of Cardinal Alessandro Albani's scholarly advisers.[53] But the ruin was clearly modelled on the much-admired 'Temple of Clitumnus' at Pissignano near Spoleto in Umbria,[54] which was long believed to be an ancient building, indeed one of the most perfect survivals of Roman architecture. Many artists in the eighteenth century drew or painted or engraved it, including Clérisseau and Piranesi. In fact, it was not recognised until the twentieth century as a mediaeval funerary oratory (of contested date, but perhaps eighth century) which made very convincing use of antique *spolia*.[55] Indeed, Cardinal Albani's 'temple' also incorporates *spolia*.[56] There is a mischievous quality in this 'ruin', since its model, the Clitumnus 'temple', was not itself a ruin at the time.

Another sham Roman ruin in Rome, a complex confected for Marc Antonio Borghese in 1791 in his landscape garden at the Villa Borghese on the Pincian Hill, has a good deal of the appearance of authenticity[57] (Figure 10.26). In the early seventeenth century, one of Marc Antonio's ancestors, Scipio Cardinal Borghese, procured two stelae inscribed with a Greek poem by Marcellus of Side in honour of Annia Regilla, wife of the wealthy sophist Herodes Atticus, who died in dreadful circumstances in AD 160. Atticus had placed the stelae in a *heroon* built in her honour somewhere near a

Figure 10.26 Villa Borghese, ruined temple. Photo: Daderot/public domain CC0 1.0.

temple he had already built by the via Appia on his estate, named Triopion, in about A D 143. This shrine was to the empress Annia Faustina, who had been consecrated upon her death as the new Ceres.[58] Marc Antonio, or more probably his architect Antonio Asprucci, had the notion of recreating the ruin-complex of temple and stelae in the garden of the Borghese family's Roman villa. So we nowadays see the handsome 'ruin' of a pronaos with its dedicatory inscription. The two stone stelae are set in front of it on either side. The antiquarian and art historian Ennio Quirino Visconti published an account of the discovery and purchase of the stelae by Cardinal Borghese (1794: 6 and 9–10), with an attractive engraving of the new monument on the title page. The original stelae are now in the Louvre, presumably part of the sale of Borghese antiquities to Napoleon in 1807, and there are copies in their place. Despite the considerable care taken in the design of the complex, Mrs Eaton typically deprecated 'the modern ruins that are tumbling about like bad actors, vainly trying to be tragical'.[59]

Italian enthusiasm for the English style of garden design was promoted by Ercole Silva in his treatise *Dell'arte de' Giardini inglesi*, first published in 1801 in Milan, and then reprinted in revised editions, most recently in 2002. As a theorist, he relied overall upon C. C. L. Hirschfeld's *Theorie der Gartenkunst* (1779–85). Silva offered a brief recommendation of the construction of ruins in gardens and he pretty clearly had Roman and Greek styles in mind for Italy.[60]

The English gardening style was also warmly embraced by Giuseppe Jappelli, who became an apostle of the picturesque thanks to his visit to England sometime during the years 1835–7. Such was his prestige as a designer that in the 1830s the banker Alessandro Torlonia commissioned him to plan the garden of his suburban villa on the via Nomentana just outside the walls of Rome. A pleasing variety of exotic structures was by now a necessary feature of the new landscape style, and clearly even 'Roman' ruins had already become something of a fashion in Rome itself. The still little-known architect Giovanni Battista Caretti designed for Torlonia an extensive complex of varied ruins. Gaetano Cottafavi engraved views of the original assemblage, which was visible to passers-by. A number of the structures were swept away in the late nineteenth century with the widening of the via Nomentana, and what was left fell into neglect after the Second World War. Conservation of the remainder is fortunately underway, and Alessandro Spila has published the fascinating results of his careful research on the nymphaeum, the remains of which have been recently restored.[61] Once again, *spolia*, some cornices of the Domitianic period and some renaissance consoles or brackets to support busts were recycled in its construction. Other parts of the structure, pilasters and their capitals, were modern work. A couple of fallen columns enhance the fiction of a genuinely antique ruin. One column even has a 'fake' repair, which prompts Spila's plausible suggestion that this was a deliberate recognition of the contemporary conservation work being done on the genuine ruins by the likes of Stern and Valadier.[62]

As Spila explains, this ruin-complex in an extensive villa garden was one of Torlonia's numerous ploys to elevate his standing among the Roman nobility. His family had only recently been ennobled, and so a lot of ground had to be made up to match the prestige of the established papal aristocracy. A palace on the piazza Venezia helped, as in due course did the purchase of the villa Albani mentioned earlier. In it was displayed an impressive collection of Roman antiquities (still occasionally accessible). Since the Albani and Borghese palace gardens had fake ruins, the villa Torlonia must not ignore the fashion. For all that, the English travel writer Augustus Hare witheringly dismissed the garden as 'ridiculous … sprinkled with mock ruins'.[63]

Landscape Gardens Further Afield

The English landscape garden, along with its sham ruins, has been transplanted even further afield than continental Europe. Both the United States and Japan boast Roman-style ruins in landscaped gardens. The National Arboretum in Washington, DC was given an impressive monument of columns of the Corinthian order in the 1980s. The columns originally formed the east portico of the Capitol building until 1958 when they had to be removed so that an addition could be made to the structure that would better support the massive dome, completed in 1866. The British landscape architect Russell Page was tasked with finding an appropriate site on which to re-erect the columns, which can now be admired as the ruins of the Temple of Flora in the Ellipse Meadow (Figure 10.27).

At the Royal Horticultural Society's annual show in the spring of 1992 the Northamptonshire company Haddonstone Ltd displayed in cast stone a ruin evocative of Chambers' Kew arch.[64] The conceit impressed, and thus inspired the commission of a full-scale English landscape garden with the ruin of a Roman bath-house to be built in Nanatsudo Park near Mito City, Japan. The park is apparently currently undergoing revitalisation.

Figure 10.27 Temple of Flora, Washington, DC. Photo: AgnosticPreachersKid, CC BY-SA 3.0.

Illustrations of the bath-house are available on the park's website.[65] The sham ruin itself was used in 2012 as a setting in a successful film based on Mari Yamazaki's manga series entitled *Thermae Romae* (2012).

This account of ruin-studded gardens may be concluded with a return to the United Kingdom. At Stonypath in the Pentland Hills, Scottish Borders, the poet Ian Hamilton Finlay, along with his first wife, designed a landscaped garden in the classical spirit of the eighteenth century. In 1980 Finlay named the garden Little Sparta; by channelling the ancient opponent of classical Athens, he marked his territory off from that of nearby Edinburgh, 'the Athens of the North'.[66] The website of the trust which maintains his garden to an exemplary standard explains its aims thus:[67] 'Imbued with a high idea content, the garden is created from the artistic fusion of poetic and sculptural elements ... Finlay's intentions are moral and philosophical as well as poetic. The themes dealt with in the garden are those which underlie the structures of society.' One group of 'ruins' comprises a fallen column with its plinth and a scatter of stone blocks, on one of which is inscribed a quotation from the French revolutionary Saint-Just: 'The world has been empty since the Romans.' Finlay had fought Strathclyde Council to ensure the survival of his garden, and he felt a strong bond with the Roman Republic's struggle for dominion.[68] His garden thus recovered that combination of aesthetic appeal and moral comment on the state of society first found in the ruined 'Temple of Modern Virtue' in the garden at Stowe.

When the novelist Ivy Compton-Burnett learned of her friend Rose Macaulay's project to chart the course of 'ruin-mindedness', she exclaimed over tea: 'She's writing not only about ruins, but about things people built to look like ruins. I don't know what she sees in them.'[69] The issue, however, was not what Macaulay saw in the sham ruins, but what pretty much the whole of Europe and beyond saw in them and still see in them right down to the present day. Sham Roman ruins are attractive and even good to think with.

11 | Conservation, Restoration and Presentation of Ruins

We saw in Chapter 5 that preservation of the ruins was occasionally mandated by the papacy, but that the mandates were evaded or ignored or overridden by permits to excavate for stone. The partial or complete restoration of ruined structures was a practice even less envisaged because there was no obvious point to it. But once it was recognised by the eighteenth century that the ruins of Rome were a lure for wealthy tourists and foreign students of architecture, the maintenance and conservation of the more conspicuous ones became an issue. As an example, the area around the Arch of Constantine was cleared and its missing portions were either restored to it or newly supplied, but its lower portion was not excavated and so remained partially buried.[1]

The discovery in that century of the buried towns of Herculaneum and Pompeii in Campania also gave an impulse to systematic excavation, an impulse further energised by the brief French occupation of Rome in the early nineteenth century. The French left behind a legacy of important measures for the excavation and care of the ruins, which was taken up and developed by the restored papacy. Indeed, one of the signal features of the papal programme of conservation is the recognition of fundamental issues in the methods of conservation that would have to be tackled later in France and England by those who wanted to restore mediaeval Gothic structures. Eugène Viollet-le-Duc and William Morris were not so much pioneers as followers (presumably unconsciously) of what had been undertaken in Rome in the early nineteenth century. Before turning to this crucial development of measures for conservation, however, some earlier steps taken to present the ruins in an appealing light can be recorded.

First Steps in Conservation

In 1536 the Holy Roman emperor, Charles V, proposed to pay a visit to Rome, a city sacked by his troops in 1527. He was returning to Europe after his conquest of Tunis in North Africa, so he would approach the city not from the north on the Flaminian Way but from the south along the Appian Way. Measures for this unusual *adventus* were entrusted to Pope Paul III's new Commissioner of Antiquities, Latino Giovenale Manetti, who seized the opportunity to clear the Campo Vaccino through which Charles was to pass.[2] The emperor's arrival from the south provided an ideal triumphal pathway through the Aurelian walls at the Porta S. Sebastiano to the foot of the Capitoline hill,[3] which he would then skirt to proceed through the Campus Martius (the densely inhabited part of the city) on his way to the Vatican.[4] Once in the archaeological sector of the city, Charles would process through a trio of ancient triumphal arches, first the Arch of Constantine, and then, after veering left, the Arch of Titus. He would be passing along the upper Sacra via, the supposed triumphal route of victorious generals and emperors in antiquity. Charles would then proceed to the Capitoline hill along a new road driven over the open space and finally through the third arch, that of Septimius Severus.

To prepare for this itinerary, the plain had to be cleared of vegetation and housing; the processional ground was levelled, and even six small churches were destroyed (the grander ones flanking the space were left). Walls between the columns of the pronaos of the Temple of Antoninus and Faustina were removed, as were the chapels of the church of S. Lorenzo in Miranda (which occupied the temple), so that the visible portion of the ancient portico could be appreciated. The Dutch artist Maarten van Heemskerck (encountered in Chapter 7, p. 144) seized the opportunity to record the changed appearance of the temple[5] (Figure 11.1). This clearance in effect created an archaeological site, from which all that was modern had been removed so as to highlight the ancient remains.[6] In this way, the ruins took on a symbolic function: in Rome the antique eclipsed the contemporary, and so on 5 April 1536 Charles was conducted along this 'restored' via Triumphalis with Manetti as his guide to the ancient structures.

In Heemskerck's and other early views of the Forum can be seen the famous trio of columns supporting a fragment of entablature, assigned at the time to the Temple of Jupiter Stator (now known to be that of Castor and Pollux, or the Dioscuri). Some two centuries later, the stability of the columns was imperilled and so scaffolding was erected to support them;[7] the scaffolding was in due course replaced with iron rings and braces to hold them in place – these appear in nineteenth-century photographs, for instance one by Giacoma Caneva (Figure 11.2).

In 1656 Pope Alexander VII had the Campo Vaccino attractively landscaped with a double alley of elm trees, which flanked the route from the Arch of Septimius to the Arch of Titus. The tree-lined avenue was drawn

Figure 11.1 Heemskerck, view of the Sacra via, ca. 1536. Photo: Staatliche Museen zu Berlin, Kupferstichkabinett/Jörg P. Anders – public domain mark 1.0.

Figure 11.2 Caneva, columns of the Temple of Castor and Pollux. Photo: this file was donated to Wikimedia Commons as part of a project by the Metropolitan Museum of Art. See the Image and Data Resources Open Access Policy, CC0, https://commons .wikimedia.org/w/index.php?curid=60498286.

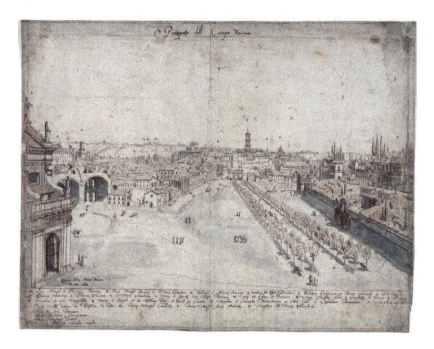

Figure 11.3 Cruyl, view of the Forum, 1665. Photo: The Cleveland Museum of Art, Dudley P. Alan Fund/public domain.

in a reversed view by Lievin Cruyl in 1665[8] (Figure 11.3). This was the 'triumphal way' driven over the Forum by Manetti for the *adventus* of Charles V, but the route, in reverse, had subsequently become that taken by the pope during his journey from the Vatican City to his cathedral church of S. Giovanni Laterano, a journey known as the *possesso*. The rows of trees were replanted in 1856 but then removed in 1883 to enable excavation of the site. It was not Alexander's intention to create an archaeological park but to show off the newly refurbished churches and to provide a shady carriage-drive (others were planted in the city). Nonetheless, the ruins benefitted by their liberation from some of the clustered hovels of former times.

The eighteenth century still witnessed a good deal of destruction of antiquities, and especially the export abroad of what was easily moved, chiefly sculpture. But there was also a growing sense that the relics of the remote past needed to be conserved as objects of interest to foreign tourists and students. Statuary, inscriptions and mosaics were now being displayed in purpose-built museums, either enlarged or newly founded by a number of popes and open to visitors.[9] The new disciplines of art history and archaeology were effectively inaugurated by the German Johann Joachim

Winckelmann in 1764 with the publication of his *Geschichte der Kunst des Alterthums* (*The History of Art in Antiquity*). The imperative need to preserve and protect Rome's classical heritage in its entirety animated Carlo Fea, who published a revised Italian translation of Winckelmann's history in 1783–4. In the third and final volume of that work, he included a still important dissertation of his own on the ruination of Rome, in which he established the paradoxical truth that the Renaissance was the most injurious period for the antiquities.[10] In 1800, Fea was appointed as Commissario delle Antichità by Pope Pius VII, a position he held until his death.[11] The pope who appointed him demonstrated an unprecedented concern for the remains of classical Rome in the early years of his reign before the second French occupation, and Fea instigated a conservation programme for major monuments.

Carolyn Springer urged that archaeological restoration at this time should be seen as a figure for the larger political and religious restoration that had to be set in train on the departure of the French in 1799, along with their dangerous notions of political liberty and secularism.[12] In 1802, Pius issued a *chirografo* (edict) mandating the protection of the monuments and antiquities.[13] From its provisions it becomes clear that Pius was chiefly concerned to prevent the export of newly discovered works of art which would help to replenish Rome's museums, depleted after the confiscation of works removed to Paris by Napoleon in accordance with the rapacious Treaty of Tolentino in 1797. Additionally, the edict urged that where possible ancient buildings be cleaned, restored and preserved. This edict was revised with new regulations in 1820 by the papal *camerlengo* (chamberlain), Cardinal Pacca, and its provisions proved to be of enduring value.[14] The edict's clauses from 39 to 45 are highly significant, since they forbade damage to ancient buildings and enjoined restoration of 'worthy monuments' at public expense.[15]

The most important works initiated by Pius VII were centred upon the arches of Constantine and of Septimius Severus. Attached structures were cleared away, the excavations were driven down to the level of the ancient pavement and an encircling wall was built to protect each of the arches[16] (Figure 11.4). The arches were in this way turned into disencumbered spectacles. Hitherto they had been hemmed in by structures which served the purposes of everyday life, for instance the stall of a vegetable seller under one of the side arches of the Severan monument. Now conserved, fully revealed and untouchably isolated by a barricade, the monument was presented just like a statue in a museum, except that the museum was now out in the open under heaven.

Figure 11.4 Rossini, Arch of Septimius Severus in 1820. Photo: The Art Institute of Chicago/CCO public domain designation.

The Colosseum gave particular concern, since the collapse of a vast portion of the southern outer wall in an earthquake in the Middle Ages had left two ragged edges in the perimeter wall of the remaining structure. These were worrisomely weak points, especially the one on the south-eastern flank, and so in 1806–7 a great buttress, designed by Raffaele Stern, was constructed to stabilise the wall's end. Barbara Nazzaro has told the full story of Stern's and other impressive early nineteenth-century feats of engineering which successfully shored up the perimeter wall of the amphitheatre[17] (Figure 11.5).

The opportunity was also seized for more extensive excavations and a good deal of earth was removed from the arcades and the surrounding area. Excavations were also carried out at the base of the Pantheon[18] and of the Temple of Vesta near the Tiber to ensure that their foundations were stable (both buildings were liable to be flooded). Attempts to clean and repair the Temple of Vesta were frustrated, however. The piazza in the front of the Pantheon was opened up, but that did not stop an obstinate baker from rebuilding his bread-shop against the temple's wall. The importance of these works must not be underestimated. Marita Jonsson stressed that the papal initiative to restore, rather than just to repair, ancient monuments for their preservation was far in advance of the times,[19] as were the methods of restoration and presentation adopted by the architects charged with

Figure 11.5 Stern, Colosseum buttress. Photo: Alessandroferri, CC BY-SA 4.0.

the works. The excavations around the triumphal arches and the attempt to stabilise the Colosseum's perimeter walls were impressive advances in practical conservation, not least because this was the first time that Rome's ruins were being looked after in situ. The restoration (indeed, over-restoration) and preservation of movable works of art in museums was a well-established practice in Rome, but care of the immovable architectural remains of antiquity was an innovative path to be followed and developed by archaeologists later in the century. It was only the anxious political situation in 1807 which brought these works to a temporary halt.

The French Occupation of Rome

In late 1808, Napoleon's troops reoccupied Rome, and would remain there until 1814. Since he was eager to forge a strong link between imperial Rome and a newly imperial France, care of the ancient monuments would provide a visible sign of the bond between the empires. In September 1809, Count Camille de Tournon was appointed prefect of Rome, and in 1810 a commission of monuments was established, the Accademia romana di Archeologia, which numbered among its Italian members the former papal commissioner Carlo Fea.[20] His knowledge and abilities were essential to the execution of the French programme of excavation and conservation. The regulations promulgated by de Tournon 'guaranteed the preservation of the monuments better than the preceding Papal regulations',[21] perhaps because the most significant feature of the regulations was that the French were in a position to enforce them. The main logistical difficulties to be faced in these impressive undertakings had already been encountered by the excavators working under the papacy: what to do with the vast quantities of rubble and soil removed from the sites and how to drain them efficiently. These problems were never satisfactorily solved. The demolition of structures built up against or within ancient buildings could moreover destabilise the original structure, as was the case with the Arch of Titus. Likewise, the removal of soil heaped about a structure was risky, as in the case of the Temple of Saturn. Over and above these logistical obstacles, there was the issue of cost. Properties with buildings to be demolished had to be purchased. The large number of workmen had to be paid; indeed, providing paid employment for the poor was one of the primary reasons for the extensive works. Needless to say, many of the French initiatives were only partially effected because of cost overruns.

In 1810, the Accademia di S. Luca, whose *principe* (director) at the time was the great sculptor Antonio Canova, was charged with the repairs and restoration of ancient architecture, in particular the Temple of Vespasian, the Colosseum and the Pantheon.[22] An earthquake on the night of 21–22 March 1812 considerably added to the Accademia's burdens, since it did much damage to the Colosseum. The amphitheatre's arena was excavated in 1813, and the disclosure of its substructure generated an impassioned debate about the purpose of the subterranean complex.[23] These works were prosecuted by Fea under the restored papacy in 1816.[24]

In 1811, a new French body, the Commission des Embellisements, replaced the Monuments Commission. It had two remits: restoration of ancient monuments and, as its name made clear, beautification of the sites. On balance, this multiplication of agencies was counterproductive, chiefly because of inadequate funding and the inevitable internecine turf wars. Nor did the inability of most of the French officials to speak or even understand Italian make their task any easier.

Nonetheless, the achievement of the French between 1809 and 1814, fully described by Marita Jonsson and Ronald Ridley, was undeniably impressive: triumphal arches, imperial fora, temples and the Colosseum were all taken in hand.[25] Perhaps even more important was the practical demonstration of what could and what ought to be done to conserve and exhibit the open-air antiquities.

Under the French, work began on the Roman Forum.[26] Its surface had to be cleared of later structures (houses, stables, granaries, churches), many of which were attached to ancient structures. Attempts to reach the ancient ground level proved optimistic. In 1813, there was a proposal not only to landscape the Forum area but also to create a circuit to be known as 'Le jardin du Capitole'. The impressive garden was designed by Louis-Martin Berthault, a devotee of the English-style landscape garden.[27] It is clear from the plan that the garden would have comprised a vast area including the Forum and the Colosseum, down the via di S. Gregorio to piazza di Porta Capena, and then along the western flank of the Palatine hill on the via dei Cerchi, with a right turn up the via di S. Teodoro back up into the Forum.[28] The circuit was planned as a carriage-drive shaded by double alleys of trees. This would indeed have been an archaeological park, studded with the more attractive fragments of ancient building. The downside was that any structure that stood in the way of the drives or the trees, whether ancient or modern, pagan or Christian, was to be removed. And of course the ground had to be levelled for the ease of riding, driving or even just walking. Fortunately, therefore, the scheme was not carried out in its entirety. The circuit of the Colosseum was, however, completed, but Britannia's daughter, Mrs Eaton, was scathing in her denunciation of the foreign landscaping:

> There are other of their [i.e. the French planners] improvements which have been suffered to remain, that we would rather have seen removed. French taste has formed a little public garden at the very base of the Colosseum, so woefully misplaced, that even I, notwithstanding my natural passion for flowers, longed to grub them all up by the roots, to carry off every vestige of the trim paling, and bring destruction upon all the fine gravel walks.[29]

The Forum Boarium with its two picturesque temples, traditionally allocated to Fortuna Virilis and to Vesta, was also taken in hand.[30] Both temples had been converted into churches, but the secular French put a stop to that. The architect Giuseppe Valadier proposed not just the isolation and basic repair of the latter structure but also a comprehensive restoration, which would have involved replacement of a missing column, raising the height of the cella wall and construction of a new entablature in marble, its design based on fragments found near the temple. Needless to say, the expense proved prohibitive and the scheme was dropped. But the temples had been deconsecrated and their ecclesiastical fittings removed. Vesta in particular was in a vulnerable condition, and so under the restored papacy more work was done by Valadier to ensure its basic conservation as an ancient temple, no longer a Christian shrine. In 1829, he oversaw the similarly basic conservation of Fortuna Virilis,[31] though it was not finally released from buildings attached to it until the 1920s.[32] In 1830, Valadier had iron fences and gates installed in and around the Basilica of Maxentius to keep out intruders.

The Forum Romanum was to be the jewel in the crown, and attention was focussed on the more conspicuous remains of the temples. Reduction of soil level revealed the lower part of all of the columns with their plinths of the pronaos of the Temple of Antoninus and Faustina.[33] The ancient level of the Sacra via in front of it had been reached in 1809. Similar deep clearances were made at the base of the three columns of the Temple of Castor and Pollux, which necessitated some stabilisation. Likewise, there were excavations at the base of the Temple of Concord (really Saturn), but with rather more spectacular results; a new road was built beside and behind it.

Far and away the boldest of the French undertakings was the restoration of the remains of the Temple of Vespasian in 1813, since the three columns supporting a fragment of the architrave on the north-east corner proved to be held upright only by the mass of soil in which their lower part was buried. To excavate the structure safely, it was therefore necessary to lift the entablature from the columns, an engineering feat recorded in a drawing, perhaps by Bartolomeo Pinelli.[34] The foundation for the columns had to be completely rebuilt.[35]

In 1812 began the task of clearing the Forum of Trajan.[36] Already in the early sixteenth century Pope Paul III had gradually cleared away accumulated debris and buildings so as to expose the pedestal on which Trajan's Column rests and to create a small piazza round it; subsequent pontiffs continued the work of clearing the area near the column.[37] The French proposed to disclose the entire forum in which that column had been raised and to open a large public space, in shape a sort of hippodrome.[38] A particular motive for their excavation of this locale was the traditional one, the hope of turning up significant works of art, a hope often disappointed; since this site was virgin territory, the hope of valuable finds seemed better founded. The stumps of the columns, still a conspicuous feature of the site to this day, began to appear, and some were re-erected by the architect Giuseppe

Camporese after the papacy was restored in 1814.[39] The excavated area was protected within an enclosure, the so-called *recinto pontificio*, following the precedent of the earlier enclosure of the arch of Septimius Severus (Figure 11.6). A fair impression of what the original Forum of Trajan looked like may be had by visiting the rebuilt nave of the basilica of S. Paolo fuori le mura, since its surface area is approximately equivalent to that of the forum.

The Pantheon was generally agreed to be the finest ancient structure to be seen in Rome, its state of preservation largely due to its conversion into a church in the seventh century (see Chapter 5, p. 85). But its surroundings were repulsive; it was hemmed in by squalid shops and there was a fish-market in the piazza (finally removed in 1823, according to an inscription).[40] In 1812 a plan was proposed to enlarge the piazza, but it proved too costly, since houses propped against the building would have had to be demolished, and others cleared away.[41] A proposal to remove Bernini's bell towers from the pronaos was unsuccessful, but at any rate the risk of damage to the structure caused by water and vegetation was checked with the repair of roofs and drains. The piazza della Rotonda was finally enlarged by demolitions in 1881–2, and the 'ass's ears' campaniles were also removed in 1882–3.[42] This was less an aesthetic than an anti-clerical gesture on the part of the secular Italian state, since without the bell towers the building no longer presented as a church.

Figure 11.6 Forum of Trajan. Photo: Mattis – own work, CC BY-SA 4.0.

The eagerness of the French occupation to improve the look of the most important ruins of Rome was encouraged by an enthusiasm for Italy in general and for Rome in particular, thanks especially to the presence there of the long-established Académie de France (see Chapter 5, p. 92). Napoleon had ensured the Académie's well-being in the revolutionary period by moving it from the Palazzo Mancini in the via del Corso to the Villa Medici on the Pincian hill. The French Revolution itself had taken on a decidedly Roman caste. Its early officials were styled aediles, tribunes and consuls. With the establishment of the Directoire and then of the empire, the Roman style was promoted in architecture and in interior design by Charles Percier and Pierre François Léonard Fontaine. Percier had secured the Académie's Rome prize in 1784, and it was in Rome that he met his life-long collaborator Fontaine. Together they turned Paris into a new Rome with the Arc du Carousel (1806–8), modelled upon the Arch of Constantine. The historiated column in the place Vendôme (not designed by Percier and Fontaine) was modelled upon Trajan's Column, in celebration of Napoleon's victory at Austerlitz. Indeed, so strong was the French attachment to Rome that in 1809 the vanquished papal states were incorporated into metropolitan France,[43] and in 1811 Napoleon gave his newly born son the title king of Rome (a city the lad would never see). Rome had thus become effectively the second city of the empire. (In 1956, Rome and Paris became 'twin cities' within what is now the European Union; Rome is twinned with no other city.) It is therefore hardly surprising that once the French found themselves actually in charge of the city of Rome, they made a considerable effort to improve its physical appearance and thus create a legacy of their dominion there. But they had pressing practical issues to resolve as well. One aim of the occupying French was political: to transfer attention from the overthrown ecclesiastical authority to a restored secular civic centre of the city. A more serious problem was created by the secularisation of religious property and the expulsion of clergy, whose charitable ministrations to the poor of the city were cancelled at a stroke. Public works on the monuments aimed to provide paid employment for labourers, who were also given a midday meal. This provision might also help to reduce the hostility of Rome's citizens to the foreign occupying forces.

The Restored Papacy

The change wrought by the French in the excavation of the monuments and their physical care was continued in 1814 under the restored papacy of Pope Pius VII, who had anticipated some of the interventions prosecuted

during the occupation.[44] In fact, one motive for further excavation and stabilisation of monuments remained pressing: public works were urgently
needed to provide paid employment for those without other work. Marita
Jonsson also pointed out that the papal undersecretary of state Ercole
Cardinal Consalvi recognised that Rome would never be an industrial or
commercial city (as a historical fact it never had been, even in antiquity),
but it could be a viable city of art that would draw tourists.[45] Once again,
we find Rome leading the way. How many modern cities, formerly mercantile and industrial, like Bilbao in Spain or Liverpool in England or Dundee
in Scotland, are repurposing themselves as destinations for tourists eager
to visit their museums and admire their architecture and works of art? By
the early nineteenth century Rome had an abundance of lures for the tourist industry, which resumed after the final defeat of Napoleon in 1815 at
Waterloo. Consalvi prudently realised the value of encouraging an influx
of visitors for the city's economy. Nor should the historical importance of
pilgrimage be forgotten. There had been no Jubilee in 1800 for political
reasons, so the city had to be prepared for the Jubilee of 1825, which is
reckoned to have drawn half a million pilgrims. Keeping the ancient ruins
in good shape and presenting them agreeably for viewing had now become
a priority of the papal administration.

Mrs Eaton was dismissive, as usual, both of the incomplete French initiatives and of the resumed excavations, including those around the Column
of Phocas in 1817–18, which were financed by Elizabeth, duchess of
Devonshire: 'I cannot but groan over the destruction of the smooth green
sod, on which the ruined temples and fallen capitals rested in such beautiful
repose';[46] but she fairly enough drew attention to the unsightly piles of earth
that were not yet carried away. (In 1819, Sir John Soane's son John Jr made
a watercolour of the excavation on the spot for his father.)[47] Mrs Eaton's
irritation was echoed in 1834 by King Ludwig of Bavaria, who expressed
dismay at the chaotic excavations in the Forum, where beauty had been
sacrificed to science.[48] Thirty years later, in 1864, the American consul in
Venice William Dean Howells made a visit to Rome and felt disgust at the
sight of the Forum: 'the first view of the ruins in the Forum brought a keen
sense of disappointment. I knew that they could only be mere fragments
and rubbish, but I was not prepared to find them so'[49] (Figure 11.7). The
disappointment of an aesthetic response to ruination becomes a burning
issue, especially to be seen in the revulsion at the removal of vegetation
from the Colosseum.

In the period 1816–18 further clearance of the Forum Romanum was
restarted under Fea, whose most important work was on the Temple of
the Dioscuri.[50] This was now excavated to its base after the basin that had

Figure 11.7 The Roman Forum ca. 1850. Photo: ImageZeno.org, ID number 20001877704, public domain, https://commons.wikimedia.org/w/index.php?curid=64901839

watered the cattle in the Campo Vaccino was transferred to a site in front of the papal palace on the Quirinal hill, where Raffaele Stern turned it into the fountain still to be seen between the two horsemen. Thanks to finds on the spot, Fea at last correctly identified the temple as dedicated not as hitherto believed to Jupiter Stator, but to the twin horsemen Castor and Pollux, who had cheered the Roman army to victory at the battle of lake Regillus in 496 BC. Fea's works also disclosed the *lacus* (pool) of the goddess Juturna in the vicinity; the *aedicula* (shrine) the visitor now sees on the spot was constructed in 1953–5[51] (Figure 11.8).

In 1817, Fea discovered the genuine Temple of Concord at the foot of the Capitoline hill.[52] This discovery at once overturned the centuries-old identification of the Temple of Saturn by that name. Fea's campaign in the Forum spurred a revival of interest in a thorough clearance of the site and excavation down to the ancient street level. Rather more pressing, however, was the need to drain the pits and to remove the unsightly and dangerous piles of earth and rubble that had been left behind by the unsystematic French excavations.[53] Much clearance and levelling

Figure 11.8 The Shrine of Juturna. Photo: author.

was done through the 1820s. Then, in 1827, Pope Leo XII inaugurated a scheme of clearance of the area bounded by the Basilica of Maxentius, the Arch of Titus, the Arch of Constantine and the Colosseum;[54] the works were to be supervised by the archaeology professor at La Sapienza Antonio Nibby (see Chapter 6, p. 115), with Valadier as architect. Ronald Ridley assessed the ambitious scheme as a failure, for the usual reasons:[55] it was too vast an undertaking for the available resources, the papal government had other matters on its mind and those most closely involved in the works were at odds over priorities. The problem of exposing the most important site in ancient Rome would only be solved after the unification of Italy.

Between 1818 and 1824, the Arch of Titus, which had received some attention from the French,[56] was freed from the buttress and the wall that hemmed it in. Since these structures also supported it, additional material had to be added to its flanks to ensure its stability once isolated. In the event, the architects Raffaele Stern, who died in 1820, and his successor Valadier took the opportunity of restoring the arch to its original size by adding an attic and reconstructing the side pylons to scale[57] (Figure 11.9). To their credit, the architects did not aim at a pastiche reproduction but at a conservative evocation of the original, made possible by the disclosure

Figure 11.9 The reconstructed Arch of Titus, 1853–6. Photo: Wikimedia Commons courtesy of the Metropolitan Museum of Art, Jane Martha St. John, CC0 1.0.

of its original footprint in the course of excavation. They made their supplementary work manifest by the use of different stone, local travertine, rather than the original thin panels of Pentelic marble from Greece, and they left the columns on the flanking pylons unfluted. (It was admitted that both measures kept down the cost of the restoration.) In this they anticipated in a way the principles later enunciated by William Morris and Philip Webb, the founders of the English Society for the Protection of Ancient Buildings (SPAB). It is surprising to one who knew him that David Watkin found the Italians' practice pusillanimous, though it has to be said that the initial reactions to Valadier's solution ranged from approval to abuse.[58]

The stability of the Colosseum continued to be a worry, even after Stern's earlier buttressing of the south-eastern flank. So, between 1822 and 1826, Valadier turned his attention to the north-western outer rim.[59] He designed a buttress which faithfully reproduced in brick the arcade and attached columns of the original, thus harmonising the support with the original. The flank buttressed by Stern is not especially conspicuous, whereas Valadier was adding to a portion of the building that generally figured in views of it from the Forum area; his solution was therefore designed to be more attractive (Figure 11.10). Presumably the perforated structure also cost less than Stern's solid buttress, thanks to the reduction in building material needed. Between 1840 and 1845 in the pontificate of Gregory XVI a further seven bays of the southern arcades were rebuilt to designs by the architect Gaspare Salvi.[60] Gregory's successor Pius IX also took up the task of stabilisation in 1852.

At this point a brief digression is needed, to draw attention to the insight given by early nineteenth-century excavations and conservation into an improved knowledge of Roman methods of design and construction. This can be seen in *The Architectural Antiquities of Rome* by the English architects George Ledwell Taylor and Edward Cresy (two folio volumes, London, 1821–2). Frank Salmon provides an engaging account of their heroic attempts to secure the most accurate measurements to date of the monuments and their decorative elements.[61] He stresses that they had two advantages over their predecessors. First, they were in a position to take account of and to illustrate what the French and subsequent papal excavations had revealed of the substructure of buildings (even though their own proposed reconstructions sometimes missed the mark). Secondly, in some of their illustrations they exploited the new technique of lithography to reproduce

Figure 11.10 Valadier's buttress. Photo: Wknight94, CC BY-SA 3.0.

their drawings of architectural details (Figure 11.11). Lithography was cheaper than engraving, and the architect could himself draw in ink directly on the stone and personally control the tone of the image without reliance on an intermediary engraver, thus ensuring superior accuracy.

Archaeologists in papal Rome continued their excavations and produced some impressive results. In 1827–9 Antonio Nibby resumed the French work on the double Temple of Venus and Roma, some extant columns of which were later re-erected on the temple's podium in the Fascist period, 1934–5.[62] In 1834 Luigi Canina started fresh excavations in the Forum of a structure which he correctly identified as the Basilica Julia. The reconstructed pier with an attached column which visitors see today was erected in the 1850s by his student, Pietro Rosa, an important figure whom we will encounter again[63] (Figure 11.12).

Figure 11.11 Taylor and Cresy, plate XC, *Capital of the Temple of Jupiter Stator*. Photo: author.

Figure 11.12 Reconstructed pier in Basilica Julia. Photo: Wikimedia Commons – MM/public domain.

In 1854, the French scheme for replanning the area around the Pantheon was to some extent implemented by Pope Pius IX. Between 1856 and 1858 he had re-erected the columns and architrave of the Portico of the Harmonious Gods (*Dei Consentes*) in the Forum[64] (Figure 11.13). The solution employed in the restoration of the Arch of Titus was repeated here, and no attempt at pastiche was made in the reconstruction. Even the additional columns added in 1942 were left unfluted, though the material of the architrave they support is original. The ancient columns are braced with unsightly rusted iron rings.

But despite these works of excavation and consolidation, the task of conserving the outdoor antiquities was in general patchy and dilatory. By mid-century, for instance, the English visitor William Forsyth complained that so little of the Forum had been excavated, reckoning that 'a body of English railway navigators would clear the whole space in a month... it does seem to be a disgrace to Rome that the whole of this spot, the cradle of her ancient glory, has not been excavated and thoroughly explored', if

Figure 11.13 Reconstructed Portico of the Harmonious Gods. Photo: Lalupa – own work, CC BY-SA 4.0.

the pope would only allow 'the diggings' to go on there.[65] Forsyth clearly had no idea of the cost of such diggings, nor did it occur to him that an ecclesiastical institution might have less worldly concerns. But his criticism also failed to take into account fresh notions of what merited the attention of the archaeologist.

Pius IX was in fact personally keen on archaeological investigation, and from 1848 he resumed the work of Pope Pius VI on the recovery of the original via Appia Antica, under the supervision of Canina. In 1855, under his authority, Pietro Ercole Visconti, son of the famous antiquarian Ennio Quirino Visconti, made rather random excavations within the town area of Rome's ancient port at Ostia at the mouth of the Tiber; this activity continued until 1870, when it was taken over by the Italian state. Russell Meiggs identified the principal motive for the work as the recovery of statuary, inscriptions and building material.[66] But once the excavations disclosed an attractive and substantial settlement, Ostia became an agreeable goal for day-trippers from Rome, as it remains to this day. Their interest prompted the construction of a site museum, which we may still visit.

The censorious Forsyth also failed to appreciate that contemporary archaeological activity in Rome was now being directed to a more systematic opening up of the underground tombs of Christians (or presumed Christians), known as the catacombs.[67] The instigator of these extensive works was the founder of Christian archaeology, Giovanni Battista De Rossi, who first investigated the Catacombs of Callixtus on the via Appia in 1850.[68] These and subsequently discovered catacombs became objects of considerable interest to both pilgrims and tourists, for whom they had to be made accessible. Presumably, resources were diverted from the care of the pagan monuments to the disclosure and presentation of the early Christian ones.

Roma Capitale

During the reign of Pius IX, Rome was absorbed in 1870 into the new Kingdom of Italy, and in the following year, to the chagrin of Florence, it became the national capital. The papacy went into a second sulky exile, this time confining itself within the Vatican City. The administration of the city of Rome became exclusively secular under the House of Savoy, which was determined to show itself worthier of its responsibilities than the ousted papacy. The new broom wielded by the northern interlopers swept very clean indeed, but not without complaints at the resultant tidiness.

The absorption of Rome into Italy entailed incalculable devastation of antiquities in the process of turning the old-fashioned papal city into a modern secular capital that might vie with its European peers.[69] The resident American sculptor William Wetmore Story feared Rome would be turned into a 'Brummagem Paris',[70] despite the gradual creation of archaeological zones and even an extensive *passeggiata* from the Forum to the Baths of Caracalla.[71] There was an undeniable need for new accommodation for the rapidly increasing population, and a now national government required buildings for its ministries and bureaucrats, all part of a process of secularisation and nation-building. Rome was no longer to present as ecclesiastical but as a part of modern secular Italy. The historic ruins, however, were not to be neglected in the process of modernisation. The impact of the new Italian state upon Roman archaeology is described by Stephen Dyson.[72] It was marked by a greater professionalism in the technology of excavation and in the presentation of the remains. A change of attitude to the purpose of excavation was effected under Pietro Rosa, the first director of the Soprintendenza agli Scavi e Monumenti della Provincia di Roma, established in 1870:[73] the recovery of statues and other valuables was less its object than the preservation of the monuments, which were to be seen as

historical documents (shades of Petrarch!) and clues to topographical studies. One of Rosa's ablest successors was Rodolfo Lanciani, who published a
stream of still engaging works of popularisation.[74] Lanciani was succeeded
by Giacomo Boni, who between 1899 and 1905 initiated the stratigraphic
approach to the excavation of the Forum, which disclosed the series of
frescos in S. Maria Antiqua (recently re-opened to the public in a splendid
display of contemporary museological wizardry) and the *lapis niger*, Black
Stone.[75] But there was a price, too high a price some felt, to be paid for the
modern approach to disclosing and displaying the ruins in the open air.

   We have already had a hint of this price in Mrs Eaton's regret that the
sod on which the marble had rested in the Forum was removed. Later in
the century, the indefatigable English travel-writer Augustus Hare never
missed an opportunity to bewail the condition of contemporary Rome
under what it pleased him to call the 'Sardinian Occupation' (the newly
minted kings of Italy were previously just the kings of Sardinia, though they
had their residence at Turin in Piedmont). His view was that 'while gaining
in historic interest, the forum ha[d] greatly lost in beauty since the recent
discoveries'. He reckoned that artists would regret the beautiful trees which
mingled with the temples, the cattle and peasants reposing in their shadow,
and above all the lovely vegetation which imparted light and colour to the
top of the ruins. He deplored the removal of every vestige of verdure as
it sprang up, leaving the appearance of nothing so much as a number of
ruined sheds in a ploughed field, with some fine columns interspersed. He
ended his tirade by quoting William Forsyth, to the effect that 'deep learning is generally the grave of taste'.[76]

   Hare's position – and he was by no means alone in adopting it, as David
Watkin noted[77] – was founded on a cornerstone of the now fully developed
aesthetic of ruin-mindedness, namely that ruination should be picturesque.
He spoke of the lament of artists, and he himself was an accomplished
watercolourist. The picturesque had now been sacrificed to scholarship and
science. His lament was echoed by W. D. Howells (again!), who paid a second visit to Rome in 1908, forty-three years after his first. The Forum still
left him unmoved: 'I cannot say that it is picturesque … it seems a hard-
ship that [stumps of columns] should not have been left lying in the kindly
earth or on it instead of being pulled up and set on end.'[78] The archaeologist
Rosa valued the ruins as historical documents which contributed to topographical research; their aesthetic appeal does not seem to have mattered to
him, as it had to hundreds of visitors for well over a century and a half. But
conservation was by now a pressing issue: vegetation growing in broken or
dislodged ashlar contributes to further damage, through water retention.

Frozen water expands as it thaws and can split stone work. So the vegetation had to be removed, according to the up-to-date professional archaeologist. And not just the archaeologist; at least one medical practitioner identified the presence of vegetation as a factor in the poisoned air (*mal'aria*) of the Colosseum and its district.[79] And so the ruin which suffered the greatest aesthetic loss from defoliation was the Colosseum.

The vast stone carcase of the Flavian Amphitheatre had over the centuries become embowered in shrubs, vines and flowering plants.[80] Serena Romano lists no fewer than four botanical studies of the ruin's vegetation, starting in the seventeenth century and including Richard Deakin's *The Flora of the Colosseum of Rome* (London, 1855).[81] The depictions of the ruin we have already seen in topographical studies or in paintings and engravings always faithfully reproduce the abundance of foliage draped over the shattered masonry. By the late eighteenth century and well into the nineteenth, in the heyday of the picturesque fashion, the Colosseum's verdure appealed strongly to artists. The German Franz Ludwig Catel depicted the structure during excavations in the 1820s. The architect Valadier bows while showing plans to Cardinal Consalvi (Figure 11.14). A number of contemporary English and Provençal artists, including Francis Towne,

Figure 11.14 Catel, 'Inside the Colosseum, 1822'. Photo: The Art Institute of Chicago/ CC0 public domain designation.

Jean-Antoine Constantin and his pupil François-Marius Granet, were also enthusiastic about the hanging garden on the stonework.[82]

In 1818 the poet Shelley started to compose a conversation piece set in the Colosseum, where a young woman described the lush vegetation to her blind father, transforming the circuit of arches and shattered stone into a scene of flowers, weeds, grass and moss.[83] Story described the building as he saw it in the 1860s in a finely rhetorical tricolon: 'thousands of beautiful flowers bloom in its ruined arches, tall plants and shrubs wave across the open spaces, and Nature has healed over the wounds of time with delicate grasses and weeds.'[84] One such plant, the ivy-leaved toadflax, now called *cymbalaria muralis*, had another common English name, Coliseum ivy, but its French name, *ruine-de-Rome*, is far more menacing (Figure 11.15).

Story's word-picture was effaced by Henry James in an essay entitled 'A Roman Holiday', written in February 1873, just three years after the beginning of the 'Sardinian occupation' of Rome: 'This roughly mountainous quality of the great ruin is its chief interest; beauty of detail has pretty well vanished, especially since the high-growing wild-flowers have been plucked away by the new government.'[85] Twenty years on, Augustus Hare was still lamenting the structure's shabby condition:

Figure 11.15 Toadflax in a wall in Frensham, Surrey, UK. Photo: author.

as late as thirty years ago, the interior of the Coliseum was (like that of an English abbey) an uneven grassy space littered with masses of ruin, amid which large trees grew and flourished. In the gaunt, bare, ugly interior of the Coliseum as it now is, it is difficult even to conjure up a recollection of the ruin so gloriously beautiful under the popes, where every turn was a picture.[86]

The loss of the picturesque quality was not compensated, for the likes of Hare, by the increase of knowledge: 'The excavations are of little interest, though they display the anatomy of the labyrinthine passages ... of the arena .... The excavations which have laid them bare have annihilated the beauty of the Coliseum.'[87]

Another monument which has undeniably suffered from the loss of vegetation (and worse) is one which it is safe to say very few tourists ever bother to track down, the so-called Temple of Minerva Medica.[88] In the eighteenth and early nineteenth centuries it was way out in the *disabitato* so that Vasi could call it very picturesque.[89] Mrs Eaton agreed, finding in the weeds that waved over the fallen masonry of the isolated building 'an interest and a charm it probably could never have owned in a state of perfect preservation' – a classic sentiment of ruin-mindedness: the ruin made an aesthetic appeal the complete structure would not have done.[90] The 'temple' attracted numerous artists, for instance the nineteenth-century German Adrian Ludwig Richter (Figure 11.16). Today the 'temple' is not only stripped of its softening vegetation but it also finds itself unfairly marooned, as Amanda Claridge put it, between a busy road and the railway tracks just outside the Termini station. No charm is left to a structure that had long captivated visitors and inspired architects and painters. It comes as no surprise that Augustus Hare, who first knew it in its once remote setting as 'indescribably picturesque', later dismissed it as not worth a visit[91] (Figure 11.17).

There is no way to reach a compromise between aesthetic appeal, now a foundation stone of ruin-mindedness, and scientific investigation and conservation, not to mention the need for modern infrastructure in an urban location. To this day, the ruins remain fairly bare, and such vegetation as gains a foothold in them owes its presence more to the neglect of the authorities than to any desire to restore a picturesque display. Perhaps the crucial consideration is that the ruins are being properly cared for, and care is the more urgent because they are now subject to the modern corrosives of stonework, acid rain and the exhaust of motor vehicles.[92]

Ruin-mindedness did not, however, exert universal appeal at the beginning of the twentieth century. There was an impassioned counter-offensive, which might be styled ruin-rage, mounted by the apostle of Italian Futurism

Figure 11.16 Richter, *View of the Temple of Minerva Medica*. Photo: Ablakok – own work/public domain – CCA-SA 4.0 International.

Figure 11.17 Contemporary view of the Temple of Minerva Medica. Photo: Lalupa, CC BY-SA 3.0.

Filippo Tommaso Marinetti. In 1909 Marinetti published his 'Manifesto of Futurism', in which he denounced Italy's absorption in its past (*passatismo*) and urged the modern nation-state to embrace the contemporary world and its future, whence the title of his manifesto. Among the objects of his scorn were the cities of Venice and Florence and Rome, the festering sores of the peninsula.[93] Rome in Marinetti's view languished under a 'leprosy of ruins', and its devotion to ruins was pilloried as *archeologismo*. Foreign tourists were the city's only lifeblood, and that in his view was a Bad Thing, because not Italian (there is an irony in Marinetti's nativism, since the manifesto was first published in Paris and in French). Marinetti's cure for the plague of ruin-mindedness was robust and original: he proposed to drive a motorcar at speed into the Arch of Constantine. That modern emblem of rapid mobility (one thinks of Mr Toad) would annihilate the ancient monument (or so Marinetti assumed; he and his four-cylinder Fiat sports car might not have survived the impact in one piece). Despite his sometimes cranky views – in his later futurist cookery book he notoriously proposed to ban pasta – his notion that contemporary Italy was ailing thanks to an absorption in its past artistic heritage was not peculiar to him. It was to be endorsed by Benito Mussolini and the Fascist political regime, with which Marinetti unsurprisingly flirted for many years. But whereas Marinetti wanted to obliterate the burdensome past, Mussolini saw a way of enhancing his own agenda by an appropriation of Rome's imperial past and above all of the city's incomparable ruins.

Mussolini's 'Liberation' of the Ruins

The founder of the Italian Fascist party and from 1922 to 1943 prime minister of the Kingdom of Italy, Benito Mussolini shared a view common among Italians of the day that Rome or rather contemporary Romans were lazy parasites, sucking resources from the rest of the country. He nonetheless reckoned that the historic city could be ransomed from its inhabitants, cleansed and refurbished, restored even to its Augustan and imperial glory, and so serve as an inspiration to a united and up-to-date Italy. This rededication of the nation's capital was to be achieved mainly by clearances around the 'millennial monuments' (including churches), and so in this respect Mussolini's urbanist schemes to some degree revived the uncompleted Napoleonic ones. The designated agent of revival, the archaeologist, was at times likened to a physician or rather to a surgeon, who removes cancerous growths to reclaim and restore a beloved body.[94] Antonio Maria

Colini's excavations of the Markets of Trajan in the 1920s, for instance, were defended as hygienic, bringing a breath of fresh air to a foetid sector of the city.

The major excavation projects of 1924–30 were the *fora* of Julius Caesar and of Augustus, the Forum and Markets of Trajan, with the via dell'Impero, now the via dei Fori Imperiali, driven over them,[95] the *area sacra* of Largo Argentina and the Theatre of Marcellus. The choice of buildings to be conserved was not haphazard as a rule, but focussed on the monumental and the imperial, so as to forge a link between the Rome of the emperors and the new empire of a Fascist Rome and Italy. But the reclamation of antiquity was not the whole story: just as the imperial *fora* had imposed a static geometric order on the urban space, so the Fascist regime would ensure motorised vehicular movement along splendid avenues, particularly the via dell' Impero and the via del Mare, both originating in the piazza Venezia. This road scheme too had precedent: Papal Rome oversaw the construction of the three great avenues radiating across the city from the piazza del Populo, but there had been no intention, as there clearly was in the Fascist period, to harmonise antiquity and modernity into a coherent entity.[96] The new highways of Fascist Rome opened up for the first time vistas of the most imposing ancient monuments, an achievement applauded by Guido Calza, an archaeologist who directed excavations in the Forum Romanum and on the Palatine hill, in an address to the Royal Institute of British Architects in 1934.[97] The downside was that the rectilinear avenues which produced the vistas were sometimes privileged over any antiquities that got in their way, and so in 1933 the *Meta Sudans* and in 1936 the brick-faced concrete base of the Colossus of Nero (both near the Colosseum) were obliterated.[98] Fascist Rome only had room for a particular sort of antiquity, and what did not fit the propagandist model was dispensed with in the names of modernity and of hygiene.

The case of the Largo di Torre Argentina and its row of four Republican victory-temples was, however, exceptional, since before their uncovering no one had imagined that so many temples existed in the area (one of them had been converted into a church, S. Nicola dei Cesarini or Calcarari (lime-burners)). This area in the centre of the *abitato* was a slum, and marked for clearance.[99] As the pickaxes started to do their work of destruction in 1926, the remains of the temples were disclosed, embedded in the modern rookeries. The temples were found to pre-date the imperial period, and since buildings of the Roman Republic were scarce, Mussolini personally decided not to proceed with the planned construction of an office complex. That the temples were recognised as votive offerings made by generals for successful military campaigns may also have favourably disposed the Duce to their preservation. So the site was excavated and landscaped as an archaeological park, which it remains to this day. The actual identity of the temples remains a matter for scholarly debate[100] (Figure 11.18).

At the same time, from 1926 to 1932, extensive works of excavation and isolation were undertaken on the Theatre of Marcellus, a structure initiated by Julius Caesar, and upon its completion by Augustus named after his nephew and son-in-law, untimely dead. The theatre's arcades were freed of the shops that had long occupied them, and the footings were exposed down to the ancient ground level. Following earlier conservation practice, a buttress was added and an extension of the arcades was constructed in a different material to give an idea of the original appearance[101] (Figure 11.19).

The chief reason for the elaborate work on this particular structure was the construction of the nearby highway to Ostia and the beaches, the via del Mare (now the via del teatro di Marcello). The road sweeps down from the piazza d'Aracoeli with the theatre in full view,[102] and it then veers past it to the left. The now isolated theatre, surmounted only by Baldassare Peruzzi's Palazzo Savelli-Orsini, which still crowns it, was intended to serve as a grand 'eye-catcher' for motorists approaching it from either direction. In

Figure 11.18 Temples in the Largo Argentina. Photo: Wikimedia Commons – Jastrow/public domain.

Figure 11.19 The Theatre of Marcellus. Photo: Palickap – own work, CC BY-SA 4.0.

1940, to complete the scenic impact of the area, the urban designer, Antonio Muñoz, who was Rome's director of antiquities and fine arts between 1928 and 1943, had three columns with entablature of the Temple of Apollo Sosianus re-erected, echoing the iconic corner grouping of the Temple of Vespasian in the Forum.[103] Thus yet again in Fascist Rome a modern piece of infrastructure, a superhighway, lived happily cheek by jowl with impressive public monuments of the Augustan city – no need for a Marinetti to ram them at speed.

It is instructive to leave Rome and pay a brief visit to Trieste, in the remote north-eastern corner of Italy, since a similar juxtaposition of ancient theatre and modern highway was engineered there too in the Fascist period. Trieste was known to the Romans as Tergeste, and the city's ancient theatre was discovered in 1814 in the modern town at the foot of the hill on which the Roman city was built. But it was not excavated until 1938, after the Fascist party had decided in 1934 to construct its local headquarters, the Casa del Fascio, in the older pre-Habsburg part of town, Cittavecchia, directly opposite the site of the Roman theatre (another instance of replacing the unhygienic dwellings in the area with something clean and up to date). Between the new building (which is now the Palazzo della Questura) and the freshly exposed Roman theatre, an arterial road was driven, the corso del Littorio (now the via del Teatro romano), just like the via del Mare in

Rome. In September 1938 Mussolini personally laid the foundation stone of the new building, the architects of which, Raffaello Battigelli and Ferruccio Spangaro, paid a gracious compliment to the curved auditorium of the theatre opposite by designing a convex portico on the flank facing the new road. So in Trieste as in Rome the Fascists aimed to forge a link between the Roman and the Italian empires, the ancient comfortably adjacent to the modern (Figure 11.20).

The Fascist fixation upon Augustus was most substantially realised in an ambitious project to 'liberate' the emperor's Mausoleum. Constructed by Augustus during his lifetime, it provided a resting place for the urns containing the ashes of members of his family. The purposes it served in later times, sketched by Amanda Claridge, were unpredictable: the Soderini family converted it into a garden during the sixteenth century, the garden became an arena for bull-fights and the Mausoleum finally served as a concert hall in the early twentieth century.[104] Works to recover its ancient core only began in earnest between 1936 and 1938, the aim being to have the restored tomb ready for the Mostra Augustea della Romanità of 1937–8, a celebration of the 2,000th anniversary of the birth of Augustus. In addition, the overall scheme for the site of the Mausoleum envisioned reconstruction of the fragments of the beautiful Ara Pacis Augustae, the Altar of Augustan Peace;[105] the restored altar was to be relocated near the conserved

Figure 11.20 Via del Teatro romano, Trieste. Photo: author.

Mausoleum. (It must also be said that the recovery of many of the altar's fragments buried under the Palazzo Fiano-Almagià on the Corso was a triumph of Italian engineering skill, described by Orietta Rossini in the official guidebook of 2006.)

Spiro Kostof, Borden Painter, Wolfgang Schieder, Stefan Altekamp, Joshua Arthurs and Stephen Dyson have all told the unhappy story of this dismal project to isolate the Mausoleum and to make it the centre-piece of an open reserve, enclosed by up-to-date, not historicist, buildings.[106] Hence the creation of the piazzale Augusto Imperatore, designed by Vittorio Ballio Morpurgo. The rebuilt Ara Pacis Augustae was re-sited in a nearby pavilion, also designed by Morpurgo, on the bank of the Tiber.[107] The complex was thus a characteristic use of Roman antiquity for Fascist ideological propaganda.[108] The clearances (*sventramenti*) necessary for the disclosure of the Mausoleum were typically justified as a sanitisation of the heart of the city.[109] Typical too was the public assurance that the works would provide employment, repeating unconsciously a reason for the French excavations in the Forum Romanum in the early nineteenth century. This scheme of urban renewal mainly failed because the Mausoleum, once freed from subsequent enhancement, proved to be, as Joshua Arthurs put it, more of a ruin than an impressive Augustan monument.[110] It was also isolated on what was to become a traffic-island, with motor vehicles whizzing round it.[111] The Ara Pacis too, for all the refinement of its embellishment and its historical interest, lacked what we would nowadays call the 'wow factor'; it was too fragmentary and too bijou, and the need to protect it within the shelter of another structure diminished its urban impact to zero. Attempts to find a new 'role' for the ruined Mausoleum, known as the 'rotten tooth' (*dente cariato*), have still proved difficult.[112] Renewed conservation work began in 2017, and the Mausoleum was supposed to reopen in April 2019; it opened in March 2021. The Ara Pacis Augustae, on the other hand, has since 2006 resided in a controversial pavilion designed by the American architect Richard Meier to replace Morpurgo's, which had weathered badly[113] (Figure 11.21).

Another disappointment from both archaeological and aesthetic points of view was the unwrapping, so to say, of the remains of the fourth-century A D Senate House (*Curia Julia*) in the Forum.[114] The original structure had been converted into the church of Sant' Adriano, consecrated in 630 by Pope Honorius I and given a Baroque makeover in 1653–6 by Martino Longhi the younger.[115] Between 1935 and 1938 the interior and exterior rinds were stripped away to reveal a plain brick cube. Apart from its fine *opus sectile* marble floor, the interior is one of the dreariest imaginable remains of ancient Rome[116] (Figure 11.22).

Figure 11.21 Meier, pavilion of the Ara Pacis. Photo: Manfred Heyde – own work, CC BY-SA 3.0.

Figure 11.22 Pavement of the Senate House. Photo: Rodrigo Caballero R. – own work, public domain.

Near the Roman Forum lies the Forum of Julius Caesar, which in 1932/3 became the object of excavation and restoration.[117] This Forum was visible from the new via dell'Impero, and so for the sake of the view from that triumphal boulevard, three columns were re-erected in the portico along with their entablature on the podium of the temple.[118] Those who post photographs on the internet often misidentify them as the columns and entablature of the Temple of Castor and Pollux, a pardonable lapse, since the decision to re-erect just a trio of columns and to crown them with a fragment of entablature was a deliberate echo of the iconic remains in the nearby Roman Forum, as Stefan Altekamp has shown[119] (Figure 11.23).

Another building in the Roman Forum partially reconstructed in 1930–1 is the round marble Temple of Vesta; following the precedent of Valadier, Alfonso Bartoli used travertine rather than the original Luna marble for the restored portions[120] (Figure 11.24).

The Fascist 'recovery' of imperial Rome thus met with mixed success: much was revealed for the first time and prominently displayed; much was brutally disposed of in pursuit of scenographic effect. There were even a few duds.

Figure 11.23 The Forum of Julius Caesar. Photo: Carole Raddato from FRANKFURT, Germany, CC BY-SA 2.0.

Figure 11.24 The Temple of Vesta, Roman Forum. Photo: Jebulon – own work, CC01.0 Universal public domain dedication.

Rome survived the Second World War largely unscathed, but post-war political, civic and economic reconstruction deflected attention from the care of the remains of antiquity, as Stephen Dyson has recently described.[121] The Fascist enthusiasm for Romanità had tarnished the esteem the once admired ruins so long enjoyed. The deterioration of this cultural heritage had become so marked by the late 1970s that the pressing need for consolidation and conservation could no longer be ignored or delayed.[122]

Efforts are now being made to devise a more sympathetic reconfiguration of the archaeological area between the Colosseum and the piazza Venezia,[123] but discord between the Italian state and the city of Rome over the ownership of the central archaeological sites, as described by Matthew Nicholls, is likely to prolong the problem of satisfactory presentation of the major ruins.[124]

*

This chapter has traced the development of an entirely new and unpredictable sense of the value of ruins. Thanks above all to tourism, it gradually became clear to the papal authorities that provision must be made both for the conservation and for the attractive presentation of such remains of Roman antiquities as could not be housed in museums. Provision had long been made for portable objects, works of sculpture in marble and bronze, mosaics and inscriptions. The latter in particular had historical value, while the former made an aesthetic appeal. All such objects could easily be removed from their find sites and brought into collections. Private collections had existed since the Renaissance, and the papal collection, exhibited in the famous Belvedere in the Vatican palace, was one such. But in the eighteenth century the Vatican also housed the Pio-Clementino Museum, which was designed to be regularly open to the visiting public. So far, so commendably customary. An unprecedented step was taken with the deliberate isolation of large structures in the open air that could not be easily moved. Isolation was an early means of conservation, which aimed to reduce the risk of damage, accidental or deliberate.

The next step, equally unprecedented for buildings, was restoration, which raised issues of method, as we saw in the case of the Arch of Titus. It would have been easy (but expensive) to produce a pastiche replica of the vanished portions, but Stern and Valadier preferred an evocation of the original structure. Its proportions and design were recoverable thanks to the regularity of classical architecture, and that was what the architects provided, with a change of the original building material and omission of the refined detail. This sensible practice became the standard in Rome, as we see in the 'spurs' (*speroni*) or buttresses used to stabilise the broken perimeter walls of the Colosseum and the Theatre of Marcellus. Stern produced a massive but rather forbidding brick structure, whereas Valadier more gracefully integrated his brick buttress into the remains of the wall he shored up, a scheme replicated a century later for the Theatre of Marcellus. The Roman practice, unusual at the time, later became standard more widely in Europe wherever the need was felt for the conservation and preservation of historic buildings or ruins. In this way, too, it was the ruins of Rome which provided the impulse and inspiration for the care of ruins elsewhere.

12 | Literary Responses to the Ruins

Up to now, the development of an aesthetic response to and engagement with the ruins of Rome in the fine arts of painting and architecture has been charted. What, moreover, may be called the applied arts of garden design and the plastic representations of ruins in cork and other materials (such as mosaic) have also been described. But from time to time, literary works have been cited as well because they helped fuel the development of an emotional aspect of ruin-mindedness: an elegy by Hildebert of Lavardin (Chapter 3, pp. 41–2), an epigram by Pope Pius II (Chapter 5, pp. 85–6), a 'literary' letter of Petrarch's (Chapter 4, pp. 56–7), Chrysoloras' rhetorical comparison (Chapter 4, pp. 63–4), the famous treatise of Poggio (Chapter 5, pp. 75–6) and the novel of Madame de Staël (Chapter 4, pp. 60–1) – all have transmitted to posterity a personal and often powerful emotional response to the ruins of Rome in language designed to evoke an echo from a reader. In fact, the literary response to the ruins becomes something of a trope in the Renaissance, when a considerable amount of poetry about the ruins was produced in Latin. Thereafter the ruins figured in vernacular literatures, especially once travel became more generally convenient. This chapter will provide a more detailed account of the many and varied imaginative responses to the ruination of Rome.

The Florentine humanist Cristoforo Landino completed a three-book collection of Latin poems, entitled *Xandra*, ca. 1460.[1] Towards the end of the second book, Landino lamented that his mistress, Xandra, had made a bolt for Rome and he of course pursued her (he had in fact spent about six months there in early 1446). The penultimate poem (29) is addressed to the letter he is writing to a friend back in Florence: if the friend wants to know what Landino is up to, the poetic epistle is to say that he is studying the city's remains (*relliquias*), an occupation which brings tears to his eyes. In the thirtieth and last poem of the book, entitled *De Roma fere diruta* ('Rome Almost Obliterated'), Landino listed a number of vanished structures, such as the Circus Maximus and the Temple of Apollo on the Palatine hill, the dedication of which was celebrated in a poem of Propertius' (4.6). Of the lofty Colosseum, he predicted its imminent pulverisation into chalk for cement.[2] He concluded by saying that if Augustus were to rise from the dead and walk across the city, he would find none of the buildings he commissioned, something of an exaggeration, as the Mausoleum of Augustus had already been identified as such.

In the 1470s, Ugolino Verino, a pupil of Landino's, wrote an epic poem on Charlemagne entitled *Carlias*. It merits a word, thanks to its recent publication.[3] In the fifteenth and final book of the epic, Charlemagne is taken on a guided tour of the ruinous landscape of the ancient city (xv.243–72). The unexpected feature of the tour is its foregrounding of the remains of the ancient city, something a contemporary tourist would want to see (like Charlemagne's successor Sigismund in 1433 (see Chapter 5, p. 78). Verino himself apparently never visited Rome, and so his topographical knowledge was entirely derived from books, such as the *Mirabilia* and Flavio Biondo's more up-to-date treatise, *Roma instaurata*. In a fuller alternative version of the tour, he regarded the ruination of the pagan city as the penalty paid for the vice and idleness (*desidia*) of its inhabitants; the new Christian city is what attracts the nations.[4] The ruins thus become admonitory, and serve as a warning, a common theme in the poetry of ruins down the ages.

Mention was made in Chapter 5 (p. 85) of Pope Sixtus IV's recycling of stone from the Colosseum for the construction of a brand new bridge across the Tiber, now known as the Ponte Sisto, in 1473–9. This spoliation met with opposition from humanists, one of whom, Evangelista Fausto Capodiferro, a pupil of Pomponio Leto, composed an epigram reviling the act. Frances Muecke has edited and discussed the text in a valuable article on contemporary neo-Latin poetry about Rome's ruins.[5]

In 1513, Andrea Fulvio completed a two-book poem in Latin, entitled *Antiquaria Urbis*, which he dedicated to Giovanni de' Medici, Pope Leo X. According to Frances Muecke, who has provided it with context and compared it to contemporary studies, it is the only poem of the early sixteenth century devoted entirely to a topographical description of Rome, including the ruins (it is here cited from Bottari 1720: v.155–231, by page and line number on each page, there being generally thirty-eight lines per page).[6] The poem so pleased the pope that he encouraged Fulvio to deal with the antiquities at greater length and in prose, the motivation for the work published in 1527 (see Chapter 5, p. 82). The poem belongs to the humanist tradition of didactic epos, and Fulvio, the *antiquarius Romanus* as he later styled himself, took his instructive function very seriously.[7] As a student of Pomponio Leto, whose house he located for the reader (205.25), he made considerable use of his master's topographical researches, sometimes, however, parting company with him where he felt he had more accurate information.[8]

Fulvio drew extensively upon ancient sources, for instance Strabo (170.16, where he even provided the book number, 5, 172.32 for the paving of the via Appia in 312 BC), Varro (at 174.34, the information on the earliest names of the Capitoline hill comes from *De lingua Latina* 5.42), Livy, Pliny the Elder and the bogus 'P. Victor'. He also cited epigraphical evidence to identify the Pyramid of Cestius, with its 'ell-long' letters (*litterae cubitales*, 223.28–33). He noted that the so-called Porta Exquilia was not really a city gate but the arch of an aqueduct, identified as such by an inscription (*epigramma* 170.13). He also frankly admitted to uncertainty or even to ignorance. After describing the pile of the so-called Temple of Minerva Medica, which, despite its ruined dome (*ruinosae ... testudinis*), he deemed a second Pantheon (187.19–26), he made a stab at identifying it as a monument built by Augustus in honour of his grandsons Gaius and Lucius, citing Suetonius for the information, *Life of Augustus* 29.4. That was a bad call because that basilica and portico were in the Forum.[9] Anyway, he conscientiously recorded that others thought the remains were of *thermae*, as indeed contemporary topographers styled it 'Terme di Galluccie'.[10] As regards another *thermae* complex, he allowed that he had no idea who built it; the remains were to be seen on the Caelian hill near the church of SS. Giovanni e Paolo and the so-called Graecostasis (181.25–6). Fulvio is clearly describing the immense platform of the Temple of Deified Claudius.[11]

In the first book, Fulvio provided a rapid survey of Rome's history from its foundation to the sovereignty of the popes, a clue to the poem's comprehensive character (158–67). He then rehearsed the circuit of the walls with its many gates, and then the hills of the city (174–91). In the second book, the material is organised topically: bridges (200–1), aqueducts (202), triumphal arches (206), theatres (207–9), obelisks (220) and libraries (222), and then some of the most imposing individual monuments are accorded separate accounts, for instance the Colosseum (209). Fulvio then moved to the Campus Martius (224) and described the great remains still to be seen there, especially the Mausoleum of Augustus (226) and the Pantheon with its lavishly marbled interior (following in the footsteps of the Roman poet Statius, *Silvae* 1.2.148–51, 1.5.34–41, 2.2.85–93, Fulvio eagerly listed the exotic marbles of the ancient city; 227–8).[12] He drew attention (226.25–33) to 'the large recently disinterred pedestal' ('ampla basis nuper tellure effossa') on which stood an obelisk, which served as the gnomon of the *Horologium Augusti* ('a barber digging a latrine in the time of Pope Julius II (1503–13) 70 m SW of S. Lorenzo hit the pedestal', which was reburied).[13]

It turns out, however, that despite the title, the material covered in the poem is not exclusively 'antique', though it is true that many of Rome's grandest basilicas are justifiably regarded as antique, since they were founded in the fourth century by Constantine and members of his family. Fulvio seems rather to be celebrating Rome's distinction both in the pagan past and in the papal present. For example, he expatiated upon Bramante's design and current work on the new S. Peter's (195.35), a structure he felt would cast the Pantheon into the shade (196). He also dwelt on Bramante's Belvedere in the Vatican, recently adorned with the famous statues of Apollo and Laocoon (196.35–197). The splendour of the ancient city is mirrored or recovered in the contemporary. In some ways the poem thus might have served as a guidebook to the city, regarded as an entity, not to be divided between then and now.

Baldassare Castiglione, who, it will be recalled, helped Raphael 'brief' Pope Leo X on the parlous state of the ruins of Rome (see Chapter 5, p. 87), composed a sonnet in 1503, 'Superbi colli et voi sacre ruine', on the triumph of time over the works of man; it was printed in 1547. It was set to music by Girolamo Conversi in 1584 and translated into French by Joachim du Bellay (Sonnet vii of the *Antiquités* cycle).[14]

> You lofty hills and sacred ruins,
> No longer bearing aught but the name of Rome,
> What pitiful vestiges you now display
> Of so many rare and sublime minds!
>
> Colossi, arches, theatres, divine works,
> Monuments to glorious and joyful triumphs,
> All reduced to a little ash,
> You tell but a mean tale to the common herd.
>
> Thus, although for a while works once renowned
> may resist the ravages of time, still, little by little,
> envious time destroys them and the very memory that they once were.
>
> Then let me live content among my torments,
> For if all earthly things must yield to time,
> Perchance my suffering too will have an end. (Translation: Mick
>   Swithinbank)

The ruination wrought by the passage of time upon even the most impressive of man's constructions encourages the writer to hope that his torments (unspecified, but perhaps erotic) will also come to an end. Rome's ruins here offer consolation.

Giovanni Vitale of Palermo, or in the better-known Latin form of his name Janus Vitalis, composed a sonnet-length elegy which was published in his *Elogia* of 1552/3.[15] The poem caught the fancy of many later poets who imitated or translated it well into the twentieth century.[16] Vitalis, like Castiglione, named no specific structure, a silence that became something of a commonplace in the poetry of ruination:[17] meditations on the flight of time as evidenced in the general ruination of the ancient city dominate, without focus on identifiable remains. In the final couplet Vitalis points a moral with an insistent imperative, *Disce hinc*, 'Learn from this' – the ruins have now become didactic, with a lesson to impart.

Vitalis' famous poem, or a version of it, was promptly put into French by Joachim du Bellay in his collection entitled *Antiquités de Rome* (1558), sonnet III;[18] his version was in its turn englished by Edmund Spenser and published in 1591. The ruin-poetry of these two can be conveniently considered in tandem, but first a preliminary word about Du Bellay himself is necessary. He went to Rome as the private secretary of his brother Jean Cardinal du Bellay in 1553. He found the contemporary city morally corrupt. The ruins were interpreted by him as material symbols of the once high civilisation of antiquity which the modern city lacked – he was also homesick! So when he said that Rome was not Rome, he meant that modern Rome was a degeneration from the ancient one (not at all the point of Vitalis' sonnet). The sonnet collection served therefore as a personal meditation upon decline, symbolised by ruination. Sabine Forero-Mendoza noted that Du Bellay had no time for specific ruins, but employed instead a generalised yet suggestive terminological vagueness:[19] ruins, structures, monuments, dust, ashes, all without specific names or locations. He thus etherialised ruination, producing a disturbing antithesis between the splendid past and its current state of decay. Du Bellay's contemplation of Rome's ruins was a meditation more upon the movement of history than the vagaries of Fortune. In the collection of sonnets, pretty much every possible cause for the fall of Rome was canvassed: hubris, idleness, moral decay, divine punishment, astrology, historic cycles, civil wars, barbarian invasions and *translatio imperii*, 'the transfer of imperial power'.

Du Bellay also had in mind a sort of subtext to his record of the depressing physical remains of a once splendid built environment, namely the still extant glories of ancient Latin poetry ('ses escrits, qui son los le plus beau', sonnet v.12). These he aimed to rival in modern French, which he was confident could match the standard set by the Latin of old. Granted success in that initiative, he could be confident that his sonnets would endure just as well as the Latin poetry which bore the image of Rome around the world.

What attracted Edmund Spenser too was the prospect of improving English as a literary language, as literary as Latin (or indeed as Du Bellay's contemporary French), and so perhaps as enduring. The conviction that literature, especially poetry, outlasts material monuments was paramount, a notion we find at the end of sonnet v. As Anne Janowitz has remarked, 'the ruins do not serve an aesthetic but a mytho-historical order', and the fame of empire is preserved and prolonged not by material ruins but in the poetry about them.[20] Here is Spenser's version of Du Bellay's version of Vitalis:

> Thou stranger, which for *Rome* in *Rome* here seekest,
> And nought of *Rome* in *Rome* perceiv'st at all,
> These same olde walls, olde arches, which thou seest,
> Olde Palaces, is that which *Rome* men call.
> Behold what wreak, what ruine, and what wast,
> And how that she, which with her mightie powre
> Tam'd all the world, hath tam'd herself at last,
> The pray of time, which all things doth devowre.
> *Rome* now of *Rome* is th' only funerall,
> And onely *Rome* of *Rome* hath victorie;
> Ne ought save *Tyber* hastning to his fall
> Remains of all: O worlds inconstancie.
> That which is firme doth flit and fall away,
> And that is flitting, doth abide and stay.

After the sixteenth century, there is apparently little or nothing in the way of ruin-poetry. Revival unsurprisingly occurs about the time when the Grand Tour is in full swing. Joseph Addison's verse epistle, 'A Letter from Italy', was written in 1701 on his way home from a tour of the country, a tour more fully described in a prose account, *Remarks on Several Parts of Italy*, published in 1705. Some of the leading traits of ruin-mindedness are combined in the following extract (lines 69–82):[21]

> Immortal glories in my mind revive,
> And in my soul a thousand passions strive,
> When Rome's exalted beauties I descry
> Magnificent in piles of ruin lie.
> An amphitheatre's amazing height
> Here fills my eye with terror and delight,
> That on its public shows unpeopled Rome,
> And held uncrowded nations in its womb:
> Here pillars rough with sculpture pierce the skies:
> And here the proud triumphal arches rise,

> Where the old Romans' deathless acts display'd,
> Their base degenerate progeny upbraid:
> Whole rivers here forsake the fields below,
> And wond'ring at their height through airy channels flow.

Addison announces the lively stimulation both of his imagination ('in my mind') and his emotions ('a thousand passions') at the sight of Rome's major ancient monuments (the Colosseum, historiated columns, triumphal arches, aqueducts). The 'magnificent' ruins now have a high aesthetic quality, 'exalted beauties'. But two lines – 'Where the old Romans' deathless acts display'd, / Their base degenerate progeny upbraid' – draw attention, not for the first time, to the writer's conviction of the degeneration of contemporary Rome from its ancient virtue. It is later explained that the degeneracy is entirely due to the 'proud oppression' and 'tyranny' of Italy's governments. To highlight this, Addison goes on to invoke Liberty, a 'goddess … Britannia's isle adores'. The British reader is thus urged to be grateful for their country's liberty and, somewhat unexpectedly, to maintain a balance of power in continental Europe. To revert to the ruins: they now scold the 'base progeny' of the 'old' Romans, who presumably would applaud the contemporary Briton.

Later in the eighteenth century, a Welsh clergyman, John Dyer, who was briefly introduced in Chapter 6 (p. 115), echoed Addison's warning to maintain British liberty after a visit to Rome. As a young man, Dyer had aspired to be a painter, but lack of support in that line prompted a transfer of his 'picturesque' skills to poetry. He secured a considerable reputation with his descriptive poem 'Grongar Hill' (1726). His visit to Rome in 1724–6 left him with reflections about the growing English empire as in some measure similar to that of Rome. Rome's fall, however, as symbolised by its present ruinous state, provided the sort of lesson the English had better learn. This lesson Dyer set out to teach in his epyllion, 'The Ruins of Rome' (1740). Dyer was the first to revive the subgenre of ruin-poetry since the Renaissance, though he may not have been aware that he was 'reviving' it, since he owes little, if anything, to either Du Bellay or Spenser,[22] though he does quote four lines from Vitalis' poem as the epigraph to his own. Like his predecessors, he was awed by the general ruinous appearance of what was left of the ancient city, but he did not hesitate to focus on particular structures, probably because they allowed him to deploy his frustrated artistic skills in descriptive passages, for instance this on the Colosseum:

> Amid the towery ruins, huge, supreme,
> Th' enormous amphitheatre behold,

Mountainous pile! o'er whose capacious womb
Pours the broad firmament its varied light;   150
While from the central floor the seats ascend
Round above round, slow-widening to the verge,
A circuit vast and high; nor less had held
Imperial Rome and her attendant realms,
When, drunk with rule, she willed the fierce delight,
And ope'd the gloomy caverns, whence out-rushed
Before th' innumerable shouting crowd
The fiery, madded, tyrants of the wilds,
Lions and tigers, wolves and elephants,
And desperate men, more fell. Abhorr'd intent!   160
By frequent converse with familiar death,
To kindle brutal daring apt for war;
To lock the breast, and steel th' obdurate heart
Amid the piercing cries of sore distress
Impenetrable.

In the exclamation, 'abhorr'd intent', he voiced a passionate moral criticism of that Roman blood-lust which the amphitheatre was built to satisfy, a criticism which became increasingly common in the later eighteenth
and well into the nineteenth centuries, as seen in the writing of Byron and
Hawthorne.[23] The fame of Dyer's description was such that a party of ladies
'of the first distinction' who visited Dubourg's Classical Exhibition of cork
models in 1785 recited passages from it (see Chapter 8, 200–1).[24]

Dyer then went on to describe the Pantheon, a structure recognised as
aesthetically pleasing, albeit most regrettably 'with erroneous aim / raised'
to the worship of false gods. At any rate, considered purely as architecture, it
provided a model for aspirant British architects, thus combining usefulness
with beauty:

And next regard yon venerable dome,
Which virtuous Latium, with erroneous aim
Raised to her various deities, and named
Pantheon; plain and round; of this our world no   180
Majestic emblem; with peculiar grace,
Before its ample orb, projected stands
The many-pillared portal; noblest work
Of human skill: here, curious architect,
If thou assay'st, ambitious, to surpass
Palladius, Angelus, or British Jones,
On these fair walls extend the certain scale,
And turn th' instructive compass: careful mark
How far in hidden art the noble plain

> Extends, and where the lovely forms commence   190
> Of flowing sculpture: nor neglect to note
> How range the taper columns, and what weight
> Their leafy brows sustain: fair Corinth first
> Boasted their order which Callimachus
> (Reclining studious on Æsopus' banks
> Beneath an urn of some lamented nymph)
> Haply composed; the urn with foliage curled
> Thinly concealed, the chapiter [= capital] informed.

In the epic's final lines, Dyer read Britain a sermon against luxury.[25] 'Liberty' is, as it was for Addison, the keyword: the Romans had lost it, and the British must learn the lesson and hang on to it. It is significant that the Roman heroes Dyer named – he seems to be gazing at busts of them, or statues – all lived under the Republic, not the empire. Dyer adduces the reason for the Romans' loss of their liberty: they sold it for a life of luxury, another snare the mercantile Briton must avoid:

> O Britons, O my countrymen, beware;   511
> Gird, gird your hearts; the Romans once were free …
>   O luxury,   535
> Bane of elated life, of affluent states,
> What dreary change, what ruin is not thine?
> How doth thy bowl intoxicate the mind!
> To the soft entrance of thy rosy cave
> How dost thou lure the fortunate and great!
> Dreadful attraction! while behind thee gapes
> Th' unfathomable gulph where Ashur lies
> O'erwhelm'd, forgotten; and high-boasting Cham;
> And Elam's haughty pomp; and beauteous Greece;
> And the great queen of earth, imperial Rome.   545

So for Dyer, as for Addison, the experience of meditating upon the ruins of Rome generated a lesson which, if not learned by his countrymen, might lead to a like decay of a once great empire. Dyer's poem also marks a stage in the development of a new sensibility in the eighteenth century, the cult of sentiment and of melancholy, which would become characteristic elements of later romanticism. Walther Rehm and most recently Susan Stewart have drawn attention to this novel feature of the poet's sentiment, found expressly in lines 344–55:[26]

> There is a mood
> (I sing not to the vacant and the young),
> There is a kindly mood of melancholy,

> That wings the soul, and points her to the skies:
> …
> How musical! When all-devouring Time,
> Here sitting on his throne of ruins hoar,
> While winds and tempests sweep his various lyre,
> How sweet they diapason, Melancholy!

Dyer's sentimental response to the ruins of Rome would be developed by his successors.

After Dyer, there was only a small crop of English ruin-poets, who are given a sympathetic reading by Bruce Swaffield,[27] who fairly reckons that, albeit undistinguished, they also prepared the way for the romantic ruin-poetry of the early nineteenth century. Oxford University set at least two ruins themes for its Newdigate prize. In 1818, Thomas Holden Ormerod won the prize with a poem on 'The Coliseum', and he surely deserves applause for lines 11–12, in which admiration for the bonding of the stonework is neatly expressed:[28]

> Though spoil'd by rapine of their binding brass,
> Self-pois'd they hang an uncemented mass.

In 1824, John Thomas Hope's poem on 'The Arch of Titus' secured the prize.[29]

It is unarguable that the ruins of Rome had their most transforming effect on one young Englishman, Edward Gibbon. They provided him with a lifetime's task and immortal fame. Gibbon started on his Grand Tour in 1763, and in his autobiography he described how and where the idea of writing his masterpiece first came to him:[30] 'It was in Rome, on the fifteenth October 1764, as I sat musing amidst the ruins of the Capitol, while the bare-footed friars were singing vespers in the Temple of Jupiter, that the idea of writing the Decline and Fall of the City first started to my mind.' Whatever the accuracy of the details in this claim, there can really be no doubt that it was the intoxication – Gibbon's own word – of finally seeing and treading 'with lofty step the ruins of the Forum' that wrought upon the young Gibbon and turned him into the historian of the protracted decline of Rome and of its empire.[31] In the final chapter of the history, the seventy-first, given at last to the world and to posterity in 1788, Gibbon again described the scene which had inspired his life's work, and he donned the mantle of Poggio in offering an account of how the city became ruinous. The inclusion of that account was entirely appropriate because it was the ruins which inspired the theme of the history in the first place.

Gibbon's famous account in its turn affected a young American visitor to Rome, Henry Adams, scion of a distinguished New England family.[32] After his graduation from Harvard College, Adams, for lack of any more specific vocation, continued his desultory education in Europe. He visited Italy in 1860 and reached Rome in May of that year. His description of the impact of the city and of its ruins upon his aimless spirit is matchless.[33] It should be borne in mind that back in the United States of 1860 there was quite as much ferment as in the Italy of the same year. Adams, the future historian of the childhood of the new Republic, was led by the passage in Gibbon's memoir to sit in the same place, upon the steps of the church of S. Maria di Ara Coeli, and ponder. Strongly moved, like Gibbon, he recorded that 'no one, priest or politician, could honestly read in the ruins of Rome any other certain lesson than that they were evidence of the just judgements of an outraged God against all the doings of man'. The ruins read Adams the lesson that Roman history was a record of immorality, but not only that: 'Rome was actual; it was England; it was going to be America.' (In 1861, Adams served as private secretary to his father, then the American ambassador in London; hence his inclusion of imperial England in the sequence of *translatio imperii*.) Gibbon, Adams maintained, had not gained an inch towards explaining the Fall. Adams presumably had in mind Gibbon's mistimed presumption that in the late eighteenth century no people would relapse into their original barbarism. For Adams, the city of Rome with its ruins remained a witness of the failures of all the great experiments of Western civilisation. This scathing critique represents less the opinions of the youthful Adams of 1860 than those of the deeply disillusioned Adams at the time of writing in 1905. At any rate, he clearly foresaw in the ruins of Rome the decline of England and then of his own homeland. Thus for both Edward Gibbon and Henry Adams the ruins provided a sort of 'careers advice' service, and turned them into historians. Reflection upon the ruins also compelled Adams to engage with and repudiate Gibbon's theory of the decline and fall which had produced them.

To return now to chronology and the late eighteenth century, tourists tended to gaze upon the ruins with the eyes of romance. A hallmark of the romantic sensibility is the attraction of the night, especially a moonlit night. It is in the late eighteenth century that visiting the ruins, especially the Colosseum, by moonlight became a trope of tourism. Serena Romano has perhaps tracked down the first reference to such a nocturnal visit in a letter of Philippina, Lady Knight to her friend Mrs Drake, dated 11 July 1778.[34] From that time on, every self-respecting tourist succumbed to what

Romano has engagingly called the 'lunar passion' (*passione lunare*), and viewed the Colosseum by moonlight; Annabel Barber extracts from a letter of J. B. S. Morritt to his aunt dated 29 March 1796 a brief account of such a visit on 'one of the finest moonlight nights ever beheld'.[35] Among the most famous was the poet Goethe, who described the visit he made by moonlight in early February of 1787 to the Colosseum (which was barred for the night) in his *Italian Journey* (see Chapter 8, p. 196), a work not published, however, until 1816–17.[36] In chapter 33 of Alexandre Dumas' novel *The Count of Monte Cristo* (1844–6), set in the early 1830s, Franz proposes to take his friend Albert a roundabout way to the moonlit Colosseum, thus avoiding the preliminary sites of the Capitol and the Forum with its arches and temples. They arrive at the beginning of chapter 34, which is devoted to their visit. The southern moonlight is said to make the vast proportions of the stupendous ruins appear twice as large.

The most influential populariser of nocturnal ruin visits must be George Gordon, Lord Byron, who stayed in Rome for nearly a month, from 29 April to 20 May 1817. His aesthetic impressions of the moonlit Colosseum were expressed by Manfred, in the act III, scene iv monologue of the eponymous tragedy *Manfred* (1816–17):

> I do remember me, that in my youth,
> When I was wandering, – upon such a night
> I stood within the Coliseum's wall
> 'Midst the chief relics of almighty Rome;
> The trees which grew along the broken arches
> Waved dark in the blue midnight, and the stars
> Shone through the rents of ruin ...
> But the gladiators' bloody Circus stands,
> A noble wreck in ruinous perfection,
> While Cæsar's chambers, and the Augustan halls,
> Grovel on earth in indistinct decay.
> And thou didst shine, thou rolling Moon, upon
> All this, and cast a wide and tender light,
> Which softened down the hoar austerity
> Of rugged desolation, and filled up,
> As 'twere anew, the gaps of centuries;
> Leaving that beautiful which still was so,
> And making that which was not – till the place
> Became religion, and the heart ran o'er
> With silent worship of the Great of old, –
> The dead, but sceptred, Sovereigns, who still rule
> Our spirits from their urns.

More extensive is Byron's account of his own visit to Rome in the fourth Canto of *Childe Harold's Pilgrimage* (April 1818), starting at stanza lxxviii. The poet contemplated the ruins of Rome in stanza lxxx: 712–20:

> The Goth, the Christian, Time, War, Flood, and Fire,
> Have dwelt upon the seven-hilled city's pride;
> She saw her glories star by star expire,
> And up the steep barbarian monarchs ride,
> Where the car climbed the Capitol; far and wide
> Temple and tower went down, nor left a site:
> Chaos of ruins! who shall trace the void,
> O'er the dim fragments cast a lunar light,
> And say, 'here was, or is', where all is doubly night?

'Doubly night' advances the notion that the ruins are beyond identification, wrapped as they are by 'Night's daughter, Ignorance' (stanza lxxxi). In a subsequent stanza, lxxxii, Byron intimated that Latin literature would survive the decay of Rome's material culture: Livy's pictured page, Cicero's voice and Virgil's lay would be 'Rome's resurrection'. (Horace had not come off quite so well in the justly famous stanzas lxxiv–vii.) But by stanza cx, the poet had changed his tune, and addressed a 'nameless column with the buried base' in the Forum, which he now found more eloquent than Cicero (lines 982–4). This crucial passage is taken to expose a tension within Byron's value system.[37] Previously Cicero's eloquence was reckoned an engine of 'Rome's resurrection', but faced now with the 'nameless column' in the Forum, the poet deemed 'Tully not so eloquent as' it, a debilitating reversal of sentiment.[38] To account for this reversal, we have to go back to the beginning of the canto, where in stanza xxv the poet proposed 'to meditate amongst decay, and stand / a ruin amidst ruins' (lines 218–19), in effect his self-identification with what he would be gazing at once in Rome. This solipsistic response to Rome's extensive ruination is interpreted as a hint at Byron's anxiety that his own poetic powers were failing.[39] Thus the ruins inspired in him a sense of personal futility, a metaphor for decline. Literary success was after all as fragile as marble. It is, however, hard to be entirely confident of such an interpretation, since by stanza cxii Cicero's 'immortal accents' still 'glow' in the Forum.

But to return to that 'nameless' column in the Forum, by the time of Byron's visit it had in fact been disinterred and even named, as that of Phocas, once its base along with its dedicatory inscription had been exposed by the French excavators a few years before, in 1813.[40] Further on (lines 986–7) the poet asked:

> Whose arch or pillar meets me in the face,
> Titus or Trajan's? No – 'tis that of Time.

The answer had long been plain enough: the arch is that of Titus, identifiable by the relief sculpture of the spoils of Jerusalem, and the pillar is Trajan's column, adorned with the carved scenes of his victories. Byron preferred, as a romantic poet must, that it all be Time's mystery, an irretrievable past.[41] His attitude was the polar opposite to that of Petrarch and of Madame de Staël, who wanted the remains to have recognisable names so that they could be embedded securely within Rome's cultural and historical context. Despite Byron's embrace of Ignorance in *Childe Harold* IV, the poem generated a digressive commentary written by his friend John Cam Hobhouse (1816 and 1818). Hobhouse was better informed than the poet, and even printed the whole of the inscription on the base of the Column of Phocas (1818: 106 and 240–1), but, as a fellow 'Trinity man', he tactfully inserted this information in parts of his commentary that did not draw attention to what Carolyn Springer has fairly called Byron's anti-archaeological bias in stanza cx.[42]

The core of the canto is the sustained meditation upon the Colosseum in stanzas cxxviii–cxlv. Timothy Webb found in Byron's imaginative interpretation of the structure a focus of his personal concerns that was complicated and perhaps contradictory.[43] Nonetheless, among its most enduringly famous passages are the romantic 'nocturnals', stanzas cxxviii–ix and cxliii–iv, lines 1147–52 and 1286–96:

> Arches on arches! as it were that Rome,
> Collecting the chief trophies of her line,
> Would build up all her triumphs in one dome,
> Her Coliseum stands; the moonbeams shine
> As 'twere its natural torches, for divine
> Should be the light which streams here, to illume
> This long explored but still exhaustless mine
> Of contemplation; and the azure gloom
> Of an Italian night, where the deep skies assume
> Hues which have words, and speak to ye of heaven,
> Floats o'er this vast and wondrous monument,
> And shadows forth its glory. …
> When the colossal fabric's form is neared
> It will not bear the brightness of the day,
> Which streams too much on all, years, man, have reft away.
>
> But when the rising moon begins to climb
> Its topmost arch, and gently pauses there;
> When the stars twinkle through the loops of time,
> And the low night-breeze waves along the air,
> The garland-forest, which the grey walls wear,
> Like laurels on the bald first Caesar's head;

When the light shines serene, but doth not glare,
Then in this magic circle raise the dead:
Heroes have trod this spot – 'tis on their dust ye tread.

Manfred and *Childe Harold* made a nocturnal visit to the moonlit Colosseum
central to the nineteenth-century experience of the building. The American
Edgar Allan Poe never visited Rome but that did not deter him from com-
posing a poem, 'The Coliseum', in 1833 in which he described 'the wan light
of the horned moon' shining on 'the swift and silent lizard of the stones'.[44]
The young American artists in Nathaniel Hawthorne's *The Marble Faun* have
Byron's lines in mind on their visit to the Colosseum, and Winterbourne, the
narrator of Henry James' novella *Daisy Miller*, recited the lines from *Manfred*
when he visited the Colosseum. A visit to the amphitheatre to see the moon
rise is a crucial event in Edith Wharton's dazzling short story, 'Roman Fever',
written in 1934 and published in a 1936 collection entitled *The World Over*.[45]

Such moonlit visits had not yet become a must for the earliest grand tourists, and so the paintings they bought did not usually depict the Colosseum
bathed in a lunar glow. The nocturnal view is clearly a spin-off of the romantic sensibility, to which Byron's poetry gave real traction. François-Marius
Granet, Joseph Mallord William Turner and Ippolito Cafi all depicted the
Colosseum in moonlight,[46] and Thomas Cole recommended an inspira-
tional visit by moonlight[47] (Figure 12.1).

Figure 12.1 Chernetsov, *The Colosseum by Moonlight*, 1842. Photo: Wikimedia
Commons/public domain.

Even early photographers, despite the inadequacies of their cumbersome apparatus, were able to satisfy the appetite for a view of the moonlit Colosseum by combining multiple negatives in a single print.[48] Nunzio Giustozzi reproduces a lovely photograph of the moonlit Forum printed from two different negatives in a technique devised by Gioacchino Altobelli in the mid-1860s (see Chapter 7, p. 155).[49]

We are not yet finished with Byron's wide influence. His phrase 'ruinous perfection' serves as a sort of definition of ruin-mindedness: the ruin is paradoxically perfect, in a way that the undamaged structure never was. The American jurist, George Stillman Hillard, echoed the sentiment in his popular travelogue of 1853, *Six Months in Italy*:[50] 'If as a building the Colosseum was open to criticism, as a ruin it is perfect. The work of decay has stopped at the exact point required by taste and sentiment.' Taste and sentiment too are hallmarks of ruin-mindedness, for they combine aesthetic judgement with a positive emotional response.

To return to Byron himself, after a personal reverie the poet reverted to the amphitheatre in stanzas cxxxviii and following. In stanza cxl, 'I see before me the Gladiator lie', he evoked the long-famous and often replicated sculpture then thought to represent a dying gladiator, but now recognised as a wounded Gaul, in Rome's Capitoline Museum. The imagined thoughts of the dying man occupy the next stanza, cxli; he recalls his homeland – Byron clearly had in mind one of Virgil's most affecting lines in the *Aeneid*, 10.782, '[Antores] remembers sweet Argos as he dies' (*dulcis moriens reminiscitur Argos*). His 'gladiator' had left behind a wife and children in Dacia, while 'he, their sire, [lay] / Butchered to make a Roman holiday'. That phrase became perhaps the most famous in the whole canto, and provided yet another trope of later visits by travellers and authors. Hawthorne quoted it, and its ritual parroting was mocked by Mark Twain at the beginning of chapter XXVII of *The Innocents Abroad* (1869).

Two of Byron's contemporaries also recorded their personal impressions of the ruins. The banker-poet Samuel Rogers visited Italy in 1815 and in 1822 published 'Italy: A Poem', which of course includes an account of a ruminative stroll through the Forum.[51] Richard Wrigley has noted that Rogers was one of the many visitors who enjoyed a 'pedestrian participation' in Rome's past glories by walking upon classic ground:[52] 'the very dust we tread stirs with life; / And not a breath but from the ground sends up / Something of human grandeur'. It is not a particularly gripping account, however, since Rogers was content to evoke wanly the figures and events of the vanished past; only in the concluding lines has he a little to say about the Forum's current condition:

> Now all is changed; and here, as in the wild,
> The day is silent, dreary as the night;
> None stirring, save the herdsman and his herd,
> Savage alike; or they that would explore,
> Discuss and learnedly; or they that come,
> (And there are many who have crossed the earth)
> That they may give the hours to meditation,
> And wander, often saying to themselves,
> 'This was the ROMAN FORUM!'

(From this extract it is easy to see why the poem only secured a readership after it was re-issued with fine engraved illustrations by Turner.) It is odd that Rogers did not draw attention to the Forum's surface, still pockmarked by the pits and hillocks left behind by Napoleon's excavators. But poetry could not be made of that!

Percy Bysshe Shelley and his wife Mary visited Rome a few years later, where he wrote *Prometheus Unbound* (1820). In the preface to the published poem, he told the reader that he wrote it 'upon the mountainous ruins of the Baths of Caracalla'; he described the 'flowery glades, and thickets of odoriferous blossoming trees, which are extended in ever winding labyrinths upon its immense platforms and dizzy arches suspended in the air'. As Christopher Woodward explained, the ruins of ancient Rome gave Shelley hope for the future, since the masonry of a structure erected by a tyrant was being steadily loosened by freely growing plants, so that in due course democratic Nature triumphs over autocratic repression.[53] Richard Wrigley found in the passage an ecological dualism:[54] the antique debris contributes materially to organic regeneration. Shelley went on to describe how 'the effect of the vigorous awakening spring in that divinest climate, and the new life with which it drenches the spirits even to intoxication, were the inspiration of this drama'. It is noteworthy that Shelley felt the intoxication of a Roman setting, just as Gibbon had done when he arrived in Rome, surely an unexpected bond between the two.

The most affecting of Shelley's evocations of the ruins is to be found in two stanzas of *Adonaïs* (1821), xlix–l, lines 433–50, an epicede lamenting the death of John Keats, who was buried in the Protestant cemetery, tucked away from the Catholic heart of Rome in the *disabitato*:[55]

> XLIX
>> Go thou to Rome – at once the Paradise,
>> The grave, the city, and the wilderness;
>> And where its wrecks like shatter'd mountains rise,
>> And flowering weeds, and fragrant copses dress

The bones of Desolation's nakedness.
Pass, till the spirit of the spot shall lead
Thy footsteps to a slope of green access
Where, like an infant's smile, over the dead
   A light of laughing flowers along the grass is spread;

L

And gray walls moulder round, on which dull Time
Feeds, like slow fire upon a hoary brand;
And one keen pyramid with wedge sublime,
Pavilioning the dust of him who plann'd
This refuge for his memory, doth stand
Like flame transform'd to marble; and beneath,
A field is spread, on which a newer band
Have pitch'd in Heaven's smile their camp of death,
   Welcoming him we lose with scarce extinguish'd breath.

The Pyramid of Cestius, itself a tomb, provided Shelley with a symbol of
eternal memory, not just of Keats but also of his son, 'my lost William', also
buried in the same cemetery.[56] The pyramid might also serve as a land-
mark or guide to the cemetery, as it was later to serve Thomas Hardy, in
the poem 'Rome at the Pyramid of Cestius Near the Graves of Shelley and
Keats' (1887, the year of his visit):

Who, then, was Cestius,
And what is he to me? –
Amid thick thoughts and memories multitudinous
One thought alone brings he.

I can recall no word
Of anything he did;
For me he is a man who died and was interred
To leave a pyramid

Whose purpose was exprest
Not with its first design,
Nor till, far down in Time, beside it found their rest
Two countrymen of mine.

Cestius in life, maybe,
Slew, breathed out threatening;
I know not. This I know: in death all silently
He does a kindlier thing,

In beckoning pilgrim feet
With marble finger high

To where, by shadowy wall and history-haunted street,
Those matchless singers lie …

– Say, then, he lived and died
That stones which bear his name
Should mark, through Time, where two immortal Shades abide;
 It is an ample fame.

For Hardy, as for Shelley, Cestius' conspicuous pyramid-tomb performed a function like the ancient monuments mentioned in the mediaeval itineraries, as a fingerpost for the modern pilgrim, now secular and literary, in quest of the marginalised shrines of the non-Catholic dead. A mid-nineteenth-century photograph by Jane Martha St John makes clear how prominent Cestius' tomb is beside the Protestant cemetery (Figure 12.2). But Hardy also seems to be channelling Byron's 'know-nothing' account of the Column of Phocas in the Forum. Hardy ascribed to the pyramid's tenant typically Roman martial behaviour. Little is known about Gaius Cestius Epulo, though it seems unlikely that he 'slew, [and] breathed out threatening'.[57]

Figure 12.2 Jane Martha St John, *The Pyramid of Cestius*. Photo: Jane Martha St John – Getty Open Content.

To return to the Shelleys, Percy's wife Mary made impressive use of the ruins of Rome in her novel *The Last Man* (1825–6), a tale of the all-but-complete annihilation of humankind by plague (the ruins had also figured in her short story of 1819, 'Valerius: The Reanimated Roman'[58]). In volume 3, chapter 2 of the novel, the leader of a handful of English survivors, Adrian earl of Windsor, apparently adopts the scheme of the novel's hero (and his brother-in-law) Lionel Verney to emigrate from England, by now depopulated after successive years of the visitation of plague, and to settle in a more cheerful climate to await extinction. Adrian fixes upon Italy, specifically 'sacred and eternal Rome'. (Those who manage to get this far with the story may be somewhat surprised that Greece was not chosen as a refuge, given the prominence of its successful revolt from Ottoman rule in the previous volumes.) Adrian's undisclosed motive for the choice is that the exiles 'might with greater patience submit to the decree, which had laid her mighty towers low' and lose their 'selfish grief in the sublime aspect of its desolation'. The ancient ruins provide consolation and induce resignation. Shelley planted a 'narrative seed' for the choice of ruinous Rome as a final refuge early in the novel, volume 1, chapter 1, where the boy Lionel, who is the narrator, describes himself in the wilds of Cumberland as being as 'uncouth a savage as the wolf-bred founder of old Rome'; Lionel cites this self-description once he finds himself alone in Rome in volume 3, chapter 10, thus bringing his life-story full circle.

Lionel Verney, now the last man, had been crossing the Apennines after the loss of his two remaining companions, Adrian and his niece Clara, in a sudden storm at sea (Mary is evoking her own husband's death). He resolves to abandon 'the wild scenes of nature, the enemy of all that lives' and to make for 'Rome, the capital of the world, the crown of man's achievements'. He now regards nature as inimical to civilisation and hopes to find consolation among Rome's 'hallowed ruins, and stupendous remains of human exertion', his emphasis clearly heard in the word 'human'. Rome, even in ruin, will restore his sense of his own humanity. He describes how he leant his burning cheek upon the cold durability of the vast columns of what he believed to be the Temple of Jupiter Stator (founded, did he know?, by Romulus). Lionel's 'sensory encounter with antiquity' relieved his present misery by calling up vivid memories of times long past.[59] His 'vivid memories' take us right back to Petrarch. Like Petrarch, he had longed to see Rome since his youth, and once there he was conscious of beholding the scene beheld by Horace, Virgil, Cicero and the heroes of Tacitus. (Tacitus is an interesting addition to the standard list of Latin classics, perhaps thanks to his detestation of tyranny, shared by the Shelleys.) For Lionel, as it was for Petrarch, it is the texts of Latin literature which enabled him to repopulate the ruins with 'the Plebeian multitude and lofty Patrician forms congregated around'. As he says, he had at length found a consolation in contemplating even the wreck of a high civilisation.

Charles Dickens devoted the tenth chapter of his travelogue, *Pictures from Italy* (1846), to his visit to Rome. His account brings to mind the older sharp division of Rome's history into pagan and Christian periods, the antique and the modern. The division is enlivened by his contrasted reactions to the cold splendour of St Peter's basilica (not a cathedral as Dickens fancied) and the Colosseum:

> When we came out of the church again (we stood nearly an hour staring up into the dome: and would not have 'gone over' the Cathedral then, for any money), we said to the coachman, 'Go to the Coliseum.' In a quarter of an hour or so, he stopped at the gate, and we went in.
>
> It is no fiction, but plain, sober, honest Truth, to say: so suggestive and distinct is it at this hour: that, for a moment – actually in passing in – they who will, may have the whole great pile before them, as it used to be, with thousands of eager faces staring down into the arena, and such a whirl of strife, and blood, and dust going on there, as no language can describe. Its solitude, its awful beauty, and its utter desolation, strike upon the stranger the next moment, like a softened sorrow; and never in his life, perhaps, will he be so moved and overcome by any sight, not immediately connected with his own affections and afflictions.
>
> To see it crumbling there, an inch a year; its walls and arches overgrown with green; its corridors open to the day; the long grass growing in its porches; young trees of yesterday, springing up on its ragged parapets, and bearing fruit: chance produce of the seeds dropped there by the birds who build their nests within its chinks and crannies; to see its Pit of Fight filled up with earth, and the peaceful Cross planted in the centre; to climb into its upper halls, and look down on ruin, ruin, ruin, all about it; the triumphal arches of Constantine, Septimus [sic] Severus, and Titus; the Roman Forum; the Palace of the Caesars; the temples of the old religion, fallen down and gone; is to see the ghost of old Rome, wicked, wonderful old city, haunting the very ground on which its people trod. It is the most impressive, the most stately, the most solemn, grand, majestic, mournful sight, conceivable. Never, in its bloodiest prime, can the sight of the gigantic Coliseum, full and running over with the lustiest life, have moved one's heart, as it must move all who look upon it now, a ruin. GOD be thanked: a ruin!
>
> As it tops the other ruins: standing there, a mountain among graves: so do its ancient influences outlive all other remnants of the old mythology and old butchery of Rome, in the nature of the fierce and cruel Roman people. ...

> Here was Rome indeed at last; and such a Rome as no one can imagine in its full and awful grandeur! We wandered out upon the Appian Way, and then went on, through miles of ruined tombs and broken walls, with here and there a desolate and uninhabited house: past the Circus of Romulus, where the course of the chariots, the stations of the judges, competitors, and spectators, are yet as plainly to be seen as in old time: past the tomb of Cecilia Metella: past all inclosure, hedge, or stake, wall or fence: away upon the open Campagna, where on that side of Rome, nothing is to be beheld but Ruin. Except where the distant Apennines bound the view upon the left, the whole wide prospect is one field of ruin. Broken aqueducts, left in the most picturesque and beautiful clusters of arches; broken temples; broken tombs. A desert of decay, sombre and desolate beyond all expression; and with a history in every stone that strews the ground.

In her introduction to the Penguin Classics edition of the work, Kate Flint emphasised Dickens' general taste for ruination and decay.[60] He showed little interest in towns that were cheerful and bustling, like Parma, and instead he 'finds his attention compulsively drawn to Italian decay, desolation and deformity ... he increasingly appears uncomfortable if decay is *not* in evidence'. Venice therefore was much to his taste, and so of course the ruins of Rome appealed more strongly to him than anything the modern city had to offer. In the final sentence of the extract Dickens recognised that the ruins had a historical context; they were not mute, but had a story to tell of which they were the material part. He also clearly much appreciated the picturesque vegetation, not yet removed, as discussed in the previous chapter.

A younger contemporary of Dickens', however, Arthur Hugh Clough, was altogether less enthusiastic about the ruins of Rome. In 1849 he composed a hexameter poem entitled 'Amours de Voyage', which was finally published in 1858. Its five cantos mostly consist of the letters of a young Englishman, Claude, sent from Rome to his friend Eustace; some other letters pass between female correspondents. Claude's Oxford-undergraduate mind-set is revealed in the first and second letters of the first canto:

> Rome disappoints me much ...
> Only the Arch of Titus and view from the Lateran please me: ...
> Rome disappoints me much; I hardly as yet understand, but
> *Rubbishy* seems the word that most exactly would suit it. ...
> Would to heaven the old Goths had made a cleaner sweep of it! ...
> Rome disappoints me still; ...
> Rome, believe me, my friend is like its own Monte Testaceo,[61]
> Merely a marvellous mass of broken and castaway wine-pots. ...
> What do I find in the Forum? An archway and two or three pillars. ...

No one can cavil, I grant, at the size of the great Coliseum.
Doubtless the notion of grand and capacious and massive amusement,
This the old Romans had; but tell me is this an idea?
Yet of solidity much, but of splendour little is extant.
'Brickwork I found thee, and marble I left thee!' their Emperor vaunted;
'Marble I thought thee, and brickwork I find thee!' the Tourist may
    answer.

Now for some contextual background, courtesy of Walter Houghton and Robindra Kumar Biswas.[62] The Rome Claude visits is the Rome in which Clough himself wrote the poem at the time of Garibaldi's occupation of the city and of the French siege which enabled the pope to recover it. Claude, like his creator, is an Oxford graduate, steeped therefore in classical literature – he will quote Horace in due course. He seems to have recently left the university, and in the vicious pride of his youth he is eager to put a considerable distance between himself and the conventional attitudes which another character in the drama, Georgina Trevellyn, expresses in the third letter: 'Rome is a wonderful place.' But as the letters progress, Claude meets some difficulty in sticking to his opinions, an insecurity those early letters reveal.

In the first letter, Claude finds Rome 'rubbishy' (the descriptor is in fact drawn by Clough from one of his own letters to his mother), but in the second the 'mass of broken and castaway wine-pots' is nonetheless 'marvellous', and the bulk of the Colosseum impresses him, even if to his Oxonian mind it is not 'an idea'. That notwithstanding, by the seventh letter of the second canto Claude is admitting that 'the great Coliseum ... at the full moon is an object worthy a visit', a sentiment as conventional as could be at that time. The seventh letter of the first canto also demonstrates Claude's appropriation of one ruin, the Pantheon. He dechristianises it by repeopling the niches with 'the mightier forms of an older, austerer worship' as he recites the roll-call of divinities from the closing lines of the fourth poem of Horace's third book of odes: Vulcan, Juno and Apollo. In his way Claude reveals himself an apt pupil of Petrarch, by using a classical text to restore the right figures to their proper place. Claude's ambivalent attitude to Rome's ruins prepares the reader for his more pressing dilemmas regarding the Risorgimento and his growing (but ultimately frustrated) affection for Mary Trevellyn. As Stephen Leach, who knows Clough's work well, explained in a personal communication: 'Clough and Claude both tend to shy away from new experiences and withhold approval until convinced that their reactions are genuine and not merely conventional.' Hence the gradually softening response to the ruins of Rome.

In 1858 the American writer Nathaniel Hawthorne went on an extended tour of Italy and arrived in Rome, where he took enthusiastically to sightseeing. This visit generated his last major work of fiction in 1860, a novel entitled *The Marble Faun* in the United States and *Transformation* in England. It is a strange work, and contemporary critics faulted its apparent defects, though many enjoyed it, and it even served as a sort of 'companion guide' to the city of Rome, like de Staël's *Corinne*.[63] The main characters are three Americans 'connected with art' in Rome and an Italian aristocrat, Donatello. One moonlit evening the foursome take a tour of the ruins, described in three chapters: 16 ('The Trevi Fountain and Trajan's Forum'), 17 ('The Coliseum') and 18 ('The Forum and the Capitol'). These chapters have a decided whiff of the travelogue, and it is clear that Hawthorne recycled a good deal of their material from his own *Italian Notebooks*, in which he recorded exactly the same tour made by himself and his wife on 25 April 1858.[64] The reuse of this material produced a curious narrative mode, in which the narrator's voice is as prominent as and to some extent blended with that of his characters.

The resident American tourists are well read. The painter Miriam, for instance, is keen to see the Trevi Fountain, not because it is a beautiful object but because that is where the lovers in de Staël's novel, Corinne and Lord Nelvil, were reconciled after an estrangement. The sculptor Kenyon cites the autobiography of Benvenuto Cellini in the Colosseum. But the most striking, and unexpected, feature of the tour is the occasional disenchantment of the visitors, a disenchantment clearly shared by the narrator too.[65] In chapter 17 the visitors disagree about the value of a vast broken column in the Forum of Trajan. Kenyon enthuses that the shaft will endure forever. The anxious Miriam finds comfort in its durability, an assurance that all human trouble appears to be but a momentary annoyance. The copyist Hilda pours cold water on this: that a dull lump of stone should outlast human happiness and beautiful art appals her. Thus the fragment prompts their personal moral reflections, which continue in the subsequent chapter when they reach the Colosseum.

Of course, on such an evening they are not the only visitors there, for the arena is thronged.[66] It is at this point that the narrator speaks in his own voice, dominating the opening paragraphs of the chapter. He describes how the moonlight 'fills and floods the great empty space', making it all 'even too distinctly visible'. None of the characters has yet spoken, nor is it their critique of excessive illumination that is being described: the disenchantment is Hawthorne's, who goes on to say that 'Byron's celebrated description is better than the reality'. His voice continues, stressing that the Colosseum is one of the earth's 'especial blood-spots'. Another party of tourists, making their way by torchlight to the highest tiers of the structure, is belittled for the inauthenticity of 'exalting themselves with raptures that were Byron's, not their own'. Once again, this reflection has nothing to do with the characters in the novel and everything to do with Hawthorne's own disappointment in the excursion he made.

The Americans, however, are for the most part delighted with the spectacle, until Kenyon recalls the bloody horrors perpetrated in the amphitheatre (this recalls Dyer's shock and Dickens' enthusiasm). But his reminder prepares the reader for the intrusion of the present horror which stalks Miriam, a horror to be increased once the party reaches the Forum.

The eighteenth chapter begins dramatically: Kenyon stamps his foot on a spot and declares that it is the very *lacus Curtius*, a pool or chasm into which the fabled horseman leapt to save his city and people.[67] Kenyon judges the act pointless, since all Rome has followed the hero into the gulf (the pious Hilda takes a different view of the act and of the memorial, naturally). Kenyon, undeterred, imagines that gulf in the Forum as a sort of receptacle of all the blood spilled in Rome's violent history, forming 'a mighty subterranean lake of gore'.[68] Kenyon's assessment of Rome's ancient remains as evidence of guilt is undeniably gothic, and suitable for a romance set in a place of 'picturesque and gloomy wrong', as Hawthorne himself put it in his preface to the novel. But there is a narrative point to Kenyon's insistence upon the sinister character of the city's chief monuments of ruination: they form an appropriate mise-en-scène for the murderous act of Donatello in the last chapter of the series.

Rome and especially the Colosseum provided the setting in a number of Henry James' stories and novels.[69] The thirteenth chapter of an early novel, *Roderick Hudson* (1875), is set in the Colosseum. *Daisy Miller: A Study* (1879) was James' break-out novella. The defining moment of naïve Daisy's life takes place in the Colosseum, moonlit of course, when she is discovered there alone with her Italian 'gentleman friend' Giovanelli by the narrator Winterbourne.[70] Daisy's social reputation had already been damaged by her flouting of decorum, and she now pays the price of her incautious freedom by catching the fatal illness 'malaria'. As William Vance neatly put it, Daisy's breaking of one convention to conform to another (Byronic romanticism) killed her.[71] J. C. Rowe registers the conventional view that 'the Roman settings in the novella evoke moral decay, objectified in the ruins of the Roman empire', further suggesting that James 'locates the problem of women's failed rebellion in the ruins of classical antiquity'.[72] However that may be, John Lyon felt that what strikes the reader of *Daisy Miller* is the lack of any substantial description of Rome; the city remains a vaguely characterised social milieu because in effect James shrugged off the burden of the past embodied in the ruins.[73] Finally, in chapter 50 of *The Portrait of a Lady* (1880–1), James set Isabel Archer among the ruins of the Colosseum, where she meets with the young man, Edward Rosier, who wants to marry her step-daughter, Pansy Osmond.[74]

Lyon's acute suggestion that James shrugged off the burden of Rome's past was anticipated by Rebecca West in her first published work, *Henry James* (1916). As a feature of his writing in general, West detected that James persistently displayed 'an odd lack of the historic sense', and that 'he had a tremendous sense of the thing that is and none at all of the thing that has been'.[75] She supported this insight with numerous examples, in particular his defective response to Roman ruins. Critics who have sought to describe James' reaction to the ruins of Rome only from his fictions were arguably on the wrong track, since in them a character might serve as the mouthpiece for a critique of the ruins, but such a critique would be inartistic if it were not germane to the narrative, as it partly was in Hawthorne. For James' personal voice, we should look rather, as West did, to his travel writing, where his own opinions are freely aired.

So, for instance, in *A Little Tour in France* (1884) James recorded his interest in the Roman ruins in Provence. Of the Pont du Gard, which he admired up to a point, he nonetheless admitted that he discovered in it 'a certain stupidity, a vague brutality'. He went on to explain that 'that element is rarely absent from great Roman work, which is wanting in the nice adaptation of the means to the end. The means are always exaggerated; the end is so much more than attained. The Roman rigour was apt to overshoot the mark'. The Pont du Gard admittedly had 'a kind of manly beauty', but after all the huge structure was built 'to carry the water of a couple of springs to a little provincial city' (Figure 12.3). West concluded that 'the man who could write those phrases was incapable of forming a philosophy', or of divining in Rome's works 'a record of the pride men felt in serviceable labour for the State'.[76] West's critique goes some way to explaining why although Rome is a favoured setting for the action in a number of James' stories, the city's ruins do not make much of a mark in them, but remain in the background as localising decor (we are in Rome, not Florence or Venice). James could find no narrative role for them, as Hawthorne had, and perhaps the reason for that was that, as West suggested, he could only see them superficially as they actually were, picturesque ruins; he could not divine in them the spirit that built them.[77]

Our final literary commentator from the 'long' nineteenth century is once again W. D. Howells, whom we encountered in the previous chapter,

Figure 12.3 The Pont du Gard, Gard, France. Photo: author.

where his grumpy comments on the state of the Forum excavations under both the papacy and the Kingdom of Italy were noted. By 1908, when he revisited the city in his seventies, he seems to have had a bad conscience about his earlier hard words on the remains of ancient Rome. His engaging travel book, *Roman Holidays and Others*, a work illustrated with stereograms by the H. C. White Company (see Chapter 7, p. 157), contains a brief palinode, entitled 'An Effort to Be Honest with Antiquity'.[78] One building, it transpires, had captured his fancy even on his first visit in 1864, 'the nobly beautiful façade … of the Temple of Neptune' (= the Temple of Deified Hadrian) (Figure 12.4). On his return to Rome forty-three years later, he had forgotten where it was exactly, but by chance as he drove through a piazza he looked up, and 'there, in awe-striking procession, stood the mighty antique columns sustaining the entablature … I could not say why their poor, defaced, immortal grandeur should always so have affected me … but no arch or pillar of them all seems so impressive, so pathetic'.[79] Once over the hurdle of his antipathy, Howells softened considerably to other remains, and the 'glorious porch' of the Pantheon and the Palatine, nearly 'the most ruinous ruin you can get', come out of his pages largely exonerated.[80] A factor in Howells' disappointment with Rome's ruins was his ignorance, a defect Mme de Staël's Corinne would have censured. For instance, he called the Theatre of Marcellus a Circus, which hardly suggests an informed interest in what he was looking at. But such was the power of

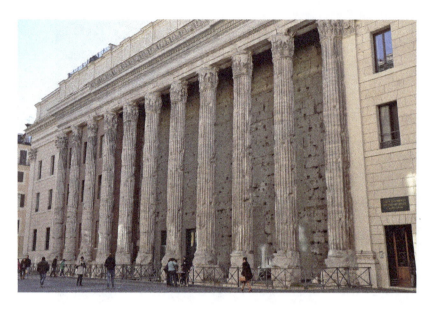

Figure 12.4 The Temple of Deified Hadrian. Photo: Following Hadrian: own work, CC BY-SA 4.0.

the shattered buildings that they managed to impress even his under-nourished imagination.

Back in Chapter 7 (pp. 137–8), attention was drawn to Giovanni Paolo Panini's tour-de-force representation of the extant ruins of Rome which now hangs in the Louvre. That painting will serve to introduce an extraordinary work of fiction, Michel Butor's *La Modification*, one of the most successful examples of the French 'new novel' (*nouveau roman*), published in 1957. Here it will be cited in the American edition of 1959 entitled *A Change of Heart*, in the translation by Jean Stewart (that title was later altered in the United States to *Changing Track* and to *Second Thoughts* in the United Kingdom).

In one passage, the protagonist and narrator, Léon Delmont, recalls having arrived very early in the morning back in Paris after one of his monthly business trips to Rome. With time on his hands, he visits the Louvre and makes his way up a small spiral stair (Butor loves such realistic detail) to the gallery of eighteenth-century pictures. The paintings Delmont 'had come so far to see and which you [Delmont is addressing himself; the entire narrative is in the second person singular] now scrutinized so lovingly were a pair of large paintings by a third-rate artist, Pannini, representing two imaginary art collections'.[81] One of the paintings, it will be recalled, comprised depictions of the famous ruins, the other of contemporary Rome's baroque beauties. Despite the dismissive epithet 'third-rate', Delmont, or perhaps Butor, indulges in an impressive analysis of Panini's manner, namely that he produced 'the absolute equivalent of reality, so that a painted capital was indistinguishable from a real capital'. This 'reality effect' he compares to that of 'the great illusionist architects of Roman baroque', whose buildings, according to Delmont, or perhaps according to Butor, are 'as impressive and as magical as the immense, authentic ruins of antiquity which they had perpetually before their eyes, putting them to shame'.[82] And it is the painting with the ruins on which Delmont's gaze first lingers, as he identifies the ones he recognises, particularly 'that mysterious round temple, called the Temple of Minerva Medica, which you see from the train as you come into the station'. He focussed on it because railway journeys between Paris and Rome are so frequent in the narrative. Later in the story Delmont recalls another visit to see the two Panini pictures, 'which you scrutinized with affectionate delight'.[83] If Panini is such a duff painter, why is Delmont so charmed by him that he scrutinised the canvases lovingly and with affectionate delight on more than one occasion?

The answer is that Delmont, successful, middle-aged and balding, with a wife and four teenage children living in the *cinquième* district of Paris, has a mistress (fifteen years younger, *naturellement*) in Rome, Cécile Darcella. His business visits are legitimate enough, but he spends much of his free time there sightseeing with her. He thus comes to see Rome through new eyes, hers, and he even learns to share her architectural taste, which is rather advanced for the mid-1950s: Borromini![84] The Panini 'diptych', one of the ruins of ancient Rome and the other of modern baroque Rome, thus synthesises Delmont's fascination with the city as a whole. But his core interest remains the ruins, albeit for Cécile's sake he had learned to love baroque Rome better than hitherto.[85] Nonetheless, he clearly prefers the Rome of antiquity (after all, he reads and mentally quotes Virgil)[86] and so he makes a point of walking one late afternoon to the Palazzo Farnese, the French Embassy where Cécile works, by way of 'that part of town where the ruins of the old imperial city are thick upon the ground, and where indeed there is little else to be seen, the modern city and the baroque city having, so to speak, withdrawn and left these ruins in their immense solitude'.[87]

The ruins are clearly not mere local decor; they have a part to play in the narrative. It is, for instance, after a joint visit to the Tomb of Caecilia Metella on the Appian Way that the eponymous Cécile invites Delmont to her flat for tea (and rather more).[88] On another occasion Delmont and Cécile wander, as they often do, in the Forum, where they try to mentally reconstruct from the remains an image of what it might have looked like undamaged, thus building as well their dream of a life together.[89] Delmont needs a solid foundation for abandoning his family and for bringing Cécile to Paris to live with him, a scheme he will come to find as 'ruinous' as the place in which it was hatched. Of course, the couple visit many other buildings, especially churches, but the classical remains are of peculiar significance to both of them. For her part, Cécile much prefers antiquity as an antidote to the priest-ridden Rome of the day.

Perhaps the most significant of his ruin visits is the one Delmont recalled having paid on his honeymoon with his bride, Henriette, to the Temple of Venus and Roma.[90] They had been to the Forum and the Palatine, and as those sites were being shut for the day, Delmont pointed out to his new wife the Colosseum, the ruins of Nero's *Domus Aurea*, the Arch of Constantine and the foundations of the Temple of Deified Claudius (he was well informed, *Guide Bleu* in hand). Delmont and Henriette sat on a bench in 'the heady evening air' when she suddenly asked him, 'Why Venus and Rome? What's the connection between the two?'. Delmont as narrator provided no answer to her question, but of course at this late point in his story the readers know exactly what the connection is between Venus and Rome for him.

The *Domus Aurea*, Golden House of Nero, is another significant ruin. As Delmont travels from Paris to Rome, an overnight journey which is the framework of the story, his fitful dozes are disturbed by dreams, one of which finds him in the 'vaults underneath Nero's golden house'.[91] Later in the narrative the significance of this is teased out: after lunch together the previous week, Delmont and Cécile had walked from their restaurant by the Tiber through the Forum Boarium and past the Colosseum to the Golden House, which she had never managed to see because of the restricted opening hours; Delmont promised to go alone and see it for her the next day.[92] Thus Delmont ended up visiting the ruin without her, but 'on her behalf', something he feels sure means that he has won her back.[93] But Nero's ruined house that troubled his dream on that sudden and unplanned rail journey back to Rome contributes to the final undermining of his resolve.

*

Obviously there can be no simple summary of the literary responses to Rome's ruins. Over the centuries, the ruins, first revitalised by Petrarch's enthusiasm, had acquired historical, cultural and finally aesthetic validation, all contributing to the enhancement of a sentiment or sensibility favourable to ruination, Rose Macaulay's 'ruin-mindedness'. Whatever an individual's reaction, it is generally founded, as was Petrarch's, on the viewer's ability to contextualise the ruins of Rome, thanks to the survival of Latin literature. The physical remains of the ancient city can be 'read' up to a point and so acquire meaning thanks to the Roman literary heritage. It is that above all which enables writers to record a varied range of nuanced responses to them that are not likely to be evoked by a ruin without a history, such as Stonehenge or Machu Picchu.

The most satisfying of the literary responses are those in which the ruins do not just afford local colour, or read a straightforward moral lesson about the ephemerality of all human endeavours or the inevitable fall of empires or the wickedness and luxury of the ancient Romans, but allow the writer to express some feeling for them. To be sure, no one can doubt the feeling for the ruins of artists like Claude or Piranesi, but putting the feeling into words helps the less imaginative among us: why else did all those nineteenth-century tourists quote Byron (even though Hawthorne felt that Byron's words surpassed the reality)? For an emotional validation of Rome's ruins, we turn chiefly to writers, who can put into words the impact the ruins made on their imaginations and feelings. The feelings are surprisingly various: sometimes elation, sometimes moral disgust, and even, in the case of Byron, 'a ruin amidst ruins', a sort of existential angst. Butor's Roman ruins rarely lack an erotic charge. The ruins of Rome are signs to be interpreted in endless ways. This cannot be said of any other ruins anywhere.

Epilogue

It may be recalled that in the Preface to this cultural history of the ruins of Rome I mentioned that Susan Stewart had posed a fundamental question: how did these particular ruins become prototypical? She offered two relevant factors: their sheer scale and the continuous presence of visitors. But there are other factors to be taken into account as well, and in this Epilogue I want to draw the threads together in the hope of providing a fuller answer to the question of why the ruins of Rome in particular are so significant.

The starting point must be that ruination in and of itself is not appealing. Settled communities try to maintain the built environment in good condition. Given this natural liking for order and a deprecation of decay, there have to be reasons why ruination is tolerated by any civic authority. Rome is just such a special case.

Rome was the metropolis of a vast territorial empire which lasted for centuries. The Romans, particularly their emperors, adorned the city with splendid public structures which were designed to defy time so long as possible. They also developed an impressive literary culture, in which the magnificence of their city was described and praised – this proved crucial for the preservation and transmission of a memory of lost splendour. Even after the city entered a long period of decline and decay, the physical remains of the ancient city were everywhere to be encountered. These remains served as the platform or armature for new structures, as we see in the Palazzo Savelli built atop the Theatre of Marcellus or other residences built against the Arch of Titus or into the Colosseum (and long since removed). The ancient was often swept away entirely, but much was embedded within the new, as was discovered in the Largo Argentina.

Tales began to be told about the purpose of the more visible ancient remains, such as the Pantheon, and they were recorded in literary works like the *Mirabilia* (a work often enlarged). The tales were usually fantastic, but their importance is to be seen in the desire to provide a quasi-historical context for the physical remains of the older culture, to account for their being there at all. A better-informed attempt to provide historical context would be initiated by Petrarch and developed by his followers, all on the basis of a wide acquaintance with the authentic literary sources of the Romans themselves.

Stewart identified the continued presence of visitors as a crucial factor in the creation of an interest in Rome's ruins. It is a fact that it is generally non-Roman visitors who express wonder in the face of the ruins: it was Hildebert of Lavardin, Master Gregory and above all the Tuscan Petrarch, with his long-nurtured desire to see Rome, who set the ball rolling. Even when Rome was at its most degraded, the city drew pilgrims to the tombs of martyrs or ecclesiastics to the papal court. So Rome could not be ignored, as Athens could be and was. The religious significance of Rome is thus also a significant factor in drawing visitors to the city. The ruins themselves were not the draw as yet, but some visitors took note of them and were favourably impressed.

A favourable impression of the ruins was enriched by other outsiders, namely architects and painters. Whether Brunelleschi visited Rome as a young man or not, he somehow or other resolved to design and build *all'antica*, as the Romans had done. Once Raphael settled in Rome, he began to introduce ruins into the background of his paintings. The ruins thus acquired, most unexpectedly, aesthetic value in addition to historic. We are now in a position to provide a fuller answer to the question of why Rome's ruins are prototypical. First, they could be provided with a reliable historical context and so counted as an important part of the Romans' general cultural achievement. Secondly, they were beautiful in themselves: 'il bello di Roma son le cose disfatte'. This aesthetic response was a unique development, and came to be extended to ruins elsewhere in the world. It is an entirely modern sensibility, unknown to antiquity and to many other cultures. It is thanks to the ruins of Rome that this sensibility exists at all.

Once the historical and aesthetic values of Rome's ruins were recognised, the need for their preservation was also recognised, and that too seems to be a first. The civic and papal authorities issued edicts enjoining the protection of some of the ruins. These edicts were generally evaded, but the recognition that a ruin should be preserved for future ages to study and enjoy is a novelty, another factor in the prototypical status of Rome's ruins. Preservation was not to be the limit. By the eighteenth century it was recognised that tourism was important to the city's economy, and that tourists, especially from northern Europe, came not as pilgrims but as students of antiquity. Thus the ruins needed conservation and attractive presentation. The papal authorities were the first to address the problem of how to conserve and present ruination, to create in effect an open-air museum of antiquities. Their initiatives would be taken up and developed elsewhere, but they deserve credit for being the first to successfully devise satisfactory means of conserving and displaying ruins. Stern's and Valadier's buttresses of the Colosseum and Valadier's reconstruction of the Arch of Titus are lasting testimony to the success of these initiatives. Attractive presentation of the archaeological sites also prompted the partial re-erection of columns and rebuilding of structures. The Roman Forum as we see it today has benefitted from such restoration, as have other classical sites such as Ephesus and Selinunte. But Rome was first in the field.

Another 'first' for Rome may well be the souvenir. In one of her earlier books, *On Longing* (1992), Susan Stewart wrote a suggestive essay on the meaning of the souvenir. She had in mind the sort of object I bought as a boy on my first visit to Paris, a model of the Eiffel Tower. So far as I know, models of the ruined buildings of Rome were the first such souvenirs devised for tourists. But unlike my cheap Eiffel Tower or the Leaning Tower of Pisa, cork models and the somewhat ludicrous Pantheon ink-wells were crafted for wealthy visitors to be displayed prominently in their homes. Perhaps the souvenir of a structure also contributes to the prototypical status of Rome's ruins.

Notes

Chapter 1 Ruins in Antiquity

1. 'Touring under the Empire', Friedländer 1907: 322–428.
2. Hartmann 2010: 191–246; Turcan 2014: 17–41.
3. Friedländer 1907: 346–8; Hartmann 2010: 225–35.
4. Sage 2000: 213–14.
5. Erskine 2001: 248–50; Hartmann 2010: 229.
6. Mortier 1974: 16.
7. Erskine 2001: 240–3, and compare Rose 2014: 222–3, with n. 30.
8. Friedländer 1907: 363–5; Hartmann 2010: 202–10; Rosenmeyer 2018.
9. Rosenmeyer 2018: 170–2.
10. Friedländer 1907: 367–94.
11. 'Ruins in Pausanias', Pritchett 1999: 195–222.
12. Schnapp 2015: 112–14.
13. Azzarà 2002: 5.
14. Porter 2001: 63–92, 2011: 685–96.
15. Schreyer 2019: 434 and 447.
16. Underwood 2019: 169.
17. Schreyer 2019: 430, and compare Hartmann 2010: 159–91.
18. Davoine 2020.
19. Johnson 1961: 157, §62.
20. Papini 2017: 126.
21. Grüner 2005: 50.
22. Claridge 2010: 132.
23. Edwards 1996: 34.
24. Suetonius, *Augustus* 37; Robinson 1992: 54–6.
25. Colpo 2010; Schreyer 2019: 158–82.
26. Colpo 2010: 160.
27. Colpo 2010: 16; Schreyer 2019: 177–9, with Abbildung 13.
28. Colpo 2010: 163, with n. 799; Schreyer 2019: 176, with Abbildung 11.
29. Settis 2006: 74–81, 2011: 717–40.
30. Settis 2006: 77, 2011: 727.
31. Weiss 1988: 66.
32. Settis 2006: 79–80, 2011: 730.
33. Devecka 2020: 80–7.

34. Settis 2006: 77–9, 2011: 728–30.
35. Hung 2012: 94.
36. Hung 2012: 18–19.
37. Hung 2012: 23.
38. Settis 2006: 80–1, 2011: 731–2.
39. Boardman 2002: 183–92.
40. Regard 1978: 881 = *Génie du Christianisme*, IIIᵉ partie, livre V, chapitre III.
41. Ottewill-Soulsby and Martínez Jiménez 2022: 1–2.
42. Stewart 2020: 202. Chapter 2

Chapter 2 How Rome Became Ruinous

1. L. Grig in *ODLA* ii.1301.
2. Claridge 2010: 299–300.
3. Claridge 2010: 234–7, with illustrations.
4. Lanciani 1899: 21–2; Coulston and Dodge 2000: 5; Grüner 2005: 42–4.
5. Carandini 2017: 318.
6. Claridge 2010: 241.
7. Coulston and Dodge 2000: 2–3; Grüner 2005: 44–5; Claridge 2010: 201–2; Dey 2021: 126.
8. Andrete 2007: 102–18.
9. Lanciani 1899: 88.
10. Galli and Molin 2014: 1301–2.
11. Carandini 2017: 318b; Underwood 2019: 105, with fig. 89 on 107.
12. *CIL* vi (1876) 1716a–b and (1902) 32094b–c; Dey 2021: 60.
13. Brentano 1974: 13.
14. Galli and Molin 2014: 1294–8.
15. Claridge 2010: 313; Galli and Molin 2014: 1296–7, with illustrations.
16. Galli and Molin 2014: 1299.
17. Claridge 2010: 185.
18. Claridge 2010: 71 and 115; Galli and Molin 2014: 1291–3, with illustrations; Dey 2021: 128.
19. Claridge 2010: 71.
20. Dey 2021: 201–5.
21. Coulston and Dodge 2000: 3–5; Coarelli 2014: 278–9, both with illustrations.
22. Claridge 2010: 243.
23. Claridge 2010: 215.
24. Coulston and Dodge 2000: 3; Claridge 2010: 212; Coarelli 2014: 299.
25. Lanciani 1899: 53–4.
26. Christie 2000: 315; Claridge 2010: 183; Dey 2021: 157–8; Kalas and van Dijk 2021: 13, n. 12 and 14, with n. 16.

27. Taylor 2016: 168; Dey 2021: 230–1.
28. Cattani 2002; Mitchell 2015: 261–71.
29. Mitchell 2015: 247–9.
30. S. Lunn-Rockliffe in *ODLA* ii.1120.
31. Ward-Perkins 1984: 85–91.
32. Ward-Perkins 1984: 92–118.
33. M. Humphries in *CAH* xiv.538–9.
34. Procopius, *Gothic War* iii.37.4 = Loeb ed. v.12–13; Claridge 2010: 300; Dey 2021: 94.
35. Underwood 2019: 103.
36. Christie 2000: 314–15; Carandini 2017: i, ills. 32 and 33; Dyson 2019: 247–50; Dey 2021: 44–5, with figs. 2.7 and 8.
37. Nash 1968: ii.187–8; Claridge 2010: 277.
38. Ward-Perkins 1984: 111–16.
39. Karmon 2011: 121–6.
40. Mitchell 2015: 335.
41. Gregorovius 1900: i.457–8.
42. Kalas and van Dijk 2021: 14, n. 14.
43. Ward-Perkins 1984: 38–48.
44. Anguissola 2002.
45. Translation from Pharr 1952: 424; Claridge 2010: 28–9.
46. Translation from Pharr 1952: 424.
47. Translation from Pharr 1952: 425; compare Kalas and van Dijk 2021: 14–15, with n. 15.
48. Translation from Pharr 1952: 427.
49. Claridge 2010: 30–1.
50. Coulston and Dodge 2000: 1; Claridge 2010: 24; M. Crawford in *OCD* s.vv. 'population, Roman'.
51. Santangeli Valenzani 2017: 116; P. Tedesco in *ODLA* ii.1209; Dey 2021: 65.
52. Claridge 2010: 67; Dey 2021: 67.
53. Mitchell 2015: 336–7 and 382; Dey 2021: 53, 66.
54. Merrills and Miles 2010: 148.
55. Underwood 2019: 84–5.
56. Ward-Perkins 1984: 41–2.
57. Underwood 2019: 88–9.
58. Lanciani 1899: 80–1.
59. Ward-Perkins 1984: 131; Underwood 2019: 72–3.
60. Taylor 2016: 187; Underwood 2019: 23; Dey 2021: 38.
61. Mitchell 2015: 336; Taylor 2016: 222–31.
62. Ward-Perkins 1984: 44.
63. *CIL* vi.1750 = *ILS* 5703.
64. *PLRE* ii.931–2.
65. Ward-Perkins 1984: 203–29.

66. Krautheimer 1980: 65–6; Dey 2021: 47–8, with figs. 2.9 and 10.
67. Eaton 1852: Letter XVI, i.168–9; Sweet 2012: 111–12.
68. Carandini 2017: i: fig. 89 and p. 319; Dey 2021: 48–50, with fig. 2.13.
69. Temple: Claridge 2010: 82; Coarelli 2014: 66–7; Porticus: Claridge 2010: 254; Pantheon: Claridge 2010: 226.
70. Claridge 2010: 172.
71. Claridge 2010: 105–6.
72. Claridge 2010: 21–3.
73. Anguissola 2002; Machado 2019: 85–7; Dey 2021: 51.
74. Barker and Marano 2017.
75. Barker and Marano 2017: 843.
76. Smallwood 1967: 93–4, §365, translation in Johnson 1961: 142–3, §172; Grüner 2005: 46–7.
77. Robinson 1992: 43–4.
78. Taylor 2016: 135.
79. Claridge 2010: 312, 237.
80. Osborne 2021: 208–9.
81. Claridge 2010: 113–14; Yegül and Favro 2019: 842–3, with figs. 12.41, 45 and 46.
82. Claridge 2010: 308–12; Ferris 2013: 38; Yegül and Favro 2019: 846–8, with figs. 12.51 and 52.
83. Claridge 2010: 373–7; McKitterick 2020: 128–9.
84. Claridge 2010: 84.
85. Gregorovius 1900: i.161–6; Krautheimer 1980: 45; Christie 2000: 318–19; Dey 2021: 39–40.
86. Ward-Perkins 1984: 220–3; Claridge 2010: 71; Dey 2021: 55, with fig. 2.15.
87. *Novels of Majorian* 4, translation from Pharr 1952: 553; Dudley 1967: 31–3; Moatti 1993: 146–8; Underwood 2019: 169.
88. Ridley 1992a: 10; Geyer 1993: 69–74; Anguissola 2002: 22–3; Cattani 2002; Karmon 2011: 33–4.
89. Arnold 2014: 220–9; Wiemer 2023: 323–6.
90. Lanciani 1899: 77–8; Gregorovius 1900: i. 296–302; R. Collins in *CAH* xiv.128; Anguissola 2002: 23–4; Claridge 2010: 30–1.
91. Geyer 1993: 65; Pergoli Campanelli 2013 and 2015: 186–251; Devecka 2020: 55–61; Dey 2021: 61–4.
92. Carandini 2017: i.263–4 for the Palatine.
93. Pergoli Campanelli 2015: 206–9.
94. Fauvinet-Ranson 2006: 106–8.
95. Fauvinet-Ranson 2006: 108–17.
96. Fauvinet-Ranson 2006: 133–41; Pergoli Campanelli 2015: 221–4.
97. Fauvinet-Ranson 2006: 135, n. 407; compare Devecka 2020: 134, n. 45.
98. Claridge 2010: 180; Santangeli Valenzani 2017: 118.
99. Arnold 2014: 205.

100. Gregorovius 1900: i.485–9; Dey 2021: 72–3.

101. Cameron in *CAH* xiv.76.

102. Santangeli Valenzani 2017: 117.

103. Gregorovius 1902: ii.150–61; Kalas and van Dijk 2021: 17–18, with n. 35.

104. Claridge 2010: 185.

105. Gregorovius 1902: ii.385–90; Dey 2021: 75.

106. Dey 2021: 294–5.

107. Gregorovius 1905: iv.1.250–4.

108. Gregorovius 1906: v.323–4; Dey 2021: 181–2.

109. Urlichs 1871: 144.

Chapter 3 Mediaeval Responses to the Ruins of Rome

1. Dey 2021: 229–30, with figs. 7.11 and 12.

2. Taylor et al. 2016: 232.

3. Dey 2021: 109–10.

4. Edwards 1996: 96–109.

5. Chapter 1, p. 28.

6. Urlichs 1871: 47; *CTCR* 1940: i.3–8, with commentary; Dudley 1967: 29–31.

7. Claridge 2010: 69–71, with illustrations.

8. Claridge 2010: 177–80, with illustrations.

9. Claridge 2010: 171–4, with illustrations.

10. Claridge 2010: 232.

11. Fane-Saunders 2016: 33, 43–4.

12. Babylonian Talmud, Pesochim 118b, trans. Isidore Epstein, cited by Graf 1882: i.150–1; Hopkins 2009: 192, n. 48.

13. Urlichs 1871: 49; Gregorovius 1900: i.142–3; *CTCR* 1940: i.302–4, with commentary; Blockley 1983: 205, fr. 41.

14. Matthews 1975: 384.

15. K. Brodersen in *OCD* 1357.

16. Urlichs 1871: 49; *CTCR* 1940: i.305–10, with commentary.

17. Wilson 2000.

18. Urlichs 1871: 1–27; *CTCR* 1940: i.89–188, with commentary; Dudley 1967: 26–9.

19. Arce 1999: 22; Coulston and Dodge 2000: 1–2 and 354.

20. Purcell 1992: 425; Dey 2021: 265.

21. J.-P. Migne, *Patrologia Latina* 90.961–2; Graf 1882: i.112; Gregorovius 1903: iii.521.

22. *Mirabilia* §16, Master Gregory, *Narracio* §8 (= Osborne 1987: 54–7 and 2021: 209–10).

23. Graf 1882: i.203–4; Versnel 1972: 57 and 61.

24. Claridge 2010: 174–5, with illustration.
25. Claridge 2010: 225, with illustration.
26. Graf 1882: i.324; Versnel 1972: 50–7.
27. 9.37–8; Dümmler 1881: 230.
28. 44.13; Dümmler 1881: 256.
29. Urlichs 1871: 59–78; *CTCR* 1942: ii.176–207, with commentary.
30. Gregorovius 1903: iii.517–19.
31. Walser 1987: 143–211; del Lungo 2004.
32. See link in the Bibliography under 'Online Citations'.
33. Blennow 2019: 51–3 and 70–1.
34. Blennow 2019: 47–8; Bogen and Thürlemann 2009: 21–4, with fig. 2.1.
35. McKitterick et al. 2015: 230–2, 2020: 58–60.
36. Rehm 1960: 45.
37. Urlichs 1871: 86–9; *CTCR* 1942: ii.138–40; Scott 2001: nos. 36 and 38.
38. Claridge 2010: 312.
39. Gibson 2017.
40. Settis 1986b: 375–8.
41. Ferero-Mendoza 2002: 30.
42. Burke: 1969: 2.
43. Urlichs 1871: 91–112; Nichols 1889: 1–117, with English translation and notes; *CTCR* 1946: iii.3–65, with notes; Accame and Dell'Oro 2004: 107–70, with Italian translation and notes.
44. Urlichs 1871: 79–81; Wickham 2015: 380, n. 176 and 322–32.
45. See Nichols 1889: 165–71 or Gregorovius 1905: iv.2.656–8 for translated excerpts.
46. Urlichs 1871: 80–1; Nichols 1889: 157–60.
47. Wickham 2015: 340.
48. Section numbers as in Urlichs 1871.
49. Graf 1882: i.116–30; Nichols 1889: ix–xix.
50. Urlichs 1871: 113–25; Wickham 2015: 380.
51. Nichols 1889: xiv–xv; Accame and Dell'Oro 2004: 27.
52. Accame and Dell'Oro 2004: 22–5; Wickham 2015: 380–1.
53. Wickham 2015: 434–45.
54. Osborne 2021: 207–8.
55. Osborne 2021: 210–11.
56. Claridge 2010: 206.
57. Nardella 2001: 437–8; Claridge 2010: 306.
58. Graf 1882: i.125.
59. Nichols' translation, 1889: 117.
60. Urlichs 1871: 106.25, 108.12, 110.6.
61. Campanelli 2011: 38.
62. Urlichs 1871: 178–9 has a Latin version of the Hebrew original; English versions in Nichols 1889: 153–6; Adler 1907; Barber 2011: 53–5.
63. Claridge 2010: 426–8.

64. Champagne and Boustan 2011: 481–7.
65. Compare Story 1871: 419; Hare 1893: i.130 with the citation of Merivale.
66. Rushforth 1919: 16–17.
67. Osborne 1987: 11–12; Nardella 1997: 29–31 and 2001: 440–7.
68. Osborne 1987; Nardella 1997; Campanelli 2011: 40–4; Hui 2016: 58.
69. James 1917.
70. James 1917: 531–7.
71. Claridge 2010: 271–2.
72. Graf 1883: ii.565–7; *CTCR* 1953: iv.360–1; Osborne 1987: 54–5.
73. Krautheimer 1980: 161–202.

Chapter 4 The Watershed: Petrarch and His Successors

1. Brentano 1974: 13–15.
2. Brentano 1974: 32.
3. Gregorovius 1906: vi.1.323.
4. Brentano 1974: 41; Dey 2021: 217.
5. Weiss 1988: 30–47; Mann 1984: 10–27.
6. Mann 1984: 11.
7. Burke 1969: 20–3; Mann 1984: 16 and 29–30.
8. Burke 1969: 23–4; Curran 2018: 650–1.
9. Mann 1984: 29–34.
10. Petrarch, *Familiares* ii.14.
11. Gregorovius 1906: vi.1.202–6; Weiss 1988: 30–8; Pisacane 2005: 105–19.
12. Mommsen 1942: 230–1.
13. Petrarch, *Familiares* xv.8.6.
14. Gibbon 1914: vii.324, with n. 40.
15. Choay 2001: 28.
16. Petrarch, *Familiares* vi.2; Urlichs 1871: 183–4; *CTCR* 1953: iv.1–10, with identification of sources; Bishop 1966: 63–6 (English translation); Boriaud 2004: 57–66 (itinerary); Hui 2016: 111–17; Legassie 2017: 169–202, especially 188–92; Fantham 2017: i.62–75, with notes on pp. 594–603.
17. Mazzocco 1977: 207, n. 13.
18. Weiss 1988: 33; Barkan 1999: 24; Chapter 3, p. 18.
19. Livy, *History of Rome*, 1.10.6 and 1.10.33.
20. Livy, *History of Rome*, 2.7.5–12.
21. Weiss 1988: 34.
22. Compare Chapter 2, p. 18.
23. Nash 1968 ii. 302–5; Claridge 2010: 158, with fig. 59; Yegül and Favro 2019: 806–7, with fig. 12.8.
24. Urlichs 1871: 196.

25. Burke 1969: 21–3.
26. Stewart 2020: 2.
27. Stewart 2020: 11.
28. Mann 1984: 110.
29. Schnapp 1996: 106.
30. Viney 2014: 140.
31. Sweet 2012: 109–11.
32. Mazzocco 1975: 357.
33. Edwards 2012: 192–3; Slaney 2016: 93–8.
34. Slaney 2016: 95 and 2020: 162–3; compare Edwards 2012: 197.
35. So Webb 1996: 31.
36. Weiss 1988: 38–42; Mann 1984: 37.
37. Uberti, *Dittamondo* ii.31 in Urlichs 1871: 244–7; Burckhardt 1890: 178; Gregorovius 1906: vi.2.717; *CTCR* 1953: iv.55–64.
38. Bibliothèque nationale de France, Paris, Ms Ital. 81; Maier 2020: 59–61, with fig. 45; Bogen and Thürlemann 2009: 59–60, with fig. 11.3.
39. So Weiss 1988: 46–7.
40. Weiss 1988: 51.
41. Urlichs 1871: 233; Burke 1969: 24; Barkan 1999: 26, 30–1; *CTCR* 1953: iv.72–3.
42. Smith 1992: 173–4; Forero-Mendoza 2002: 61–4.
43. *Epistola* 86 in Smith 1934: 211–20 = *CTCR* 1953: iv.89–100; Smith 1992: 174–6; McManamon 1996: 82–5.
44. Smith 1934: 216; Viti 2005: 133.
45. Weiss 1988: 56–7; Barkan 1999: 33–4; Campanelli 2011: 49–51.
46. Graf 1882: i.54–5, with n. 24.
47. Weiss 1988: 45.
48. Urlichs 1871: 234–5, extracts in Greek; Gregorovius 1906: vi.2.676–7, précis of content; Smith 1992: 150–70 and 199–21.
49. Smith 1992: 158–60; Viti 2005: 133–4; Stewart 2020: 70–1.
50. Smith's translation, 1992: 200–1.
51. Smith 1992: 159.
52. Smith 1992: 201–2.
53. Webb 2012: 130–3.
54. Schnapp 2017: 8–10.
55. Graf 1882: i.52; Rehm 1960: 81; Viti 2005: 137 from Mehus, L. (ed.), 1759. *Ambrosii Traversarii … Latinae Epistolae*, Florence (reprinted 1968, Bologna), Lib. XI, Epist. XIII, vol. II col. 492.
56. *Tractatus de rebus antiquis et situ urbis Romae* in Urlichs 1871: 149–69; *CTCR* 1953: iv.101–50.
57. Weiss 1988: 61.
58. Cassiodorus: Urlichs 1871: 158; *CTCR* 1953: iv.140; Suetonius: Urlichs 1871: 159, 160, 163; *CTCR* 1953: iv.117, n. 3 and 132, n. 2.
59. Urlichs 1871: 167; *CTCR* 1953: iv.146.

60. Claridge 2010: 382–3.
61. *CTCR* 1953: iv.109; Weiss 1988: 62; Campanelli 2011: 47–9.
62. Smith 1992: 151.
63. Baron 1955: i.282–3, with n. 43; Buddensieg 1965: 54, with n. 28; Weiss 1988: 57–8; Barkan 1999: 34–5; Viti 2005: 135–6.

Chapter 5 The Battle for the Ruins

1. Claridge 2010: 285; Riccioni 2011: 457–61, with fig. 3; Wickham 2015: 235–8; Dey 2021: 223–4, with figs. 7.5 and 6.
2. Forsyth 1865: 63–4.
3. Compare Chapter 3, p. 41.
4. Compare Chapter 3, p. 45.
5. Karmon 2011: 39; Riccioni 2011: 456; Dey 2021: 209.
6. *De antiquis edificiis non diruendis*: Gregorovius 1898: vi.1.410–11; Karmon 2011: 42, with n. 47.
7. Weiss 1988: 62–3; Fane-Saunders 2016: 158; Schnapp 2017: 17a.
8. Murray 1969: 51.
9. Saalman 1970: 26 and 132, with n. 30.
10. Trachtenberg 1985 and 1996: 171.
11. Trachtenberg 1985: 680.
12. Burns 1971: 277.
13. Chernetsky 2022: 53–8.
14. Burns 1971: 283–4.
15. Murray 1969: 50.
16. Burns 1971: 277.
17. *CTCR* 1953: iv.399–419.
18. Weiss 1988: 78–81; Grafton 2000: 230–3 and 258.
19. Grafton 2000: 261–92.
20. Grafton 2000: 262 and 286.
21. Burns 1971: 286; Grafton 2000: 274–5 and 283.
22. Grafton 2000: 275.
23. Fane-Saunders 2016: 254.
24. Grafton 2000: 316–17.
25. Murray 1969: 102.
26. Borsi 1985: 144–6; Claridge 2010: 68–71.
27. Murray 1969: 137; Watkin 2009: 144–5.
28. Briggs 1927: 142–4.
29. Weiss 1988: 63 and 147.
30. Urlichs 1871: 235–43; Gregorovius 1898: vi.2.713–26; *CTCR* 1953: iv.223–45; Weiss 1988: 64–6.

31. Weiss 1988: 105–30.
32. Weiss 1988: 137–42.
33. Mitchell et al. 2015: 42–9.
34. Fane-Saunders 2016: 230–44.
35. Weiss 1988: 141.
36. Piccoli 2017: 226–7; Brilliant 1984: 224–6.
37. Mitchell et al. 2015: 92–3.
38. Graf 1882: i.52–3; Viti 2005: 137.
39. Latin text in Della Schiava 2020.
40. Raffarin[-Dupuis] 2005 and 2012.
41. Weiss 1988: 66.
42. Burke 1969: 25–7.
43. Viti 2005: 140.
44. Raffarin [-Dupuis] 2005: L–LXIV.
45. Raffarin [-Dupuis] 2005: LXXIX–LXXXVI (inscriptions), LXXXVII–LXXXIX (coinage), LXXXIX–XCI (autopsy).
46. Compare Weiss 1988: 67–8.
47. Compare Chapter 6, p. 100.
48. Schnapp 2017: 16b.
49. Scaglia 1964; Weiss 1988: 90; best illustration in Bogen and Thürlemann, 2009: 51–5.
50. Scaglia 1964.
51. *CTCR* 1953: iv.423–36.
52. *CTCR* 1953: iv.426, 7–9.
53. Fane-Saunders 2016: 68–70.
54. Weiss 1988: 86–9.
55. See Bibliography for a link to the 1588 edition.
56. *Il bello di Roma son le cose disfatte*; Fabronius 1788: ii, 165–6; Burckhardt 1890: 179–80.
57. Ridley 1992a: 12–31.
58. Karmon 2011: 56.
59. Karmon 2011: 55, with n. 20.
60. Karmon 2011: 58–63.
61. Compare Chapter 2, p. 17.
62. Lanciani 1902: 50–1 = 1989: 58–9.
63. Weiss 1988: 99.
64. Grafton 2000: 303–4.
65. Gregorovius 1898: vi.2.665–73.
66. Compare Chapter 3, p. 45.
67. Gregorovius 1900: vii.2.666.
68. Weiss 1988: 100.
69. *Carmina* 1.51 *De Roma*; Gregorovius 1900: vii.2.584–8; Rehm 1960: 82–3; Mortier 1974: 32–3.

70. Thurley 2013: 38–41.
71. Briggs 1952: 228–9.
72. Thurley 2013: 55–8 and 66–83; Harney 2017: 287–9.
73. Fry 2014: 3–4.
74. Compare Chapter 3, p. 42.
75. Rubinstein 1988: 199; D'Onofrio 1989: 25–7 (Latin text with Italian translation); Karmon 2011: 67–71; Hui 2016: 72.
76. Karmon 2011: 74–5.
77. Gerding 2002: 14; Karmon 2011: 258, with n. 73.
78. Weiss 1988: 99–100.
79. Rubinstein 1988: 203.
80. Barkan 1999: 37; Karmon 2011: 88–9.
81. Barkan 1999: 38–42; Hart and Hicks 2009: 177–92 (complete English translation); Maier 2015: 49–60 and 2020: 90–1.
82. Urlichs 1871: 169; Ridley 1992a: 20.
83. Burns 1984: 396–9; Nesselrath 1984: 407.
84. Ridley 1992b.
85. Rubinstein 1985: 425; Karmon 2011: 80 and 99–100, with nn. 69 and 79.
86. Ridley 1992a: 13–14 and 1992b: 117–18.
87. Ridley 1992a: 20–1; Karmon 2011: 111; Fritsch 2017.
88. Claridge 2010: 100.
89. Ridley 1992a: 182–6.
90. Forero-Mendoza 2002: 118–20; Dacos 2004: 17–32; Makarius 2011: 50; Hui 2016: 74; Curran 2018: 645, with fig. 32.2; DiFuria 2019: 95–6, with fig. 3.7; Stewart 2020: 127–8, with plate 5.
91. Rubinstein 1985: 425.
92. Weiss 1988: 103–4.
93. D'Onofrio 1992; Ridley 1992a: 22, with n. 64, and 29.
94. Osborne 2013: 279–83.
95. Hopkins 2005: 157.
96. Ridley 1992a: 24, with n. 68.
97. Italian text in Ridley 1992a: 15.
98. Toynbee 1903: i.63.
99. Frommel 2006: 418 and 2007: 94–6 with illustrations.
100. *CTCR* 1953: iv.489, 18–21.

Chapter 6 From Topographical Treatise to Guidebook

1. Burns 1988: 21; Carpo 2001: 225–6.
2. Jacks 1993: 158–61; *CTCR* 1953: iv.437–56.
3. Eisenstein 1983: 22.

4. Bunbury 1846: 378–81; Urlichs 1871: 31–4; *CTCR* 1940: i.201–6.
5. Extracts with commentary in *CTCR* 1953: iv.462–98; Murray 1972 is a photographic reprint.
6. Amato 2012: 168.
7. *CTCR* 1953: iv.488: 24–5 and 9–11.
8. Amato 2012: 171; Tschudi 2019: 90.
9. Bulletti 1931: x.
10. *CTCR* 1953: iv.488: 5–8 and 498: 14–18.
11. Marshall 2002: 17.
12. Partner 1976: 115.
13. Jacks 1993: 191–204; Bogen and Thürlemann 2009: 64–70; Cellauro 2014: 54–5; Maier 2015: 61–2; Piccoli 2017: 231a, with fig. 4.
14. Compare Chapter 5, p. 82.
15. For a copy online, see the Bibliography.
16. Jacks 1993: 206–14; Long 2018: 123–6.
17. Blunt 1958: 8; Lazard 1993: 64–6.
18. See M. Albanese in *DBI* 70 (2008), 598.
19. Weiss 1988: 88–9, 93.
20. Marshall 2002: 20.
21. Partner 1976: 54–5.
22. Marshall 2002: 23.
23. Cellauro 2014: 58–9; Maier 2015: 120–1 and 2020: 92–5, with figs. 72–4; Long 2018: 124–6, with illustration; Tschudi 2019: 109, fig. 2.6.
24. Maier 2015: 77–118 and 2020: 74–7, with figs. 55–60; Long 2018: 121–3.
25. Maier 2015: 114.
26. Schudt 1930: 374–5 and 508.
27. Coffin 2004; compare Schreurs 2014.
28. Reprinted by Negri 1989 with illustrations and maps.
29. Piccoli 2017: 231b; Campbell 2023.
30. Chapter 4, p. 58.
31. Coffin 2004:17; Bogen and Thürlemann 2009: 85, with fig. 16.1; Cellauro 2014: 59–60, with illustration; Maier 2015: 122–4, with illustration; Long 2018: 131, with illustration on p. 132.
32. Jacks 1993: 216–18, with illustration; Bogen and Thürlemann 2009: 85, with fig. 16.2; Cellauro 2014: 60–1, with a large illustration; Maier 2015: 124–6; Long 2018: 131–3, with illustration on p. 134.
33. Coffin 2004: 17–18.
34. Claridge 2010: 261.
35. Muecke 2003.
36. See Huelsen 1909: 42–4; Coffin 2004: 18; Long 2018: 127–37.
37. See Laureys and Schreurs 1996.
38. See his 'antico Foro Romano' in *Vedute di Roma*, ca. 1756.
39. Bogen and Thürlemann 2009: 86–9, with fig. 16; Cellauro 2014: 64–6; Maier 2015: 126–33 and 2020: 95–9, with figs. 75–8; Long 2018: 137–8.

40. Burns 1988.
41. Burns 1988: 77, with figs. 41–3; Hill 1989: 40; Bocciarelli and Bizet 2016.
42. Burns 1988: 36–9.
43. Cellauro 2014: 66–8; Long 2018: 155–8.
44. Ligthbown 1964: 175, n. 36; Gampp 2011: 227–8.
45. Bogen and Thürlemann 2009: 90–1, with fig. 16.4.
46. Lightbown 1964: 175; Gampp 2011: 227.
47. Ferrary 1996: 139–45.
48. Piccoli 2017: 233; Long 2018: 150.
49. Bogen and Thürlemann 2009: 96, with fig. 17.2 [Dupérac's orientation]; Cellauro 2014: 60–3, with illustrations; Maier 2015: 110–11.
50. Jacks 1993: 223.
51. Heenes 2014.
52. Bogen and Thürlemann 2009: 91–9, with fine illustrations; Long 2018: 151–3, with illustration.
53. Meier 2011: 152; Tucci 2017: ii.782–3.
54. Bogen and Thürlemann 2009: 17–21; Claridge 2010: 173–4, with fig. 65 on p. 171; Coarelli 2014: 127–8; Tucci 2017: i.126–54, with fig. 46.
55. Claridge 2010: 170, fig. 64; Coarelli 2014: 126, fig. 34; Maier 2020: 32–4, figs. 21 and 23.
56. Caldana 2003: 54–8.
57. Tschudi 2017: 10.
58. Caldana 2003: 76.
59. Lanciani 1985: 168.
60. Marshall 2002: 33–4 and 36–7.
61. Claridge 2010: 118–21.
62. Sweet 2012: 112; Bortolozzi 2019: 132–8.
63. Long 2018: 147–9; Bortolozzi 2019: 144–51.
64. Richardson 1992: xxiii.
65. Bunbury 1846: 338.
66. Campbell 2004: i.236–7 and 258, with fig. 80 on p. 260.
67. Caldana 2003: 81–94; Sweet 2012: 103 with n. 16.
68. Benz 2014.
69. Bogen and Thürlemann 2009: 152–6, with the usual fine illustration.
70. Bogen and Thürlemann 2009: 153; compare Chapter 4, p. 57.
71. Miller 1776: ii.390.
72. Compare Chapter 9, pp.180–1.
73. Sweet 2012: 104–7.
74. Venuti 1763: ii.139–41.
75. Sweet 2012: 103; Gleadhill 2022: 78–81.
76. Miller 1776: iii.30.
77. Sweet 2012: 104.
78. Compare Chapter 7, p. 151.
79. Caldana 2003: 83.

80. Vasi 1970.
81. Vasi 1820: 117.
82. Woodward 2001: 123.
83. Compare Chapter 12, pp. 283–6.
84. Barbanera 2015: 34–6.
85. Compare Chapter 11.
86. Caldana 2003: 88–94.
87. Salmon 2000: 60–1.
88. Compare Chapter 10, p. 238.
89. Caldana 2003: 91–4.

Chapter 7 The Ruins Visualised

1. Settis 1986b: 379–80; Ferero-Mendoza 2002: 47–50; Makarius 2011: 24; Stewart 2020: 67–8.
2. Forero-Mendoza 2002: 92–5, with plates IV and V; Makarius 2011: 26–9.
3. Woodward 2001: 92.
4. Clark 1958: 677.
5. Hui 2015: 321–2.
6. Burckhardt 1890: 186.
7. Forero-Mendoza 2002: 156–8.
8. Compare Forero-Mendoza 2002: 135–46; Makarius 2011: 35–9; Frommel 2013: 97; Stewart 2020: 76.
9. Covi 2005: 204–5.
10. Weiss 1988: 65.
11. Mortier 1974: 33–5; Forero-Mendoza 2002: 102–5; Makarius 2011: 15–22; Hui 2016: 131–43; Stewart 2020: 86–92.
12. Godwin 1999: vii.
13. McGowan 2000: 133–6, with n. 12.
14. Turner 1966: 153–74; Nesselrath 2014: 121–35.
15. Nesselrath 2014: 124, with illustration on p. 65.
16. Nesselrath 1984: 408, with illustration on pp. 406 and 442, and 2014: 133, with illustration on p. 135.
17. DiFuria 2019: 103–4, with fig. 3.12.
18. Turner 1966: 160–1.
19. McGowan 2000: 155–6, 161–86; Forero-Mendoza 2002: 129–31; Castorio 2019: 186–95.
20. Turner 1966: 173.
21. Wagenberg-Ter Hoeven 2018: 150–1, no. 52.
22. Marshall 1993: 30.
23. Marshall 1993: 23.

24. See Weingarten and Howard 2017: 18–19 for an illustration.
25. Marshall 1993: 32–4.
26. Wittkower 1999: ii.154 and iii.101; Busiri Vici 1992; Weingarten and Howard 2017: 26–7 for an illustration.
27. Marshall 2014a: 148–51.
28. Sonnabend 2011: 133–5.
29. Sonnabend 2011: 134–5.
30. Busiri Vici 1987: 162–99.
31. Busiri Vici 1987: 247.
32. Arisi 1993: 12.
33. Arisi 1993: 16.
34. Mayernik 2014: 35.
35. Stéphane Loire in Arisi 1993: 53–70, especially 63–7.
36. Arisi 1993: 27–52.
37. Watkin 1982: 53.
38. Wittkower 1999: iii.101–2.
39. Viney 2014: 155–7; Schnapp 2016.
40. Makarius 2011: 117.
41. Woodward 2001: 153; Schnapp 2016: 86; Stewart 2020: 214.
42. Seznec 1983: 221–49, especially 227.9, 230.16.
43. Mortier 1974; compare Faroult and Voiriot 2016: 50; Schnapp 2016: 87.
44. Seznec 1983: 227.3–4.
45. Seznec 1983: 246.26–30.
46. Seznec 1983: 228.20–2, 233.6, 234.18–20, 228.22–4.
47. Seznec 1983: 242.34–6 to 243.1–8.
48. Makarius 2011: 121–3; Schnapp 2016: 91.
49. Woodward 2001: 153–4.
50. Junod 1982–3; Makarius 2011: 117–20.
51. Watkin 1982: 55–6.
52. Woodward 1999: 22–3 and 34, cat. nos. 11 and 10.
53. Claridge 2010: 205–6.
54. Harris, 'Introduction', in Harris and Snodin 1996: 3.
55. Faroult and Voiriot 2016: 392–3, cat. no. 125 with illustration; Stewart 2020: 215–16 and 322, n. 51, with plate 8.
56. Faroult and Voiriot 2016: 419.
57. Woodward 2001: 154–6, with illustration; Makarius 2011: 117–18, with fig. 38; Faroult and Voiriot 2016: 437–41, cat. no. 144 with illustration.
58. King 2007: 310.
59. Settis 2011: 723.
60. Hans and Blanc 1871: 8.
61. Green 2011: 147–67.
62. Woodward 1999: 28–9 and 38–9; Lukacher 2006: 161–5, with n. 69 and illustrations; Viney 2014: 157–9; Dorey 2015: 50–1, 53; Stewart 2020: 216–18.

63. Dorey 2015.
64. Lukacher 2006: 15.
65. Hell 2019: 378–88.
66. Hell 2019: 369–72.
67. Scobie 1990: 93–6.
68. Nesselrath 2014.
69. Nesselrath 2014: 152–93.
70. DiFuria 2019: 2.
71. Forero-Mendoza 2002: 125.
72. Turner 1966: 166–9; Dacos 2004: 79–81; DiFuria 2019: 169–83, with fig. 6.1.
73. Forero-Mendoza 2002: 120–2; Dacos 2004: 85; DiFuria 2019: 217–42, with fig. 7.1.
74. Watkin 1977: 1–3.
75. Zänker 1994: 93.
76. Chevtchenko 1995.
77. Watkin 1977: 3 and 2000: 106; Thornton and Dorey 1992: 48–9, with fig. 42; Stainton in Wilton 1996: 274–5.
78. Watkin 1977: 3.
79. McCormick 1990: 103–12.
80. Rubach 2016; Long 2018: 142–4.
81. Parshall 2006: 11.
82. See Bibliography; Zorach 2008: 11–23.
83. Rubach 2016: 280–3 and 284–315.
84. Parshall 2006: 3.
85. Riggs 1977: 263–4; DiFuria 2019: 235–6.
86. Riggs 1977: 260; Heuer 2009: 393.
87. Zorach 2008: 71.
88. Turner 1966: 208–9; Oberhuber 1968; Heuer 2009: 399, with n. 48.
89. Riggs 1977: 265; Stewart 2020: 159–161, with figs. 36–8.
90. Zorach 2008: 71–3; Stewart 2020: 135–6.
91. Long 2018: 155.
92. Wittkower 1963: 5–6; compare Bogen and Thürlemann 2009: 97; Stewart 2020: 161, 306, with n. 13.
93. Nash 1968: i.7.
94. Wilton-Ely 1978.
95. Barbanera 2015: 10–12.
96. Stewart 2020: 162–94.
97. See Bibliography for link.
98. Pinto 2012: 107–10.
99. Wilton-Ely 1978: 10.
100. Coen 1996; University of Oregon's Vasi digital project (see Bibliography).
101. Wilton-Ely 1978: 12.
102. Wilton-Ely 1978: 8.
103. Wilton-Ely 1978: 45; Pinto 2012: 99.

104. Wilton-Ely in Wilton 1996: 112–13, no. 68.

105. Wilton-Ely 1978: 48.

106. Wittkower 1938–9; compare M. Bevilacqua in *DBI* 84 (2015), 155.

107. Murray 1971: 50–5; and Wilton-Ely 1978: 65–9, amply illustrated.

108. Lawrence 1938: 135–6.

109. Sweet 2012: 123–4.

110. Wilton-Ely 1978: 43 and plate 114.

111. Pinto 2012: 100–6.

112. Mayer 2007: 171–2.

113. Seznec 1983: 235.34–5.

114. Ruskin 1895: 27.

115. Wilton-Ely 1978: 123–4.

116. Pirazzoli 1990: 91.

117. Becchetti 1977: 31–7; Dyson 2019: 79–80; Einaudi 1978.

118. Becchetti 1977: 39; Ritter 2005: 97–105.

119. Carrandini 2017: i. fig. 154.

120. Crawford 1999: 363.

121. Crawford 1999: 389 and 394.

122. Becchetti 1977: 35, 40, 46–7 and 1987; Crawford 1999: 376–8 and 402; Ritter 2005: 164–71.

123. Story 1871: 400 n.

124. See Bibliography for link.

125. Ritter 2005: 26–95.

126. Carrandini 2017: i. figs. 202a and 207.

127. Becchetti 1977: 36–7; Crawford 1999: 395.

128. Klinge 2020.

129. Anita Margiotta in Cavazzi 1990: 14.

130. Brizzi 1975; Cavazzi 1990: 8; Kuhn 2000.

131. Nash 1968: ii.360–9.

132. Cameron and Schimmelman 2016.

133. Piantoni 1994.

Chapter 8 'Virtual' Rome

1. The seal is illustrated in Bogen and Thürlemann 2009: 34–8, 35, fig. 6.1 and Rea 2019: 152–3, fig. 163.

2. Gregorovius 1906: vi.1: 140–8; Rodocanachi 1906: 76, n. 4.

3. Massing 1990: 8–9.

4. Forero-Mendoza 2002: 85–7.

5. Fane-Saunders 2016: 88.

6. Cametti and Falcucci 1996.

7. Marshall 2002: 32.

8. Marshall 2002: 38.
9. Tschudi 2017: 34–73.
10. See L. di Callisto in *DBI* 64 (2005), 115–17.
11. Claridge 2010: 250.
12. Piccoli 2017: 235.
13. Montagu 1985: i.100, with fig. 98, ii.455, with fig. 82.
14. Aurenhammer 1973: 154–7.
15. Aurenhammer 1973: 155, plate 106, 157–8.
16. Wilton-Ely 1978: 45, with n. 8.
17. Miranda 2000.
18. Wilton-Ely 1978: 45–6 and 60, with illustration 10.
19. Wulf-Rheidt in Cain 2011: 256.
20. Compare Chapter 6, p. 104.
21. Mielke 1991: 82.
22. Wilton-Ely 1978: 73–6.
23. Salmon 2000: 98–105, with illustration 76.
24. Reproduction in Tyack 1992: plate 7 and colour plate 1.
25. Tyack 1992: 15.
26. Tyack 1992: plate 19.
27. Salmon 2000: 89–90.
28. Sorrell and Birley 1970.
29. Connolly 1998.
30. Golvin and Lontcho 2008.
31. Comment 1999/2002; Kockel 2011: 26–9.
32. Comment 1999/2002: 196–200, with illustrations.
33. See Bibliography for link.
34. Illustration in Kockel 2011: 26–7.
35. Kockel 2011: 46–7, with illustration.
36. Cain 2011.
37. Kockel 2011: 39, with illustration.
38. Altekamp 2011: 218.
39. See Bibliography for links.
40. Packer 1997 and 2001.
41. Packer 1997: 137–215 = 2001: 86–143, with abundant illustrations.
42. Packer 2001: 193–9.
43. Gorski and Packer 2015.
44. Gorski and Packer 2015: xvi–xvii.
45. Meneghini 2007 and 2009; Packer 2001: 373, n. 11.
46. Hinard and Royo 1991; Ciancio Rosetto 1991: 241–2; Piccoli 2017: 244.
47. Tschudi 2012: 388, with fig. 2; Rocha 2018: 281, with fig. 2.
48. Royo in Hinard and Royo 1991: 201–21; David 2002: 204, with illustration; Fleury 2005 and 2014, with illustration; Tschudi 2012: 388; Piccoli 2017: 244; Rocha 2018: 282, with figs. 4–6.
49. See Bibliography for link.

50. Bernard in Hinard and Royo 1991: 165–84.
51. Reproduction in David 2002: #82.
52. Ciancio Rossetto in Hinard and Royo 1991: 237–56.
53. Balty in Hinard and Royo 1991: 223–36.
54. Ciancio Rossetto in Hinard and Royo 1991: 244.
55. See Bibliography for link; Dudley 1967: plates 104–9; David 2002: 205; Filippi 2007; Bogen and Thürlemann 2009: 199–202; Tschudi 2012; Piccoli 2017: 244–5; Maier 2020: 39–41.
56. Pisani Sartorio in Hinard and Royo 1991: 262.
57. Prieto Arciniega 2015: 175.
58. Wyke 1997: 140–1, with illustration 5.8; McGeough 2022: 99, with fig. 3.2.
59. Theodorakopoulos 2010: 110.
60. See Bibliography for link.
61. Cyrino in Holleran and Claridge 2018: 699–713.
62. Prieto Arciniega 2015: 175–6; Cyrino 2018: 704–6; McGeough 2022: 36.
63. Prieto Arciniega 2015: 165.
64. Bondanella 1987: 239, with fig. 68.
65. Theodorakopoulos 2010: 125–6; Prieto Arciniega 2015: 178–9.
66. Dyson 2019: 225–6.
67. Bondanella 1987: 247, with fig. 75; Dyson 2019: 252.
68. Junkelmann 2004: 272–4, with fig. 158; Winkler 2009: 142–3, with plates 9–15; Prieto Arciniega 2015: 176–7, with fig. 9.1.
69. Llewellyn-Jones 2018: 174–8.
70. Winkler 2009: 216.
71. Winkler 2009: 215.
72. Packer 2001: 135.
73. Piccoli 2017: 242–3, with fig. 12.
74. Cyrino 2018: 710.
75. Junkelmann 2004: 294–9.
76. McGeough 2022: 289–93, with fig. 9.4.
77. Cyrino 2018: 712.
78. Prieto Arciniega 2015: 177–8, with fig. 9.2.

Chapter 9 Remembering the Grand Tour: Paintings, Models and Other Souvenirs

1. Soane Museum Collections ARC 6224: it may be viewed online via the museum's website.
2. Hibbert 1987: 155–81; Sweet 2012: 107–29; Wilton 1996; Makarius 2011: 95–130.
3. See Bibliography for link and Ceserani et al. 2017.
4. Haskell in Wilton and Bignamini 1996: 10.

5. Wilton and Bignamini 1996: 271–303.

6. Hibbert 1987: 180–1.

7. Bowron 2016: 414–17, catalogue no. 335.

8. Miller 1776: ii.391–2; Weingarten and Howard 2017: 70–1 for an illustration; Gleadhill 2022: 1, 81.

9. Briganti 1996; Moore 1985: 117–18, with illustrations.

10. Murray 1971: 17, with fig. 13; Wittkower 1999: iii.102.

11. Haskell 1980: 287–91 and 405–6.

12. Whitaker 2017: 88–9.

13. Whitaker 2017: 100; compare Debenedetti 1987: 117.

14. See Weingarten and Howard 2017: 12–13 for illustrations.

15. Whitaker 2017: nos. 34 and 37.

16. Laing 1993; Weingarten and Howard 2017: 32–3 for illustrations.

17. Moore 1985: 125.

18. Sutton 1982: 22, with frontispiece and figs. 9–11.

19. Illustrations in Moore 1985: 122 and 124.

20. Debenedetti 1987: 120–1.

21. Haskell 1980: 307.

22. Compare Debenedetti 1987: 119.

23. Whitaker 2017: 196–207.

24. Lindsay Stainton in Wilton and Bignamini 1996: 296–7.

25. Sutton 1982: 25, with figs. 24 and 26.

26. Croft-Murray 1970: 296–300 for a list.

27. Stillman 1966: fig. 32; Croft-Murray 1970: plate 83; Watkin 1982: 59–60.

28. Stillman 1966: 21–2; Hatchlands: Stillman 1966: fig. 12; Lansdowne (Shelburne) House: Stillman 1966: fig. 30.

29. Stillman 1966: figs. 28 and 29.

30. Stillman 1966: fig. 24.

31. Croft-Murray 1970: 55, with plate 84.

32. Russell 1977; Robinson 2018; Retford 2023.

33. Taylor 2018: 123–7, with fig. 5.8 and plates 16–17.

34. Teynac et al. 1982: 76–9 with illustrations.

35. Croft-Murray 1970: 63 and 159–61, with figs. 119 and 120; Watkin 1982: 60–1; Oswald 1938, with illustrations; and see Bibliography for a weblink.

36. See Bibliography for link.

37. Goldstein 1977: 226–31.

38. Jenkins in Wilton 1996: 236–8; Tedeschi 2011: 257–69 with illustrations.

39. Hawcroft 1988: 40–7.

40. Stephens 2015: 3.

41. Petochi 1981.

42. Eaton 1852: Letter LXXXVI, ii.310–12.

43. See Weingarten and Howard 2017: 56–7 for illustrations.

44. See Bibliography for link.

45. Wilton and Bignamini 1996: 285–9.
46. Gleadhill 2022: 77–103, especially 65–6, with plate 6.
47. Tedeschi 2011: 259; Gillespie 2017b: 120.
48. Story 1871: 396.
49. Gillespie 2017b: 123.
50. Goethe 1962: 116; compare Chapter 12, p. 288.
51. See Bibliography for link.
52. Kockel in Helmberger and Kockel 1993: 11–31 and Kockel 2010: 421–6; Schingo 2001: 105–6; Lecocq 2008: 227–33; Gillespie 2017b.
53. Zänker 1994: 94–6; Gercke 2001; Schingo 2001: 106.
54. Büttner 1974 and 1986.
55. See Bibliography for link.
56. Helmberger and Kockel 1993: 63–89; Lecocq 2008: 233–45, with illustrations; Rieche 2012: 59–60.
57. Helmberger and Kockel 1993: 240–4; Yegül and Favro 2019: 811–12, with fig. 12.11.
58. Schingo 2001: 111; Lecocq 2008: 235.
59. Kockel in Helmberger and Kockel 1993: 99–117 and 193–5; Lecocq 2008: 239.
60. Compare Chapter 11, pp. 255–6.
61. Watkin 2000.
62. Richardson 1989; the publication of Valentin Kockel's catalogue of the collection is imminent.
63. Thornton and Dorey 1992: 80, with illustration; Dorey 2022: 81.
64. Dorey 2022: 90–5; see Bibliography for link.
65. Wilton and Bignamini 1996: 298.
66. Silva 2002: 169.
67. Kockel 1998; Tatarinova 2006.
68. Gillespie 2016, 2017a and 2017b: 126–36, with illustrations.
69. Richardson 1989: 225; Dorey 2022: 88.
70. Thornton and Dorey 1992: 67, with illustration.
71. Gillespie 2017a: 260b.
72. Gillespie 2017a: 262a, with fig. 4.
73. Eaton 1852: Letter VII, i.67.
74. Gillespie 2017b: 136–40 provides a list of shame.
75. Gillespie 2016 and see Bibliography for link.
76. Lecocq 2008: 244–5, with nn. 97 and 98.
77. Schingo 2001: 110–11; Conti 2001 and 2017, with illustrations; compare Dudley 1967, plate 47; see Bibliography for link.
78. Ridley 2000: 135.
79. Schingo 2001: 109, with illustration; Lecocq 2008: 238, with n. 73; Conti 2017: 221, with illustrations; Rea 2019: 190–2, with illustrations.
80. Lecocq 2008: 238; Kockel 2010: 423–4.
81. Richardson 1989: 225; Salmon 2000: 75, with illustration; Dorey 2022: 93.

82. Roberts 2002: 139–42; Lecocq 2008: 238; see Bibliography for link.
83. See Weingarten and Howard 2017: 28–31 and 34–5 for illustrations.
84. See Bibliography for link.
85. Claridge 2010: 365–8.
86. See Weingarten and Howard 2017: 21 for an illustration.
87. Forsyth 1865: 110.
88. See Bibliography for link.
89. Teolato 2016; Weingarten and Howard 2017: 14–17, 38–9 and 50 for illustrations.
90. Salmon 2000: 49 and 73–5.
91. Forsyth 1865: 62–3.
92. Puetz 2004: 21.
93. Benson 2004: 18.

Chapter 10 Ruins in the Landscape Garden

1. Negri 1965: 31–48; Mortier 1974: 107–25; Baridon 1985; Makarius 2011: 133–49.
2. Harris 1990: 262–80.
3. See Bibliography for link.
4. Hartmann 1981: 13, 33 and 124.
5. Zimmermann 1989: 90–1; Woodward 1999: 19, with cat. no. 3 and 2001: 186; Floud 2020: 76.
6. Kitz 1984: 60–3; Symes 2010: 81–3; Floud 2020: 73–5.
7. Kitz 1984: 63.
8. Kitz 1984: 61–2, with illustration 18.
9. Toynbee 1927–8: 36–7; Jones 1974: 42; Kitz 1984: 73.
10. Watkin 1982: 56–7; Harris and Snodin 1996: 64.
11. Einberg in Wilton 1996: 276.
12. Woodward 1999: 23 and 36, cat. no. 14.
13. See Bibliography for link.
14. Fleming 1962: plate 69 and p. 229, with plates 72 and 73.
15. Fleming 1962: 258, with plate 80; Watkin 1982: 57; Stainton in Wilton 1996: 275.
16. Woodward 1999: 23 and 35, cat. no. 12.
17. Watkin 1982: 62 and in Woodward 1999: 13; Dorey in Woodward 1999: 54 and Dorey 2015: 5.
18. Woodward 1999: 29–31, 42–3 and 2001: 167.
19. Woodward 1999: 29 and Dorey 2015: 4, both with illustrations.
20. Woodward 1999: 42, cat. no. 28.
21. See Bibliography for link.

22. Woodward 1999: 31 and 42–3, with illustrations, as well as in the article just cited.

23. Jones 1974: 141–2; Watkin 1982: 63–4; Woodward 2001: 136–9; Viney 2014: 148–9.

24. Roberts 1997: 458–9.

25. Roberts 1997: 461.

26. Illustrated in Roberts 1997 and Woodward 1999: 45, with fig. 15.

27. See Bibliography for link.

28. Jones 1974: 277–8.

29. See Bibliography for link.

30. Gibberd 2004: 12–13, with illustrations, the drawing on p. 15.

31. Zucker 1968: 220 has an illustration.

32. Watkin in Woodward 1999: 13.

33. Curl 1995; Mikocki 1995; Jaskulska-Tschierse et al. 1998; see Bibliography for link to website.

34. Hartmann 1981: 319–21.

35. See Bibliography for link.

36. See Bibliography for link.

37. Watkin in Woodward 1999: 10.

38. Mielke 1991: 68 and 404, with fig. 74.

39. Mielke 1991: 95, with fig. 114; Watkin in Woodward 1999: 10–11, with fig. 6.

40. Claridge 2010: 174–6.

41. Bergau 1885: 383.

42. Watkin and Mellinghoff 1987: 29–34.

43. Hartmann 1981: 141 and 173, with fig. 89.

44. Hartmann 1981: 169–72.

45. Hartmann 1981: 135–47.

46. Zimmermann 1989: 53 and 168; Zänker 1994: 92–3; Dahm 2003.

47. Hartmann 1981: 33.

48. Mambriani 2006: 67–9.

49. Conforti 2013: 114.

50. Zänker 1994: 87–92.

51. Debenedetti 1987: 124, with fig. 10; Watkin in Woodward 1999: 12, with fig. 9.

52. Spila 2006: 127.

53. Zucker 1968: 228–9, with illustration.

54. Spila 2006: 107.

55. Emerick 2014.

56. Spila 2006: 116–21 and 133–5.

57. Spila 2014: 110, n. 6.

58. Claridge 2010: 418; Coarelli 2014: 392–3.

59. Eaton 1852: Letter LXIX, ii.153.

60. Silva 2002: 166–9.

61. Spila 2014.
62. Spila 2014: 127–30, with fig. 25.
63. Hare 1893: ii.15.
64. Woodward 1999: 48, with illustration.
65. See Bibliography for link.
66. Sheeler 2003: 16–17.
67. See Bibliography for link.
68. Sheeler 2003: 73, with illustration.
69. Spurling 1984: 449.

Chapter 11 Conservation, Restoration and Presentation of Ruins

1. Jonsson 1986: 25; Ridley 2000: 133.
2. Partner 1976: 197–8; Madonna 1997, with fine illustrations; Watkin 2009: 141–3; Karmon 2011: 102–6; Scott 2014: 81–97; Hell 2019: 119.
3. Claridge 2010: 369–71.
4. Madonna 1997: 52 provides a map.
5. Illustrated in Ridley 1992a: 22, plate 1; DiFuria 2019: 107 and 293–6, cat. no. 1.
6. Karmon 2011: 109–10.
7. Salmon 2000: 38.
8. Krautheimer 1985: 109–13, with illustrations; Watkin 2009: 156–8; Scott 2014: 86–7, with illustration.
9. Ridley 1992a: 24–8; Dyson 2019: 8–32.
10. Ridley 2000: 38–9.
11. Ridley 2000: 79–99.
12. Springer 1987: 75 and 87.
13. Jonsson 1986: 17–18 and 146–7; Springer 1987: 75–7; Ridley 1992a: 16–17 and 2000: 101–23; Barbanera 2015: 23.
14. Dyson 2019: 54–5.
15. Ridley 2000: 221–2.
16. Jonsson 1986: 21–6; Springer 1987: 78; Ridley 1992a: 35–46 and 2000: 125–6.
17. Jonsson 1986: 28–38; Ridley 2000: 134–7; Rea 2019: 197; Nazzaro 2017.
18. Jonsson 1986: 26–8.
19. Jonsson 1986: 11.
20. Dyson 2019: 48.
21. Ridley 1992a: 53.
22. Ridley 1992a: 78–86.
23. Ridley 1992a: 217–37 and 2000: 156–8.
24. Jonsson 1986: 117.
25. Jonsson 1986: 41–96; Ridley 1992a: 94–216, summary on 242–6; Salmon 2000: 54–5; Tucci 2018: 673–5.

26. Ridley 1992a: 137–48.
27. Jonsson 1986: 69–72; Watkin 2009: 184.
28. Jonsson 1986: 71, with fig. 36.
29. Eaton 1852: Letter IX, i.83.
30. Ridley 1992a: 205–16.
31. Jonsson 1986: 141–5.
32. Claridge 2010: 285–6.
33. Ridley 1992a: 182–7.
34. Jonsson 1986: 80–7, with fig. 42; Ridley 1992a: 196–205, with plate 70; Salmon 2000: 55.
35. Nash 1968: ii.501.
36. Jonsson 1986: 62–5 and 74–8; Ridley 1992a: 152–66; Packer 2001: 20–6; Bernacchio 2021: 84–90.
37. Packer 2001: 11–15, with figs. 9 and 10.
38. Dyson 2019: 43–4.
39. Jonsson 1986: 139–41.
40. Dyson 2019: 49.
41. Jonsson 1986: 66–7 and 72–4; Ridley 1992a: 173–9; Marder and Wilson Jones 2015: 41.
42. Hare 1893: ii.129; Nash 1968: ii.175, with illustration.
43. Ridley 1992a: 5.
44. Ridley 1992a: 238–40; Dyson 2019: 49.
45. Jonsson 1986: 98.
46. Eaton 1852: Letter XIX, i.132.
47. Woodward 1999: 32 and 49.
48. Huelsen 1909: 52.
49. Howells 1901: 130; compare Vance 1989: i.1–2.
50. Ridley 2000: 187.
51. Claridge 2010: 98–9; Nash 1968: ii.14–15.
52. Ridley 2000: 194.
53. Ridley 2000: 309–13.
54. Ridley 2000: 313.
55. Ridley 2000: 321.
56. Ridley 1992a: 95–9.
57. Jonsson 1986: 99–117; Ridley 1992a: 241; Salmon 2000: 58, with illustration; Caffiero 2021: 102–14.
58. Watkin 2009: 190; Rossi Pinelli 2009: 145, n. 10; and compare Lanciani 1901: 231.
59. Jonsson 1986: 119–30; Ridley 1992a: 241–2; Nazzaro 2017: 281–3.
60. Hopkins and Beard 2005: 171; Nazzaro 2017: 287.
61. Salmon 2000: 64–72, with illustration on p. 70, plate 48.
62. Nash 1968: ii.496.
63. Claridge 2010: 92; Gorski and Packer 2015: 257, with fig. 14.9.

64. Gorski and Packer 2015: 215.
65. Forsyth 1865: 47–8.
66. Meiggs 1973: 102–10, especially 106–8.
67. Judith Toms in Claridge 2010: 449; Dyson 2019: 73–7.
68. Ghilardi 2022.
69. Arthurs 2012: 14; Tucci 2018: 676–80; Dyson 2019: 83.
70. Story 1871: vi.
71. Dyson 2019: 88, 91–2.
72. Dyson 2019: 81–128.
73. Tucci 2018: 679–80; Dyson 2019: 86–7.
74. Dyson 2019: 93–4.
75. Nash 1968: ii.21–3; Claridge 2010: 75–7, with illustration; Namer 2019: 94–8, with Tavola IV; Dyson 2019: 94, 96–9.
76. Hare 1893: i.105.
77. Watkin 2009: 196–7.
78. Howells 1908: 95, but compare Lanciani 1901: 231–2.
79. Wrigley 2013: 185.
80. Insolera 2000: 90–105.
81. Romano 2017: 202; Woodward 2001: 23; Wrigley 2013: 185.
82. Insolera 2000; Romano 2017: 205–8.
83. Stewart 2020: 278–9; compare Romano 2017: 208.
84. Story 1871: 232.
85. James 1875: 121.
86. Hare 1893: i.141.
87. Hare 1893: i.138.
88. Claridge 2010: 389–90; Dyson 2019: 194; Yegül and Favro 2019: 855–7, with figs. 12.58, 59 and 60.
89. Vasi 1820: i.143.
90. Eaton 1852: Letter XXIII, i.245.
91. Hare 1893: ii.49.
92. Coulston and Dodge 2000: 9.
93. Arthurs 2012: 16–19.
94. Arthurs 2012: 61.
95. Schieder 2006: 717–19; Scott 2014: 88–90; Dyson 2019: 168–73.
96. Painter 2005: 22; Arthurs 2012: 66.
97. Painter 2005: 24.
98. Nash 1968: ii.61–3 and i.268–9; Dyson 2019: 173–4.
99. Painter 2005: 7–9; Schieder 2006: 712; Dyson 2019: 162–4.
100. Claridge 2010: 241–6; Coarelli 2014: 275–80.
101. Claridge 2010: 275.
102. Painter 2005: 9–12, with illustrations; Dyson 2019: 164–7.
103. Altekamp 2011: 209–11, with illustration; Rieche 2012: 45.
104. Claridge 2010: 207.

105. Claridge 2010: 207–14; Coarelli 2014: 299–302.
106. Kostof 1978; Painter 2005: 73–5 and 2018: 691–2; Schieder 2006: 712–16; Altekamp 2011: 215–16; Arthurs 2012: 68–74; Dyson 2019: 174–9.
107. Kostof 1978: 303–4.
108. Claridge 2010: 204–7; Coarelli 2014: 302–4; Hell 2019: 319.
109. Arthurs 2012: 61.
110. Arthurs 2012: 74.
111. Kostof 1978: 317.
112. Watkin 2009: 208.
113. Bosworth 2011: 200.
114. Claridge 2010: 71–5.
115. Scott 2014: 88; Osborne 2021: 216.
116. Altekamp 2011: 215; Gorski and Packer 2015: 122–3; Dyson 2019: 157.
117. Claridge 2010: 163–9.
118. Nash 1968: i.426.
119. Altekamp 2011: 208–10, with illustration.
120. Claridge 2010: 105–6; Coarelli 2014: 85–6; Gorski and Packer 2015: 317, with figs. 20.9–11; Dyson 2019: 158.
121. Dyson 2019: 221, 233, 235.
122. Dyson 2019: 236–58.
123. Panella 2013.
124. Nicholls 2017.

Chapter 12 Literary Responses to the Ruins

1. Mortier 1974: 37–9; Forero-Mendoza 2002: 105–6; Viti 2005: 138; Chatfield 2008: 136–9.
2. Rehm 1960: 81.
3. Thurn 1995 and 2002: 725–7; De Beer 2017: 35–40.
4. De Beer 2017: 38.
5. Muecke 2007: 122–3; compare Barkan 1999: 36.
6. Muecke 2007.
7. Muecke 2007: 109.
8. Laureys 2006: 209–14.
9. Claridge 2010: 69–70.
10. Hare 1893: ii.49; Claridge 2010: 390; Nash 1968: ii.127–9, 'Nymphaeum hortorum Licinianorum'.
11. Claridge 2010: 349–50.
12. Barry 2020: 280.
13. Claridge 2010: 214–16.
14. Rehm 1960: 98–9.

15. Graf 1882: i.53; Rehm: 1960: 95–6; Mortier 1974: 46–59; Forero-Mendoza 2002: 108–9.
16. Stewart 2020: 123–5.
17. Forero-Mendoza 2002: 105.
18. Rehm 1960: 96–7; Tucker 1990: 157–73; Edwards 1996: 13; McGowan 2000: 187–227.
19. Forero-Mendoza 2002: 109–10 and 175–8.
20. Janowitz 1990: 24–7.
21. Swaffield 2009: 52–3 and 87.
22. Swaffield 2009: 52–3 and 87.
23. Swaffield 2009: 94; Sweet 2012: 125–9.
24. Gillespie 2017a: 259a.
25. Goldstein 1977: 25–42; Janowitz 1990: 30–40; Edwards 1996: 13; Woodward 2001: 185; Swaffield 2009: 37–8.
26. Rehm 1960: 155–66; Stewart 2020: 199 and 220.
27. Swaffield 2009: 49–71.
28. Swaffield 2009: 94–5.
29. Swaffield 2009: 95–6.
30. Birkbeck Hill 1900: 167.
31. Birkbeck Hill 1900: 163; Barber 2011: 13.
32. Vance 1989: i.35.
33. Adams 1918: 89–92.
34. Romano 2017: 205.
35. Barber 2011: 84.
36. Goethe 1962: 156–7.
37. Sachs 2010: 138.
38. Sachs 2010: 143.
39. Springer 1987: 11; Janowitz 1990: 42.
40. Ridley 1992a: 123–6.
41. Slaney 2020: 201.
42. Springer 1987: 5–7.
43. Webb 1996: 31–3.
44. Vance 1989: i.60.
45. Vance 1989: ii.318–19; Barber 2011: 88–91.
46. Romano 2017: 207–8 and 212 with illustrations.
47. Romano 2017: 215, n. 17.
48. Szegedy-Maszak 1992: 127.
49. Giustozzi 2019: 138.
50. Vance 1989: i.47.
51. Swaffield 2009: 103.
52. Wrigley 2013: 210–12.
53. Woodward 2001: 66–7.
54. Wrigley 2013: 182.

55. Barber 2011: 221–3.
56. Woodward 2001: 70.
57. Claridge 2010: 399.
58. Hurst 2007: 133–6.
59. Slaney 2020: 202–6.
60. Flint 1998: xviii–xix.
61. Claridge 2010: 402–3.
62. Houghton 1963: 119–55; Biswas 1972: 298–321, especially 312–13.
63. Edwards 2018: 130.
64. Simpson 1968: xxxv–xxxvii; Edwards 2018: 129.
65. Vance 1989: i.31.
66. Vance 1989: i.60–1.
67. Claridge 2010: 88–91, with figs. 28–9.
68. Edwards 2018: 141–5.
69. Vance 1989: i.61–2.
70. Woodward 2001: 20–1; Barber 2011: 91–5.
71. Vance 1989: i.62.
72. Rowe 2018: 193 and 202.
73. Lyon 1999: 146–7.
74. Lyon 1999: 154.
75. West 1916: 27.
76. West 1916: 62.
77. West 1916: 61.
78. Howells 1908: 110–21.
79. Howells 1908: 115.
80. Vance 1989: i.173–4.
81. Butor 1959: 51.
82. Butor 1959: 52.
83. Butor 1959: 158.
84. Butor 1959: 99–100.
85. Butor 1959: 56.
86. Butor 1959: 67, 43, 228.
87. Butor 1959: 70.
88. Butor 1959: 101.
89. Butor 1959: 141.
90. Butor 1959: 233–4.
91. Butor 1959: 222.
92. Butor 1959: 230–1.
93. Butor 1959: 244.

Bibliography

Accame, M. and E. Dell'Oro. 2004. *I 'Mirabilia Urbis Romae'*, Rome.

Acer, J. 1999. 'El inventario de Roma: Curiosum y Notitia', in Harris 1999: 15–22.

Adams, H. 1918. *The education of Henry Adams*, Boston, MA.

Adler, M. N. 1907. *The itinerary of Benjamin of Tudela*, London.

Alcock, S. E., J. F. Cherry and J. Elsner (eds.). 2001. *Pausanias: travel and memory in Roman Greece*, Oxford.

Altekamp, S. 2011. 'Die visuelle Konzeption der Stadt Rom zur Zeit des Faschismus', in Cain et al. 2011: 203–22.

Altekamp, S., C. Marcks-Jacobs and P. Seiler (eds.). 2017. *Perspektiven der Spolien-forschung 2: Zentren und Konjekturen der Spolierun* (Berlin Studies of the Ancient World, 40), Berlin.

Altick, R. D. 1978. *The shows of London*, Cambridge, MA.

Amato, L. 2012. 'Francesco Albertini e l'*Opusculum de Mirabilibus Urbis Romae*: modelli e fonti', in *Acta Conventus Neo-Latini Upsaliensis* (Proceedings of the Fourteenth International Congress of Neo-Latin Studies (Uppsala 2009)), volume 14: 167–76, Leiden.

Andrete, G. S. 2007. *Floods of the Tiber in ancient Rome*, Baltimore, MD.

Anguissola, A. 2002. 'Note alla legislazione su spoglio e reimpiego di materiali da costruzione ed arredi architettonici, I Sec. A.C.–VI Sec. D.C.', in Cupperi 2002: 13–29.

Arisi, F. 1993. *Giovanni Paolo Panini 1691–1765*, Milan.

Arnold, J. J. 2014. *Theoderic and the Roman imperial restoration*, New York.

Arthurs, J. 2012. *Excavating modernity: the Roman past in Fascist Italy*, Ithaca, NY.

Aurenhammer, H. 1973. *J. B. Fischer von Erlach*, London.

Azzarà, S. 2002. 'Osservazioni sul senso delle rovine nella cultura anitica', in Cupperi 2002: 1–12.

Balty, J.-C. 1991. 'Henry Lacoste et la maquette de Bruxelles', in Hinard and Royo 1991: 223–36.

Barbanera, M. (ed.). 2009. *Relitti riletti: trasformazione delle rovine e identità culturale*, Turin.

　2015. *Storia dell'archeologia classica in Italia*, Rome.

Barber, A. 2011. *Blue Guide literary companion Rome*, London.

Baridon, M. 1985. 'Ruins as a mental construct', in *Journal of Garden History* 5: 84–96.

Barkan, L. 1999. *Unearthing the past: archaeology and aesthetics in the making of Renaissance culture*, New Haven, CT.

Barker, S. J. and Y. A. Marano. 2017. 'Demolition laws in an archaeological context: legislation and architectural re-use in the Roman building industry', in Pensabene et al. 2017: 833–50.

Baron, H. 1955. *The crisis of the early Italian Renaissance: civic humanism and republican liberty in an age of classicism and tyranny*, Princeton, NJ.

Barry, F. 2020. *Painting in stone: architecture and the poetics of marble from antiquity to the enlightenment*, New Haven, CT.

Becchetti, P. 1977. 'Early photography in Rome up to the end of Pius IX's reign' (pp. 31–8) and 'Photographers in Rome' (pp. 39–51), in *Rome in early photographs: the age of Pius IX – photographs 1847–78 from Roman and Danish collections* (trans. Ann Thornton), Copenhagen.

　1993. *Roma nelle fotografie della Fondazione Marco Besso, 1850–1920*, Rome.

Becchetti, P. and C. Pietrangeli. 1987. *Un inglese fotografo a Roma: Robert MacPherson*, Rome.

Benson, S. 2004. 'Reproduction, fragmentation, and collection: Rome and the origin of souvenirs', in Medina Lasansky and McLaren 2004: 15–36.

Benz, M. 2014. 'Venuti, Ridolfino', in *Brill's new Pauly supplements: history of classical scholarship – a biographical dictionary*, vol. 6: 630–1, Leiden.

Bergau, R. 1885. *Inventar der Bau- und Kunstdenkmäler in der Provinz Brandenburg*, Berlin.

Bernacchio, N. 2021. 'Napoleone: L'Italia, il Papato e Roma', in Parisi Presicce et al. 2021: 75–90.

Bernard, B. 1991. 'Paul Bigot, mon patron', in Hinard and Royo 1991: 165–84.

Bernardo, A. S. and S. Levin (eds.). 1990. *The classics in the Middle Ages*, Binghamton, NY.

Birkbeck Hill, G. (ed.). 1900. *The memoirs of the life of Edward Gibbon*, London.

Bishop, M. 1966. *Letters from Petrarch*, Bloomington, IN.

Biswas, R. K. 1972. *Arthur Hugh Clough: towards a reconsideration*, Oxford.

Blennow, A. 2019. 'Wanderers and wonders: the medieval guidebooks to Rome', in Blennow and Fogelberg Rota 2019: 33–89.

Blennow, A. and S. Fogelberg Rota (eds.). 2019. *Rome and the guidebook tradition from the Middle Ages to the twentieth century*, Berlin.

Bloch, H. 1984. 'Der Autor der "Graphia aureae urbis Romae"', in *Deutsches Archiv für Erforschung des Mittelalters* 40: 55–175.

Blockley, R. C. 1983. *The fragmentary classicising historians of the later Roman empire: Eunapius, Olympiodorus, Priscus, and Malchus*, Liverpool.

Blunt, A. 1958. *Philibert De L'Orme*, London.

Boardman, J. 2002. *The archaeology of nostalgia: how the Greeks re-created their mythical past*, London.

Bocciarelli, D. and M. Bizet. 2016. 'Le *macellum Magnum* et les *dupondii* de Néron', in *Revue numismatique* 173: 271–81.

Bogen, S. and F. Thürlemann. 2009. *Rom. Eine Stadt in Karten von der Antike bis Heute*, Darmstadt.

Bolgar, R. R. (ed.). 1971. *Classical influences on European culture*, A.D. *500–1500* (proceedings of an international conference held at King's College, Cambridge, April 1969), Cambridge.

Bolgia, C., R. McKitterick and J. Osborne (eds.). 2011. *Rome across time and space: cultural transmission and the exchange of ideas c. 500–1400*, Cambridge.

Bondanella, P. 1987. *The eternal city: Roman images in the modern world*, Chapel Hill, NC.

Boriaud, J.-Y. 2004. 'L'Image de Rome dans la Lettre Familière VI.2', in Boriaud and Lamarque 2004: 57–66.

Boriaud, J.-Y. and H. Lamarque (eds.). 2004. *Pétrarque épistolier* (Les Cahiers de l'Humanisme, 3), Paris.

Borsi, S. 1985. *Giuliano da Sangallo: I disegni di architettura e dell'antico*, Rome.

Bortolozzi, A. 2019. 'Architects, antiquarians, and the rise of the image in Renaissance guidebooks to ancient Rome', in Blennow and Fogelberg Rota 2019: 115–61.

Bosworth, R. J. B. 2011. *Whispering city: Rome and its histories*, New Haven, CT.

Bottari, G. G. (ed.). 1720. *Carmina illustrium poetarum Italorum*, Florence.

Bowron, E. P. 2016. *Pompeo Batoni: a complete catalogue of his paintings*, New Haven, CT.

Brentano, R. 1974. *Rome before Avignon: a social history of thirteenth-century Rome*, London.

Brezzi, P. and M. de Panizza Lorch (eds.). 1984. *Umanesimo a Roma nel Quattrocento*, Rome.

Briganti, G. 1996. *Gaspar van Wittel* (2nd ed. by L. Laureati and L. Trezzani), Rome.

Briggs, M. S. 1927. *The architect in history*, Oxford.

    1952. *Goths and Vandals: a study of the destruction, neglect, and preservation of historical buildings in England*, London.

Brilliant, R. 1984. 'Ancient Roman monuments as models and as topoi', in Brezzi and de Panizza Lorch 1984: 223–33.

Brizzi, B. 1975. *Roma cento anni fa nelle fotografie della raccolta Parker*, Rome.

Buberl, B. (ed.). 1994. *Roma antica: römische Ruinen in der italienischen Kunst des 18. Jahrhunderts*, Munich.

Buddensieg, T. 1965. 'Gregory the Great, the destroyer of pagan idols', in *Journal of the Warburg and Courtauld Institutes* 28: 44–65.

Buddensieg, T. and M. Winner (eds.). 1968.*Munuscula discipulorum: Kunsthistorische Studien, Hans Kauffmann zum 70. Geburtstag 1966*, Berlin.

Büttner, A. 1974. *Korkmodelle von Antonio Chichi. Vollständiger Katalog der Korkmodelle, Hessisches Landesmusem Darmstadt Staatliche Kunstsammlungen Kassel*, Kassel.

    1986. *Antike Bauten in Modell und Zeichnung um 1800*, Kassel.

Bulletti, P. E. (ed.). 1931. *Fra Mariano da Firenze, Itinerarium Urbis Romae*, Rome.

Bunbury, E. H. 1846. 'On the topography of Rome: with an appendix on the Regionarii', in *The Classical Museum* 3: 319–81.

1847. 'On the topography of Rome: the Roman Forum', *in The Classical Museum* 4: 1–35.

Burckhardt, J. 1890. *The civilisation of the Renaissance in Italy* (trans. S. G. C. Middlemore) (2nd ed.), London.

Burke, P. 1969. *The Renaissance sense of the past*, London.

Burns, H. 1971. 'Quattrocento architecture and the antique: some problems', in Bolgar 1971: 269–87.

1984. 'Verso la ricostruzione della Roma antica', in Frommel et al. 1984: 437–50.

1988. 'Pirro Ligorio's reconstruction of ancient Rome: the *Anteiquae Vrbis Imago* of 1561', in Gaston 1988: 19–92.

Busiri Vici, A. 1987. *Peter, Hendrik e Giacomo Van Lint: tre pittori di Anversa del '600 e '700 lavoravano a Roma*, Rome.

1992. *Giovanni Ghisolfi (1623–1683): un pittore milanese di rovine romane*, Rome.

Butler, S. (ed.). 2016. *Deep classics: rethinking classical reception*, London.

Butor, M. 1959. *A change of heart* (= *La modification*, 1957, Paris; trans. J. Stewart), New York.

Caffiero, M. 2021. 'Valadier at the Arch of Titus: papal reconstruction and archaeological restoration under Pius VII', in Fine 2021: 103–14.

Cain, H.-U., A. Haug, and Y. Asisi. 2011. *Das antike Rom und sein Bild* (Transformationen der Antike 21), Berlin.

Caldana, A. 2003. *Le guide di Roma. Ludwig Schudt e la sua bibliografia. Lettura critica e Catalogo ragionato*, Rome.

Cameron, J. B. and J. G. Schimmelman. 2016. *The glass stereoviews of Ferrier & Soulier, 1852–1908*, Rochester, MI.

Cametti, C. and C. Falcucci (eds.). 1996. *Meraviglie della Roma antica*, Rome.

Campanelli, M. 2011. 'Monuments and histories: ideas and images of Antiquity in some descriptions of Rome', in Bolgia et al. 2011: 35–51.

Campbell, I. 2004. *Ancient Roman topography and architecture* (The Paper Museum of Cassiano dal Pozzo: Series A – Antiquities and Architecture, Part Nine), London.

2023. 'Pirro Ligorio's *Paradosse* and the location of the Forum', in Davis et al. 2023: 157–66.

Carandini, A. 2017. *The atlas of ancient Rome: biography and portraits of the city*, Princeton, NJ.

Carpo, M. 2001. 'How do you imitate a building that you have never seen? Printed images, ancient models, and handmade drawings in Renaissance architectural theory', in *Zeitschrift für Kunstgeschichte* 64: 223–33.

Carter, M., P. N. Lindfield and D. Townshend (eds.). 2017. *Writing Britain's ruins*, London.

Castorio, J.-N. 2019. *Rome réinventée: L'antiquité dans l'imaginaire occidental de Titien à Fellini*, Paris.

Cattani, P. 2002. 'La distruzione delle vestigia pagane nella legislazione imperiale tra IV e V secolo', in Cupperi 2002: 31–44.

Cavazzi, L., A. Margiotta and S. Tozzi. 1990. *An Englishman in Rome, 1864–77: the Parker Collection in the Municipal Photographic Archives*, Rome.

Cellauro, L. 2014. 'Roma antiqva restored: the Renaissance archaeological plan', in Marshall 2014b: 52–75.

Cellauro, L. and G. Richaud. 2008. *Antoine Desgodets: les édifices antiques de Rome*, Rome.

Ceserani, G., G. Caviglia, N. Coleman et al. 2017. 'British Travelers in eighteenth-century Italy: the Grand Tour and the profession of architecture', in *The American Historical Review* 122(2): 425–50.

Champagne, M. T. and R. S. Boustan. 2011. 'Walking in the shadows of the past: the Jewish experience of Rome in the twelfth century', in *Medieval Encounters* 17: 464–94.

Chatfield, M. P. (trans.). 2008. *Cristoforo Landino, poems*, Cambridge, MA.

Chernetsky, I. 2022. *The mythological origins of Renaissance Florence: the city as new Athens, Rome, and Jerusalem*, Cambridge.

Chevtchenko, V., S. Cotté, M. Pinault Sorensen et al. (eds.). 1995. *Charles-Louis Clérisseau (1721–1820): Dessins du musée de l'Ermitage, Saint-Petersbourg*, Paris.

Choay, F. 2001. *The invention of the historic monument*, Cambridge (Eng. trans. of 1992. *Allégorie du patrimoine*), Paris.

Christie, N. 2000. 'Lost glories? Rome at the end of the empire', in Coulston and Dodge 2000: 306–31.

Ciancio Rossetto, P. 1991. 'La reconstitution de Rome antique: du plan-relief de Bigot à celui de Gismondi', in Hinard 1991: 237–56.

Claridge, A. 2010. *Rome: an Oxford archaeological guide* (2nd ed.), Oxford.

Clark, K. 1958. 'Andrea Mantegna', in *Journal of the Royal Society of Arts* 106: 663–80.

Coarelli, F. 2014. *Rome and environs: an archaeological guide*, Berkeley, CA.

Coen, P. 1996. *Le magnificenze di Roma nelle incisioni di Giuseppe Vasi*, Rome.

Coffin, D. R. 2004. *Pirro Ligorio: the Renaissance artist, architect, and antiquarian*, University Park, PA.

Colpo, I. 2010. '*Ruinae … et putres robore trunci*': paesaggi di rovine e rovine nel paesaggio nella pittura romana (I secolo a.C.-I secolo d.C.) (*Antenor Quaderni* 17), Rome.

Comment, B. 1999/2002. *The panorama*, London.

Conforti, C. 2013. 'Spazio, tempo e rovine nel giardino del rinascimento', in Kaderka 2013: 109–18.

Connolly, P. 1998. *The ancient city: life in classical Athens and Rome*, Oxford.

Conti, C. 2001. 'Il modello ligneo dell'Anfiteatro Flavio, di Carlo Lucangeli: osservazioni nel corso del restauro', in La Regina 2001: 117–25.

　　2017. 'Il modello di Carlo Lucangeli: un colosseo di legno', in Rea et al. 2017: 216–25.

Coulston, J. and H. Dodge (eds.). 2000. *Ancient Rome: the archaeology of the eternal city* (Oxford University School of Archaeology Monograph 54), Oxford.

Covi, D. A. 2005. *Andrea del Verrocchio: life and work*, Florence.

Crawford, A. 1999. 'Robert Macpherson 1814–1872, the foremost photographer of Rome', in *Papers of the British School at Rome* 67: 353–403.

Croft-Murray, E. 1970. *Decorative painting in England 1537–1837: Volume two, the eighteenth and early nineteenth centuries*, Feltham.

Cupperi, W. (ed.). 2002. *Senso delle rovine e riuso dell'antico*, Pisa = *Annali della Scuola Normale Superiore di Pisa. Classe di lettere e filosofia, serie 4, Quaderni 14, 2*.

Curl, J. S. 1995. 'Arkadia, Poland: garden of allusions', in *Garden History* 23: 91–112.

Curran, B. A. 2018. 'The Renaissance: the "discovery" of ancient Rome', in Holleran and Claridge 2018: 643–71.

Cyrino, M. S. 2005. *Big screen Rome*, Oxford.

    (ed.). 2008. *Rome, season one: history makes television*, Oxford.

    2015. *Rome, season two: trial and triumph*, Edinburgh.

    2018. 'The city of ancient Rome on screen', in Holleran and Claridge 2018: 699–713.

Dacos, N. 2004. *Roma quanta fuit, ou l'invention du paysage de ruines*, Brussels.

Dahm, F. 2003. *Die römische Ruine im Schlosspark von Schönbrunn: Forschungen, Instandsetzung, Restaurierung* (Wissenschaftliche Reihe Schönbrunn 8), Vienna.

David, M. (ed.). 2002. *Ruins of ancient Rome: the drawings of French architects who won the Prix de Rome 1786–1924*, Los Angeles, CA.

Davis, G. J. C., J. DeLaine, Z. Kamash and C. R. Potts (eds.). 2023. From the Palatine to Pirro Ligorio: architectural, sculptural and antiquarian studies in memory of Amanda Claridge (1949–2022), in *Journal of Roman Archaeology Supplementary Series* 111, Portsmouth, RI.

Davoine, C. 2020. 'Les ruines contre la ville: l'idéale urbain à l'épreuve des destructions dans le monde romain', in *Histoire urbaine* 58: 15–28.

De Beer, S. 2017. 'In the footsteps of Aeneas: humanist appropriations of the Virgilian walk through Rome in *Aeneid* 8', in *Humanistica Lovaniensia: Journal of Neo-Latin Studies* 66: 24–55.

Debenedetti, E. 1987. 'Le rovine nel 700 romano: vedute e immagini di repertorio archeologico', in De Caprio 1987: 113–30.

De Caprio, V. (ed.). 1987. *Poesia e poetica delle rovine di Roma: momenti e problemi*, Rome.

Della Schiava, F. (ed.). 2020. *Blondus Flavius. Roma Instaurata* (Edizione nazionale delle opera di Biondo Fabio, 7), Rome.

Del Lungo, S. 2004. *Roma in età carolingia e gli scritti dell'anonimo Augiense*, Rome.

Devecka, M. 2020. *Broken cities: a historical sociology of ruins*, Baltimore, MD.

Dey, H. 2021. *The making of medieval Rome: a new profile of the city, 400–1420*, Cambridge.

DiFuria, A. J. 2019. *Maarten van Heemskerck's Rome: antiquity, memory, and the cult of ruins*, Leiden.

Disselkamp, M., P. Ihring, and F. Wolfzettel (eds.). 2006. *Das alte Rom und die neue Zeit*, Tübingen.

D'Onofrio, C. 1989. *Visitiamo Roma nel Quattrocento*, Rome.

   1992. *Gli obelischi di Roma*, Rome.

Dorey, H. (ed.). 2015. *Crude hints towards an history of my house in Lincoln's Inn Fields by Sir John Soane*, London.

   2022. 'The place of models and drawings in Sir John Soane's house and museum', in Goffi 2022: 80–99.

Dotti, U. (ed.). 1974. *Francesco Petrarca Le familiari* (libri I–XI) (2 vols), Urbino.

Dudley, D. R. 1967. *Urbs Roma: a source book of classical texts on the city and its monuments selected and translated with a commentary*, London.

Dümmler, E. (ed.). 1881. *Poetae Latini Aevi Carolini* I, in *Monumenta Germaniae Historica*, Berlin.

Dufallo, B. 2018. *Roman error: classical reception and the problem of Rome's flaws*, Oxford.

Dyson, S. 2019. *Archaeology, ideology, and urbanism in Rome from the Grand Tour to Berlusconi*, Cambridge.

Eaton, C. A. 1852 *Rome, in the nineteenth century* (2 vols) (5th ed.), London.

Edwards, C. 1996. *Writing Rome: textual approaches to the city*, Cambridge.

   (ed.). 1999. *Roman presences: receptions of Rome in European culture, 1789–1945*, Cambridge.

   2011. 'Possessing Rome: the politics of ruins in Roma capitale', in Hardwick 2011: 346–59.

   2012. 'The return to Rome: desire and loss in Staël's *Corinne*', in Saunders et al. 2012: 183–202.

   2018. 'The romance of Roman error: encountering antiquity in Hawthorne's *The Marble Faun*', in Dufallo 2018: 127–51.

Einaudi, K. Bull-Simonsen. 1978. *Fotografia archeologica, 1865–1914*, Rome.

Eisenstein, E. 1983. *The printing revolution in early modern Europe*, Cambridge.

Emerick, J. J. 2014. 'The Tempietto del Clitunno and San Salvatore near Spoleto: ancient Roman imperial columnar display in medieval contexts', in Reeve 2014: 41–71.

Erskine, A. 2001. *Troy between Greece and Rome: local tradition and imperial power*, Oxford.

Fabrizio-Costa, S. (ed.). 2005. *Entre trace(s) et signe(s): quelques approaches herméneutiques de la ruine* (= Leia: Université de Caen 7), Bern.

Fabronius, A. 1788–9. *Magni Cosmi Medicei Vita* (2 vols), Pisa.

Fagiolo, M. (ed.). 1997. *La festa a Roma dal Rinascimento al 1870*: I 50–65, Turin.

   2013. *Roma barocca: i protagonisti, gli spazi urbani, i grandi temi*, Rome.

Fane-Saunders, P. 2016. *Pliny the Elder and the emergence of Renaissance architecture*, Cambridge.

Fantham, E. (ed., trans.). 2017. *Francesco Petrarca: selected letters*, Cambridge, MA.

Faroult, G. and C. Voiriot (eds.). 2016. *Hubert Robert (1733–1808): un peintre visionnaire* (exhibition catalogue), Paris.

Fauvinet-Ranson, V. 2006. *Decor civitatis, decor Italiae: monuments, travaux publics et spectacles au VIe siècle d'après les Variae de Cassiodore*, Bari.

Ferrary, J.-L. 1996. *Onofrio Panvinio et les antiquités romaines* (Collection de l'École française de Rome 214), Rome.

Ferris, I. M. 2013. *The arch of Constantine: inspired by the divine*, Stroud.

Filippi, F. (ed.). 2007. *Ricostruire l'Antico prima del virtuale: Italo Gismondi, un architetto per l'archeologia (1887–1974)* (exhibition catalogue), Rome.

Fine, S. (ed.). 2021. *The arch of Titus: from Jerusalem to Rome – and back*, Leiden.

Fiore, F. P. and A. Nesselrath (eds.). 2005. *La Roma di Leon Battista Alberti; umanisti, architetti e artisti alla scoperta dell'antico nella città del Quattrocento*, Milan.

Fleming, J. 1962. *Robert Adam and his circle in Edinburgh and Rome*, London.

Fleury, P. 2005. *La Rome antique: plan relief et reconstruction virtuelle*, Caen.

2014. 'Le plan de Rome de Paul Bigot: de la maquette en plâtre de Paul Bigot à la maquette virtuelle de l'Université de Caen', in *Civiltà Romana* 1: 109–24.

Fleury, P. and O. Desbordes (eds.). 2008. *Roma illustrata: représentations de la ville*, Caen.

Flint, K. (ed.). 1998. *Charles Dickens, Pictures from Italy*, Harmondsworth.

Floud, R. 2020. *An economic history of the English garden*, London.

Forero-Mendoza, S. 2002. *Le temps des ruines: le goût des ruines et les formes de la conscience historique à la Renaissance*, Champ Vallon.

Forsyth, W. 1865. *Rome and its ruins*, London.

Fracassetti, G. (ed.). 1859–63. *Francisci Petrarcae epistolae de rebus familiaribus et variae* (3 vols), Florence.

Frederiksen, R. and E. Marchand (eds.). 2010. *Plaster casts: making, collecting and displaying from classical antiquity to the present*, Berlin.

Friedländer, L. 1907. *Roman life and manners under the early empire* (authorised translation of the seventh enlarged and revised edition of the *Sittengeschichte Roms* by Leonard A. Magnus, vol. I), London.

Fritsch, B. 2017. 'The ancient monuments of Rome and their use as suppliers of remnants for construction of new St. Peter's basilica: building activity in Rome during the Renaissance', in Altekamp et al. 2017: 335–56.

Frommel, C. L. 2006. *Architettura e committenza da Alberti a Bramante*, Florence.

2007. *The architecture of the Italian Renaissance*, London.

Frommel, C. L., S. Ray and M. Tafuri (eds.). 1984. *Raffaello architetto*, Milan.

Frommel, S. 2013. 'Tradition religieuse contre invention à l'antique: ruines dans la peinture de la deuxième moitié du *Quattrocento*', in Kaderka 2013: 95–108.

Fry, S. 2014. *A history of the national heritage collection, volume 5: 1931–1945*, London.

Galli, P. and D. Molin. 2014. 'Beyond the damage threshold: the historic earthquakes of Rome', in *Bulletin of Earthquake Engineering* 12(3): 1277–1306.

Gampp, A. 2011. 'Rom zwischen Tivoli und Washington. Die Visualisierung des antiken Rom in der Frühen Neuzeit', in Cain et al. 2011: 225–43.

Gantner, C., R. McKitterick and S. Meeder (eds.). 2015. *The resources of the past in early medieval Europe*, Cambridge.

García Morcillo, M., P. Hanesworth and O. Lapeña Marchena (eds.). 2015. *Imagining ancient cities in film: from Babylon to Cinecittà*, New York.

Gaston, R. W. (ed.). 1988. *Pirro Ligorio: artist and antiquarian*, Florence.

Gercke, P. 2001. *Antike Bauten: Korkmodelle von Antonio Chichi 1777–1782: Katalog*, Kassel.

Gerding, H. 2002. *The tomb of Caecilia Metella: tumulus, tropaeum and thymele*, Lund.

Geyer, A. 1993. 'Ne ruinis urbs deformetur: Ästhetische Kriterien in der spätantiken Baugesetzgebung', in *Boreas* 16: 63–77.

Ghilardi, M. 2022 'Giovanni Battista de Rossi, *Archaeologiae Christianae Fundator, nel* Bicentenario della Nascita', in *Augustinianum* 62: 485–96.

Gibberd, P. 2004. *Sir Frederick Gibberd and his garden*, Harlow.

Gibbon, E. 1909–14. *The history of the decline and fall of the Roman empire* (edited in seven volumes with introduction, notes, appendices and index by J. B. Bury) (2nd ed.), London.

Gibson, B. 2017. 'Hildebert of Lavardin on the monuments of Rome', in Woodman and Wisse 2017: 131–54.

Gillespie, R. 2016. 'From "trash" to treasure: Museum Victoria's Colosseum model', in *Iris: Journal of the Classical Association of Victoria* 29: 22–31.

  2017a. 'Richard Du Bourg's "Classical Exhibition", 1775–1819', in *Journal of the History of Collections* 29: 251–69.

  2017b. 'The rise and fall of cork model collections in Britain', in *Architectural History* 60: 117–46.

Ginsberg, R. 2004. *The aesthetics of ruins*, Amsterdam.

Giustozzi, N. 2019. *The Roman Forum book*, Milan.

Gleadhill, E. 2022. *Taking travel home: the souvenir culture of British women tourists, 1750–1830*, Manchester.

Godwin, J. (trans.). 1999. *Francesco Colonna, Hypnerotomachia Poliphili, The Strife of Love in a Dream*, London.

Goethe, J. W. von. 1962. *Italian Journey: 1786–1788* (trans. W. H. Auden and E. Mayer), London.

Goffi, F. 2022. *The Routledge companion to architectural drawings and models: from translating to archiving, collecting and displaying*, London.

Goldstein, L. 1977. *Ruins and empire: the evolution of a theme in Augustan and Romantic literature*, Pittsburgh, PA.

Golvin, J.-C. and F. Lontcho. 2008. *Rome antique retrouvée: L'Vrbs/Ostie/Villa Hadriana/Palestrina/Villa de Tibère*, Paris.

Gorski, G. J. and J. E. Packer. 2015. *The Roman Forum: a reconstruction and architectural guide*, New York.

Graf, A. 1882–3. *Roma nella memoria e nelle immaginazioni del Medio Evo* (2 vols), Turin.

Grafton, A. 2000. *Leon Battista Alberti: master builder of the Renaissance*, New York.

Grafton, A., G. Most and S. Settis (eds.). 2010. *The classical tradition*, Cambridge, MA.

Green, A. 2011. *Changing France: literature and material culture in the Second Empire*, London.

Greene, T. M. 1982. *The light in Troy*, New Haven, CT.

Gregorovius, F. 1894–1912. *History of the city of Rome in the Middle Ages* (trans. A. Hamilton) (vols 1–4, 2nd revised ed.), London.

Grüner, A. 2005. 'Ruinen ohne Romantik: Zerstörte Gebäude als urbanistisches Problem der frühen Kaiserzeit', in Neudecker and Zanker 2005: 39–50.

Hall, J. 2019. *The conquest of ruins: the third Reich and the fall of Rome*, Chicago, IL.

Hans, L. and J. J. Blanc. 1871. *Guide à travers les ruines: Paris et environs*, Paris.

Hardwick, L. and C. Stray (eds.). 2011. *A companion to classical receptions*, Chichester.

Hare, A. J. C. 1893. *Walks in Rome* (13th ed.), London.

Harney, M. 2017. 'Conclusion: conserving Britain's ruins, 1700 to the present day', in Carter 2017: 275–96.

Harris, E. 1990. *British architectural books and writers 1556–1785*, Cambridge.

Harris, J. and M. Snodin (eds.). 1996. *Sir William Chambers, architect to George III*, New Haven, CT.

Harris, W. V. (ed.). 1999. 'The transformation of Vrbs Roma in late antiquity', in *Journal of Roman Archaeology Supplementary Series* 33, Portsmouth, RI.

Hart, V. and P. Hicks. 2009. *Palladio's Rome: a translation of Andrea Palladio's two guidebooks to Rome*, New Haven, CT.

Hartmann, A. 2010. *Zwischen Relikt und Reliquie: Objektbezogene Erinnerungspraktiken in antiken Gesellschaften* (= Studien zur alten Geschichte 11), Berlin.

Hartmann, G. 1981. *Die Ruinen im Landschaftsgarten: ihre Bedeutung für den frühen Historismus und die Landschaftsmalerei der Romantik*, Worms.

Haskell, F. 1980. *Patrons and painters: a study in the relations between Italian art and society in the age of the Baroque* (2nd ed.), New Haven, CT.

Hawcroft, F. W. 1988. *Travels in Italy, 1776–1783, based on the memoirs of Thomas Jones* (exhibition catalogue), Manchester.

Heckscher, W. S. 1936. *Die Rom-Ruinen: die geistigen Voraussetzungen ihrer Verwertung im Mittelalter und in der Renaissance*, Würzburg.

Heenes, V. 2014. 'Dupérac, Étienne', in *Brill's new Pauly supplements: history of classical scholarship – a biographical dictionary*, vol. 6: 168–9, Leiden.

Hell, J. 2019. *The conquest of ruins: the third Reich and the fall of Rome*, Chicago, IL.

Helmberger, W. and V. Kockel (eds.). 1993. *Rom über die Alpen tragen: Fürsten sammeln antike Architektur: Die Aschaffenburger Korkmodelle*, Landshut.

Heuer, C. P. 2009. 'Hieronymus Cock's aesthetic of collapse', in *Oxford Art Journal* 32(3): 389–408.

Hibbert, C. 1987. *The Grand Tour*, London.

Hill, P. V. 1989. *The monuments of ancient Rome as coin types*, London.

Hinard, F. and M. Royo (eds.). 1991. *Rome: l'espace urbain & ses representations*, Paris.

Hobhouse, J. C. 1818. *Historical illustrations of the Fourth Canto of Childe Harold: containing dissertations on the ruins of Rome; and an essay on Italian literature* (2nd ed.), London.

Holleran, C. and A. Claridge (eds.). 2018. *A companion to the city of Rome*, Chichester.

Hopkins, K. 2009. 'The political economy of the Roman empire', in Morris 2009: 178–204.

Hopkins, K. and M. Beard. 2005. *The Colosseum*, London.

Hornsby, C. (ed.). 2000. *The impact of Italy: the Grand Tour and beyond*, London.

Houghton, W. E. 1963. *The poetry of Clough: an essay in revaluation*, New Haven, CT.

Howells, W. D. 1901. *Italian journeys*, London.

    1908. *Roman holidays and others*, New York.

Huelsen, C. 1909. *The Roman Forum, its history and its monuments*, Rome.

Huet, V. 1999. 'Napoleon I: a new Augustus?', in Edwards 1999: 53–69.

Hui, A. 2015. 'The birth of ruins in Quattrocento adoration paintings', in *I Tatti Studies in the Italian Renaissance* 18: 319–48.

    2016. *The poetics of ruins in Renaissance literature*, New York.

Hung, W. 2012. *A story of ruins: absence and presence in Chinese art*, Princeton, NJ.

Hurst, I. 2007. 'Reanimating the Romans: Mary Shelley's response to Roman ruins', in Wrigley 2007: 125–36.

Insolera, I. and A. M. Sette (eds.). 2000. *Frondose arcate: il Colosseo prima dell'archeologia* (exhibition catalogue), Milan.

Jacks, P. 1990. 'The *Simulachrum* of Fabio Calvo: a view of Roman architecture *all'antica* in 1527', in *The Art Bulletin* 72: 453–81.

    1993. *The antiquarian and the myth of antiquity: the origins of Rome in Renaissance thought*, Cambridge.

James, H. 1875. *Transatlantic sketches*, Boston, MA.

James, M. R. 1917. '*Magister Gregorius de Mirabilibus Urbis Romae*', in *English Historical Review* 32: 531–54.

Janowitz, A. F. 1990. *England's ruins: poetic purpose and the national landscape*, Oxford.

Jaskulska-Tschierse, A., J. Kolendo and T. Mikocki. 1998. *Arcadiana. Arcadia in Poland. An 18th century antique garden and its famous sculptures*, Warsaw.

Jenkyns, R. (ed.). 1992. *The legacy of Rome: a new appraisal*, Oxford.

Johnson, A. C., P. Robinson Coleman-Norton and F. C. Bourne. 1961. *Ancient Roman statutes*, Austin, TX.

Jones, B. 1974. *Follies and grottoes*, London.

Jonsson, M. 1986. *La cura dei monumenti alle origini: restauro e scavo di monumenti antichi a Roma 1800–1830*, Stockholm.

Junkelmann, M. 2004. *Hollywoods Traum von Rom. 'Gladiator' und die Tradition des Monumentalfilms* (Kulturgeschichte der antiken Welt 94), Mainz.

Junod, P. 1982–3. 'Ruines anticipées ou l'histoire au futur antérieur', in *L'homme face à son histoire*, Lausanne = 2007. *Chemins de traverse. Essai sur l'histoire des arts*, Lausanne.

Kaderka, K. (ed.). 2013. *Les ruines: entre destruction et construction de l'Antiquité à nos jours*, Rome.

Kalas, G. and A. van Dijk (eds.). 2021. *Urban developments in late antique and medieval Rome: revising the narrative of renewal*, Amsterdam.

Karmon, D. E. 2011. *The ruin of the eternal city: antiquity and preservation in Renaissance Rome*, Oxford.

King, R. 2007. *The judgement of Paris*, London.

Kinney, D. 1990. 'Mirabilia Urbis Romae', in Bernardo 1990: 207–21.

Kitz, N. and B. 1984. *Pains Hill Park: Hamilton and his picturesque landscape*, Cobham.

Klinge, M. 2020. 'Rome in early photographs', in *Rom in frühen Photografien: Sammlung Orsola und Filippo Maggia* (Lempertz auction 1161 catalogue, 7 December), Cologne.

Kockel, V. 1998. *Phelloplastica: modelli in sughero dell'architettura antica nel XVIII secolo nella collezione di Gustavo III di Svezia*, Stockholm.

2010. 'Plaster models and plaster casts of classical architecture and its decoration', in Frederiksen and Marchand 2010: 419–33.

2011. '"Wissenschaft und Kunst sind, wie selten, eine glückliche Verbindung eingegangen": Das Rom-Panorama von Josef Bühlmann im Kontext des 19. Jahrhunderts', in Cain et al. 2011: 23–48.

Kocziszky, E. (ed.). 2011. *Ruinen in der Moderne: Archäologie und die Künste*, Berlin.

Kostof, S. 1978. 'The emperor and the Duce: the planning of Piazzale Augusto Imperatore in Rome', in MIllon and Nochlin 1978: 270–325.

Krautheimer, R. 1980. *Rome: profile of a city, 312–1308*, Princeton, NJ.

1985. *The Rome of Alexander VII, 1655–1667*, Princeton, NJ.

Kuhn, C. 2000. *Italienische Fotographien aus der Sammlung John Henry Parker (1806–1884)*, Berlin.

Laing, A. 1993. 'O Tempera, O Mores! The ruin paintings in the dining room at Shugborough', in *Apollo* 137(374): 227–32.

Lanciani, R. 1899. *The destruction of ancient Rome: a sketch of the history of the monuments*, London.

1901. *New tales of old Rome*, London.

1902. *Storia degli scavi di Roma* (first volume: A. 1000–1530), Rome; reprinted 1989, Rome.

1985. *Rovine e scavi di Roma antica*, Rome.

La Regina, A. (ed.). 2001. *Sangue e arena* (exhibition catalogue), Milan.

Laureys, M. 2006. 'Das alte und das neue Rom in Andrea Fulvios *Antiquaria Urbis*', in Disselkamp et al. 2006: 201–20.

Laureys, M. and A. Schreurs. 1996. 'Egio, Marliano, Ligorio, and the Forum Romanum in the 16th century', in *Humanistica Lovaniensia* 45: 385–405.

Lawrence, L. 1938. 'Stuart and Revett: their literary and architectural careers', in *Journal of the Warburg Institute* 2: 128–46.

Lazard, M. 1993. *Rabelais l'humaniste*, Paris.

Lecocq, F. 2008. 'Les premières maquettes de Rome: L'exemple des modèles réduits en liège de Carl et Georg May dans les collections européennes aux XVIIIe–XIXe siècles', in Fleury and Desbordes 2008: 227–60.

Legassie, S. A. 2017. *The medieval invention of travel*, Chicago, IL.

Lichtenberger, A. and R. Raja (eds.). 2017. *The diversity of classical archaeology*, Turnhout.

Lightbown, R. W. 1964. 'Nicolas Audebert and the Villa d'Este', in *Journal of the Warburg and Courtauld Institutes* 27: 164–90.

Liversidge, M. and C. Edwards (eds.). 1996. *Imagining Rome: British artists and Rome in the nineteenth century*, London.

Llewellyn-Jones, L. 2018. *Designs on the past: how Hollywood created the ancient world*, Edinburgh.

Long, P. O. 2018. *Engineering the eternal city: infrastructure, topography, and the culture of knowledge in late sixteenth-century Rome*, Chicago, IL.

Lukacher, B. 2006. *Joseph Gandy: an architectural visionary in Georgian England*, London.

Lyon, J. 1999. 'Henry James and the anxiety of Rome', in Edwards 1999: 140–56.

Macaulay, R. 1953. *Pleasure of ruins* (numerous reprints), London.

Machado, C. 2019. *Urban space and aristocratic power in late antique Rome*, A D 270–535, Oxford.

Madonna, M. 1997. 'L'ingresso di Carlo V a Roma', in Fagiolo 1997: I 50–65.

Maier, J. 2015. *Rome measured and imagined*, Chicago, IL.

   2020. *The eternal city: a history of Rome in maps*, Chicago, IL.

Makarius, M. 2011 [2004]. *Ruines. Représentations dans l'art de la Renaissance à nos jours*, Paris.

Mambriani, C. 2006. *Il giardino di Parma*, Reggio Emilia.

Mann, N. 1984. *Petrarch*, Oxford.

Marder, T. A. and M. Wilson Jones (eds.). 2015. *The Pantheon from antiquity to the present*, Cambridge.

Marshall, A. 2002. *Mirabilia Urbis Romae: Five centuries of guidebooks and views* (exhibition catalogue), Toronto.

Marshall, D. R. 1993. *Viviano and Niccolò Codazzi and the baroque architectural fantasy*, Rome.

   2014a. 'The Campo Vaccino: order and the fragment from Palladio to Piranesi', in Marshall 2014b: 140–61.

   2014b. *The site of Rome: studies in the art and topography of Rome 1400–1750* (Melbourne Art Journal 13), Rome.

Marshall, D. R., S. Russell and K. Wolfe (eds.). 2011. *Roma Britannica: art patronage and cultural exchange in eighteenth-century Rome*, London.

Martínez Jiménez, J. and S. Ottewill-Soulsby (eds.). 2022. *Remembering and forgetting the ancient city*, Oxford.

Massimiliano, D. (ed.). 2002. *Ruins of ancient Rome: the drawings of French architects who won the Prix de Rome 1786–1924*, Los Angeles, CA.

Massing, J. M. 1990. '"The Triumph of Caesar" by Benedetto Bordon and Jacobus Argentoratensis: its iconography and influence', in *Print Quarterly* 7: 2–21.

Matthews, J. 1975. *Western aristocracies and imperial court*, A.D. 364–425, Oxford.

Mayer, R. 2007. 'Impressions of Rome', in *Greece and Rome* 54: 156–77.

Mayernick, D. 2014. 'The *capricci* of Giovanni Paolo Panini', in Steil 2014: 33–7.

Mazzocco, A. 1975. 'Petrarca, Poggio, and Biondo: humanism's foremost interpreters of Roman ruins', in Scaglione 1975: 353–63.

    1977. 'The antiquarianism of Francesco Petrarca', in *Journal of Medieval and Renaissance Studies* 7: 203–24.

McClellan, A. 1994. *Inventing the Louvre: art, politics, and the origins of the modern museum in 18th-century Paris*, Berkeley, CA.

McCormick, T. 1990. *Charles-Louis Clérisseau and the genesis of neo-classicism*, Cambridge, MA.

McGeough, K. M. 2022. *Representations of antiquity in film from Griffith to Grindhouse*, Sheffield.

McGowan, M. M. 2000. *The vision of Rome in late Renaissance France*, New Haven, CT.

McKitterick, R., J. Osborne, C. M. Richardson and J. Story (eds.). 2013. *Old Saint Peter's, Rome*, Cambridge.

    2015. 'Transformations of the Roman past and Roman identity in the early Middle Ages', in Gantner et al. 2015: 225–44.

    2020. *Rome and the invention of the papacy: the Liber Pontificalis*, Cambridge.

McManamon, J. M. 1996. *Pierpaolo Vergerio the Elder: the humanist as orator*, Tempe, AZ.

Medina Lasansky, D. and B. McLaren (eds.). 2004. *Architecture and tourism: perception, performance and place*, Oxford.

Meier, H.-R. 2011. 'Visuelle Konzeptionen der antiken Stadt Rom in der Frühen Neuzeit: Ruinenlandschaften versus Rekonstruktionen – ein Überblick', in Cain et al. 2011: 139–57.

Meiggs, R. 1973. *Roman Ostia* (2nd ed.), Oxford.

Meneghini, R. and R. Santageli Valenzani. 2007. *I Fori imperiali: gli scavi del Comune di Roma (1991–2007)*, Rome.

    2009. *I Fori imperiali e i mercati di Traiano*, Rome.

Merrills, A. and R. Miles. 2010. *The vandals*, Chichester.

Mielke, F. 1991. *Potsdamer Baukunst: das klassische Potsdam* (2nd ed.), Frankfurt.

Mikocki. T. 1995. *Collection de la Princesse Radziwill. Les monuments antiques et antiquisants d'Arcadie et du Château de Nieborow*, Wroclaw.

Mikocki, T. and W. Piwkowski (eds.). 2001. *Et In Arcadia Ego. Muzeum Ksiezny Heleny Radziwillowej*, Warsaw.

Miller, A. R. (Lady) 1776. *Letters from Italy, describing the manners, customs, antiquities, paintings, etc. of that country, in the years MDCCLXX and MDCCLXXI, to a friend residing in France*, London.

Millon, H. A. and L. Nochlin (eds.). 1978. *Art and architecture in the service of politics*, Cambridge, MA.

Miranda, S. 2000. *Francesco Bianchini e lo scavo farnesiano del Palatino (1720–1729)*, Pavia.

Mitchell, C., E. W. Bodnar and C. Foss (eds.). 2015. *Cyriac of Ancona, life and early travels* (The I Tatti Renaissance Library 65), Cambridge, MA.

Mitchell, S. 2015. *A history of the later Roman empire, AD 284–641* (2nd ed.), Chichester.

Moatti, C. 1993. *The search for ancient Rome*, London.

Mommsen, T. E. 1942. 'Petrarch's conception of "The Dark Ages"', in *Speculum* 17: 226–42.

Montagu, J. 1985. *Alessandro Algardi* (2 vols), New Haven, CT.

Moore, A. W. 1985. *Norfolk and the Grand Tour: eighteenth-century travellers abroad and their souvenirs*, Norwich.

Morris, I. and W. Scheidel (eds.). 2009. *The dynamics of ancient empires: state power from Assyria to Byzantium*, Oxford.

Morrogh, A., F. S. Gioffredi, P. Morselli et al. (eds.). 1985. *Renaissance studies in honor of Craig Hugh Smith*, Florence.

Mortier, R. 1974. *La Poétique des ruines en France: ses origines, ses variations de la Renaissance à Victor Hugo*, Geneva.

Muecke, F. 2003. 'Humanists in the Roman Forum', in *Papers of the British School at Rome* 71: 207–33.

    2007. 'Poetry on Rome from the ambience of Pomponio Leto: topography, history, encomium', in *L'Ellisse* 2: 101–26.

Murray, P. 1969. *The architecture of the Italian Renaissance*, London.

    1971. *Piranesi and the grandeur of ancient Rome*, London.

    1972. *Five early guides to Rome and Florence*, Farnborough.

Namer, M. P. 2019. *Giacomo Boni: storia memoria archeonomia*, Rome.

Nardella, C. (ed., trans.). 1997. *Il fascino di Roma nel Medioevo: Le Meraviglie di Roma di maestro Gregorio*, Rome.

    2001. 'L'antiquaria romana dal "Liber Pontificalis" ai "Mirabilia Urbis Romae"', in Zerbi 2001: 423–47.

Nash, E. 1968. *Pictorial dictionary of ancient Rome* (revised ed., 2 vols), London.

Nazzaro, B. 2017. 'I "grandi" restauri dell'ottocento e i "grandi" architetti: Stern, Valadier, Salvi, Canina', in Rea et al. 2017: 272–91.

Negri, D. 1989. *Pirro Ligorio, Delle antichità di Roma: circi, theatri, amphitheatri con numerose tavole e la pianta cinquecentesca di Roma*, Rome.

Negri, R. 1965. *Gusto e poesia delle rovine in Italia fra il sette e l'ottocento*, Milan.

Nesselrath, A. 1984. 'Raffaello e lo studio dell'antico nel Rinascimento', in Frommel 1984: 381–96 and 397–421.

    2014. *Der Zeichner und sein Buch: Die Darstellung der antiken Architektur im 15. und 16. Jahrhundert*, Mainz.

Neudecker, R. and P. Zanker (eds.). 2005. *Lebenswelten: Bilder und Räume in der römischen Stadt der Kaiserzeit*, = Palilia 16, Wiesbaden.

Nicholls, M. 2017. 'Fiddling with Rome', in *Apollo* 186(656): 40–2.

Nichols, F. M. 1889. *Mirabilia Vrbis Romae: the marvels of Rome or a picture of the golden city*, London (2nd ed. by E. Gardiner, 1986, New York).

Oberhuber, K. 1968. 'Hieronymus Cock, Battista Pittoni und Paolo Veronese in Valla Maser', in Buddensieg 1968: 207–24.

Odorico, P. and C. Messis (eds.). 2012. *Villes de toute beauté: l'ekphrasis des cités dans les littératures Byzantine et Byzantino-Slaves* (Dossiers Byzantins 12), Paris.

Osborne, J. (ed., trans.). 1987. *The marvels of Rome/Master Gregorius*, Toronto.

2013. '*Plus Caesare Petrus*: the Vatican obelisk and the approach to Saint Peter's', in McKitterick et al. 2013: 274–86.

2021. 'The re-invention of Rome in the early Middle Ages', in Kalas and van Dijk 2021: 205–35.

Oswald, A. 1938. 'Bretton Park', in *The Country Life* 83: 530–5 and 554–9.

Ottewill-Soulsby, S. and J. Martínez Jiménez. 2022. 'Zimbabwe and Rome: remembering and forgetting ancient cities', in Martínez Jiménez and Ottewill-Soulsby 2022: 1–20.

Packer, J. E. 1997. *The Forum of Trajan in Rome: a study of the monuments*, Berkeley, CA.

2001. *The Forum of Trajan in Rome: a study of the monuments in brief*, Berkeley, CA.

Painter, B. W. 2005. *Mussolini's Rome: rebuilding the eternal city*, New York.

2018. 'Mussolini and Rome', in Holleran and Claridge 2018: 683–97.

Panella, R. 2013. *Roma la città dei Fori: Rome the city of Forums*, Rome.

Papini, M. 2009. 'Etiam periere ruinae: Lucano, Bellum Civile IX 969. Le rovine nella cultura antica', in Barbanera 2009: 89–111.

2011. *Città sepolte e rovine nel mondo greco e latino*, Rome.

2017. 'The Romans' ruins', in Carandini 2017: 122–8.

Parisi Presicce, C., N. Bernacchio, M. Munzi and S. Pastor (eds.). 2021. *Napoleone e il mito di Roma* (exhibition catalogue), Rome.

Parshall, P. 2006. 'Antonio Lafreri's *Speculum Romanae Magnificentiae*', in *Print Quarterly* 23: 3–28.

Partner, P. 1976. *Renaissance Rome, 1500–1559: a portrait of a society*, Berkeley, CA.

Pensabene, P., M. Milella and F. Caprioli (eds.). 2017. *Decor. Decorazione e architettura nel mondo romano* (Thiasos Monografie 9), Rome.

Pergoli Campanelli, A. 2013. *Cassiodoro alle origini dell'idea di restauro*, Squillace.

2015. *La nascita del restauro dall'antichità all' Alto Medioevo*, Milan.

Petochi, D., M. Alfieri and M. Branchetti. 1981. *I mosaici minuti romani dei secoli xviii e xix*, Rome.

Pharr, C. 1952. *The Theodosian code and novels: and the Sirmondian constitutions*, Princeton, NJ.

Piantoni, F. (ed.) 1994. *Roma in stereoscopia*, Rome.

Piccioni, C. (ed.). 1993. *Le antichità della città di Roma*, Rome.

Piccoli, C. 2017. 'Visualizing antiquity before the digital age: early and late modern reconstructions of Greek and Roman cityscapes', in *Analecta Praehistorica Leidensia* 47: 225–57.

Pinto, J. A. 2012. *Speaking ruins: Piranesi, architects and antiquity in eighteenth-century Rome*, Ann Arbor, MI.

Pirazzoli, N. 1990. *Luigi Rossini 1790–1856: Roma antica restaurata*, Ravenna.

Pisacane, C. 2005. 'Pétrarque à Rome: l'image des ruines entre mémoire du passé et promesse de *renovatio*', in Fabrizio-Costa 2005: 105–19.

Pisani Sartorio, G. 1991. 'Le plan-relief d'Italo Gismondi: méthodes, techniques de realisation et perspectives futures', in Hinard 1991: 256–77.

Porter, J. I. 2001. 'Ideals and ruins: Pausanias, Longinus, and the Second Sophistic', in Alcock et al. 2001: 63–92.

    2011. 'Sublime monuments and sublime ruins in ancient aesthetics', in *Antiquity and the Ruin: L'Antiquité et les ruines*, Special Issue of *European Review of History: Revue europeenne d'histoire* 18: 685–96.

Prieto Arciniega, A. 2015. '"Rome is no longer Rome": in search of the eternal city in cinema', in García Morcillo 2015: 163–83.

Pritchett, W. K. 1999. *Pausanias periegetes* II, Amsterdam.

Puetz, A. 2004. 'Robert Hancock', in *Dictionary of National Biography* 25: 20–1.

Purcell, N. 1992. 'The city of Rome', in Jenkyns 1992: 421–53.

Raffarin-Dupuis, A. (ed.). 2005/2012. *Flavio Biondo, Roma Instaurata (Rome restaurée)* (2 vols), Paris.

Rea, R. 2019. *The Colosseum*, Milan.

Rea, R., S. Romano and R. Santangeli Valenzani (eds.). 2017. *Colosseo* (exhibition catalogue), Milan.

Reeve, M. (ed.). 2014. *Tributes to Pierre du Prey: architecture and the classical tradition, from Pliny to posterity*, London.

Regard, M. (ed.). 1978. *Chateaubriand: Essai sur les révolutions, Génie du christianisme*, Paris.

Rehm, W. 1960. *Europäische Romdichtung* (2nd ed.), Munich.

Retford, K. 2023. 'Cutting and pasting: the print room at Woodhall Park', *British Art Studies* 24, https://doi.org/10.17658-5462/issue-24/kretford (unpaginated).

Riccioni, S. 2011. 'Rewriting antiquity, renewing Rome: the identity of the eternal city through visual art, monumental inscriptions and the *Mirabilia*', in *Medieval Encounters* 17: 439–63.

Richardson, L. 1992. *A new topographical dictionary of ancient Rome*, Baltimore, MD.

Richardson, M. 1989. 'Model architecture', in *Country Life* 183(38): 224–7.

Ridley, R. T. 1992a. *The eagle and the spade: archaeology in Rome during the Napoleonic era*, Cambridge.

    1992b. 'To protect the monuments: the papal antiquarian (1534–1870)', in *Xenia Antiqua* 1: 117–54.

    2000. *The pope's archaeologist: the life and times of Carlo Fea*, Rome.

Rieche, A. 2012. *Vom Rom nach Las Vegas: Rekonstruktionen antiker römischer Architektur*, Berlin.

Riggs, T. A. 1977. *Hieronymus Cock: printmaker and publisher*, New York.

Ritter, D. 2005. *Rom 1846–70: James Anderson und die Maler-Fotografen, Sammlung Siegert*, Heidelberg.

Roberts, J. 1997. *Royal landscape: the gardens and parks of Windsor*, New Haven, CT
     (ed.). 2002. *Royal treasures: a Golden Jubilee celebration* (exhibition catalogue),
     London.

Robinson, J. M. 2018. 'Refreshing the palette: Woodhall Park, Hertfordshire', in
     Country Life 212(7): 51–2.

Robinson, O. F. 1992. *Ancient Rome: city planning and administration*, London.

Rocha, I. E. 2018. 'Rome models: between history and representations', in *Heródoto:
     Revista do Grupo de Estudos e Pesquisas sobre a Antiguidade Clássica e suas
     Conexões Afro-asiáticas* 3: 276–87.

Rodocanachi, E. 1906. *The Roman Capitol in ancient and modern times*, London.

Romano, S. 2017. 'Delle fronde e del chiaro di luna, degli agguati e delle febbre: il
     Colosseo romantico', in Rea et al. 2017: 202–15.

Rose, C. B. 2014. *The archaeology of Greek and Roman Troy*, Cambridge.

Rosenmeyer, P. A. 2018. *The language of ruins: Greek and Latin inscriptions on the
     Memnon Colossus*, Oxford.

Rossetti, S. 2000. *Rome: a bibliography from the invention of printing through 1899,
     I: The guide books*, Florence – 2,457 items.

Rossi, V. (ed.). 1933–42. *Francesco Petrarca Le familiari* (4 vols), Florence.

Rossini, O. 2006. *Ara Pacis*, Milan.

Rossi Pinelli, O. 2009. '"La bellezza involontaria": dalle rovine alla cultura del fram-
     mento tra Otto e Novecento', in Barbanera 2009: 140–57.

Rowe, J. C. 2018. 'The Roman aura in Henry James's *Daisy Miller: a study* (1878)', in
     Dufallo 2018: 191–208.

Royo, M. 1991. 'La mémoire de l'architecte', in Hinard and Royo 1991: 201–21.

Rubach, B. 2016. *Ant. Lafreri Formis Romae: Der Verleger Antonio Lafreri und seine
     Druckgraphikproduktion*, Berlin.

Rubinstein, R. O. 1985. 'Tempus Edax Rerum: a newly discovered painting by
     Hermannus Posthumus', in *The Burlington Magazine* 127: 425–33 and 435–6.

Rubinstein, R. 1988. 'Pius II and Roman ruins', in *Renaissance Studies* 2: 197–203.

Rushforth, G. McN. 1919. 'Magister Gregorius *de mirabilibus urbis Romae*: a new
     description of Rome in the twelfth century', in *Journal of Roman Studies* 9:
     14–58.

Ruskin, J. 1895. *The harbours of England*, London.

Russell, F. 1977. 'Microcosm of 18th-century taste: the engravings room at Woodhall
     park', in *Country Life* 162(4188): 924–6.

Saalman, H. 1970. *The life of Brunelleschi by Antonio di Tuccio Manetti*, University
     Park, PA.

Sachs, J. 2010. *Romantic antiquity: Rome in the British imagination, 1789–1832*,
     Oxford.

Sage, M. 2000. 'Roman visitors to Ilium in the Roman imperial and late antique
     period: the symbolic functions of a landscape', in *Studia Troica* 10: 211–31.

Salmon, F. 2000. *Building on ruins: the rediscovery of Rome and English architecture*,
     Aldershot.

Santangeli Valenzani, R. 2017. 'The end of the ancient city', in Carandini 2017: 116–21.

Saunders, T., C. Martindale, R. Pite and M. Skoie (eds.). 2012. *Romans and romantics*, Oxford.

Scaglia, G. 1964. 'The origin of an archaeological plan of Rome by Alessandro Strozzi', in *Journal of the Warburg and Courtauld Institutes* 27: 137–63.

Scaglione, A. 1975. *Francis Petrarch, six centuries later: a symposium*, Chapel Hill, NC.

Scherer, M. R. 1955. *Marvels of ancient Rome*, London.

Schieder, W. 2006. 'Die Repräsentation der Antike im Faschismus', in Stein-Hölkeskamp 2006: 701–21.

Schingo, G. 2001. 'I modelli del Colosseo', in La Regina 2001: 105–15.

Schnapp, A. 1996. *The discovery of the past: the origins of archaeology*, London (Eng. trans. of *La conquête du passé*, 1993).

   2003. 'Vestiges, monuments, and ruins: the East faces West', in Zimmermann 2003: 3–24.

   2011. 'Les ruines dans l'antiquité classique', in Cain et al. 2011: 115–37.

   2015. *Ruines: essai de perspective comparée*, Lyon.

   2016. '"Robert des ruines": le peintre face aux monuments antiques', in Faroult and Voiriot 2016: 85–95.

   2017. 'La révolution des images: la figuration des ruines et la naissance de l'idée de relevé dans l'archéologie classique', in Lichtenberger and Raja 2017: 7–21.

Schreurs, A. 2014. 'Ligorio, Pirro', in *Brill's new Pauly supplements: history of classical scholarship – a biographical dictionary*, vol. 6: 370–1, Leiden.

Schreyer, J. 2019. *Zerstörte Architektur bei Pausanias. Phänomenologie, Funktionen und Verhältnis zum zeit genössischen Ruinendiscurs* (Studies in Classical Archaeology 5), Turnhout.

Schudt, L. 1930. *Le guide di Roma: Materialien zu einer Geschichte der römischen Topographie*, Vienna.

Scobie, A. 1990. *Hitler's state architecture: the impact of classical antiquity*. University Park, PA.

Scott, A. B. (ed.). 2001. *Carmina minora/Hildebertus Cenomannensis Episcopus*, Leipzig.

Scott, J. B. 2014. 'Uses of the past: Charles V's Roman triumph and its legacy', in Reeve 2014: 81–97.

Settis, S. (ed.). 1986a. *Memoria dell'antico nell'arte italiana, vol. 3: Dalla tradizione all'archeologia*, Turin.

   1986b. 'Continuità, distanza, conoscenza. Tre usi dell'antico', in Settis 1986a: 373–486.

   2006. *The future of the 'classical'*, Cambridge = 2004: 82–91, *Futuro del 'classico'*, Turin.

   2011. 'Nécessité des ruines: les enjeux du classique', in *Antiquity and the Ruin: L'Antiquité et les ruines, Special Issue of European Review of History: Revue européenne d'histoire* 18: 717–40.

Seznec, J. 1983. *Diderot: Salons, Volume 3: 1767* (2nd ed.), Oxford.

Sheeler, J. 2003. *Little Sparta, the garden of Ian Hamilton Finlay*, London.

Silva, E. 2002. *Dell'arte de' Giardini inglesi* (G. Guerci, C. Nenci and L. Scazzosi (eds.)), Florence.

Simpson, C. M. (ed.). 1968. *Nathaniel Hawthorne, The marble faun: or, the romance of Monte Beni* (The Centenary Edition of the Works of Nathaniel Hawthorne IV), Columbus, OH.

Slaney, H. 2016. 'Perceiving (in) depth: landscape, sculpture, ruin', in Butler 2016: 87–105.

  2020. *Kinaesthesia and classical antiquity 1750–1820: moved by stone*, London.

Smallwood, E. M. 1967. *Documents illustrating the principates of Gaius, Claudius and Nero*, Cambridge.

Smith, C. 1992. *Architecture in the culture of early humanism: ethics, aesthetics, and eloquence 1400–1470*, New York.

Smith, L. (ed.). 1934. *Pier Paulo Vergerio, Epistolario* (Fonti per la storia d'Italia pubblicate dall'Istituto Storico Italiano per il Medio Evo 74), Rome.

Soane Museum. 2017/18. 'Past perspectives: future practice', *Annual Review* 58; reference: SM vol. 92 fol. 21.

Solkin, D. H. 1982. *Richard Wilson*, London.

Sonnabend, M. and J. Whiteley. 2011. *Claude Lorrain: the enchanted landscape*, Oxford.

Sorrell, A. and A. Birley. 1970. *Imperial Rome*, London.

Spila, A. 2006. 'Il tempio diruto di Villa Albani e il tema delle finte rovine nella Roma del Settecento', in Materiali e strutture 3/2005, 5/6: 104–39.

  2013. 'Il ponte ruinante di Palazzo Barberini e il giardino della Guglia', in Fagiolo 2013: 663–5.

  2014. 'The false ruins of Villa Torlonia: the Nymphaeum/Sui falsi ruderi di villa Torlonia: il ninfeo', in *ArcHistoR* I, 1: 108–33.

Springer, C. 1987. *The marble wilderness: ruins and representation in Italian romanticism, 1775–1850*, Cambridge.

Spurling, H. 1984. *Ivy: the life of Ivy Compton-Burnett*, London.

Steil, L. (ed.). 2014. *The architectural capriccio: memory, fantasy and invention*, Farnham.

Stein-Hölkeskamp, E. and K.-J. Hölkeskamp (eds.). 2006. *Errinerungsorte der Antike: die römische Welt*, Munich.

Stekelenburg, A. V. von. 1990. 'The Colosseum from late antiquity till the end of the Middle Ages: a case of lost identity', in *Akroterion* 35: 126–33.

Stephens, R. 2015. *Light, time, legacy: Francis Towne's watercolours of Rome* (exhibition brochure), London.

Stewart, S. 2020. *The ruins lesson: meaning and material in western culture*, Chicago, IL.

Stillman, D. 1966. *The decorative work of Robert Adam*, London.

Story, W. W. 1871. *Roba di Roma* (6th ed.), London.

Striker, C. L. (ed.). 1996. *Architectural studies in memory of Richard Krautheimer*, Mainz.

Sutton, D. (ed.). 1982. *Souvenirs of the Grand Tour* (exhibition catalogue), London.

Swaffield, B. C. 2009. *Rising from the ruins: Roman antiquities in neoclassic literature*, Newcastle.

Sweet, R. 2012. *Cities and the Grand Tour: the British in Italy, c. 1690–1820*, Cambridge.

Symes, M. 2010. *Mr Hamilton's Elysium: the gardens of Painshill*, London.

Szegedy-Maszak, A. 1992. 'A perfect ruin: nineteenth-century views of the Coliseum', in *Arion* ser. 3, 2(1): 115–42.

Tatarinova, I. 2006. 'Architectural models at the St Petersburg Academy of Fine Art', in *Journal of the History of Collections* 18: 27–39.

Taylor, C. 2018. *The design, production and reception of eighteenth-century wallpaper in Britain*, London.

Taylor, R., K. W. Rinne and S. Kostof. 2016. *Rome: an urban history form antiquity to the present*, Cambridge.

Tedeschi, L. 2011. 'Vincenzo Brenna and his drawings from the antique for Charles Townley', in Marshall et al. 2011: 257–69.

Teolato, C. 2016. *Hopfgarten and Jollage rediscovered: two Berlin bronzists in Napoleonic and restoration Rome*, Rome.

Teynac, F., P. Nolot and J.-D. Vivien. 1982. *Wallpaper, a history*, London.

Theodorakopoulos, E. 2010. *Ancient Rome at the cinema: story and spectacle in Hollywood and Rome*, Bristol.

Thornton, P. and H. Dorey. 1992. *A miscellany of objects from Sir John Soane's Museum*, London.

Thurley, S. 2013. *Men from the ministry: how Britain saved its heritage*, New Haven, CT.

Thurn, N. 1995. *Ugolino Verino, Carlias: ein Epos des 15. Jahrhunderts erstmals herausgegeben*, Munich.

2002. *Kommentar zur Carlias* des Ugolino Verino, Munich.

Toynbee, P. (ed.). 1903. *The letters of Horace Walpole, earl of Orford*, Oxford.

1927–8. *Walpole's journals of visits to country seats*, etc. (The Volume of the Walpole Society 16), London.

Trachtenberg, M. 1985. 'Brunelleschi, "Giotto" and Rome', in Morrogh et al. 1985: 675–97.

1996. 'On Brunelleschi's choice: speculations on medieval Rome and the origins of Renaissance architecture', in Striker 1996: 169–73.

Tschudi, V. P. 2012. 'Plaster empires: Italo Gismondi's model of Rome', in *Journal of the Society of Architectural Historians* 71: 386–403.

2017. *Baroque antiquity: archaeological imagination in early modern Europe*, Cambridge.

2019. 'Two sixteenth-century guidebooks and the *bibliotopography* of Rome', in Blennow and Fogelberg Rota 2019: 89–115.

Tucci, P. L. 2017. *The Temple of Peace in Rome* (2 vols), Cambridge.

  2018. 'Napoleonic Rome and "Roma Capitale"', in Holleran and Claridge 2018: 673–81.

Tucker, G. H. 1990. *The poet's Odyssey: Joachim Du Bellay and the Antiquitez de Rome*, Oxford.

Turcan, R. 2014. *L'Archéologie dans l'antiquité: tourisme, lucre et découvertes*, Paris.

Turner, A. R. 1966. *The vision of landscape in Renaissance Italy*, Princeton, NJ.

Tyack, G. 1992. *Sir James Pennethorne and the making of Victorian London* (Cambridge Studies in the History of Architecture), Cambridge.

Underwood, D. 2019. *(Re)using ruins: public building in the cities of the late antique West, A.D. 300–600* (*Late antique archaeology* supplementary series, vol. 3), Leiden.

Urlichs, C. L. 1871. *Codex Urbis Romae Topographicus*, Würzburg.

Vance, W. L. 1989. *America's Rome* (2 vols), New Haven, CT.

Vasi, M. 1820. *Itinèraire instructif de Rome*, Rome.

  1970. *Roma del Settecento: itinerario istruttivo di Roma di Mariano Vasi romano con note di Guglielmo Matthiae*, Rome.

Venuti, R. 1763. *Accurata e succinta descrizione topografica delle antichità di Roma*, Rome.

Versnel, H. S. 1972. 'The ancient Roman origin of the *salvatio Romae* legend', in *Talanta* 4: 46–62.

Viney, W. 2014. *Waste: a philosophy of things*, London.

Visconti, E. Q. 1794. *Iscrizioni greche triopee ora borghesiane*, Rome.

Viti, P. 2005. 'La rovina di Roma come coscienza della rinascita umanistica', in Fabrizio-Costa 2005: 121–58.

Wagenberg-Ter Hoeven, A. A. van. 2018. *Jan Baptist Weenix: the paintings – a story of versatility, success and bankruptcy in seventeenth-century Holland*, Zwolle.

Walser, G. 1987. *Die Einsiedler Inschriftensammlung und der Pilgerführer durch Rom (Codex Einsiedlensis 326): Facsimile, Umschrift, Übersetzung und Kommentar* (*Historia* Einzelschrift 53), Wiesbaden.

Ward-Perkins, B. 1984. *From classical antiquity to the Middle Ages: urban public building in Northern and Central Italy, AD 300–850*, Oxford.

Watkin, D. 1977. *Triumph of the classical: an exhibition in the Graham Robertson Room, 27 September–20 November 1977*, Cambridge.

  1982. *The English vision: the picturesque in architecture, landscape and garden design*, London.

  1999. 'Built ruins: the hermitage as a retreat', in Woodward 1999: 5–14.

  2000. 'Sir John Soane's Grand Tour: its impact on his architecture and his collections', in Hornsby 2000: 101–21.

  2009. *The Roman Forum*, London.

Watkin, D. and T. Mellinghoff. 1987. *German architecture and the classical ideal, 1740–1840*, London.

Webb, R. 2012. 'Describing Rome in Greek: Manuel Chrysoloras' *Comparison of old and new Rome*', in Odorico and Messis 2012: 123–33.

Webb, T. 1996. '"City of the soul": English romantic travellers in Rome', in Liversidge and Edwards 1996: 20–37.

Weingarten, D. and L. Howard. 2017.*All roads lead to Rome: 17th–19th century architectural souvenirs from the collection of Piraneseum* (exhibition catalogue), San Francisco, CA: San Francisco Airport Museums, https://issuu.com/piraneseum/docs/all_roads_lead_to_rome_exhibit_-_sa.

Weiss, R. 1959. 'Andrea Fulvio antiquario Romano c 1470–1527', in *Annali della Scuola Normale Superiore di Pisa* 28: 1–44.

1988. *The Renaissance discovery of classical antiquity* (2nd ed.), Oxford.

West, R. 1916. *Henry James*, London.

Whitaker, L. 2017. *Canaletto and the art of Venice* (exhibition catalogue), London.

Wickham, C. 2015. *Medieval Rome: stability and crisis of a city, 900–1150*, Oxford.

Wiemer, H.-U. 2023. *Theoderic the Great: king of Goths, ruler of Romans* (trans. J. N. Dillon), New Haven, CT.

Wilson, A. 2000. 'The water-mills on the Janiculum', in *Memoirs of the American Academy in Rome* 45: 219–46.

Wilton, A. and I. Bignamini (eds.). 1996. *Grand Tour: the lure of Italy in the eighteenth century* (exhibition catalogue), London.

Wilton-Ely, J. 1978. *The mind and art of Giovanni Battista Piranesi*, London.

2010. 'Ruins', in Grafton et al. 2010: 853–4.

Winkler, M. M. (ed.). 2009. *The fall of the Roman empire: film and history*, Chichester.

Wittkower, R. 1963. *Disegni de le ruine di Roma e come anticamente erono*, Milan.

1999. *Art and architecture in Italy 1600–1750*, revised by Joseph Connors and Jennifer Montagu, New Haven, CT.

Woodman, A. J. and J. Wisse (eds.). 2017. *Word and context in Latin poetry: studies in memory of David West. Cambridge Classical Journal* supplement no. 40. Cambridge.

Woodward, C. (ed.). 1999. *Visions of ruin: architectural fantasies and designs for garden follies* (exhibition catalogue), London.

2001. *In ruins: a journey through history, art, and literature*, London.

Wrigley, R. (ed.). 2007. *Regarding romantic Rome*, Bern.

2013. *Roman fever: influence, infection and the image of Rome, 1700–1870*, New Haven, CT.

Wulf-Rheidt, U. 2011. 'Die Darstellung komplexer räumlicher Gebilde als Grundlage für bauforscherische Untersuchungen – das Beispiel Kaiserpalast auf dem Palatin', in Cain et al. 2011: 245–58.

Wyke, M. 1997. *Projecting the past: ancient Rome, cinema and history*, New York.

Yamazaki, M. 2012. *Thermae Romae* (English version), New York.

Yegül, F. and D. Favro. 2019. *Roman architecture and urbanism from the origins to late antiquity*, Cambridge.

Zänker, J. 1994. 'Künstliche Ruinen: gebaute, gemalte und phelloplastische Ruinenmodelle', in Buberl 1994: 84–97.

Zerbi, P. (ed.). 2001. *Roma antica nel medioevo. Mito, rappresentazione, sopravviven-ze nella 'Respublica Christiana' dei secoli IX–XIII* (Atti della quattordicesima Settimana internazionale di studio, Mendola, 24–28 August 1998), Milan.

Zimmermann, M. F. (ed.). 2003. *The art historian: national traditions and institu-tional practices*, Williamstown.

Zimmermann, R. 1989. *Künstliche Ruinen: Studien zu ihrer Bedeutung und Form*, Wiesbaden.

Zorach, R. (ed.). 2008. *The virtual tourist in Renaissance Rome: printing and collect-ing the Speculum Romanae Magnificentiae*, Chicago, IL.

Zucker, P. 1968. *Fascination of decay: ruins – relic, symbol, ornament*, Ridgewood, NJ.

Online Citations

Belli's triumphal arches: www.rct.uk/collection/43916/arch-of-septimius-severus

Bigot's maquette of ancient Rome in Caen: www.unicaen.fr/cireve/rome/pdr_maquette.php?fichier=histoire

Bretton Hall decoration: www.bretton-hall.com/archive/college-days/mansion_revisited/murals

Calvo's *Antiquae Urbis Romae cum regionibus simulachrum*: https://archive.org/details/ARes61118

Caracciolo's Rome Panorama: https://collections.vam.ac.uk/item/O134168/panorama-of-rome-oil-painting-caracciolo-lodovico

G. Ceserani et al., grand tourist architects: https://grandtour.stanford.edu

http://republicofletters.stanford.edu/publications/grandtour

Château de Beloeil, Belgium: www.chateaudebeloeil.com/en/the-gardens

Chichi's cork Pantheon in Ghent: www.gum.gent/en/news/the-conservation-of-a-unique-masterpiece-antonio-chichis-cork-model-of-the-pantheon

Computer-generated images of reconstructed Rome (Rome Reborn): https://romereborn.org

Digitales Forum Romanum: www.digitales-forum-romanum.de

DuBourg's Colosseum in Melbourne: https://collections.museumvictoria.com.au/items/715107

Einsiedeln Itinerary: www.e-codices.unifr.ch/en/list/one/sbe/0326

Fulvio's *Antiquitates* 1588: https://archive.org/details/bub_gb_iRR2Bl8iSRoC

Gismondi's *Plastico*: www.museociviltaromana.it/collezioni/percorsi_per_sale/plastico_di_roma_imperiale

Hallswell Park, Temple of Harmony: https://halswellpark.wordpress.com/2016/01/22/the-temple-of-harmony

Hodnet Hall Folly: https://thefollyflaneuse.com/the-folly-hodnet-hall-hodnet-shropshire

Janus Quadrifrons micromosaic: http://collections.vam.ac.uk/item/O157687/the-arch-of-janus-quadriffons-picture-raffaelli-giacomo

Klein Glienicke Park, Potsdam: https://de.wikipedia.org/wiki/Park_Klein-Glienicke

Lafreri's *Speculum*: http://speculum.lib.uchicago.edu/index.html

Langley's *New Principles of Gardening* (1728): https://archive.org/details/mobot 31753000819141

Lazienki Garden, Warsaw: www.lazienki-krolewskie.pl/en/architektura/amfiteatr

Little Sparta garden: www.littlesparta.org.uk/visit

Lucangeli's Colosseum model: https://parcocolosseo.it/en/marvels/carlo-lucangelis-wooden-model-of-the-colosseum

Macpherson's photographs: www.luminous-lint.com/app/vexhibit/_PHOTO GRAPHER_Robert__Macpherson_01/6/1/83755831483275234480797166

Marliani's *Antiquae Romae Topographia*: https://archive.org/details/antiqvaer omaetop00marl

Mirabilia Romae etc. website curated by Claudia Bolgia and Maurizio Campanelli: www.linkingevidence.it/project

Nanatsudo Park, Japan: www.nanatsudo.net/foreigners/english

Nicholls' virtual Rome: https://research.reading.ac.uk/virtualrome

Piraneseum souvenirs of the Grand Tour www.piraneseum.com

Piranesi: University of South Carolina, The Digital Piranesi project: https://scalar.usc.edu/works/piranesidigitalproject/index?path=index

Quarenghi's Kitchen Ruin Pavilion, Catherine Park, Russia https://tzar.ru/en/objects/ekaterininskypark/landscape/ruinedkitchen

https://life-globe.com/en/kitchen-ruin-tsarskoe-selo-petersburg

Rife's 'Gravely Speaking' blogsite for 12 September 2014: https://gravelyspeaking.com/2014/09/12/scipios-tomb-classical-exemplar

Soane Museum Model Room: http://explore.soane.org/#/section/modelroom

Soane Museum Plaster Model of Temple of 'Jupiter Stator' (= Castor and Pollux) http://collections.soane.org/object-l70

Soane's garden ruins, Pitzhanger: 'Sir John Soane and gardens …', The Gardens Trust Blog for August 2014: https://thegardenstrust.blog/2014/08

Theo Fennell's Colosseum ring: www.theofennell.com/product/slain-gladiator-opening-ring

Vasi project: http://vasi.uoregon.edu

Vienna 'Karthago'/Roman ruin https://notallarchaeologistshavebeards.wordpress.com/2017/11/17/almost-better-than-the-real-thing-some-thoughts-on-fake-ruins-from-the-18th-century-to-the-modern-day

Virginia Water 'Temple of Augustus': www.thecrownestate.co.uk/media/5311/leptis-magna-ruins.pdf

Wetmore Parlor, Wadsworth Atheneum: https://5058.sydneyplus.com/argus/final/Portal/Public.aspx?lang=en-US

Index

Académie de France, 92, 136, 140, 144, 168, 172, 173, 174, 233, 252
Accademia di S. Luca, 152, 167, 248
Adam, Robert, 144, 187, 219
Adams, Henry, 287
Addison, Joseph, 282
adventus, 28, 30, 31, 242, 244
Aetna, anonymous poem, 1
Aglio, Agostino, 191
Alaric, 29, 36
Albani, Alessandro, 91
Alberti, Leon Battista, 72, 73, 78, 84, 93
Albertini, Francesco, 94, 97
Alberto degli Alberti, 83, 118
Alcuin, 39, 41, 52
Alexander VII, 91, 242
Algardi, Alessandro, 163
alluviation, 18
Alpheios of Mitylene, 5
Altieri, Giovanni, 198
Altobelli, Gioacchino, 155, 292
Ambrose, 19
Amici, Domenico, 117
Ammianus Marcellinus, 28, 35
Ancient Monuments Protection Act, UK, 86
Anderson, James, 155
annona, 23, 30
Anonymus Magliabecchianus, 65
Anson, Thomas, 224
aqueducts, 23, 24, 30, 31, 32, 34, 36, 37, 46, 54, 76, 79, 80, 83
Ara Pacis Augustae, Altar of Augustan Peace, 18, 271
Arch of Augustus, Rimini, 63
Arch of Constantine, 46, 83, 116, 197, 202, 241, 242, 245, 252, 255, 267
Arch of Gordian, 94
Arch of Janus Quadrifrons, 194
Arch of Septimius Severus, 38, 65, 242, 245
Arch of the Argentarii, 198
Arch of Titus, 48, 103, 198, 242, 248, 255, 259, 276, 290

Arch of Trajan, Ancona, 77
archaeology, 10, 76, 92, 112, 115, 117, 151, 164, 167, 244, 255, 261, 267
architectural models, 196, 198, 200, 202, 203, 207
Arkadia Park, Poland, 225
Asprucci, Antonio, 237
Audebert, Nicolas, 106
Augustus, 7, 14, 19, 22
Aurelian walls, 24
Aventine hill, 25, 103, 110

Banco, Maso di, 120
Barbarasa, Hercole, 100
Bartoli, Alfonso, 274
Basevi, George, 220
Basilica Aemilia, 17, 18, 29, 36, 73
Basilica Julia, 258
Basilica of Maxentius, 17, 116, 125, 152, 250, 255
Basilica of St John Lateran, 28
Basilica Ulpia, 17
Basilius, 16
Baths of Caracalla, 14, 25, 36, 37, 176, 261, 293
Baths of Constantine, 25
Baths of Diocletian, 36, 50, 80, 85
Batoni, Pompeo, 180
Battigelli, Raffaello, 271
Belisarius, 31
Bellavite, Innocente, 226
Belli, Giovacchino and Pietro, 203
Benedict XIV, 91
Benedict, supposed author of *Mirabilia*, 43, 44, 45, 46, 47, 51, 52
Benjamin of Tudela, 47
Bernini, Gian Lorenzo, 235, 251
Berthault, Louis-Martin, 249
Bianchini, Francesco, 165, 174
Bigot, Paul, 173
Biondo, Flavio, 9, 36, 58, 75, 78, 79, 80, 81, 82, 84, 95, 97, 101, 118, 278
Boccaccio, Giovanni, 63

Boissard, Jean-Jacques, 108
Boni, Giacomo, 262
Boniface IV, 45
Bordone, Benedetto, 125, 160
Borromini, Francesco, 163
Boston Manor House, Middlesex, 189
Botticelli, Sandro, 124
Bracciolini, Poggio, 75, 277, 286
Bramante, Donato, 74, 280
Brancaleone degli Andalò, 32
Brenna, Vincenzo, 193, 196
Bretton Hall, Yorkshire, 191
Bridge of Cestius, 21
Brunelleschi, Filippo, 70, 121
Buckingham House, 186
Bufalini, Leonardo, 101
Bühlmann, Josef, 170, 174
Bulla Aurea, the Golden Bull, 158
Bunbury, Edward, 112
Burgess, Richard, 116
Busiri, Giovanni Battista, 184
Butor, Michel, 137, 304, 307
Byron, George Gordon, Lord, 284, 288, 292, 300

Cafi, Ippolito, 291
Calvo, Marco Fabio, 70, 88, 98, 102, 108
Calza, Guido, 268
Campano, Giannantonio, 63
Campidoglio, 82
Campo Vaccino, 18
Camporese, Giuseppe, 251
Campus Martius, 16, 18, 54
Canaletto, Giovanni Antonio, 185
Cancelleria nuova, Rome, 93
Caneva, Giacomo, 155, 242
Canina, Luigi, 166, 172, 258, 260
Canova, Antonio, 248
Capitoline hill, 279
Capodiferro, Evangelista Fausto, 278
Caracciolo, Ludovico, 169
Caravaggio, Polidoro da, 126
Caretti, Giovanni Battista, 238
Carmontelle, Louis Carogis, 224
Caron, Antoine, 127
Cartaro, Mario, 105
Casa dei Crescenzi, 68, 150
Casa Romuli, hut of Romulus, 7
Caserta, Naples, 235
Cassiodorus Senator, 30, 37, 65
Castiglione, Baldassare, 87, 280
Castle Ashby, Northamptonshire, 188
Castle Howard, Yorkshire, 185

catacombs, 261
Catherine Park, Pushkin (Tsarskoye Selo), 225
Cencio de'Rustici, 66
ceramics, 208
Chambers, William, 140, 144, 152, 217
Charlemagne, 32
Charles V, 88, 89, 241, 244
Château de Beloeil, Mons, 225
Chateaubriand, François-René de, 11
Chichi, Antonio, 198, 200
China, ruins of no concern, 9, 10, 120
Chrysoloras, Manuel, 63, 66, 277
Cicero, 289
Cinecittà, 176, 177
Circus Flaminius, 41, 163
Circus Maximus, 14, 19, 22, 36, 47, 277
Circus of Maxentius, 48
Claude Lorrain, 133, 134, 135
Clement VII, 82
Clement X, 91
Clement XI, 91
Cleopatra, 176
Clérisseau, Charles Louis, 144, 187, 219, 230, 236
Cleve, Hendrick van, 148
Clough, Arthur Hugh, 298
Cock, Hieronymus, 147
Cockerell, Charles Robert, 167
Codazzi, Viviano, 131
Codex Coner, 73
coinage, 78, 80, 92, 104, 164, 165, 172
Cole, Thomas, 191, 291
Colini, Antonio Maria, 268
Cöllen, Dieter, 201
Colonna di S. Vito, Giovanni, 56
Colonna, Francesco, 125
Colonnacce, 228
Colosseum, 11, 16, 21, 27, 28, 30, 32, 34, 37, 42, 44, 46, 48, 51, 53, 54, 57, 61, 63, 73, 76, 82, 84, 85, 90, 114, 115, 116, 160, 176, 177, 180, 202, 209, 246, 247, 248, 249, 253, 255, 256, 263, 264, 275, 276, 277, 278, 279, 283, 287, 288, 290, 297, 300, 301, 306
Colossus of Nero, 268
Column of Phocas, 121, 157, 253, 289, 290
Column of Trajan, 47, 69, 207, 252, 290
Condulmer, Gabriele, 77
Connolly, Peter, 168
Consalvi, Ercole Cardinal, 253, 263
conservation, 6, 12, 67, 75, 83, 84, 85, 86, 88, 89, 90, 91, 175, 201, 222, 238, 241, 245, 247, 248, 250, 257, 262, 265, 269, 272, 275, 276
Constans II, 32

Constantin, Jean-Antoine, 264
Constantine, 14, 19, 21, 28, 32
Constantius II, 28, 35
Conversi, Girolamo, 280
corso del Littorio, Trieste, 270
Cottafavi, Gaetano, 117, 238
Cresy, Edward, 257
Cruyl, Lievin, 244
Crypta Balbi, 21
Curia Julia, Senate House, 65, 272
Curzon, Lord, Viceroy of India, 12
Cyriac of Ancona, 75, 76, 80, 159, 188

de Bry, Theodor, 108
De Rossi, Giovanni Battista, 261
de Staël, Germaine, 60, 277, 290, 303
defoliation, 88, 253, 263, 265
Delille, Jacques, 215
Dessau-Anhalt, Leopold Friedrich Franz von, 230
Dickens, Charles, 297, 301
Diderot, Denis, 138, 154
Dio Chrysostom, 6
Diribitorium, voting hall, 36
disabitato, 24, 34, 40, 54, 265, 293
Dodd, Alan, 191
Domus Augustana, 50
Domus Aurea, 46, 235, 306
Donati, Alessandro, 109
Dondi dall'Orologio, Giovanni, 62
Dosio, Giovanni Antonio, 112
du Bellay, Joachim, 280, 281
du Cerceau, Jacques Androuet, 147
Dubourg, Richard, 198, 200, 201, 284
Ducros, Abraham Louis, 186
Dumas, Alexandre, 288
Duncombe Park, Yorkshire, 214
Dupérac, Étienne, 105, 107, 146, 148, 174
Dyer, John, 115, 283, 284, 285, 301

earthquake, 4, 14, 16, 17, 18, 33, 54, 248
Eaton, Charlotte, 25, 194, 201, 207, 237, 249, 253, 265
École des Beaux-Arts, Paris, 202
Egio, Benedetto, 103
Einsiedeln Itineraries, 40, 43, 52
Erdmannsdorff, Friedrich Wilhelm von, 230
Eugenius IV, 77, 79, 84
Evelyn, John, 106, 109

fans, 195
Fauno, Lucio, 101
Fea, Carlo, 202, 245, 248, 253, 254

Felbrigg Hall, Norfolk, 131, 184
Fellini Satyricon, 176
Fellini's Roma, 176
Fennell, Theo, 209
Fiano, Francesco da, 66
Fiennes Pelham-Clinton, Henry, 184
Finlay, Ian Hamilton, 240
fire, 15
Fischer von Erlach, Johann Bernhard, 164
Fischer, Reinhard Heinrich Ferdinand, 228
Flavian amphitheatre. *See* Colosseum
flooding, 16
Fontaine, Pierre François Léonard, 252
Forma Urbis, 107
Fornasetti, Pietro, 209
Forsyth, William, 68, 204, 208, 259, 260, 262
Forum Boarium, 306
Forum of Julius Caesar, 170, 274
Forum of Nerva, 38
Forum of Peace, 31
Forum of the Deified Augustus, 36
Forum of Trajan, 18, 28, 37, 82, 164, 171, 250, 300
Fouquet, Jean-Pierre and François, 202
Franzini, Girolamo, 111
Frontinus, 76, 92
Fulgentius, African monk, 31
Fulvio, Andrea, 82, 88, 98, 278, 279, 280
Futurism, 265

Gamucci, Bernardo, 111
Gandy, Joseph Michael, 142
Gartenreich, Wörlitz, 230
Gatteschi, Giuseppe, 168, 172, 177
Gatti, Guglielmo, 174
Ghent University Museum, 198
Ghirlandaio, Domenico, 124
Ghisolfi, Giovanni, 132, 185
Gibberd, Frederick, 222
Gibbon, Edward, 56, 75, 111, 286, 287, 293
Gismondi, Italo, 165, 170, 172, 174
Gladiator, 175, 177
Goethe, Johann Wolfgang von, 196, 288
Golvin, Jean-Claude, 169
Gontard, Carl Philipp Christian von, 226
Graecostasis, 279
grand tourists, 60, 92, 114, 136, 145, 179, 216, 219, 282, 286, 291
Granet, François-Marius, 264, 291
Gratian, 19
Great Zimbabwe, 13
Gregory XVI, 257
Grove Street Cemetery, New Haven, 206

guidebook, 40, 94, 108, 109, 111, 113, 114, 115, 116, 117, 166, 280, 300
Guiscard, Robert, duke of Apulia, 32, 54

Hadrian's Wall, Northumberland, 86
Halswell Park, Somerset, 217
Hamilton, Charles, 215
Hamilton, William, 188
Hancock, Robert, 208
Hannan, William, 216
Hardy, Thomas, 294
Hare, Augustus, 262, 264, 265
Harewood House, Yorkshire, 187
Hatchlands, Surrey, 188
Hawthorne, Nathaniel, 235, 291, 292, 300
Heemskerck, Maarten van, 144, 242
Herodes Atticus, 236
Herzogliches Museum, Gotha, 198
Hetzendorf von Hohenberg, Johann Ferdinand, 233
Higden, Ranulph, 49
Hildebert of Lavardin, 41, 47, 52, 87, 277
Hillard, George Stillman, 292
Hiyya bar Abba, rabbi, 36
Hoare, Richard Colt, 186
Hobhouse, John Cam, 290
Hodnet Hall, Shropshire, 222
Holkham Hall, Norfolk, 131, 182
Home, Henry, Lord Kames, 215
Honorius, 16
Honorius I, 272
Hope, John Thomas, 286
Hopfgarten, Wilhelm, 207
Horace, 8, 9, 16, 49, 299
Horologium Augusti, 279
horrea, warehouses, 36
Howard, Henrietta, 185
Howard, Henry, 185
Howells, William Dean, 253, 262, 302

inscriptions, 13, 16, 25, 40, 61, 63, 68, 75, 76, 77, 78, 80, 92, 97, 111, 139, 237, 244, 260, 276, 279, 289, 320
interior decoration, 129, 132, 179, 181, 187, 188
Isidore of Seville, 49

Jackson, John Baptist, 189
Jacob of Strasbourg, 160
James, Henry, 264, 291, 301, 302
Janiculum Hill, 16, 37
Jappelli, Giuseppe, 238
Jeremiah Lee Mansion, Marblehead, MA, 189

Jubilee, 53, 54, 72, 91, 100, 101, 107, 163, 253
Jussow, Heinrich Christoph, 231
Justinian, 19, 31, 32
Juvenal, 16

Kammsetzer, Johann Chrystian, 225
Keats, John, 293
Kedleston Hall, Derbyshire, 188, 219
Kensal Green Cemetery, 206
Kent, William, 215, 219
Knobelsdorff, Georg Wenzeslaus von, 226

La Dolce Vita, 176
lacus Curtius, 301
Lady Knight, 287
Lafréry, Antoine, 128, 145
Lamy, Ernest, 157
Lanciani, Rodolfo, 262
Landino, Cristoforo, 277
Langley, Batty, 213
Lansdowne (Shelburne) House, 188
lapis niger, Black Stone, 262
Largo Argentina, 18, 20, 268
Lauro, Giacomo, 161
Lazienki Park, Warsaw, 225
Le Roy, Julien-David, 152
Lego, 210
Lenné, Peter Joseph, 228
Leo X, 82, 87, 278
Leo XII, 255
Leto, Pomponio, 81, 82, 95, 97, 278
Liber Pontificalis, 40, 76
Ligorio, Pirro, 100, 101, 102, 103, 104, 105, 110, 174
Lint, Hendrik Frans van, 136
lithography, 257
Little Sparta, Scotland, 240
Livy, 3, 55, 57, 76, 150, 279, 289
Longhi, Martino, 272
Lubbock, John, 86
Lucan, 2, 3, 49
Lucangeli, Carlo, 202
Lucatelli, Andrea, 185
Ludwig, king of Bavaria, 253

Macaulay, Rose, 12, 240, 306
Macellum Magnum, Great Market of Nero, 104, 165
Macpherson, Robert, 155
Majorian, 29
Manetti, Antonio di Tuccio, 71
Manetti, Latino Giovenale, 88, 242, 244
Mantegna, Andrea, 121

maps of ancient Rome, 40, 46, 61, 80, 81, 98, 100, 102, 104, 107, 110, 113, 162, 322
Marble hill, 185
Marcelliani, Giuseppe, 173
Marcellus of Side, 236
Mariano da Firenze, 97
Marinetti, Filippo Tommaso, 267
Markets of Trajan, 268
Marliani, Bartolomeo, 80, 99, 100, 103, 108
Marmorpalais, Potsdam, 226
Martial, 16, 37
Martin V, 54, 83
Martin, Jean, 126
Marylebone Cemetery, 206
Masaccio, 121
Mason, William, 214
Master Gregory, 47, 48, 49, 50, 51, 52
material culture, 6, 12, 53, 55, 64
Mausoleum of Augustus, 45, 48, 140, 271, 278, 279
Mausoleum of Hadrian/Castel Sant' Angelo, 81
Maxentius, 27
May, Carl Joseph, 198
May, Georg, 198
McSwiny, Owen, 182
Megalopolis, 5
Meier, Richard, 272
melancholy, 138, 215, 216, 285
Memnon, statue in Thebes, Egypt, 3
Meta Sudans, 268
Miller, Lady, 114, 180, 195
Mirabilia Urbis Romae, 38, 43, 44, 46, 47, 51, 52, 57, 58, 62, 65, 80, 81, 278
Mithraeum, London, 18
Moglia, Domenico, 194
Montecitorio, 18
moonlight, 287, 290, 291, 300
Morpurgo, Vittorio Ballio, 272
Morritt, J. B. S., 288
Muffel, Nikolaus, 50
Muñoz, Antonio, 270
Museums Victoria, Melbourne, 201
Mussolini, Benito, 267, 268, 271
Mycenae, 5

Nanatsudo Park, Mito City, Japan, 239
Nardini, Famiano, 111
Nash, John, 202
National Arboretum, Washington, 239
Nibby, Antonio, 115, 166, 255, 258
Nicholas V, 84
Nuremberg Chronicle, 86

obelisk, Vatican, 51, 90
Olympiodorus, Greek historian, 36
Ordo Romanus, 43
Ormerod, Thomas Holden, 286
Osterley Park, 188
Ostia, 18, 87, 174, 260, 269
Overbeke, Bonaventura van, 150
Ovid, 47, 49, 51, 52, 65, 90

P. Victor, 96, 103, 107, 108, 279
Page, Russell, 239
Paine, James, 185
Painshill, Surrey, 215, 233
Palace of Pilate, 41
palatia, 44, 50
Palazzo Rucellai, Florence, 73
Palazzo Spada, 129
Palladio, Andrea, 111
Palmyra, 13
Paltronieri, Pietro, 184
Panini, Giovanni Paolo, 136, 137, 138, 144, 145, 151, 185, 189, 208, 233, 304
panorama, 169
Pantheon, 26, 28, 32, 45, 47, 50, 51, 61, 71, 79, 85, 104, 118, 188, 189, 198, 210, 228, 246, 248, 251, 259, 279, 284, 299
Panvinio, Onofrio, 107, 108
Parc Monceau, Paris, 224
Parker, John Henry, 156
Parmigianino, 127
Parrhasius, Janus, 96
Patel, Pierre, 136
Paul III, 88, 250
Pausanias, 4, 6, 52, 76
Pennethorne, James, 167
Percier, Charles, 252
Peruzzi, Baldassare, 126, 269
Peter and Paul Fortress, St Petersburg, 186
Peter the Deacon, 45
Petitot, Ennemond Alexandre, 233
Petrarch, Francesco, 17, 51, 52, 53, 54, 55, 56, 58, 60, 61, 62, 63, 64, 65, 69, 75, 76, 102, 113, 118, 151, 262, 277, 290, 296, 299
phelloplasty, 197
Phocas, 45
photographs, 155, 157, 170, 242, 274, 292
Piazza Navona, 14
piazzale Augusto Imperatore, 272
Piccolomini, Aeneas Silvius, 85, 277
picturesque, 115, 129, 140, 145, 147, 153, 156, 212, 213, 216, 219, 238, 262, 263, 265, 298
Pigage, Nicolas de, 231
pigna, bronze pine-cone, 45

Pilate, Pontius, 41, 68
Pinelli, Bartolomeo, 250
Piranesi, Giovanni Battista, 104, 114, 137, 138, 145, 147, 150, 151, 152, 153, 154, 155, 165, 180, 198, 201, 228
Pittoni, Battista, 147
Pitzhanger Manor, Middlesex, 220
Pius IX, 257, 259, 260
Pius VII, 245, 252
plaster cast, 207
Pliny the Elder, 35, 36, 37, 38, 70, 78, 79, 279
Pliny the Younger, 6
Poe, Edgar Allan, 291
Poelenburgh, Cornelis van, 130
Polemius Silvius, 37
ponte ruinante, Palazzo Barberini, 236
Pontelli, Baccio, 93
population, 20, 22, 23, 24, 30, 53
Porena, Filippo, 117
Porta S. Sebastiano, 242
Portico *ad nationes*, 38
Portico of the Harmonious Gods, 259
Porticus of Octavia, 26, 87
Portland vase, 8
Posthumus, Herman, 89
Pragmatic Sanction, 31
Prattware, 209
presentation, 246, 253, 261, 275, 276
preservation, 261
Price, Robert, 184
print rooms, 188
Procopius, 31
Propertius, 8, 277
Protestant Cemetery, 293
Prowse, Thomas, 219
Pyramid of Cestius, 51, 63, 76, 91, 184, 279, 294

Quadratianus, 25
Quarenghi, Giacomo, 225
Quo Vadis, 175, 176

Rabelais, François, 100
Raffaelli, Giacomo, 194
Raphael, 70, 82, 87, 88, 98, 126
Re, Lorenzo, 115
regionary catalogues, 14, 37, 44, 47, 92, 96, 104, 107
restoration, 22, 25, 30, 42, 158, 198, 222, 241, 245, 246, 248, 249, 250, 256, 259, 274, 276
Ricci, Marco, 151, 182
Ricci, Sebastiano, 189
Richardson, Charles, 220

Richter, Adrian Ludwig, 265
Rienzo, Cola di, 61, 68
Robert, Hubert, 136, 138, 140, 141, 154
Rogers, Samuel, 292
Roman Bar, Alexandra Palace, 191
Roman Forum, 18, 27, 28, 29, 35, 36, 57, 88, 103, 110, 116, 167, 172, 179, 242, 249, 250, 253, 254, 258, 259, 261, 262, 268, 270, 274, 292
Romanis, Antonio de, 115
Romano, Giulio, 126
Rome, 177
Rometta Fountain, Villa d'Este, 105
Rosa, Augusto, 197
Rosa, Pietro, 258, 261
Rossini, Luigi, 154, 170
rubble, 17
Rucellai, Bernardo, 95
Rucellai, Giovanni, 72, 73
ruina, 'collapse', 16
ruin-aesthetic, 6, 42, 56, 64, 67, 74, 83, 87, 88, 114, 115, 119, 120, 125, 126, 128, 133, 141, 178, 213, 216, 240, 253, 262, 265, 282, 283, 284, 288, 292, 302, 306
ruin-mindedness, 12, 56, 58, 60, 64, 67, 76, 115, 119, 133, 152, 212, 240, 262, 265, 277, 282, 292, 306
Ruminal Fig Tree, 113
ruralisation, 53
Ruskin, John, 86, 124, 154, 156

S. Lorenzo in Miranda, 88
S. Maria Antiqua, 262
S. Maria in Trastevere, 25
S. Pietro in Vincoli, 25
S. Spirito, Florence, 71
Saciara v, 88
Sacra via, 27, 89, 242, 250
Sadeler, Aegidius, 148
Sadeler, Marco, 180
Saint-Just, Louis Antoine Léon de, 240
Salvatio Civium, Safeguard of the Citizens, 38, 49
Salvi, Gaspare, 257
Sangallo family, 73, 93, 94
Sans Souci, Potsdam, 226
Sarcophagus of Scipio, 204, 205
Scalae Gemoniae, Stairs of Groaning, 103, 110
Scalamonti, Francesco, 77
Scamozzi, Vincenzo, 147
Schloss Hohenheim, Stuttgart, 228
Schloss Johannisburg, Aschaffenburg, 198
Schloss Klein-Glienicke, Potsdam, 228

Schloss Schwetzingen, Rhinepfalz, 231
Schlossküche, Marmorpalais, 233
Schönbrunn Palace, Vienna, 231
Senatus Consultum Hosidianum, 26
Seneca, 49
Septimius Severus, 25
Septizodium, 51, 58, 102, 110, 127
Serlio, Sebastiano, 161
Sessorian palace, 65
Seth Wetmore House, 191
Seven Wonders, 37, 38
sewers, 36, 37
Sex. Rufus, 107
sham ruins, 212, 213, 220, 226, 233, 235, 236
Shelley, Mary, 293, 296
Shelley, Percy Bysshe, 264, 293
Shrine of Juturna, 254
Shugborough Hall, Staffordshire, 183, 223
Sigismund of Luxembourg, 78, 278
Silva, Ercole, 200, 237
Sixtus IV, 85, 278
Sixtus V, 87, 91
slave trade, 34
Soane Museum, London, 73, 179
Soane, John, 142, 145, 198, 201, 202, 207, 220, 253
Solinus, 61
Sorrell, Alan, 168
souvenirs, 179, 181, 193, 197, 200, 210
Spangaro, Ferruccio, 271
Speer, Albert, 143
Spenser, Edmund, 281, 282
spolia, 25, 26, 27, 28, 68, 71, 225, 228, 236, 238
Ss. Cosmas and Damian, 27, 107
St Peter's Basilica, 14, 87, 88, 90
Staccioli, Romolo Augusto, 170
Stadium of Domitian, 41
Statius, 279
Statue of Marcus Aurelius, 83
Stendhal, 115
stereogram, 157, 303
Stern, Raffaele, 238, 246, 254, 255, 256, 276
Stonehenge, 13
Story, William Wetmore, 261, 264
Stourhead, Wiltshire, 186
Stowe, Buckinghamshire, 215, 240
Strabo, 3, 140, 279
Strawberry Hill, 185
Strozzi, Alessandro, 80
sublimity, 114, 296
Suetonius, 49, 51, 65, 279
Symmachus, 22, 30

Tabularium, Record Office, 49, 159
Tacitus, 16, 296
Taylor, George Ledwell, 257
Tempietto d'Arcadia, Parma, 233
Temple of Antoninus and Faustina, 88, 242, 250
Temple of Apollo on the Palatine Hill, 277
Temple of Apollo Sosianus, 270
Temple of Castor and Pollux, 191, 242, 250, 253, 274
Temple of Clitumnus, Pissignano, 236
Temple of Concord, 76, 254
Temple of Deified Claudius, 279
Temple of Deified Hadrian, 38, 303
Temple of Deified Julius, 88
Temple of Deified Romulus, 27
Temple of Fortuna Virilis, 198, 249
Temple of Jupiter Optimus Maximus, 28
Temple of Jupiter Tonans, 228
Temple of Mars Ultor, 30
Temple of Minerva Medica, 185, 220, 265, 279, 305
Temple of Peace, 26, 28, 36, 107, 116, 125, 152
Temple of Saturn, 28, 76, 248, 250, 254
Temple of the Sun, 44
Temple of Venus and Cupid, 65
Temple of Venus and Roma, 28, 46, 111, 188, 258, 306
Temple of Vespasian, 26, 228, 248, 250, 270
Temple of Vesta, 161, 246, 249
Temple of Vesta, Roman Forum, 26, 274
Temple of Vesta, Tivoli, 198
Templum Canapare, 84
Tertullian, 19
The Fall of the Roman Empire, 176
Theatre of Marcellus, 21, 34, 52, 126, 269, 276
Theatre of Pompey, 16, 28, 38, 79, 94
Theoderic, 24, 27, 30, 31
Theodosius, 19
thermae, 14, 24, 30
toadflax, 264
Tomb of Caecilia Metella, 76, 87, 305
Tomb of Remus, 76
topography, 59, 78, 79, 80, 92, 95, 96, 101, 108, 111, 112, 262, 278
Totila, king of the Ostrogoths, 20, 22, 31
Totti, Pompilio, 109, 113
tourism, 1, 3, 4, 13, 25, 34, 55, 57, 66, 72, 78, 82, 85, 89, 91, 95, 101, 108, 112, 116, 119, 147, 148, 156, 157, 163, 179, 184, 186, 204, 212, 241, 244, 253, 260, 261, 262, 265, 267, 275, 278, 287

Tournon, Camille de, 248
Towne, Francis, 193, 263
Townley, Charles, 192, 196
translatio imperii, 281, 287
Traversari, Ambrogio, 64
Trieste, 270
Triopion, 237
Troy, 1, 2, 3, 7, 13
Turner, Joseph Mallord William, 291, 293
Twain, Mark, 292

Uberti, Fazio degli, 61
Unger, Georg Christian, 165

Valadier, Giuseppe, 116, 198, 238, 249, 255, 256, 263, 274, 276
Valadier, Luigi, 166
Vandals, 23, 24, 31
Vanvitelli, Gaspare, 182
Varagine, Iacopo da, 120, 125
Varro, M. Terentius, 279
Vasi, Giuseppe Agostino, 114, 151
Vasi, Mariano, 115, 142, 265
vedute, 129, 132, 137, 145, 148, 151, 155, 156, 157
Venuti, Ridolfino, 113
Vergerio, Pier Paulo, 58, 63, 92
Verino, Ugolino, 278
Veronese, Paolo, 147
Verrocchio, Andrea del, 124
Vespasian, 28
via Appia, 48, 63, 260, 279
via del Mare, 268, 269

via dell'Impero, 268, 274
via Papalis, 43
Villa Albani, 236
Villa Borghese, 236
Villa Torlonia, 238
Virgil, 2, 35, 49, 51, 55, 289, 292
Virginia Water, Surrey, 221
Visconti, Ennio Quirino, 237
Visconti, Pietro Ercole, 260
Vitalis, Janus, 281, 283
Vitruvius, 63, 70, 73, 93
Volpato, Giovanni, 186, 233

Wagner, Alexander von, 170
wallpaper, 189
Walpole, Horace, 92, 131, 132, 185, 217
water mills, 37
Weenix, Jan Baptist, 131
West, Rebecca, 302
Wharton, Edith, 291
Wigan, Willard, 209
Wilhelmshöhe, Kassel, 231
William of Malmesbury, 41
Wilson, Richard, 217
Winckelmann, Johann Joachim, 245
Windham, William, 184
Wood, Robert, 13
Woodhall Park, Hertfordshire, 188
Wyatville, Sir Jeffrey, 221

Yamazaki, Mari, 240

Zucchi, Antonio Pietro Francesco, 187, 188

For EU product safety concerns, contact us at Calle de José Abascal, 56–1°, 28003 Madrid, Spain or eugpsr@cambridge.org.

www.ingramcontent.com/pod-product-compliance
Lightning Source LLC
Chambersburg PA
CBHW080802080126
37904CB00044B/9